Power and Diplomacy in Northern Nigeria 1804-1906

Ibadan History Series

Published by Northwestern University Press

CHRISTIAN MISSIONS IN NIGERIA 1841–1891
by J. F. A. Ajayi

THE ZULU AFTERMATH
by J. D. Omer-Cooper

Published by Humanities Press

THE MISSIONARY IMPACT ON MODERN NIGERIA 1842–1914
by E. A. Ayandele

THE SOKOTO CALIPHATE
by Murray Last

BRITAIN AND THE CONGO QUESTION 1885–1913
by S. J. S. Cookey

BENIN AND THE EUROPEANS 1485–1897
by A. F. C. Ryder

NIGER DELTA RIVALRY
by Obaro Ikimẹ

THE INTERNATIONAL BOUNDARIES OF NIGERIA
by J. D. Anene

In preparation (to be published by Humanities Press)

REVOLUTION AND POWER POLITICS IN YORUBALAND
by S. A. Akintove

THE SEGU TUKULOR EMPIRE 1848–1893
by B. O. Ọlọruntimẹhin

THE NEW OYO EMPIRE
by J. A. Atanda

Ibadan History Series
General Editor J. F. A. Ajayi, Ph.D.

Power and Diplomacy in Northern Nigeria 1804-1906

The Sokoto Caliphate and its Enemies

R. A. Adeleye, Ph.D.
Department of History, University of Ibadan

Humanities Press

First published
in the United States of America 1971
by Humanities Press Inc.
303 Park Avenue South
New York, N.Y. 10010

SBN 391-00169-8

Printed in Great Britain

In memory of Iya,
my mother

Contents

Plates *facing page*

The author and publishers are grateful to the following for permission to reproduce photographs: plate 1, The Public Record Office, London; plates 2–8, the University of Ibadan Library.

Abbreviations

A.S.	*Al-Aḥkām al-Sulṭaniyya*
Acc.	Accumulation number
A.N.S.E.	Archives Nationales; Section Etrangère for the Archives Diplomatiques et Documents, Paris
A.N.S.O.M.	Archives Nationales; Section d'Outre-Mer, Paris
A.O.F.	Afrique Occidentale Française
B.C.A.D.	*Bulletin of the Centre of Arabic Documentation*, University of Ibadan
B.C.A.F.	*Bulletin du Comité de l'Afrique Française*
B.N.	Bibliothèque Nationale, Paris
B.S.O.A.S.	*Bulletin of the School of Oriental and African Studies*, London
B.W.	*Bayān Wujūb al-Hijra*
C.M.S.	Church Missionary Society, London
C.A.D.	Centre of Arabic Documentation, University of Ibadan
C.O.	Colonial Office (British)
Corr.	Correspondence
C.S.O.	Chief Secretary's Office
D.H.	*Ḍiyā' al-ḥukkām*
D.M.	*Ḍabṭ al-Multaqaṭāt*
F.O.	Foreign Office (British)
G.O.K.	Governor's Office, Kaduna
H.C.	High Commissioner (British)

Ib.	Ibadan University Library
I.D.W.O.	Intelligence Division of the War Office
I.F.A.N.	Institut Français d'Afrique Noire (*Bull. IFAN*, Bulletin)
I.M.	*Infāq al-Maisūr fī Tarīkh bilād al-Takrūr*
J.A.H.	*Journal of African History*
J.H.S.N.	*Journal of the Historical Society of Nigeria*
J.A.S.	*Journal of the African Society*
J.R.G.S.	*Journal of the Royal Geographical Society*
N.A.C.	National African Company (became R.N.C. in 1886)
N.A.I.	National Archives, Ibadan
N.A.K.	National Archives, Kaduna
R.A.	*Rauḍāt al-Afkār*
R.G.S.	Royal Geographical Society (*Journal* and *Proceeding*)
R.H.B.E.	Rhodes House, Oxford: British Empire MSS
R.N.C.	Royal Niger Company (previously N.A.C.)
S.N.P.	Secretary Northern Provinces
T.I.	*Tanīs al-Ikhwān*
T.W.	*Tazyīn al-Waraqāt*
U.A.C.	United African Company
W.A.F.F.	West African Frontier Force

Glossary

Amān	safe-conduct
ʿAjam	non-Arabic
Amīr	Emir, commander, title-holder, prince
Amīr al-jaish	Commander of the army
Amīr al-Mu'minīn	Commander of the Faithful (i.e. Caliph or Imām)
balogun	General (Yoruba)
bayʿa	act of homage to the Caliph
Bughāt	dissenters
Dan	son of (Hausa)
Dār al-ḥarb	a land of Unbelievers on which war by Muslims is obligatory
Dār al-Islām	Muslim territory
dhimmi	non-Muslim under protection in Muslim territory
Ḥadīth	tradition of the Prophet
ḥarbī	person from Dār al-ḥarb
hijra	emigration for the sake of Islam
ijmāʿ	concensus of opinion
jamāʿa	community (of Muslims)
jangali	cattle tax (Hausa)
jihād	war for the sake of Islam
jizya	poll tax

kharaj	land tax
khums	one-fifth
maṣlahā	public welfare
muhājirīn	participants in a *hijra*
mujāddidūn	reformers
mujāhidūn	participants in a *jihād*
musta'mīn	holder of an amān
Nasara	Christians (Arabic, used in Hausa)
nuwwāb	deputies, representatives
ribāṭ	frontier stronghold
sarauta	throne, public office (Hausa)
sarki	king or chief (pl. sarakuna)
(*masu sarauta*)	office-holders
sharī'a	the law of Islam
shirk	polytheism
sunna	orthodox Islam, i.e. according to the practice of the Prophet
sunnī	following the *sunna*
taqīyya	dissembling for the sake of the faith
'Ulamā'	learned men
Umma	the Muslim community or nation
zaure	entrance-hall (hausa)
zakāt	canonical alms—one of the pillars of the faith
wa	Hausa suffix at end of place name meaning 'native of', e.g. Kanawa means native of Kano

Preface

The study of Northern Nigerian history has engaged the attention of serious scholars only during the last decade. Attention has been focused particularly on the Sokoto Caliphate owing, no doubt, to the relative richness of its archives as well as the fact that it embraced by far the greater part of the old Northern Region of Nigeria. Nonetheless, a comprehensive history of the Caliphate has yet to be written. But this is scarcely feasible until the history of the component emirates has been studied in far greater detail than at present. This book, which is the outcome of my thesis for the Ph.D. of the University of Ibadan, is a study in power relations. Within this framework it attempts a comprehensive history of the whole of the Sokoto Caliphate. It is an attempt to fill existing gaps and to re-examine certain current claims.

For convenience, this book may be seen in three sections. A general history of the Caliphate, with special reference to its establishment, structure and organization, defence and problems of security, is presented in chapters 1 to 4. The question of relations between Sokoto and its emirates is examined while the defence and expansion of the Caliphate is seen as synonymous with the problem of each emirate defending and expanding its domains. Decentralization was most apparent in the Caliphate's defence arrangements. While the adequacy of the Caliphate's system for its nineteenth-century needs is stressed the overall picture that emerges is that 'there was nothing particularly weak or strong' about the Caliphate. Albeit its remarkable unity and the intactness of its machinery of government up to the European conquest are demonstrated.

Against the general background provided by Part I, the manner of European penetration, the problems which it raised for the various parts of the Caliphate and how these were handled, are discussed in Part II (chapters 5 and 6). European imperial policies and diplomatic exchanges between imperial rivals are strictly avoided except where the picture would be blurred without a mention of them. Attention is focused on the activities of Europeans actually within the Caliphate as the events which have direct relevance to this study.

Chapters 7 to 10 (Part III) deal with the British overthrow of the Caliphate. The reasons for the vehemence of the resistance and the antagonism of the masses to British occupation are analysed. Thus, the main emphasis is on how and why the Caliphate met the European challenge the way it did. More importantly, in this connection, I have attempted to demonstrate that in order to have a sound understanding of the European conquest—a major turning point in the history of Northern Nigeria—the whole stirring event must be seen not as an isolated episode in the Caliphate's history but rather in the perspective of its nineteenth-century history.

A general review of sources used is made in the 'Notes on Sources'.

It is not possible for me to thank all those from whom I received assistance in various forms. I particularly wish to thank Professor H. F. C. Smith, whose knowledge of Northern Nigerian history is unrivalled, for his invaluable help and kindliness. In the University of Ibadan I wish to thank Dr E. A. Ayandele of the Department of History, who read through all my drafts and made very valuable suggestions. In the same Department I thank Dr Obaro Ikimẹ and Dr R. J. Gavin, who read through my drafts at the thesis stage. My thanks are also due to Professor J. F. Ade. Ajayi, who read through chapters 1 to 4 of my final draft, for his assistance. I owe many thanks to the staff of the various archives and libraries in which I worked for their kind assistance. In this regard I wish to specifically mention: the Africana Library of the University of Ibadan; the Ahmadu Bello University Library (Zaria); the Ibadan and Kaduna branches of the Nigerian National Archives, the Public Records Office, London; C.M.S. House, London; Rhodes House, Oxford; Archives du Ministère des Affaires Etrangères, Quai D'Orsay, Paris; Archives Nationales, Paris. I would like to thank Messrs Oye Akinbọade and E. Kẹhinde for typing the manuscript. I owe more thanks to my friends, too numerous to name, than I can adequately express.

Above all I wish to express my deep gratitude to Adedoyin, my wife, who, during the final stages of this work, patiently and with great understanding, put up with far less attention than she is entitled to so soon after our wedding.

R. A. Adelẹyẹ

Ibadan,
December 1969

Part I
The Caliphate in the Nineteenth Century

Chapter 1
Introduction

THE 'UTHMĀN DAN FODIYE JIHĀD

The old Northern Nigeria, as well as certain areas in present-day Niger Republic, was the scene of a violent and decisive revolution at the beginning of the nineteenth century. The movement known variously as the Sokoto, the Fulani and the 'Uthmān dan Fodio *jihād* marked a crucial turning point patently unprecedented in the history of the area. Over the ruins of the numerous polities of this vast area of about 250,000 square miles, it established a new political organization—the Sokoto Caliphate—based primarily on Islamic law and values. Hausaland was the main theatre of this revolution which had repercussions on the peoples of the Western and Central Sudan from the Senegal in the west to Lake Chad in the east and from the Sahel in the north to the borders of the tropical rain forests in the south.

This study is concerned with the consequences of the *jihād* for the Hausa and their neighbouring peoples brought within the Sokoto Caliphate, as well as those who became its enemies. East of Hausaland were the Kanuri who formed the core of the Bornu empire, which for close on a thousand years had been under the rule of the Seifawa dynasty. At the beginning of the nineteenth century Bornu was still strong at its core but the Mais (i.e. kings of Bornu) were becoming less and less able to maintain an effective control over their subject provinces. On the surface, however, there were no obvious signs of impending disintegration. But although the *jihād* failed to integrate Bornu in the Sokoto Caliphate, it initiated a political revolution in the kingdom, which ultimately swept away the Seifawa dynasty and profoundly affected the history of the old empire for the rest of the century. On the northern frontiers of the Caliphate the *jihād* failed to win all Hausa-speaking peoples, some of whom subsequently remained its inveterate enemies, as will be seen later. To the west of Hausaland is a region comprising Zaberma, Dendi, Fogha,

Yagha and Gurma peoples who are non-Hausa. This region, against which the *jihād* was only partially successful, was fragmented into numerous splinter polities.

To the south of Hausaland and Bornu the number of ethnic groups was legion.[1] Ethnic heterogeneity reached its highest peak in the regions of the Bauchi plateau and what is now known as Adamawa province. The vast majority of the ethnic groups south of Hausaland and Bornu seem not to have organized themselves into closely integrated states. In this politically fragmented region, the Jukuns (Kwararafa) of the Gongola-Benue valleys, the Igala, the Igbira-Panda, the Nupe, the Ọyọ Yoruba of the savanna belt as well as the Borgawa were organized into comparatively powerful kingdoms and 'empires'. By the end of the eighteenth century, the glorious age of the Jukun empire already lay in the past. Nupe was apparently still strong; but it was already falling on evil days with the inception of a bitter succession rivalry which set in there towards the close of the century. The once powerful Ọyọ empire had entered on a period of decline and gradual disintegration since the mid-eighteenth century. The Ẹgba broke away towards the end of that century while whatever influence Ọyọ may have had over Nupe and Borgu had been definitely overthrown. The core of the Ọyọ empire had become dangerously enfeebled by internal dissensions. As the nineteenth century opened, it appears, there was an interregnum which lasted many years, during which the spirit of local independence among the subject provinces had scope to consolidate. The *jihād* administered the death-blow to the already tottering empire. Only the northern fringes of the old Ọyọ empire ultimately formed part of the Sokoto Caliphate. But the history of the Yoruba has been profoundly affected in various ways by the *jihād*.

1. It is not possible to enumerate all the tribes here. C. L. Temple, *Notes on the tribes, provinces, emirates and states of the Northern provinces of Nigeria* (Cape Town, 1919) provides a rough though sometimes unreliable guide. The Hausa, Kanuri, Fulani, Tiv, Yoruba, Nupe, Igala, Igbira, Jukun, Gwari, Bassa, Idoma, Gwandara, Mandara, Jarawa, Ningi, Birom, Montol, Ankwe, Yergam, Bolewa, Batta, Bachama, Borgawa, Dan Kerkeri, are some of the numerous tribes (see map on p. 8).

THE SEARCH FOR POLITICAL ENTITIES

Two major themes, one political, the other religious, can be traced in Hausa historical development up to the beginning of the nineteenth century. As I have shown elsewhere,[2] the search for larger and more secure political entities stands out as the dominant theme of Hausa political life. Thus from about the fifteenth century there had been intense rivalry and conflict between Katsina, Kano and Zazzau (Zaria) the leading three of the traditional seven Hausa states. Between the fifteenth century and the nineteenth there had been a number of unsuccessful attempts to build lasting empires by welding together many of the numerous states. Consequently during various phases one power rose to pre-eminence only to be supplanted by another.

During the fifteenth century Zazzau, under the legendary Queen Amina, established what was, in effect, the first Hausa empire. Zazzau dominion is said to have extended over territories as far as the Benue and the Niger and in some form over Bauchi, Kano and Daura. Amina's epoch was succeeded by the imposition of Bornu overlordship on the Hausa states. In spite of challenge by Songhay at the beginning of the sixteenth century Bornu's suzerainty over Hausaland survived, though in a very much weakened form, to the end of the eighteenth century. The remote hegemony of Bornu did not stop imperial conflict among the Hausa. From the second decade of the sixteenth century the state of Kebbi, founded by Kanta Kotal, soon imposed its imperial control not only over the Hausa states but also on some of their non-Hausa neighbours to the west and the Nupe (perhaps northern Nupe only) to the south. From the mid-seventeenth century the sultanate of Ahir (Asben), founded about 200 years earlier, had attained a position of strength sufficient to support the ambition of acquiring dominion over the more fertile territories of her Hausa neighbours to the south.[3] From then to the nineteenth century the Tuareg factor was an important element in the history of Kebbi, Gobir, Zamfara and indeed Bornu.

Perennial conflict with Ahir sapped Kebbi's strength. The rapid growth of both Zamfara and Gobir during the seventeenth

2. R. A. Adeleye, 'Hausaland and Bornu 1600–1800', in *History of West Africa*, ed. J. F. A. Ajayi and M. Crowder vol. i, (London, forthcoming).
3. *Ibid.*

century involving conflict between each of them and Kebbi resulted in the overthrow of the latter as an imperial power about the end of the seventeenth century or the beginning of the eighteenth.[4] During the first half of the eighteenth century Zamfara was the leading power of the Hausa states, or at least the most aggressive. Though its pursuit of power brought it into collision with neighbours like Kebbi, Gobir, Katsina and Kano from which it emerged victorious, it failed to found an empire. Early in the second half of the century, Zamfara was forcibly supplanted by Gobir from its position of dominance. For the rest of the century Gobir was locked in conflict with Zamfara, Kebbi, Ahir, Katsina and Kano. Its armies carried conquest beyond these states to Shira in the Western Marches of Bornu and westward into Zaberma. For over three decades to the end of the century, Zamfara and Katsina were in an alliance of convenience against Gobir, their common enemy, but to no avail. However, Gobir never reaped the fruits of conquest. Half a century of constant warfare had not only served to isolate her politically from other Hausa states, it had also, no doubt, depleted her physical resources. In spite of military pre-eminence Gobir's immoderate expansion left no room for the proper establishment and organization of an empire.

Although the details of the degree of solidarity that existed in the 'tentative empires' of Northern Nigeria before the nineteenth century are still to be discovered, the evidence available indicates that there was little cohesion. The successive empires, Bornu apart, were therefore transient. Pre-nineteenth-century pursuit of empire in Northern Nigeria seems to have depended for success largely on the continued military supremacy of the conquering state. The mode of warfare and the weapons used (mainly bows and arrows, spears and swords, with few firearms, if any) were the same for both the victor and the vanquished. Added to this, the vastness of the area over which the conquerors' efforts were diffused meant that the defeat or even devastation of a state did not prevent relatively rapid recovery. Hence warfare tended to be endemic. Such a situation was incompatible with effective administration of a conquered territory. Long distances from the centre of supreme authority coupled with the heterogenous ethnic groups with their disparate and often competing economic interests further rendered adminis-

4. *Ibid.*

tration precarious and the evolvement of a common ethos elusive. Moreover, common cultural identity among the Hausa as well as among the other ethnic groups did not provide a basis for political unity. In the overwhelming majority of cases political boundaries divided rather than united ethnically homogeneous peoples. Ideas of allegiance to the traditional but small polity and the ideal of the prosperous self-sufficient state, though mutually contradictory, superseded ethnic loyalty. Politically the tendency towards apparently monolithic ethnic cohesiveness is a contemporary development of Nigerian history, not least in the region presently under study. In the absence of any powerful state or group of states willing and able to act together to impose a common pax by military means over the numerous states and peoples, a common need or unifying ideology was a prerequisite for guaranteeing the cohesion of any multi-ethnic or multi-state political entity. These unifying factors cannot be traced in the history of Northern Nigeria before the *jihād.*

THE GROWTH OF ISLAM

It was to another crucial development in Western Sudan history —the growth of Islam—that the Sokoto Caliphate was to owe its foundation. Without denying the vital importance of success in war for the initial establishment of the Caliphate, its consolidation and survival depended far more on the common bond provided by Islam than on any military superiority of the *mujāhidūn* over their adversaries. The *jihād* itself was the upshot of a long process of evolutionary development of Islamic acculturation in the Western Sudan states.

Islam had been introduced into Bornu from about the eleventh century and into Hausaland from the fifteenth. The earliest protagonists of Islamization were foreign savants and merchants, while the patrons were kings and their courtiers. The supposed mystical powers of the faith, the dazzle and obvious advantages of writing, the use of Arabic as the *lingua franca* of diplomatic relations outside the ethnic group, the probable attractiveness of the laws as an instrument of political integration as well as a badge of identification with an internationally accepted religion, all seem to have commended Islam readily to the kings and their courts. Embracing Islam did not involve, and was not seen as

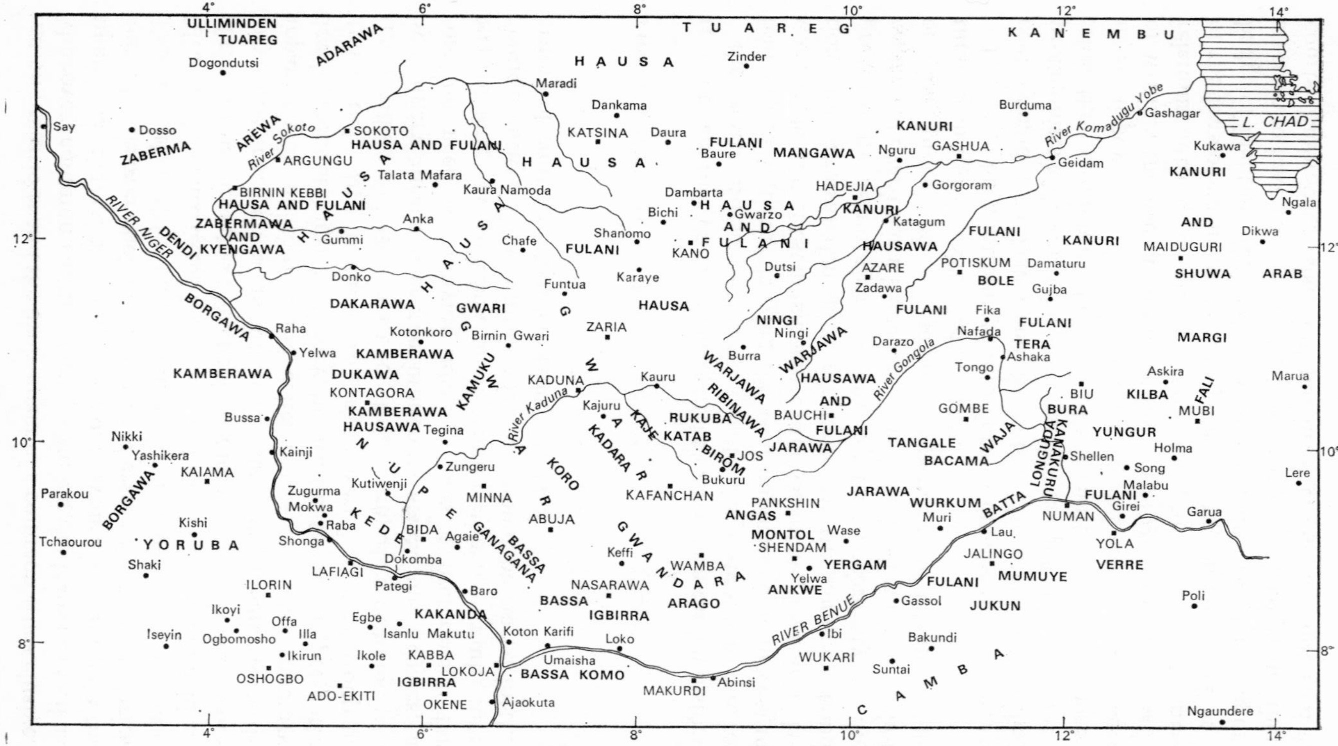

Ethnographic map of Northern Nigeria

involving, a radical overthrow of important aspects of traditional systems and values. Many rulers were noted for their piety and were zealous for the spread of the faith in their domains. Writing in the sixteenth century, the famous Timbuktu scholar Aḥmad Bābā, referred to Bornu, Katsina and Kano as Islamic states.[5] However, Islam appears to have remained a religion of the minority top echelons of society until perhaps well into the seventeenth century. Official Islam apparently emerged as a syncretic blending of the faith with traditional culture types. Indeed, it might be said that if there was pollution in the process of acculturation, it was Islam that was corrupting the traditional cultures. Because of the power of traditional culture the syncretic forms that attained currency as the norm varied from one locality to another. Yet the values of Islam are antithetical at many points to the indigenous cultures. The areas of conflict relate not only to the private life of the individual but also to the whole corpus of political, social, economic and other forms of public organizations and observances. So long as Islam was only marginally conditioning traditional values, the necessary conflict implicit in the continued development of this process remained latent.

The growth of education in the Islamic sciences among Western Sudanese peoples was perhaps the most far-reaching factor in the transformation of the religion from a thing accepted on the basis of mere belief to a faith based on a true awareness of the stipulations of the Qur'ān and other sources that govern its practice. Leadership of this intellectual development was not provided by the kings but by a rising class of educated élite known as the *'Ulamā'*—learned men. Islam thus grew out of the royal courts and soon left them lagging behind in the pursuit of true knowledge and practice. This is not to deny that learned men remained in the courts as household and state functionaries. Understandably many of the *'Ulamā'* appear to have identified themselves with the *status quo*, and such men are known to have made significant contribution to the promotion of Islamic education in court circles. However, the real storm-troopers of the spread of Islam in terms of the number of adherents and depth of knowledge were those *'Ulamā'* outside the official court circles. Learning and preaching, these men were instrumental in

5. See 'Uthmān b. Fodiye, *Tanbīḥ al-Ikhwān* (Ibadan, 82/212), quoting from Aḥmad Bābā's *Kashf wa'l-bayān li Aṣnāf Majlūb al-Sūdān.*

calling into existence an ever-widening circle not only of other learned men but also of a generality that progressively became better informed about the *sharīʿa* (the Muslim law) and Islamic values as these governed all aspects of the believer's life. Muḥammad Bello b. ʿUthmān b. Fodiye listed some of the most famous representatives of the *ʿUlamā'* from the seventeenth century to his days in Baghirmi, Bornu, Ahir and Hausaland.[6] During this period works written by the *ʿUlamā'* also became a powerful addition to the intellectual armoury of their class. Muḥammad Bello also listed many of such works while, more recently, Bivar and Hiskett have made a survey of the leading pre-*jihād* authors of Hausaland and Bornu.[7] Pre-*jihād* authorship appears to have reached its peak of development during the second half of the eighteenth century.

Consequent on this growth in intellectual and missionary fervour, a powerful searchlight was turned on society. In these circumstances, innovations (*bidʿa*) in contemporary Islamic practice were, no doubt, viewed as resulting from the syncretic and totally un-Islamic laws and values which governed the societies in which the Muslims lived. Preaching reform in this context involved, no matter how indirectly, criticism of existing political order. Since this order constituted the heritage to which contemporary rulers succeeded, they apparently felt committed to defend it as the only guarantee they knew of security and political stability in the face of the new Muslim 'radicalism'. No matter what they themselves might have thought, the activities of puritan Muslims demanding no more than freedom to practise their faith in its pure form constituted, in these circumstances, plain rebellion. Conflict between religion and politics, a logically inherent development in such a situation, turned the evolutionary Islamic acculturation into the revolution which gave birth to the Sokoto Caliphate.[8] Any interpretation of subsequent events of

6. Muḥammad Bello, *Infāq al-maisūr* (*I.M.*), ed. C. E. J. Whitting (London, 1957), pp. 5–14, and 22–9.
7. *Ibid.*, and M. Hiskett and A. D. H. Bivar, 'The Arabic literature of Northern Nigeria to 1804, a provisional account', *B.S.O.A.S.* xxv (1962) 104–48.
8. The course of the outbreak of the *jihād* in Gobir furnishes the best illustration of this phenomenon. D. M. Last, *The Sokoto Caliphate* (London, 1967), pp. 1–29; H. A. S. Johnston, *The Fulani Empire of Sokoto* (Oxford, 1967), pp. 26–46; and M. R. Waldman, 'The Fulani *Jihād*, a reassessment', *J.A.H.* vi, no. 3, 1965, pp. 333–55.

the *jihād* which seeks completely to divorce political from religious considerations is open to grave risks of distortion.

THE SCATTERED JAMĀʿAS

Other side factors also aided the success of the revolution. The spread and growth in depth of Islamization cut across the strife-ridden political and human divides. Against the age-old divisiveness Islam was fostering a community that was united by a common ideology even though this unity had as yet no chance of overt political expression. By the second half of the eighteenth century this community existed in widely dispersed units all over Northern Nigeria. Regular contacts with the heartland of Islam (Mecca, Medina and the Middle East generally) through the annual pilgrimage, and regular commercial connections across the Sahara provided scholars with access to books, new ideas and materials for writing. The leading local seats of learning were Birnin Gazargamu, Agades, Katsina and Kano, with other state capitals following behind them at varying levels. Besides, there were numerous mallam (*muʿalim*) settlements with followers known as their *jamāʿas*. From their headquarters the mallams (*muʿallimū*) journeyed over long distances, while students also moved from one master to another to learn their various specialities and obtain from them the necessary licence (*ijāza*) to teach.

At first, the scattered *jamaʿas* lacked coordinated existence and central leadership. This was, however, remedied with the emergence during the last quarter of the eighteenth century of the Shaikh Muḥammad b. ʿUthmān b. Muḥamad b. ʿUthmān b. Ṣalīh known to history as ʿUthmān dan Fodio (i.e. *Fulfulde-Fodiye*, learned man) as the most outstanding Islamic pundit and preacher in all Hausaland and Bornu and possibly in the whole of Western Sudan. Born on Sunday 15 December 1754, the Shaikh ʿUthmān dan Fodiye was heir of a centuries-old family tradition of learning and social respectability.[9] He received his education following the traditional pattern of the training of a

9. F. H. El-Masri: 'A critical edition of Dan Fodio's Bayān Wujūb al-Hijra ʿAla 'l-ʿIbad' (unpublished Ph.D. thesis, Ibadan, 1968), p. 6 ff. In this work he will be referred to as ʿUthmān b. Fodiye, the Shaikh Uthmān, or simply as the Shaikh.

mallam.[10] He grew up to be a very learned theologian and a pious *ṣufi*. Based at Degel in Gobir about sixty miles west of Alkalawa —the capital of that state—he began his preaching career in 1774/75.[11] His activities were not confined to his community at Degel or even to Gobir; he travelled to Kebbi, Zamfara, Zaberma and to the Niger, as well as to Daura.

With his background, his learning and his position as a leading *ṣufi*,[12] he had all the attributes of a successful charismatic leader. Because of his towering personality the Shaikh's movement rapidly attracted adherents from over a wide area. His mysticism, in itself an aspect of his charisma, compelled the reverence, if not the awe, of many for him and the movement which he led. The depth of learning which he brought into interpreting Islam to his audience placed his movement on a much higher intellectual and spiritual plane than the other widely scattered Muslims and their communities could attain. An obvious model, the Shaikh's movement naturally drew into its orbit communities aiming at a goal identical with his own (i.e. the purification and spread of the practice of Islam) but unequipped and/or lacking the power to present their aims with the same force and clarity.

Initially the Shaikh directed his efforts to those who already accepted Islam,[13] exhorting them to purify their practice of the religion in accordance with *sunnī* orthodoxy. This phase was apparently soon merged with wide-scale proselytization among the masses. Although he shunned the courts of kings, the implied criticism of the established political order which his reformist movement involved soon alerted the King of Gobir, Bawa jan Gwarzo, to attempt curbing the activities of the Muslim community which he regarded as incipient rebellion. In 1788–89, Bawa summoned the Shaikh to join the 'Id al-Kabīr prayers at Magami. The reported desertion on this occasion of the king's mallams to join the Shaikh's followers, bringing up the total number of mallams present to over a thousand,[14] attests to the Shaikh's tremendous influence. It also showed up the numerical strength of the '*Ulamā*' class in Gobir alone as well as the poten-

10. See 'Abdullāh b. Fodiye, '*Idā' al-Nusūkh*', ed. M. Hiskett, *B.S.O.A.S.* xix (1957), pp. 551–9.
11. *T.W.* p. 85.
12. El-Masri, *op. cit.*, pp. 9–15.
13. The most substantial study of the various phases of 'Uthmān b. Fodiye's preaching career is that made by El-Masri, *op. cit.*, pp. 42–4.
14. *T.W.* pp. 88–9; Last, *op. cit.*, p. 7.

tial threat that the Shaikh posed to the King's authority. Although Bawa is said to have intended to harm the Shaikh and the cause of Islamic reform, he was apparently overawed by this display of strength into granting all the five requests of the Shaikh:[15] freedom to preach, freedom of the king's subjects to respond to the call, concession that all those who wore the turban—the badge of membership of the *jamāʿa*—should be treated with respect, that all prisoners be freed and that excessive taxation be alleviated.

The successors of Bawa were, however, openly hostile to the movement of reform which was fast creating a state within the state. Nafata, who ascended the throne in 1794–95, following the death in battle with the Katsinawa of Bawa's successor, Yaʿqūb, now made a widely published proclamation which amounted to a complete reversal of the concessions earlier granted by Bawa.[16] This attempt to enforce solidarity in the state merely aggravated an already tense situation and hastened the development of an open clash between the *jamāʿa* and the state. As a measure of self-defence the Shaikh had ruled in 1794–95 that the making ready of weapons of war by the Muslim community was *sunna* (*inna istiʿdād al-silah sunna*).[17] As this was a fundamental difference between the Shaikh's movement at Gobir and the other scattered *jamāʿas* which looked to him for leadership, so also did it raise the movement of reform from the plane of mere exhortation and protest to one of a positive determination that the Muslim community and its ideals must survive, if need be by fighting for that survival. By this ruling, the Shaikh's *jamāʿa* turned into a potential fighting force. Its general acceptance was a revolution in the history of Islam in the Hausa states. It marked the first definite departure of the course of Islamic revivalism in those lands from mere preaching to the fighting of *jihād*. From self-defence it was an easy step to offence.

Subsequent harrying of Muslims under Nafata and his successor Yunfa (1802–08) brought matters to the brink of war.[18] The permanent breach was precipitated by open hostility between Yunfa and the community of ʿAbd al-Salām (a follower of the Shaikh) settled at a place called Gimbana in Kebbi

15. *Ibid.*
16. *I.M.* p.67; Last, p. 12.
17. *T.W.* pp. 51, 105.
18. *I.M.* p. 67 f., *T.W.* pp. 107–8, Muḥammad Bello, *Sard al-Kalām* (Ibadan 82/212).

territory.[19] 'Abd al-Salām had earlier fled to Gimbana with his *jamā'a* for fear of molestation by the Sarkin Gobir. Following his refusal to return to Gobir, Gimbana was sacked by an expeditionary force sent by Yunfa. The Muslim prisoners taken were freed by the Degel community, much to the chagrin of Yunfa. Consequently he ordered the Shaikh and his family to evacuate Degel as he intended to attack it. The Shaikh refused to leave his community in the lurch. Since they had not the power to withstand Gobir attack the Muslims found refuge in flight. On 21 February 1804 the emigration of the Degel community to Gudu in the west began.[20] Conceived and executed as a *hijra*, basically on the pattern of the Prophet Muḥammad's flight from Meccan persecution to Medina, this apparently minor accident of history proved the signal for the outbreak of the *jihād*.

It seems clear that the Shaikh's revivalist movement was, in a general sense, simply the most important and the most profound of similar movements in various parts of the old Northern Nigeria during the second half of the eighteenth century. At about the same time as 'Uthmān b. Fodiye was preaching reform and winning fame and the veneration of pious Muslims from far and wide, Abubakar b. 'Uthmān, known to history as Buba Yero, was, according to tradition, engaged in similar activities in the Gombe (Old Gombe) region.[21] Having received his education in Gazargamu, he had returned to Shellen to preach Islam. When his community grew large he founded a settlement for them which he called 'Furakoyo' ('welcome' in Janafulu Fulfulde). Later, he travelled like many itinerant mallams of his day to the neighbouring countries to the south until he heard of the Shaikh 'Uthmān b. Fodiye and went to him.[22]

Local leaders like Buba Yero were quite common. A large number of them were to be found in Hausaland generally and in the territories which later became the emirates of the eastern frontiers of the Caliphate. In general the latter looked to Bornu for their Islamic education. Gazargamu was the centre to which their zealots resorted before the *jihād*. Scholars from Bornu made

19. *Sard al-kalām*.
20. *I.M.* p. 68.
21. Babagoro, *History of Gombe* (copy obtainable from the Divisional Office, Gombe).
22. *Ibid.* The settlement of Buba Yero among the Janafulu Fulani is corroborated by *Tabyīn Amr Bubu Yero* (copy in possession of Professor H. F. C. Smith, Ahmadu Bello University, Zaria).

itinerant journeys through the 'eastern emirates' of the future. Two of such mallams were Adamu (Adam) and Isḥāq, whose travels took them to Bauchi territory where they met Mallam Daṭī, a Jarawa, father of Ya'qūb, the future Emir of Bauchi. Mallam Daṭī gave Ya'qūb to Mallam Isḥāq to study under him. Both master and student later studied under the Shaikh 'Uthmān.[23] Modibo Adam b. Al-Ḥasan, the future Emir of Adamawa, first studied under a Mallam Kiari in Bornu and later under the Shaikh.[24] Gwoni Mukhṭar, who led the *jihād* against Bornu, had been educated there while Mallam Zaki, leader of the *jihād* in Katagum was a learned man of great repute.

Besides the well-known names there were in various other places *jamā'as* with mallams who enjoyed considerable local fame and deep respect. Even south of the Hausa states proper, where Muslims were significantly fewer in number, *jamā'as* antedating the *jihād* were to be found. The first Etsu of Nupe to embrace Islam with seriousness was Jibrīl who reigned about the mid-eighteenth century.[25] An Etsu Nupe who reigned about the second half of the seventeenth century bore a Muslim name, Muḥammad Wari, like many Etsus after him and before Jibrīl.[26] Thus the introduction of Islam into Nupe could not have been later than some time during the seventeenth century. It is well known that both Nupe and the old Ọyọ empire enjoyed contact through commerce with Hausaland, Bornu, the regions of Dendi and the old Songhay and Mali empires. Indeed, Palmer records that Mallam 'Umar, leader of a Muslim community of Kulumfardo in Bornu, visited Nupe during the 1680s.[27] Judging by Nupe's importance on the southward extension of the trans-Saharan trade routes since the times of Amina of Zazzau and Ya'qūb of Kano in the fifteenth century, as well as the Kantas of

23. Imām Muḥammad b. Muḥammad Bello b. Aḥmad b. Idrīs al-Sudānī, *Tarīkh Bauchi* (Ibadan 82/378), p. 2. Also R. M. East, *Labarun Hausawa da Makwabtansu* (Zaria, 1932), vol. i, p. 45; 'Labarin Asalin Bauchi' by Mallam Mustafa, teacher of Ya'qūb's sons.
24. H. K. Strumpell, *A History of Adamawa compiled from Verbal information* (Hamburg, 1912, mimeographed). See also Capt. C. Vicars-Boyle 'Historical Notes on the Yola Fulanis', *J.A.S.* x (1910), p. 75.
25. S. F. Nadel, *A Black Byzantium* (Oxford, 1961), King List of Nupe, p. 406.
26. *Ibid.*
27. Tilho, *Documents scientifiques de La Mission Tilho*, vol. ii (Paris, 1911), pp. 397–8.

Kebbi in later years, it is reasonable to suppose that Islam may have been introduced there well before the seventeenth century.

There had been other renowned mallams in Nupe before Dendo came there. The most outstanding of these, Mallam Musa and Mallam ʿAbd al-Raḥmān, were contemporaries of Dendo.[28] Mallam Musa is said to have had a larger *jamāʿa* than Dendo. ʿAbd al-Raḥmān was credited with mystical powers which indicate the esteem and reverence in which he was held by his contemporaries. He was known personally to the Shaikh ʿUthmān b. Fodiye and the core of the reformist community around him. Indeed Dendo's fame as a mallam does not seem to have become predominant in Nupe until after the death of ʿAbd al-Raḥmān, *c.* 1818–19.[29]

At Iṣẹyin—in the old Ọyọ empire—tradition has it that Islam was introduced by the Malawa (men from Mali).[30] At the old Ọyọ metropolis, Alfa Yigi, who is said to have brought Islam, was reputedly an Arab.[31] It appears that a powerful Muslim community already existed in Ọyọ since it is reported that a work in Arabic, *Shifāʾ al-rubā fī tahrīr fuqahāʾ Yaruba*, was composed for them during the 1660s in answer to an enquiry which they had sent to Katsina about methods of determining the precise moment of sunset.[32] Ṣāliḥ (known to history as Mallam Alimi) met Muslims in Ọyọ, Ikoyi, Iṣẹyin, Kuwọ, as well as in Ilọrin during his itinerant travels in northern Yorubaland.[33] At Ilọrin, his chief collaborator, one Ṣọlagbẹru of Oke-suna, was even said to have been a Tījanī.[34]

The vitality of local mallams and their *jamāʿas*, who stood out

28. East, *op. cit.*, vol. i; account of Mallam Musa, pp. 76–7, and ʿAbd al-Raḥmān, pp. 77–82.

29. *Ibid.*, p. 81.

30. G. O. Gbadamọsi, 'The Growth of Islam among the Yoruba' (unpublished Ph.D. thesis, Ibadan, 1968), p. 12.

31. *Ibid.*, pp. 12–13.

32. Hiskett and Bivar, *op. cit.*, p. 116. Work composed by Abū ʿAbdullāh b. Muḥammad b. Masanih.

33. Gbadamọsi, *op. cit.*, p. 19. Alimi is said to have been expelled from Ọyọ by the Alafin on account of his growing influence in the town. The King feared that the cleric might be tempted to usurp the throne. See also Aḥmad b. Abī Bakr (Ọmọ Kokoro) *Taʾlif Akhbār al-Qurūn min ʿUmarāʾ bilād Ilọrin* (uncatalogued photocopy in C.A.D., Ibadan).

34. Gbadamọsi: personal communication of oral evidence collected by him. Strange as this assertion may seem, it is none the less worthy of further investigation.

as beacons of revivalism, provided the basis on which the establishment of the Sokoto Caliphate ultimately depended. The activities of the mallams had called into existence communities which, when the time came, needed only to be galvanized into action. The Shaikh's revivalist movement canalized the energies of the scattered communities into a single channel out of which grew a general Muslim rising. He turned their protests into a revolution. It was, indeed for our area, an age of a general Islamic revivalism that varied merely in degree and intensity from one place to another. The widespread enthusiasm with which the scattered Muslim *jamāʿas* embarked on the *jihād* supplied the initial momentum which carried the revolution to success. Their dependence on guidance from the Shaikh established that common allegiance to the Caliph which was to hold the Caliphate together.

The case of the persecution of the Shaikh's followers in Gobir illustrates the position of Muslims who embraced the purification of the practice of Islam in the *jamāʿas* of the various states. The disabilities which the Muslim suffered by living under governments that were not based on the *sharīʿa* gave rise to deep-seated grievances which provided Muslims with a common cause to fight for. This factor auspiciously prepared the ground for the success of reforming preachers. In Gobir, for instance, as tension mounted between the Shaikh's community and the state authorities the grievances of the community were aggravated and this had a corresponding effect on their solidarity and further enhanced the progress of the reformist movement. Besides obvious causes of grievance, details of departures from the *sharīʿa* only needed pointing out to the generality to be seen as un-Islamic and therefore unjust.

The heretical observances of the rulers of Hausaland, as the Shaikh saw them, are enumerated in his *Kitāb al-Farq*[35] and a number of other works. He emphasizes that these rulers administered oppressive laws contrary to the *sharīʿa*, that they did whatever they liked heedless of whether or not their actions were in accordance with the *sharīʿa*. These rulers imposed uncanonical and excessive taxation, took bribes to pervert justice, forcibly seized property of their subjects and forced Muslims to fight in uncanonical wars or pay heavily for failure to comply. They prohibited Muslims from doing things that were *sunna* for them,

35. See tr. by M. Hiskett, *B.S.O.A.S.* xxiii (1960).

such as wearing of the turban by men and the veil by women. Further, the rulers indulged in luxurious and voluptuous living; revelling in illegal music, wearing ornamented fineries and accumulating women, often as many as 1,000, in their harems. The officers of state, the methods of their appointment and the administrative structure and functions, were regarded as plain illegalities.

The rulers either indulged in or condoned heathen practices like pouring dust on the head as a sign of respect when greeting the king. More heinous was the charge of polytheism—*shirk*—the most reprehensible departure from Islam. The reformers frowned at the practice of worshipping spirits and gods and making sacrifices to them. These charges were substantially valid. Among Hausa goddesses were *Uwandowa* (goddess of hunting), and *Uwargona*, goddess of agriculture.[36] To these, sacrifices were offered. Some communities believed in a water spirit—*Sarkin Rafi*—to whom the sacrifice appears to have been a virgin girl.[37] Other Hausa communities had their totems and there was widespread belief in divination, 'black magic' and conjuring.[38] The charge of polytheism against Bornu during the early years of the *jihād* was not denied by the learned Shaikh Muḥammad el-Amīn el-Kānemī. Large communities of heathens (known as *maguzawa* in Hausa) existed among the various ethnic groups in Hausaland and Bornu including even the Fulani, reputedly the most highly Islamized. In Katsina and Kano the state possessed talismans similar to the ancient sacred *Mune* of Bornu in the belief attached to them as palladiums of state security. The *Dirki* of Kano was the Qur'ān turned into a fetish to which sacrifices of cattle were offered.[39] When the talismans of Katsina and Kano were opened towards the end of the eighteenth century the action was not taken in deference to Islam. The inference drawn from the event was that it presaged the impending destruction of the two kingdoms. These anti-Islamic practices no doubt existed in a higher degree in the region south of Hausaland and Bornu where Islam exercised a markedly lighter influence on most of the societies and in some, none at all.

36. A. J. N. Tremearne, *Hausa Superstitions and Customs: An Introduction to the folk-lore and the folk* (London, 1913), pp. 111–19.
37. *Ibid.*, p. 111.
38. *Ibid.*, p. 169 f.
39. See 'Kano Chronicle' in H. R. Palmer, *Sudanese Memoirs*, vol. iii (Lagos, 1928), p. 127.

The foregoing aberrations from the path of Islam especially in the realm of administration and the laws of the state meant tensions and difficulties for the pious Muslim who, though anxious to be orthodox, was compelled to compromise his faith. The non-Islamic aspects and practices of the contemporary societies aptly represent the dilemma of the Muslim and the magnitude of the forces with which he had to contend.

THE PLACE OF THE FULANI IN THE JIHĀD

Another aspect of the *jihād* which demands attention is the phenomenon that it was Fulani-inspired, that it was in the main Fulani-led, and that the government it established was dominated by the Fulani. The obvious question is whether or not it was fought to achieve Fulani domination. The Fulani were aliens in the Hausa and other states in which they had settled for three or more centuries before the *jihād*.

With a few exceptions they had remained aliens, denied effective and direct participation in the government of their adopted homes. This isolation of the Fulani may, in part, be ascribed more to the difficulty of aliens fitting into an already existing structure of authority and functions in an indigenous society than to any deliberate antagonism of the indigenes to them. Such a situation could, nevertheless, provide a fertile ground for fostering Fulani solidarity and separate identity. It was easy, in the circumstances, for the Fulani to see any form of oppression by the government as hatred for their ethnic group. More important than this factor was that the outlook and way of life of the Fulani, the bulk of whom were nomads, differentiated them from their host peoples, who were mostly peasants and townsmen. The basic animosity between nomads and townsmen completed the Fulani isolation and partly explains the tension between them and the indigenous peoples under whose rule they lived.

This animosity was apparently expressed in fighting in some places before the *jihād*. It is related, for instance, that a certain Fulani called Bauchi-Gordi, had raided 'Adamawa' territory before the *jihād* and that after him Buba Yero did likewise.[40] In addition, the Fulani were better Islamized than their host peoples. Injustices against them would therefore tend to be seen

40. Strumpell, *op. cit.*, pp. 13–14.

as injustices not only against their ethnic group but also against the religion of Islam. Being largely outside the pale of government, the pious Fulani were more favourably placed to identify abuses against Islamic tenets than their counterpart indigenous Muslims, many of whom had vested interests in the existing system. It is therefore not strange that religious reform should have found its staunchest votaries among the Fulani. The prompt acceptance of the *jihād* by the Bornu Fulani and other Fulani communities in the Hausa states tend to make the *jihād* appear as a struggle for Fulani political freedom.

To what extent the Fulani reaction was ethnocentric rather than religious cannot be definitely decided since the distinction between loyalty to kin and to religion cannot be demarcated beyond doubt. Like the Arabs in the history of Islam or the Jews in that of Christianity, the fortunes of the reformist movement seem to have been identified with those of a people—the Fulani—who filled the role of a chosen people. That many Fulani joined the *jihād* from a sense of racial solidarity cannot be ruled out. Fulanis were conscious of their separate identity and, as D. M. Last points out, they seldom had internal feuds and their mallams maintained contact over long distances.[41] Without going into the details of those who did and those who did not support the *jihād*—and it is clear that both Fulani and non-Fulani fought on both sides of it—it suffices to note that the reformers made their appeal basically on religious grounds. Since the Fulani were not superior in arms or political organization to their opponents their numerical inferiority alone would have ensured the failure of the *jihād* if they had not enjoyed the active support of non-Fulani allies and associates.

That the Caliphate was largely Fulani-ruled was a direct result of the fact that the *jihād* leaders were mainly Fulani. Non-Fulani like ʿAbd al-Salām, the release of whose followers was an immediate cause of the *jihād*, Yaʿqūb of Bauchi, Jattau, Sarkin Zazzau who supported the *jihād*, were not denied position in the new scheme of things. If there was subsequent antagonism among the Hausa people within the Caliphate against the Fulani as well as resentment at the overthrow of Habe authority, it was never sufficiently strong to constitute a major threat to Fulani rule. Apart from the ʿAbd al-Salām revolt there is, so far as I know, no record of any other Hausa revolt, worthy of note,

41. Last, *op. cit.*, p. lxxx.

against Fulani rule within the Caliphate that may conceivably be construed as ethnically motivated.[42] Even in the ʿAbd al-Salām revolt, it is difficult to disentangle racial grievances from his personal ambition or rightful indignation. This, however, is not to say that ethnic considerations played no significant role in the founding and subsequent history of the Caliphate.

The role of leadership of the scattered *jamāʿas* which the Fulani played makes clear the decisive contribution of their ethnic group to the success of the *jihād*. Yet another element in the success of the *jihād* was that the evils of society against which the reforming Muslims raved were significant even for the non-Muslim who felt oppression keenly. To this class of people, as much as to Muslims, the reform movement held up a manifesto for the reorganization of government on the principles of primordial Islam. To the Muslims this was the only worthy alternative to contemporary governments and the promise of a better life. In this way, once conflict which seemed likely to overthrow unjust and oppressive governments broke out the reform movement could draw support from a wider circle than its immediate Muslim following. As will be seen later, the *jihād* canalized the divisive forces within various states. This, perhaps no less than commitment to Islam, accounts for its success over a vast territory.

Even though the original aim was the reform of Islam, 'the most lasting consequences of the movement was a profound political, social, cultural, religious, economic, demographic and intellectual revolution totally unprecedented in its scope and intensity in the history of the West-Central Sudan'.[43] Whatever side motives can be traced in the revolution it was on the basis of the integrating force of the Islamic ideology of the *Umma* that the Caliphate was established and sustained. Yet large-scale political integration was an incidental result of the *jihād*; unforeseen and therefore not specifically prepared for by the leaders of the reform movement.

42. The allusion made here is to those Hausa that accepted the authority of the Caliphate *ab initio*. The rejection of this authority by substantial numbers of Hausa from Katsina and Zaria is of course well known. Outside Hausaland the rejection of Fulani rule by various ethnic groups is again well known, the most apt example being the Nupe emirate.

43. R. A. Adeleye, 'The Sokoto Caliphate in the nineteenth century', in ed. Ajayi and Crowder, *History of West Africa*, vol. ii (London, forthcoming).

An important aspect of the history of the Caliphate is that the integrating ideology was successfully rejected by many states and communities both outside and inside its peripheral frontiers. Many of such groups threatened the very existence of the Caliphate in its early years. These enemies were mostly those against whom the *jihād* had initially been waged but who were not subjugated thereby. Within the peripheral frontiers, there were pockets of enemy territory which resisted the Caliphate's control throughout its existence of ninety-nine years. Even within the perimeter of each emirate the degree of acquiescence of various groups differed.

In a significant way, therefore, the Caliphate was faced with problems of integrating disparate peoples under its sway similar to earlier attempts in the region to found large states. The Caliphate was a community bound together and to the Caliph by Islamic values. This bond did not depend on territorial unity which the Caliphate never attained. The preservation and, where possible, the enlargement of *Dār al-Islām* against enemies never ceased to be its preoccupation.

Chapter 2
The Establishment of the Sokoto Caliphate

The breach between the Gobir state and the Muslim community came about, paradoxically enough, in spite of the King, Yunfa, and the Shaikh, 'Uthmān b. Fodiye.[1] For either leader to yield ground on any essential aspect of the cause he championed was to compromise it to the point of ruin and to undermine the morale of his faction. But both leaders seem to have been thoroughly aware of the grave consequences for his side to which an armed conflict could lead. On the one hand, Yunfa must have known that, besides the Muslim threat at home, he could not count on friendship with Kebbi. Zamfara was, as it had been for four decades, in open rebellion while Katsina's traditional enmity with Gobir was as lively as ever. With these neighbours as potential allies for the Muslims, the risk involved in precipitate action could not have been discounted. On the other hand, in spite of the phenomenal growth of tension between his community and the state, it must have been obvious to the Shaikh that the Muslims were ill-prepared militarily. In fact, the *hijra* was the answer to their weakness.

For about two months after 21 February 1804, crowds of the *muhājirīn* from Degel and many other places were converging on Gudu. Force and brutal repression having failed to stop them Yunfa tried conciliation. The Shaikh's terms for peace and for the return of his community to Degel, if accepted by Yunfa, would have amounted to a volte face on his part, involving his full conversion to the reformer's viewpoint. He rejected the peace proposals on the advice of his '*Ulamā*' and his councillors.[2] Forthwith, the community of Gudu appointed the Shaikh as their

1. *T.W.*, tr. M. Hiskett (Ibadan, 1963), pp. 85–109; Muḥammad Bello, *I.M.*, ed. C. E. J. Whitting (London, 1951), pp. 65–71. The theme of the 'inevitability' of the outbreak of the *jihād* can be grasped from M. R. Waldman: 'The Fulani *jihād*: a re-assessment'. *J.A.H.* vi, no. 3 (1965), pp. 333–55 and D. M. Last, *The Sokoto Caliphate* (London, 1967), pp. 1–24.
2. *I.M.* p. 69.

Amīr al-Mu'minīn and paid the *bay'a* (homage) to him accordingly.[3] The permanence of the breach was confirmed. The Sokoto Caliphate was born.

THE JIHĀD IN GOBIR

The details of the course of the *jihād* in Gobir are now sufficiently well known.[4] The first two years, 1804–05, were the most decisive in the struggle of the jihadists. During this period their army inflicted notable defeats on the Gobir army as well as suffering a number of heavy reverses. Successive victories in the opening battles of Matankari, Konni and Tabkin Kwotto (between April and June 1804)[5] manifestly improved the chances of success for the jihadists, strengthened their morale immensely and sapped that of their enemy. Moreover, since the jihadists had the disadvantage of inferior numbers and equipment, the victory was seen as due to God's intervention on their side. Both Muḥammad Bello and 'Abdullāh b. Fodiye (son and brother respectively of the Shaikh) have compared Tabkin Kwotto with the celebrated battle of Baḍr[5a] in which the forces of the Prophet Muḥammad decisively defeated a Meccan army in similar circumstances. Late in 1804 an abortive attempt by the jihadists to take the Gobir capital, Alkalawa, by storm was followed by a severe reverse for them at the battle of Tsuntsua, a short distance from the city. About two thousand jihadists, two hundred of whom knew the Qur'ān by heart, were reported killed in the Tsuntsua encounter.[6]

In March 1805 the *mujāhidūn* established their base at Sabongari in south-western Zamfara from where they launched fierce attacks on Kebbi territory. In April 1805 the capital town of Kebbi, Birnin Kebbi, was sacked.[7] The submission of numerous

3. *I.M.* pp. 70–1, *T.W.* (tr.), p. 108.
4. See Last, *op. cit.*, pp. 1–45, and H. A. S. Johnston, *The Fulani Empire of Sokoto* (London, 1967), pp. 35–59.
5. Last, *op. cit.*, pp. 25–6; *I.M.* p. 71; *T.W.* p. 109 and Johnston, *op. cit.*, p. 43.
5(a). *I.M.* pp. 73–9, *T.W.* pp. 109–11; for the comparison of Tabkin Kwotto with Baḍr, see p. 110 and *I.M.* p. 77. Last, pp. 26–7 and Johnston, pp. 44–6, describe Tabkin Kwotto battle in detail.
6. *I.M.* pp. 87–8. Last, *op. cit.*, pp. 31–2, Johnston, *op. cit.*, p. 50.
7. *I.M.* p. 93.

Kebbi towns followed apace. Meanwhile a similar reduction of southern Zamfara towns was going on. The Muslims again moved camp to Gwandu and settled there. A combined force comprising Gobirawa, Kebbawa and Tuareg launched a heavy attack on the new base late in 1805. At the battle of Alwasa (about twenty miles west of Gwandu) the Muslims suffered a terrible reverse in which about a thousand of them were killed.[8] Defeat was soon turned into victory in the gallant defence of Gwandu which culminated in the rout of the allies in 1806. Alkalawa finally fell to the Muslims at their fourth attempt in October 1808. Thenceforth the triumph of the Muslim cause was assured. In 1809 Sokoto, which became the capital of the Caliphate, was built by Muḥammad Bello.[9] Wurno, also built during his reign as a *ribāṭ*, assumed more and more the character of a twin capital with Sokoto in subsequent years.

From 1805 to 1812 the army of the Shaikh also won many victories in Arewa, Dendi, Zaberma, Gwariland, Borgu and north-western Nupe. However, the claims thus staked out by the jihadists over these places had yet to be made good. The problem of consolidation was, for long after the initial conquest, an important preoccupation of the Caliphate not only in the outlying emirates but even in its heartland. Despite the fall of Alkalawa, the conquest of Gobir was partial. It was neither accepted by Gobir nor was it ever completed by Sokoto. Throughout the century, Gobir remained an implacable enemy of the Caliphate.

The course of the *jihād* in Gobir reveals more than the stubborn defence of two conflicting ideologies by their respective votaries. Other more mundane considerations were at work in determining which of the opposing parties claimed the allegiance of the various groups in the area at any particular time. This, in turn, often decided who was the victor and who the vanquished. With variation in details the course of the *jihād* in the different emirates revealed similar factors.

During the early phase of the *jihād* the king of Gobir had appealed to the other Hausa states for assistance to quell the revolt.[10] When every allowance has been made for the fact that these states had difficulties with their Muslim communities, the

8. *I.M.* pp. 99–100.
9. *D.M.*, f. 31; *I.M.* p. 119.
10. *I.M.* pp. 73–4.

basic point remains that the spirit of united action to which Gobir appealed was not there to be invoked. The ravages of these states by Gobir up to the end of the eighteenth century rendered it highly unlikely that, even in the face of a common enemy, they would rally to save it from defeat. Nevertheless the Muslims could not automatically count on the support of the erstwhile enemies of Gobir, or even of some Muslim and Fulani groups, while, as yet, it seemed unlikely that they could achieve victory. The victory at Tabkin Kwotto was an important landmark in the history of the *jihād* because, among other things it brought the Sullebawa Fulani to the camp of the jihadists.[11] Dissident groups in south-western Zamfara such as those of Mafara, Burmi and Donko declared for the Shaikh.[12] Their support was not for the cause of Islamic reform as such. Tabkin Kwotto was an excellent opportunity for them to continue their previous hostility to Gobir on the side of the victors.[13] The Kebbi Fulani gave their support to the Shaikh apparently for similar reasons.

After the reverses suffered by the Muslims in their first assault on Alkalawa and at Tsuntsua, the Tuareg who had hitherto supported them deserted.[14] When after this the jihadists moved to Zamfara in search of a secure base, they found ready support from Abarshi, a claimant to the Zamfara throne. In fact, he had already thrown off his allegiance to the reigning *sarkin* Zamfara. The dispute over the Zamfara succession was resolved by the Shaikh in favour of Abarshi.[15] In Sabongari which was the base of the jihadists in Zamfara there was, among the Shaikh's community, a group of Kebbawa under the leadership of ʽUthmān Masā, a pretender to the Kebbi throne. It was in consultation with this group that the jihadists had decided to attack Kebbi.[16] The Shaikh also appointed ʽUthmān Masā emir over the conquered southern portion of Kebbi.

In the Gobir–Zamfara–Kebbi region, the Fulani, perhaps for racial considerations, were the most consistent in their support for the *jihād*. Last and Johnston have demonstrated how difficult

11. Last, *op. cit.*, pp. 28–9.
12. *Ibid.*; *I.M.* p. 82.
13. *Ibid.*
14. Last, *op. cit.*, p. 35.
15. *Ibid.*, pp. 32–3; for other details of the first Zamfara campaign see *I.M.* p. 90.
16. *I.M.* p. 91. For details of the Zamfara and Kebbi campaigns, see *I.M.* p. 91 f., Last, pp. 32–4, 36–8 and Johnston, pp. 50–8.

it was for the jihadists to find food, and how this determined their movements and actions.[16a] Their search and demand for food in Zamfara soon became oppressive to the population. While Kebbi was still being subdued in 1805, the Zamfarawa rose in rebellion. It is seldom that in the struggle to sustain an ideal by recourse to arms the ethics which that ideal dictates are respected in the actual fighting. Thus, although Muḥammad Bello unequivocally admitted the charge of oppression over the Zamfarawa, this did not stop him from ruthlessly stamping out their rebellion.[17] During some of the darkest periods for the jihadists, between the battles of Alwasa and Gwandu, the southern Kebbi revolted with ʿUthmān Masā at their head. He was killed later in battle against the jihadists.[18] While the jihadists were carving out a base for their power in Gobir, Zamfara and Kebbi, permanent enmity was being consolidated against them in substantial parts of those states.

KATSINA, KANO AND DAURA

The *jihād*, originally a revolt against Gobir authority, had meanwhile spread to other Hausa states. The *Sarakuna* of the Hausa states, such as those of Katsina and Kano, had refused an appeal from the Shaikh contained in a letter he addressed to them late in 1804 to support his *jihād* and the reform of Islam.[19] Only Zaria, whose Sarki Jattau[20] accepted the appeal, was not attacked. Not until it revolted after Jattau's death (1806) was the *jihād* begun against it. As the rulers of the other Hausa states took the offensive against their subjects who joined the Shaikh's revivalist movement, the local revolt in Gobir became general throughout Hausaland and beyond. From 1805 onwards, leaders of Muslim communities came from far and wide to pay homage (*bayʿa*) to the Shaikh and to be appointed by him as his *nuwwāb* (deputies or agents) charged with waging the *jihād* against the recalcitrant

16(a). Last: pp. 27, 31, 32, 33, 34, 35; Johnston: pp. 43, 46, 50, 52, 54.

17. *I.M.* pp. 94, 95; Last, p. 34.

18. *I.M.* p. 104.

19. *I.M.* p. 83; the kings of Katsina and Kano were said to have torn their copies of the letter.

20. The *Labarun Hausawa*, vol. i, p. 44, 'Lisafin sarakuna Zakzak', refers to him as Ishaku (Isḥāq) called Jattau (literally 'red-skinned', meaning 'fair in complexion').

rulers and peoples in their various localities.[21] The Shaikh gave out flags to these leaders as a symbol of his authority. By the Shaikh's acceptance of the submission of these leaders, their scattered communities were formally brought under one central authority.

The *jihād* against Katsina was begun during the dry season of 1805. Daura, Katsina and Kano allied to oppose the Muslims, but the military collapse of the allied forces early in the struggle led to the fall of each of these states. A bitter struggle, which claimed the lives of several successive Katsina kings both in Katsina and Dankama—to which the Katsina Habe had retreated—could not prevent the Muslim occupation of Katsina.[22] A like fate overtook Daura whose King, Abdu, was fiercely attacked by his Muslim subjects and made to flee into Bornu territory.[23] About the same time (1807) the King of Kano, Al-Walī, was finally put to flight by Muslims and Fulani clans living in the suburbs of Birnin Kano. He was killed at a place called Burum-Burum.[24]

The towns of Dankama, Maradi and Tessawa, to which the Katsina Habe had retreated, allied with Damagaram (a vassal of Bornu). Together they became the inveterate enemies of the Caliphate and a source of threat to the emirates of Katsina, Daura, Kano, and even Zaria throughout the nineteenth century.

THE JIHĀD IN ZARIA

Following the revolt of Zaria against the Shaikh's authority after Sarki Jattau's death, a force under Mallam Musa, a former

21. *I.M.* pp. 104–5. Bello records the swearing of allegiance to the Shaikh (represented by Bello) at Birnin Gada. See also *D.M.* f. 29. Bello is said to have appointed Suleiman of Kano at this time (i.e. third year after *hijra*—1805/6). See Last, *op. cit.*, pp. 53–4 for list of recipients of flags from the Shaikh.
22. For the conquest of Katsina, see *I.M.* p. 95 f.; Henry Barth, *Travels and Discoveries in North and Central Africa* (London, 1857), vol. ii, pp. 40, 80–1. F. Daniel, *History of Katsina* (mimeographed, 1937), and *Labarun Hausawa da Makwabtansu*, vol. i, p. 41, 'Wandansu Labarun Katsina' collected by Magajin Gari Zaiyanu from Liman Zagami, Kasar Kogo.
23. *I.M.* p. 97; cf. S. J. Hogben, *Muhammedan Emirates of Nigeria*, p. 80; Hogben states that Sarkin Daura lost his title in this encounter.
24. *Tarīkh Kano* (Ibadan, 82/165, pp. 95–6), reign of Al-Wali, Al-Wali reigned for three years during the Fulani trouble (i.e. d. *c.* 1807).

student of the Shaikh, was sent against it.[25] Before the *jihād*, Fulanis settled in Zaria are said to have revolted against the King. According to an oral tradition related by M. G. Smith, Musa received the support of some Habe vassals of Zaria on his way to the capital.[26] The breaking of Zaria resistance and the putting to flight of the *sarki* with his loyal followers seem to have been accomplished with little difficulty. The pursuit of fugitive Zaria forces to Kajuru and Zuba (vassal states of Zaria) ended in the overthrow of the Habe rulers of those places.[27] Lapai, another vassal state of Zaria, surrendered without fighting and thus retained its dynasty.

After many military campaigns lasting until *c.* 1812,[28] Musa was sufficiently entrenched in Zaria to undertake extension of his authority over all the former vassals of Zaria to the south. He accomplished this by giving flags to leading Muslim fighters authorizing them to subjugate the states to the south in his name. The local Fulani leaders of Jema'a and 'Abdullāh Zanga of Keffi were prevented from obtaining flags direct from Sokoto and compelled to accept Zaria authority.[29] Nasarawa was brought under Zaria through the agency of Makama Dogo who had been a notable helper of Musa during the conquest of Zaria.[30]

Zaria, with Adamawa, was unique among the emirates of the Caliphate in its size. Within the confines of this sprawling emirate were tribes whose allegiance was at the best nominal. The far-flung exploits of Musa's agents among numerous heathen peoples merely enabled outposts of Islam to be founded. These outposts became centres of military operations against surrounding heathen enemy peoples. Keffi, one of the more powerful of

25. The appeal to the *Sarakuna* of Hausaland which the Shaikh sent out from Magabchi was in 1805; it is therefore certain that Jattau, Sarkin Zazzau, and not his successor Makkau, accepted the Shaikh's appeal. Makkau rejected it. Musa was not named *Amīr* of Zaria until 1808—see *D.M.* f. 30; see also D. M. Last, 'A solution to the Problems of Dynastic chronology in 19th Century Zaria and Kano', *J.H.S.N.* iii, no. 3 (1966). Jattau most probably died in 1806 and not in 1802 as contained in the Zaria King list.

26. M. G. Smith, *Government in Zazzau* (Oxford, 1960), p. 139.

27. *A Chronicle of Abuja*, p. 5.

28. *D.M.* f. 30.

29. J. C. Sciortino, *Notes on Nassarawa Province* (London, 1920), p. 6; M.G. Smith, *op. cit.*, p. 140.

30. *Labarun Hausawa da Makwabtansu*, vol. i, p. 44.

Zaria vassals, for example, continued to fight pagan peoples till the British occupation in 1902.[31]

BORNU AND THE EMIRATES ON ITS WESTERN FRONTIERS

In the meantime emirates of the Caliphate were being founded to the east of Daura, Katsina, Kano and Zaria, while the Fulani in Bornu had revolted. Bornu survived as an independent state after a protracted and gruelling struggle marked by several reverses.[32] Thenceforth it showed itself an inveterate enemy of Sokoto and its emirates on its western frontiers as well as a willing ally of Sokoto's enemies until *c.* 1880.

Besides Ardo Lerlima who led the *jihād* in Bornu, Gwoni Mukhtar, Ibrahīm Zaki, Bi-Abdur (ʿUmar) and his brother Muḥammad Sambo (Digimsa) all received the white flags from the Shaikh ʿUthmān to wage the *jihād* in their various localities on the western frontiers of Bornu.[33]

By 1808 the foundation of the emirate of Hadejia had been laid under the leadership first, of Bi-Abdur and then of his brother, Muḥammad Sambo, both of whom had been fighting in Auyo since 1805.[34] Bi-Abdur had died in *c.* 1806, leaving the leadership to Muḥammad Sambo, who became the first Emir of Hadejia. Katagum was founded by Ibrahīm Zaki (*c.* 1810).[35] The third principal emirate in this region, Missau, was not founded until after 1830 following protracted wars said to have lasted three years[36] with the joint army of the Emir of Gombe, Buba Yero, and the Emir of Hadejia, Dankawa, attacking the district. The then Caliph, Muḥammad Bello, appointed Muḥammad Manga, son of Gwoni Mukhtar, as the first Emir of Missau. The type of co-operative effort thus shown by the emirates on the

31. D. J. M. Muffet, *Concerning Brave Captains* (London, 1964), p. 64; record of oral traditions collected from Hassan Keffi. Pagans referred to are the Riri, Toni of Dari and the Mada.
32. *I.M.* p. 122 ff.; J. M. Fremantle: 'History of Katagum Emirate in Kano Province', *J.A.S.*, x (1911), p. 308; and Y. Urvoy, *Histoire de l'Empire du Bornou*, Mémoire de l'IFAN, no. 7 (Paris, 1949), p. 99 ff.
33. Last, *op. cit.*, p. 54.
34. Fremantle, as above, *J.A.S.* x, p. 196.
35. *Ibid.*, p. 315.
36. *Ibid.*, p. 399.

eastern frontiers of the Caliphate in the conquest of Missau seems to have generally characterized relations between them for the greater part of the century. The three major emirates together with the smaller ones of Dambam and Jama'ari continued to live under the shadow of the threat of Bornu and Bedde, immediately to the east of them. With the insecurity of the eastern frontier, united action in times of danger would seem to have found acceptance among the emirates there.

THE JIHĀD IN GOMBE, BAUCHI AND ADAMAWA

The eastern emirates of the Caliphate, those of Gombe, Bauchi, and Adamawa[37] shared a common peculiarity of having been established amid multifarious heathen tribes. The establishment and defence of these emirates against the opposition of numerous tribes involved protracted fighting. After receiving their flags from the Shaikh 'Uthmān the *jihād* leaders, Buba Yero, Ya'qūb b. Daṭi and Adam b. Al-Ḥasan for Gombe, Bauchi and Adamawa respectively, had to assert their authority among their own peoples. Ya'qūb was not enthusiastically accepted by his own people, the Jarawa.[38] The intervention of the Shaikh was necessary to uphold the authority of Modibo Adam, who came from the small Fulani Ba clan, against the contention of the leaders of the more powerful clans like the Wollarbe and the Jillaga.[39] In the latter case the uneasy allegiance of the chiefs of the numerous Fulani clans to Modibo Adam broke into open revolt during the reigns of his sons in the second half of the nineteenth century.

Owing to the numerous fronts on which the *jihād* had to be fought to preserve their emirates, Gombe, Bauchi and Adamawa gave full expression to a policy of delegating authority to subordinates to conquer and superintend their various districts and tribes. Buba Yero, with a large number of Fulani clans in his emirate, appointed no less than thirteen deputies besides his

37. 'Eastern emirates' means the emirates directly under Sokoto as distinct from the Gwandu emirates. The Emir of Adamawa was normally referred to as Amīr al-Yamān (Emir of the south).
38. *Labarun Hausawa da Makwabtansu*, vol. i, p. 46, 'Labarin Asalin Bauchi'.
39. H. K. Strumpell, *A History of Adamawa*, p. 18.

immediate relations and close companions.[40] His battles and raids were numerous,[41] extending from Jukunland across the Gongola to beyond Shellen in the north, and from towns in Biu and Fika districts to towns now in Bauchi emirate.[42] A dispute between Yaʿqūb and Buba Yero, leading to war, broke out because of Yero's encroachment on lands west of the Gongola to which Yaʿqūb laid claims. Bauchi defeated Gombe although they both amicably ironed out their differences thereafter.[43] But the question of confirming Gombe's hold on the tribes over which Buba Yero had laid claims by attack remained to baffle his sons after his death in *c.* 1841.[44]

In Bauchi Yaʿqūb fought several lengthy wars against, among many others, the Yergam, Montol, Angas, and the tribes of the Dass mountains.[45] The mountainous terrain and the consequent difficulty of finding access, the ease with which the enemy tribes could find refuge in the hills for launching counterattacks, made pagan resistance to the Muslim forces so difficult to suppress that Yaʿqūb had to concede to some of them permission to persist in paganism so long as they paid *jizya* to him as *dhimmis*.[46]

All along, Yaʿqūb's search for a secure capital had continued. From his initial settlement at Warinje he moved to Inkil and finally he built Garun Bauchi close by, apparently during the later years of his life. At Bauchi different peoples like Fulani, Bornawa, Hausawa, gathered round him until the population grew so great that the original city, with a wall in which were four

40. *Tabyīn Amr Buba Yero, op. cit.*
41. *Ibid.* This short document is devoted mainly to an account of the wars of the Emirs of Gombe throughout the nineteenth century.
42. *Ibid.*; also Babagoro, *op. cit.*
43. *Labarun Hausawa da Makwabtansu*, vol. i, p. 47; 'Labarin Asalin Bauchi'; also C. L. Temple, *Notes on the Tribes, Provinces, Emirates and States of Northern Nigeria* (Cape Town, 1919), p. 420. The account given by Temple on the authority of Mallam Mustafa, teacher to the children of Yaʿqūb of Bauchi, seems identical with the account in *Labarun Hausawa*.
44. *Tabyīn Amr Buba Yero.*
45. For detailed account of the wars of Yaʿqūb b. Daṭi, see Imām Muḥammad's *Tarīkh ʿUmarāʾ Bauchi* and also 'Labarin Asalin Bauchi'. Yaʿqūb fought as far as Bukuru to the west and Lafia Beriberi to the south-west.
46. *Tarīkh ʿUmarāʾ Bauchi*; see also Gerhard Rohlfs: *Quer Durch Afrika*, 2 vols (Leipzig, 1874), vol. ii, p. 53. I am grateful to Dr Victor Low for an English translation of extracts from this book.

gates, had to be considerably expanded. The expanded city had a new wall with nine gates.[47]

Modibo Adam b. Al-Ḥasan had the same problems that faced the *mujāhidūn* of Gombe and Bauchi. His wars were waged over an extensive area and he is said to have had no respite from fighting until his death[48] in 1848. From his first capital, Gurin, he fought against the Battas (a powerful tribe) who fled to the mountains, whence they persistently challenged Fulani authority throughout the nineteenth century. Modibo Adam obtained the initial but doubtful submission of Mandara. He raided the Yanguru, Fali, Kilba, Muffu and Daba pagans to the north and the Verre, Chamba and Dui, to the south.[49] In view of the many-sided pagan opposition he had to face and the keen rivalry for power and position among the Fulani clans, he had to concede considerable independence of action to his lieutenants. He therefore depended on a large number of local heads for the success of his *jihād*. During his lifetime, Modibo Adam is said to have given out twenty-four flags to such local leaders.[50] He later moved capital from Gurin to Joboliwo and finally settled in Yola during the last decade of his life (*c.* 1840). Like Bauchi, he recognized the strength of some of the pagan tribes by granting them independence while contenting himself with their paying tribute to him as their suzerain.[51]

At Adam's death, his authority was effectively established over Ngaundere, Bubban jidda, Tibati, Banyo, Madagalli, Golumba, Fali, the Marua districts and Yola. The vehement insubordination of local Fulani clan heads, to which Modibo Adam had made concessions and which he had thereby unwittingly strengthened, was to break out in revolts under his son Lawal, and to weaken further the unconsolidated conquests. Gombe, Bauchi and Adamawa emirates had to fight wars of survival and consolidation in the period before 1880. They thus became some of the chief suppliers of slaves within the Caliphate.

47. *Tarīkh 'Umarā' Bauchi*, p. 38.
48. Strumpell, *op. cit.*, p. 21.
49. *Ibid.*, p. 20.
50. Captain C. Vicars-Boyle, 'Historical notes on the Yola Fulanis', *J.A.S.* x, no. 27 (1910), pp. 82–4.
51. *Ibid.*, p. 77.

THE GWANDU EMIRATES

In the western emirates (those which fell under Gwandu from 1812) the process of establishing Muslim dominance was slower and, even in the end, apparently less complete than in the east. Besides, large tracts of territory remained unsubjugated well into the nineteenth century. Although the Shaikh's army conquered many towns in Dendi, Gwari (including the capital—Birnin Gwari), Nupe and Zaberma territories from 1809 to 1810,[52] Kuta in Gwariland was unsuccessfully assailed in 1811 and expeditions into Borgu in 1813–14 failed to establish the basis of permanent Muslim rule there.[53]

It seems that the planting of Islam in the regions to the south of Gwandu and Kebbi had been difficult because they had less solid traditions of Islam and consequently an insufficiently strong core of Muslims to lead and wage the *jihād* locally. Islam did, however, find strong outposts in Nupe and Iḷọrin. Although traditions of Islamization had been present in both places, the success of the *jihād* there seems to have been owed far more to their internal political situations than to any burning desire on the part of Muslims to reform religion. These same political situations left a legacy of baffling problems which plagued both emirates throughout the nineteenth century.

Mallam Dendo, the founder of Nupe emirate, arrived in Nupe about 1810,[54] and probably even later, at a time when two cousins, Majiya and Jimada, had declared themselves rival Etsus, a situation which precipitated civil war. Dendo came as an itinerant preacher capable of making *asiri*[55]—charms with magic power. It is difficult to know whether or not he was, to begin with, ambitious to establish his rule over Nupe, but it is clear that

52. *I.M.* pp. 120 and 121; *T.W.* pp. 124–30; *R.A.* p. 27; *D.M.* f. 31.
53. *I.M.* p. 111.
54. Nadel, *op. cit.*, pp. 76, 406, gives two dates, 1778–95 and 1810 respectively. It is possible that Dendo visited Nupe before the *Jihād* but Nadel's dates for the beginning of the nineteenth century are so confused and definitely call for considerable revision. Cf. E. J. Arnett, *Rise of the Sokoto Fulani*, p. 26.
55. *'Umar b. Muḥammad b. al-Ḥasan b. Adam*, Imām of Bida. *Tarīkh min bilād Bida wa Tarīkh al-bilād min bilād Gbara*: N.A.K. KADCAPTORY, Box 2, item 22. Hausa version of this document is in *Labarun Hausawa*, vol. i, p. 49 ff. 'Litafin Chude' (Tsoede).

the opportunity he had of playing one Etsu cousin against the other very soon decided the goal of his ambitions.

From being Majiya's guest Dendo became the arbiter in the Nupe dynastic rivalry.[56] Having successfully put himself at the head of Fulani strength in Nupe he threw his forces into the balance on Majiya's side. An engagement with Jimada at Ragada ended in the latter's defeat. Dendo's followers and power grew so much and so fast that Majiya felt compelled to remove the obvious threat to his own position by expelling him from his capital, Raba.

Majiya's failure to conciliate Dendo, not being able to crush him, seems in the circumstances to have been the real basis from which the success of the *jihād* in Nupe derived. Dendo allied with Idrīs, Jimada's son. Together they fled to Iḷorin where they allied with the Muslim forces against the Nupe army which came to attack them.[57] The news of the approach of the victorious army of Dendo and Idrīs led to panic in Raba and evacuation of the town, which then fell easily to Dendo.

Dendo, firmly established in Raba, instructed his sons to start collecting *jizya* from the native Nupe population. This led to disagreements with Idrīs. When the latter subsequently allied with Majiya against Dendo, it was too late. Both allies were by then too weak to check Dendo's growing power. Their sons after them were appointed figurehead Etsus by Dendo, who by the time of his death in 1833[58] was the effective ruler of Nupe. Resentment among the old Nupe dynasties against the Fulani who deprived them of power, and bitter rivalries among Dendo's children, meant for the emirate of Nupe a long unsettled period of internecine wars before it was consolidated. Until Masaba (Muḥammad Saba) succeeded as emir (Etsu) in 1859, it could not be said that the emirate's survival had been guaranteed beyond doubt.

The conquest of Iḷorin was made possible by political tensions and divisions which on the eve of the *jihād* had broken out into

56. The summary of the events which led to the founding of the Nupe emirate is based on Imām 'Umar, *Tarīkh Bida*; E. G. M. Dupigny, *Gazetteer of Nupe Province* (London, 1920), and Nadel, *op. cit.*, p. 76 f.

57. *Tarīkh Bida*, p. 2. *Gazetteer of Nupe Province*, p. 9 f.

58. Dendo was still alive though ailing in 1832 when the Lander brothers visited Raba. He died in the following year.

open revolt in the rapidly tottering Ọyọ empire. The revolt of Afọnja, the Arẹ Ọna Kakanfo (Field-Marshal) against the Alafin of Ọyọ, is a familiar story. Important to the founding of the Ilọrin emirate was Afọnja's invitation to Alimi, a powerful itinerant Muslim leader who had once been expelled from Ọyọ by the Alafin. Alimi drew Muslims, slaves converted to Islam and the few local Fulani[59] to his *jamā'a* which, allied with Ṣọlagbẹru's community of Oke-Suna ward in Ilọrin, became an effective fighting force. Afọnja was therefore able to defy Ọyọ.

When, soon afterwards, Afọnja tried to curb the excesses of the members of the *jamā'a*, who rapidly learnt to indulge in molesting innocent Ilọrin citizens, Alimi turned against him. Hostilities broke out. It was a moment of decision for Ṣọlagbẹru. Probably because he was dissatisfied with Afọnja for refusing to change to Islam or even to destroy sacred groves and other open symbols of the old religion, he gave his loyalty to the Muslims. In the meantime he remained neutral in the actual fighting, perhaps because he was reluctant to join in an attack on his liege-lord. Afọnja died in the ensuing battle between him and the Muslims. Thenceforth, Ṣọlagbẹru's unflinching support for Alimi vitiated the efforts of surrounding Yoruba towns to co-operate in order to expel the foreigners.[60]

After Alimi's death (*c.* 1823) rivalry for power broke out between Ṣọlagbẹru and the former's son, 'Abd al-Salām. The foreign conquerors, who now obtained a flag from Gwandu, could not be expelled, largely because Ṣọlagbẹru failed to rally powerful Yoruba towns like Ikoyi and Ogbomọshọ round him against 'Abd al-Salām. On the contrary, he neglected the more urgent issue of Fulani conquest in favour of allying with Ogbomọshọ against Ikoyi, thus further dividing and weakening the already enfeebled Yoruba resistance. Completely misjudging his own strength, it must be admitted, Ṣọlagbẹru attempted to assert his supreme authority in the Ilọrin area by demanding tribute from the Onikoyi. He did not get the tribute, and, worse still, the Onikoyi defected to his enemy. 'Abd al-Salām's forces attacked the isolated Ṣọlagbẹru soon after and killed him. The position of

59. According to Aḥmad b. Abū (Abī) Bakr—*Ta'lif Akhbār al-Qurūn min 'Umarā' bilād Ilọrin*: there were cattle Fulani in Ilọrin many of whom were converted to Islam by Mallam Alimi.

60. Rev. Samuel Johnson, *The History of the Yorubas* (London, 1960), pp. 197–9, 200–2.

'Abd al-Salām was thus assured as the undisputed Emir of Iḷọrin[61] (*c.* 1830).

Because of lack of co-operation among the states of the tottering Ọyọ empire, the Fulani attack on Iḷọrin could not be nipped in the bud, but the emirate thus established had to defend itself against constant attacks from southern Yorubaland. For some years after 'Abd al-Salām's succession, and again towards the end of the century, Iḷọrin tended to be relatively isolated from the Caliphate. For much of the nineteenth century Iḷọrin's military preoccupation was with the Yoruba to the south.

A number of observations can be made from the course of the establishment of the Caliphate and its emirates. In many parts of the Caliphate, the Muslim conquest was not accomplished until the third decade after the outbreak of the *jihād* of the Shaikh. This fact not only underlines the difficulties encountered in the founding of the emirates, but it also meant that the process of consolidating the Muslim conquests, in many places, was pushed further still into the century. Even when established, all the emirates were faced with problems of self-preservation because their conquests gave rise to opposition from different groups. None of them, even at the peak of religious enthusiasm, was able to achieve such a complete victory through the *jihād* as could have stifled all opposition.

The task of suppressing opposition was to become the preoccupation of the emirates throughout the Caliphate's existence. For most of the emirates, the task of founding had been a local one; preoccupation with local problems, particularly of defence, was to become traditional among them. Inter-emirate co-operation, not unknown, was the exception rather than the rule, even though common loyalty to the Caliph and a sense of belonging to one community minimized inter-emirate conflicts. These were, however, not entirely unknown.[62] Within the Islamic communities there were, during the founding phases, signs of internal conflicts between the leaders of the *jihād* in the various localities. These conflicts came into the open soon after the initial establishment of the emirates.

All these meant that the elements of strength and weakness in the Caliphate were to be determined by the extent of the military

61. *Ibid.*, pp. 201, 203–5.
62. See above, p. 32; also below, p. 89f.

commitments of the various emirates and the effectiveness of the organization of the Caliphate's government. For each emirate, in addition, the extent to which its internal conflicts could be reconciled went a long way to determine its strength. It is now necessary to take a look at the framework of the organization of the Caliphate.

THE STRUCTURE OF THE CALIPHATE

The problem of consolidating the newly founded emirates of the Caliphate, including as it did, the establishment of an effective administrative machinery, was extremely difficult. In an age of slow communications, the enormous distances[63] between the various emirates and Sokoto did not render administrative control from the centre easy. Yet it was possible through the application of Islamic norms of state organization to evolve a structurally coherent administrative system for the Caliphate. In the arrangement that emerged, the Caliph was the effective source of all authority and, certainly, the common bond which held the component parts together as one polity.

The coming together of the Islamic communities in the various localities of the Caliphate under one authority—the Caliph—was, as earlier stated, the result of their acceptance of the supreme

63. To anyone who has travelled extensively in Northern Nigeria, this is obvious. Present road distances between some centres of the nineteenth-century Sokoto Caliphate are as follows:

Sokoto–Kano	339 miles	Sokoto–Gombe	684 miles
Sokoto–Bauchi	587 ,,	Sokoto–Yola	838 ,,

all the above are on the same route—Sokoto to Yola.

Sokoto–Missau	402 miles	Bida–Zaria	253 miles
Sokoto–Zaria	250 ,,	Ilọrin–Kano	519 ,,
Sokoto–Keffi (via Zaria)	514 ,,		

Distances worked out from Northern Nigeria Road Map, Ministry of Works' Plan No. 12266/8 of November 1962, revised February 1966. Barth, vol. ii, gave the following nineteenth-century figures in days:

Kano–Zaria	(163 miles)	9 days	pp. 562–3
Kano–Keffi	(427 ,,)	25 ,,	pp. 562–4
vol. iv:			
Kano–Bauchi	(188 ,,)	8 ,,	pp. 571–2
Kano–Sokoto	(339 ,,)	17 ,,	pp. 571–2

Distances given in brackets are based on 1966 roads.

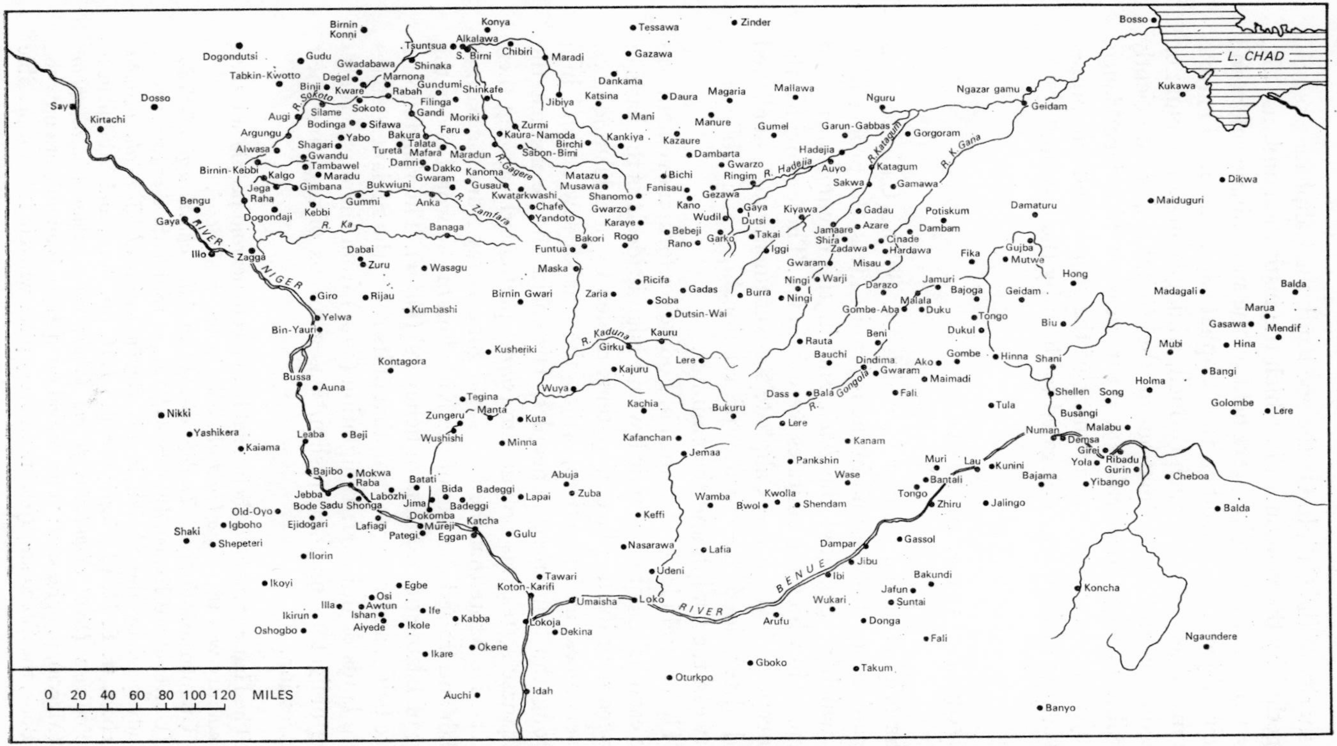

The Sokoto Caliphate and neighbouring states: place names

authority of the Caliph. On the one hand, the Caliphate was held together by the veneration in which the institution and, usually, the person of the Caliph were held by the subordinate rulers and their subjects. On the other, the Caliphate derived cohesion from its machinery of government which, while placing a premium on obedience and subordination to the Caliph, was sufficiently flexible to allow local rulers a great measure of independence, subject to their non-infringement of the *sharīʿa* and the proper discharge of functions delegated to them by the Caliph.

REFORMIST IDEAS OF STATE

The origins of the manner in which the Sokoto Caliphate was organized are to be found in the reformist ideas, the propagation of which precipitated the *jihād* and in the circumstances and manner in which the emirates were founded. These provided the concepts on which the Caliphate's government was established and determined the nature of relationships and obligations between the Caliph and the emirates.

The central idea of ʿUthmān b. Fodiye's reform movement was the establishment of Islamic law and Islamic ideals as the basis of government in the place of systems ridden by non-Islamic laws, observances, and practices, which the Shaikh saw around him among the 'Sudanese'[64] peoples. His main charge against the Sudanese states was polytheism (*shirk*) particularly among their rulers. He wrote that the rulers had gone astray from the path of Allah and 'raised the flag of the Kingdom of the world above the flag of Islam and are thus unbelievers' (*kufār*). The religion of a state being, according to him, that of its ruler, the Sudanese states were lands of unbelief. Emigration (*firār*) from them was therefore obligatory on the Muslim,[65] as a means of avoiding their oppression.

64. The Hausa states and their neighbours were negroid people and their country was therefore *bilād al-sūdān* hence 'Sudanese'.
65. ʿUthmān b. Fodiye, *Tanbīḥ al-Ikhwān ʿala aḥwāl arḍ al-Sudān* (University of Ibadan Library 82/212), p. 18, identical arguments are advanced by the Shaikh in his *Bayān wujūb al-hijra ʿala al-ibād*, ch. 1, tr. F. H. El-Masri; see also *I.M.* pp. 8–11, and ʿAbdullāh b. Fodiye's *Ḍiyā' al-ḥukkām fī ma lahum wa alaihim min al-aḥkām* (Mecca), p. 6, he says: 'The obligation of *Hijra* is an obligation by the Book, the *Sunna* and *Ijmāʿ* from every place wherein it is not possible

To the Muslims, those who opposed or harassed Muslims who accepted the ideals and standards of the faith as preached by 'Uthmān b. Fodiye rendered themselves unbelievers by such overt acts. To abolish the illegalities of the Sudanese states, the Shaikh drew attention to the legality of first calling unbelievers to the right path, and if this proved ineffective, of waging the *jihād* against them, in accordance with classical traditions of the faith.[66]

The Shaikh 'Uthmān and his helpers sought therefore to restore the practice of Islam among the 'Sudanese' to the classical pattern of the early rightly guided Caliphs (*Al-Khulafā' al-Rashidūn*). Their concern for orthodoxy is evident in the *jihād* literature of the Shaikh, 'Abdullāh his brother, and Muḥammad Bello.[67] The concern of the reformers was to expound the pristine clarity of Islamic jurisprudence as it touched the various obligations of the individual as well as the whole of society in an orthodox Islamic *Umma*.

The concern of the reformers for legal orthodoxy is discernible in their preparations for and prosecution of the *jihād* and in the establishment of the Caliphate. While talking of the attempt of the Sokoto *mujāddidūn* to mirror the early Caliphate of the golden

for the Muslim to uphold his religion and unbelievers' laws are imposed on him'.

66. 'Uthmān b. Fodiye, *Wathīqat ahl al-Sudān*, tr. A. D. H. Bivar, *J.A.H.*, iii (1961), pp. 235–48; clauses 1, 2, 12, 15. The legality of calling unbelievers to the faith before waging the *jihād* against them if they refuse is in accordance with classical Islamic traditions. See Qur'ān VIII, 4, IX, 5 and 29, XVII, 18. M. Khadduri, *War and Peace in the Law of Islam* (Baltimore, 1965)—quotation from al-Bukhārī's *Ṣaḥiḥ* 'I have been ordered to fight polytheists until they say there is no God but Allah; if they say it they are secured in their blood and property.' See also A. H. Al-Mawardi, *al-aḥkām al-sulṭaniyya*, tr. into French by E. Fagnan (Alger, 1915), pp. 75–6, 98–9 and *Encyclopaedia of Islam* (London, 1913), *jihād*. 'Uthmān b. Fodiye in *Bayān wujūb al-hijra*, ch. 13, 14, 15, 16, 17, 32, stresses that the obligation of *jihād* on the Muslim community is binding 'until the religion is God's'.

67. See, e.g., Muḥammad Bello, *Infāq al-Maisūr*, 'Uthmān b. Fodiye, *Bayān wujūb al-hijra*, *Wathīqat ahl al-sudān*, *Kitāb al-Farq*, *Tanbīḥ al-Ikhwān 'ala al-aḥkām al-amān*, *Tanbīḥ al-Ikhwān 'ala aḥwāl arḍ al-Sudān*, *Nasā'iḥ al-'Ummat al-Muḥammadiyya*, *Ta'līm al-Ikhwān bi 'l-umūr allatī Kafarnā bihā Mulūk al-sudān*; 'Abdullāh b. Fodiye, *Ḍiyā' al-ḥukkām fī ma lahum wa 'alaihim min al-aḥkām; Tazyīn al-Waraqāt*. The writings of the Shaikh are generally apologetic; explaining the grounds on which the *jihād* was legally justified.

age of Islam, it is relevant here to note Hiskett's observation that the written sources they read seem to have been predominantly works of the late Abbāsid theorists of the Malikī school of legists.[68] Since these jurists were concerned with what was the legally correct constitutional position of the Abbāsid Caliphate according to God's word and the traditions of the Prophet, they were preoccupied with what would be legally correct according to the practices of the early Caliphate of the first four Caliphs. This they therefore mirrored in their writings.

In the preparations of the Muslim community before the *jihād*, the Shaikh sought legal justification for the Muslim's acquisition of war weapons even in a situation in which common sense and necessity dictated such action.[69] The persecution of Muslims by Gobir which gave rise to the Shaikh's *hijra*, except for the fact that the Shaikh himself was not immediately threatened, bears striking parallels with the circumstances which led to the Prophet's *hijra* from Mecca. Indeed, the Shaikh ʿUthmān, like many reformers of Islamic practices, thought the circumstances were similar.[70]

The fortunes of the Shaikh's wars are seen by him as similar to the fortunes attendant on the Prophet's wars.[71] Concern for legal classical orthodoxy, almost an obsession, was again shown after the first raids to Matankari and Konni. On this occasion the booty—*ghanima*—was not distributed according to the *sharīʿa*.

68. M. Hiskett claims that he can recognize only about three of a total of about sixty authorities quoted in *Ḍiyā'al-ḥukkām* as not belonging to the Malikī school and also that the Sokoto *Mujāddidūn's* most oft-quoted authorities were jurists of the late Abbāsid epoch; see M. Hiskett, 'An Islamic tradition of reform in the Western Sudan', *B.S.O.A.S.* xxv (1962), p. 592.

69. ʿUthmān b. Fodiye declared *c.* 1794/95 that the making ready of weapons by the Muslims was *sunna*. By that time the Shaikh's community had become a state within the state of Gobir pregnant with rebellion and Gobir authorities were already adopting strong-arm methods to suppress them.

70. See R. A. Adeleye *et al.*, 'Sifofin Shehu', *Bulletin of the Centre of Arabic Documentation* (Ibadan) ii, no. 1 (1966). In lines 7–11 of this poem the Shaikh draws a parallel between his *hijra* and the Prophet's, vide, notes to the translation, p. 32, note 3. Note 4 on line 10; the Shaikh draws a parallel between his age and that of the Prophet at the beginning of their missions.

71. *Ibid.* line 12; the Muslim victory at the battle of Tabkin Kwotto (Rabiʿ al-awal 1219 A.H.) is compared with the Prophet's victory at Baḍr, vide also *T.W.* p. 55.

A treasurer, 'Umar al-Kammu, was thereupon appointed to prevent the recurrence of such a breach of the *sharī'a*.[72]

The depth of the ideological background and the purist religious norms on which the 'Sokoto' reformers attempted to build the *jihād* demonstrate clearly their desire to set up a state which would properly mirror the early Caliphate. D. M. Last and M. Hiskett have endeavoured to show the great extent to which they successfully did this.[73]

The position and duties of the Caliph. Right from the inception of the *jihād* the politico-religious needs of the nascent community had been appreciated and attempts were made to meet them. Soon after the Shaikh accomplished his *hijra* the *muhājirīn* (emigrants) composing his community paid homage (*bay'a*) to him as their *Imām* (i.e. *Khalifa* or *Amīr al-Mu'minīn*) as an obligation enjoined by the Qur'ān and the *Sunna*.[74] The *sunnī* viewpoint is that the appointment of an *Imām* is compulsory for the Muslims wherever there is no visible *Imām* and that it is obligatory to give obedience to him if he is visible.[75]

72. *I.M.* p. 73.
73. Last, *op. cit.*, pp. 46–60; Hiskett, 'An Islamic tradition of reform in the Western Sudan'. Many of the offices in the Caliphate were derived from later developments in Muslim history after the early Caliphate. However, the office of the chief Qāḍī dates from the time of 'Umar (the second Caliph); see Ibn Khaldun, *Muqaddima*, tr. F. Rosenthal (London, 1958), vol. i, p. 455. The office of Wazir attained full development under the Abbāsid Caliphs—(*Muqaddima*, vol. ii, p. 10) —while the office of chief of Police, Ṣaḥib al-Shurṭa, was a creation of the Abbāsids (*Muqaddima*, vol. ii, p. 36) even though it attained full development under the Ummayyad in Spain and the Fatimids in Egypt—(q.v. *Muqaddima*, vol. i, pp. 456–7). These offices with that of tax collector are the offices specifically mentioned by 'Uthmān b. Fodiye in *Kitāb al-farq*.
74. 'Uthmān b. Fodiye: *T.I.* p. 25; the appointment of the *Imām* or *Amīr al-mu'minīn* (the terms are interchangeable, see *Muqaddima*, vol. i, p. 388, and *al-Aḥkām al-sulṭaniyya*, pp. 5–7) is a necessity for the Muslim community. At the Prophet's death, Abu Bakr was immediately chosen as his *Khalīfa* (successor); the community paid homage and swore allegiance to him. The practice was continued thereafter: see *Muqaddima*, vol. i, p. 389. 'Uthmān b. Fodiye pointed out that the appointment of the *Imām* is obligatory by *Ijmā'*, see *Wathīqat ahl al-Sudan*, clauses v and vi, and *B.W.*, ch. 6; see also 'Abdullāh b. Fodiye, *D.H.* p. 10.
75. M. Khadduri and H. J. Liebesny, *Law in the Middle East* (Washington, 1955), vol. i, pp. 7–8.

The appointment of the Shaikh as the *Amīr al-Mu'minīn* was the central act in the foundation of the Caliphate. Obedience was due to him from all his subjects as a matter of obligation enjoined by the *sharī'a*. His duty was to uphold the religion and exercise political leadership.[76] Spelt out in greater detail,[77] the Caliph was to ensure that religious practice conformed with principles of Islam as maintained under the orthodox Caliphs. In this respect, he had to see to it that the prohibitions enjoined by Allah were adhered to and that the rights of Muslims remained inviolate. Not only must he protect the rights of citizens within the Muslim community, but he must also address himself to the question of adequate protection of the Islamic territory. One of the ways an Imām can do this is by providing the frontiers with garrisons or causing them to be garrisoned in order to obviate surprise enemy attack. It was the Caliph's duty to promote the expansion of Islam by conversion of unbelievers. In this respect, he was duty bound to see that the Muslims fought against unbelievers who refused peaceful invitation to embrace Islam until they were converted or agreed to pay tribute.

In the realm of political administration, the Caliph must be vigilant in ensuring that only canonical taxes are collected from the Islamic state and also that the revenue of the state is disbursed properly—according to the *sharī'a*—and where nothing specific is laid down, in accordance with *maṣlahā* (public welfare). To ensure efficient application of the *sharī'a*, the Caliph must appoint only the right and loyal people into offices of state, and must himself keep a vigilant eye on the affairs of state in order that reliance on his officers should not result in negligence on his part.

The *bay'a* symbolizes a contract of allegiance, entered into by those who make it as an act of surrender to the Caliph of the supervision of their own affairs and their obedience to him in all things.[78] The Caliph's position as the supreme constitutional authority (though not above the law, of which he was the chief

76. *Muqaddima*, vol. i, p. 388.
77. For the duties of the Caliph see Al-Mawardi, pp. 30–1.
78. *Ibid.*, p. 428; see also Qur'ān, IV, 62: 'Oh you who believe, obey Allah, Obey his Prophet and those who have authority among you.' Al-Mawardi quotes *ḥadīth* related by Abu Ḥuraira in which the Prophet said 'He who obeys me obeys God and he who obeys my Amīr obeys me'. *A.S.* p. 96; the same *Ḥadīth* is quoted by 'Uthmān b. Fodiye in *B.W.* ch. 6, and also by 'Abdullāh b. Fodiye in *D.H.* p. 11.

agent) was the central binding force in the Caliphate. The Caliph was the ultimate source of all authority and all powers were exercised in his name.[79]

The officers of state as laid down in the *kitāb al-farq* were appointed in Sokoto.[80] It would be misleading to expect that the offices of the early *Umma* were reflected without variation or modification in the Sokoto Caliphate. Just as the offices of the state had developed out of the circumstances of the early Caliphate and its successors as well as with the growing complexity of administrative problems and the variation of these problems with different localities, so did many offices in the emirates of the Sokoto Caliphate derive of necessity from the Habe and other administrative systems before the *jihād.* Many of the local titles such as the Nupe Etsu and Ndegi, the Bornu Galadima, the Hausa Madaki and the Yoruba Balogun, to name a few, were for instance retained. This did not necessarily entail compromising Islamic principles of administration.

The Caliph and the emirates. Early in the *jihād c.* 1805–06 the first emirs of the provinces were appointed by the Shaikh's authority.[81] They depended on this authority for their acceptability to their communities. Thus only the Shaikh's ruling could quell the dispute for leadership of the *jihād* among the 'Adamawa' Fulani. In Kano similar rivalries showed up early in the *jihād* among the various Fulani clans. The appointment of Suleiman as Emir of Kano on the authority of the Shaikh once again settled the Kano dispute. It is conceivable that reverence for the Shaikh's authority might have prevented similar disputes from coming to the surface in some other emirates.

The dependence of the first emirs on the Shaikh's investiture

79. See *D.H.* pp. 19–37 on the various offices of state. For the necessity of the *Imām* delegating his authority because he cannot perform all functions and in all places together, see pp. 19–20.

80. See *Kitāb al-farq, faṣl.* 3, and *D.H.* ch. 3; Hiskett, 'An Islamic tradition of reform', p. 592, observes that the hierarchy of offices which the Fulani sources reflect from the Wazīr to the lower-ranking offices like the inspector of markets is not that of the early *Umma* of Medina but a re-enactment of the later developments of the organization of the *Umma.*

81. *I.M.* pp. 104–5. Muḥammad Bello received the homage of the 'Eastern Emirs' (from provinces to the East of Gobir) on behalf of the Shaikh 'Uthmān.

to give legal validity to their local *jihād* laid a firm foundation of loyalty to Sokoto, which made any assertion of independence by any emirate an act which would effectively brand the government of that emirate illegal. What the communities in the outlying territories outside Gobir had done in willingly submitting to the Shaikh may be seen as paying homage to a 'visible' Imām. This, as already mentioned, was obligatory for them as *sunnī* Muslims. It must be stressed that this loyalty which the Shaikh received from the various communities was freely given, not imposed.

The theory of what is obligatory for the Muslim apart, this voluntary submission to the Shaikh and, by implication, to his successors, was in practice a deeper basis for lasting loyalty to the Caliph than a forcible integration of the provinces with Sokoto. Furthermore, the Shaikh earned the submission of the various provincial communities because the latter had realized that they shared the same ideals and aspirations with him and his *jam'ā* and that he best and most effectively represented these ideals and aspirations. The likelihood of any properly established emirate successfully asserting its independence was throughout the nineteenth century remote in the extreme.[82]

A further factor which made for cohesion in the Caliphate was the fact that quite a number of the early *jihād* leaders in the emirates, including Ya'qūb of Bauchi, Buba Yero of Gombe, 'Umar Dallaji of Katsina, Modibo Adam of Adamawa, Suleiman of Kano, Musa of Zaria and possibly Mallam Dendo of Nupe, among others, were either personally known to the Shaikh or had been students under him.[83] The more or less personal basis of relationship thus established with the Caliph at the foundation of several emirates would have meant so much more depth to the emirates' loyalty to Sokoto.

The official hierarchies in the emirates were, while not entirely discarding the old Habe and other titles, reflections of the Sokoto model. Like all ideals it is to be expected that the Sokoto Caliphate could, in practice, do no more than approximate to the conceptualized Caliphate of their *jihād* literature. It was impor-

82. See below, p. 95 ff. Even during the Bukhārī and Tukor revolts neither Bukhārī (from all known facts) nor the sons of the Emir 'Abdullāh in Kano respectively talked of declaring their independence of the Caliph.

83. The number of the leaders who had direct contact with the Shaikh still has to be worked out.

tant that a foundation was laid for the *de jure* centralization of authority in the hands of the Caliph. Recognition by subordinates of their *de jure* responsibilities and duties, and their positions *vis-à-vis* the Caliph, provided the guidance necessary to keep the system going. In practice centralization meant no more than a general supervision and intervention directed towards arresting or correcting local departures from expected standards. Such interventions could be and often were crucial.

The writings of the Shaikh and ʿAbdullāh were the sources on the constitution and the law. ʿAbdullāh's *Ḍiyā' al-ḥukkām*,[84] for instance, can be regarded as a comprehensive digest of the constitution and government of the Caliphate and the *Bayān wujūb al-hijra* of the Shaikh as a concise reference book covering diverse aspects of religion and the state. For intellectual, religious and political leadership, the emirates looked up to, and depended on, Sokoto.

> In comparison with imperial expansions generally and particularly with the expansion of the early Arab-Muslim Caliphate, the Sokoto Caliphate's expansion was marked by the peculiar feature that it was not achieved through expeditions organized and sent out from one centre. Its expansion was achieved through a coming together voluntarily rather than through forcible integration by Sokoto. There was therefore no necessity to create a standing or regular army for the overall conquests or for overall defence thereafter.[85]

Because of the vast distances mentioned earlier between most of the emirates and Sokoto, and the preoccupation of each emirate with its own establishment and defence in the early days, the emirates were in most cases founded single-handed by the first emirs without material assistance from Sokoto, or neighbouring emirates. As local defence problems and security against enemies remained, in one degree or the other, with each emirate throughout the century, co-operation in defence matters between a number of neighbouring emirates of Sokoto was the exception rather than the rule. Subordinate emirates were in the habit—in fact it was an obligation—of sending military contingents (*maddād*) to Sokoto to participate in major wars or in the annual dry season raids of Sokoto against its traditional enemies. The continued presence of enemy peoples on the other hand did not

84. The book was in fact written *c.* 1806/7 in answer to a request by the Muslims of Kano for a book of guidance; see *T.W.* pp. 108–9.
85. Adeleye, 'The Sokoto Caliphate in the nineteenth century'.

lead to the creation of professional armies. Military contingents, however, were not usually sent from Sokoto to the emirates. The same reasons which accounted for the founding of most of the emirates without material support from Sokoto also led to their enjoying a relatively high degree of independence in day-to-day affairs. Localism in government and its personnel tended to be emphasized above common policies and organic political integration from Sokoto.

The emirates were controlled from Sokoto through a system of supervision. In *c.* 1812, the Shaikh divided the Caliphate into two: the eastern provinces (east of Sokoto) he gave to his son, Muḥammad Bello, and the western provinces to his brother, ʿAbdullāh.[86] Besides this act, whereby the basis for more effective control over the emirates was laid, a further measure of control was later introduced in the eastern emirates whereby particular emirates came under the supervision of particular office-holders in Sokoto.

Under this arrangement the Caliph's Wazir was the chief officer of state to whom much of the Caliph's power over the eastern emirates was delegated. The unique position of the Wazir and his functions are concisely but effectively stated by ʿAbdullāh b. Fodiye. The Wazir, he wrote:

> is the one to whom the Imām delegates [entrusts with] all affairs, he is like the father to the Imām to wake him when he sleeps, to give him sight when he is blind, to remind him when he forgets. He is the partner in the ordering and clarification of policies and the one who sounds the alarm when danger threatens. He [the Imām] gains from him [the Wazir] knowledge of what he is ignorant of and strengthening of what he knows.[87]

The Shaikh ʿUthmān saw the Wazir as the first pillar of the state and considered that the greatest calamity which could befall a state is that it be deprived of good and honest wazirs.[88] The Wazir was the direct ultimate link between the Caliph and the emirates.

In the course of the nineteenth century, as the practical problems of administration became clarified and ordered, the Wazir

86. See Muḥammad Bello, *Sard al-kalām* (Ibadan, 82/212), *majmūʿ* Haliru Binji. This arrangement, made for the Shaikh's lifetime, became permanent after his death. After an initial quarrel ʿAbdullāh, the first Emir of Gwandu, accepted and paid homage to Muḥammad Bello as Caliph.
87. *D.H.* ch. 3, *faṣl.* 1.
88. *B.W.* ch. 9.

had seven provinces—Kano, Zaria, Hadejia, Gombe, Katagum, Missau, Adamawa—under his direct supervision.[89] Other Sokoto officials supervised the other emirates like Katsina, Daura, Gusau, Zamfara, Muri and, later on in the century, Kontagora.[90] The Wazir, however, had general supervision over those eastern emirates not directly under his charge. The vastness of the territory made the delegation of supervisory authority to officials other than the Wazir a necessity. The Wazir travelled round his emirates on his supervisory rounds, armed with the Caliph's authority. The official confirmation of the appointment of the emirs of the provinces was delegated to him.

As shown by D. M. Last, the Wazir carried with him on his tours blank papers bearing the Caliph's seal, with which he would write out letters of appointment for an emir if he was on the spot at his selection. If there were no disputes the Wazir could make appointments without reference to Sokoto but where there was doubt, he had to ascertain the Caliph's decision.[91] For depositions, if the Wazir was on the spot, he could take action but if not, the local electors could act and seek Sokoto's ratification later. Such ratification was no mere formality. In the absence of the Wazir at the time of selection of an emir by the local electors, if Sokoto approved, the Wazir or some other high state dignitary would be sent out to instal the new emir.

Thus in the theory of the Caliphate's constitution, the emirs held their offices at the good pleasure of the Caliph. The Caliph's court was the final court of appeal to which appeals from the emirates came, through the officer in Sokoto (known as the Door: Hausa—*kofa*) responsible for overseeing the affairs of the particular emirate.[92] Through appointments and through overseeing the affairs of the emirates Sokoto had a potentially wide scope for intervention in the emirates.

The emirates were, in the theory of the constitution, expected to pay certain taxes to Sokoto. These included *zakāt*, *kharaj*, *jizya* (from *dhimmi*), *irth* (inheritance money), and the *khums* (fifth) of the booty. *Fai'* and property whose owner cannot be

89. Last, *op. cit.*, p. 158. My account of the Wazir's role in the emirate is, as will be seen in the footnotes, based on Last. See also Barth, vol. iv, p. 155—footnote.
90. Last, *op. cit.*, pp. 100–1.
91. *Ibid.*, p. 180.
92. *Ibid.*, p. 102.

traced were in addition legitimate sources of revenue for the treasury. In practice it seems that many of the taxes regarded as uncanonical by the Shaikh in his *Kitāb al-Farq* (certainly the cattle tax—*jangali*) continued to be levied in the Caliphate.

Besides supervision, the Caliph informed the emirates about important events like the declaration of war against an enemy or the infiltration of foreigners.[93] For the discharge of his duties to the communities in the emirate, the Caliph depended on the use of the powers he delegated to the emirs. The Shaikh gives us a good example of the kind of guidance the Caliph gave his emirs. In his letter of appointment to Yaʿqūb b. Daṭi of Bauchi, the Shaikh commanded the Emir to observe the following stipulations: (1) that his community should be one in speech and in action and should have no dissensions among them, (2) to be zealous in the repair of mosques, (3) to be zealous in praying in them, (4) to study and teach the Qur'ān, (5) to study and teach the sciences (Islamic), (6) to improve the markets and prohibit illegalities in them, (7) to wage the *jihād* as a duty imposed on Muslims.[94]

It is reasonable to assume that similar letters were sent to other emirs on appointment. The concern to see the Sokoto standards followed in the emirates (as indicated in this letter) is again echoed in a letter from Muḥammad Bello to Yaʿqūb[95] during the former's Caliphate. The Caliph, Bello, took the occasion of reporting an expedition he had embarked upon to remind the Emir, in emphatic terms, of the obligations of *jihād* on the Muslim community and the duty of every able individual to fight in it or be persuaded, and even threatened to fight if he refused. Bello explained the law as regards the disabled to Yaʿqūb and admonished him to follow his (Bello's) example by waging the *jihād* on his most important frontiers.

The set-up in the Gwandu section of the Caliphate is not documented to the same extent as the Sokoto section. Gwandu, however, followed the Sokoto pattern. The only important qualification which must be made is that even though Gwandu was by and large independent, its Emir recognized the supreme

93. See below, pp. 96, 100, 102, 188.
94. Copy in Imām Muḥammad, *Tarīkh 'Umarā' Bauchi*, pp. 26–7.
95. From Muḥammad Bello to Yaʿqūb b. Daṭi, tr. A. D. H. Bivar, 'Arabic documents of Northern Nigeria', Letter No. 4, *B.S.O.A.S.* xxii (1959), pp. 339–40.

authority of the Caliph, consulted him and carried out instructions from him.[96] Indeed the first Emir of Gwandu, ʿAbdullāh b. Fodiye, was the first and most senior Wazir to the Shaikh. The position of the Emir of Gwandu throughout the nineteenth century was that of an unusually independent Wazir of the Caliph, exercising a near-complete delegated authority. But his subordinate position to Sokoto was never in doubt. As late as 1895, the Emir of Gwandu ʿUmar, known as Bakatara, described himself as the Emir in charge of the Western Emirates[97]—that is, of the Sokoto Caliphate.

We shall, in due course, see to what extent the structure of authority outlined here was reflected in the relations that actually existed between the Caliph and the emirates, especially during the last twenty years before the overthrow of the Caliphate. But the pattern analysed here supplied the basic framework of relations within the Caliphate. This framework sought to reflect the concept of state organization and relations within the Islamic community embodied in the *sharīʿa*.

It must be admitted that in the day-to-day life of the Caliphate, the *sharīʿa* did sometimes have to concede precedence to local customs and practices such as were not deemed reprehensible. That the Sokoto Caliphate did not, as I have shown elsewhere,[98] administer the pure *sharīʿa* does not detract from its standing as an Islamic state. It was established on the highest ideals of the *sharīʿa* but, 'the laws that rule the lives of the Islamic peoples have never been co-extensive with pure Islamic law'.[99] The momentous problems with which the Sokoto Caliphate had to grapple, and that with difficulty, were not those of keeping its emirates together but of those peoples both inside and outside its perimeter who not only refused to accept its authority but often threatened its existence with war.

96. See below, pp. 77–9.
97. See below, p. 79.
98. R. A. Adeleye, 'The Sokoto Caliphate in the nineteenth century'.
99. Khadduri and Liebesny, *op. cit.*, pp. 80–1.

Chapter 3
Expansion and consolidation to *c.* 1880

Although Islamic reform was the prime factor behind the founding of the Sokoto Caliphate and the values of the faith provided the strongest bond of unity within it, its expansion and consolidation alike ultimately depended on the effectiveness of the physical force which all parts of it could muster. In many localities, including the Sokoto heartland, there was no assurance that the territorial claims initially staked out by means of the *jihād* would not be reversed. To the casual observer, the prevalence of wars in nineteenth-century Northern Nigeria proves that the Caliphate was incapable of maintaining peace within its domains. This view is based on the fallacy that all the territory within the perimeter of the Caliphate formed part of it. Another wrong view to take is to suppose that the component emirates were all founded in the early years (i.e. first and second decades) of the nineteenth century. Seen in this light, the wars after the supposed period of establishment were simply civil wars resulting from revolts against the authority of the Caliphate.

However, even at the height of the Caliphate's territorial expansion, the area within its perimeter did not wholly come under its jurisdiction. Its optimum limits comprised the Sokoto and Gwandu heartlands, carved out of the states of Gobir, Zamfara and Kebbi; Kebbi itself (what was left of it), Arewa, Zaberma, Dendi and Gurma, while the Caliph exercised some influence over Adar and Ahir (Asben). The foregoing territories were to the north, west and south-west of Sokoto. Immediately east and south-east of the Sokoto heartland were the emirates of Daura, Katsina, Kano and Zazzau, the last having sub-emirates extending as far as the Benue. Farther east and south-east were the emirates of Hadejia, Katagum, Jama'ari, Danbam, Missau, Gombe, Bauchi, Muri and Adamawa. Yauri (semi-independent and enjoying a *dhimmī* status), Kontagora, Nupe, Agaie, Lafiagi, Shonga and Ilọrin lay to the far south and south-west.

These emirates were not geographically contiguous. Interspersing them, unsubjugated and recalcitrant, were pockets of enemy states and peoples. This situation persisted throughout the nineteenth century. Thus there were heathen groups and states such as Zuru (between Zamfara and Yauri); a part of Gwariland, bordering on the emirates of Kontagora, Zazzau and Nupe; an extensive area of the Bauchi plateau, bordering the Bauchi emirates to the north and stretching as far as Shendam to the south. There were other centres, Muslim or quasi-Muslim, such as Gobir, Kebbi (after *c.* 1849), the Hausa state of Abuja and the Ningi sultanate (between Kano and Bauchi), which persisted in open hostility against the Caliph to the end of the nineteenth century.

The problem of expansion and consolidation of *Dār al-Islām* (i.e. the Caliphate) against its enemies was, perhaps, as mentioned earlier, the most outstanding single problem which the Caliphate had to face throughout its existence. Another vital aspect of this problem was the existence of ethnic groups within the perimeter of certain emirates, notably Bauchi, Gombe, Adamawa and south of Zaria, who rejected political integration with those emirates. The problem of internal consolidation varied from one emirate to another. But a general distinction must here be made between the Hausa states, with an Islamized political and cultural pre-*jihād* tradition and the emirates south of them created from a predominantly and often overwhelmingly non-Islamic antecedents. Consolidation within the latter followed a far more painful process than in the former, as is aptly exemplified by the continued restiveness of the indigenous rival Nupe dynasties under the Fulani–Muslim hegemony.

On the peripheral frontiers of the Caliphate there were other sources of opposition resulting from the initial *jihād* conquests. To the west were, Borgu, Gurma, Dendi, Zaberma, Arewa, Kebbi and Gobir, which could either not be conquered or had persisted as undigested and rebellious conquests and regular sources of vexatious attacks on the Caliphate. To the north of Katsina and Daura were the Katsina successor states of Tessawa and Maradi, founded by the fugitive pre-*jihād* rulers of Katsina and their loyalist followers. These, allied with Damagaram (with its capital at Zinder) and often with Gobir, remained inveterate enemies of the Caliphate. Bornu, which apart from direct assaults on its power had lost territory to the Caliphate at the beginning of the *jihād*, also remained an irreconcilable enemy on the eastern frontiers of the Caliphate. Mandara, between Bornu and Adamawa, was a hotly contested no-man's-land throughout the century, while numerous heathen tribes on the banks of the Benue, particularly the Jukun and the Tiv, constituted other sources of opposition on the southern frontiers of the Caliphate. On Nupe's frontiers south of the Niger was an extensive area comprising presentday Kogi, Kabba and Igbira Divisions of Kwara state, the Afenmai division of the mid-west state and the Akoko division of the western state. This region, characterized by a remarkably high degree of political fragmentation, provided an area over which Nupe could conveniently impose its authority. Ilọrin's southern frontier was also an area of expansion for that emirate, owing to the upheaval and the unsettled nature of political relations among the Yoruba following the collapse of the Ọyọ empire.

The vital fact must be carefully noted, that whereas the oldest emirates—particularly those created out of Hausaland and the western and southern marches of Bornu (Missau excepted)—had been founded by *c.* 1810, Ilọrin and Nupe were not founded until the late 1820s, Missau in 1830, Muri in *c.* 1833 and Kontagora in *c.* 1859. So the *jihād* specifically directed to the founding of *Dār al-Islām* lasted for more than half a century. This protracted process gradually reduced the unconquered or undigested areas that separated the component emirates of the Caliphate.

With all the factors mentioned above in mind, it becomes evident that what was going on within and on the frontiers of the Caliphate was a series of military conquests which were not completely successful. Consequently, in terms of territorial expansion and consolidation, the *jihād* was an uncompleted revolution which virtually persisted until the overthrow of the Caliphate. Besides, the revolution also involved far-reaching religious, political, economic and social reforms which, of their nature, could not be completely achieved and which therefore provoked many different types of opposition. All the foregoing considerations had a direct bearing not only on the defence system and the ultimate strength of the Caliphate but also on the varied aspects of the organization and actual working of the central government of the Caliph and that of each emirate.

The forces that tended to weaken or limit the strength of the Caliphate both militarily and in terms of political and other forms of relations within it may be divided into external and internal.

There was the problem of maintaining and expanding the boundaries of the early Caliphate against the various enemies briefly analysed above. Internally the problem assumes two aspects. First was the problem of controlling or integrating undigested conquests which revolted within the emirates. Secondly was the question, from one emirate to another, of rivalries among the leaders of the *jihād*, their groups of followers and, as the century wore on, their descendants. The internal problems will be examined first.

RIVALRIES WITHIN EMIRATES

The administrative arrangements of the various emirates were worked out at the same time as the usually protracted wars of conquest and consolidation were going on. Under the first emirs, these wars were a more urgent consideration than the details of the administrative structure. Indeed, most of the first emirs were noted and respected more for their role as learned and religious leaders (hence mallams) than as rulers.[1] As agents of the Shaikh 'Uthmān, each emir was regarded primarily as the *Amīr Al-Jaish* (Commander of the Army) for his particular locality. In the militarily unsettled state of the early Caliphate, such administrative arrangements as emerged, particularly with regard to distribution of authority and functions within each emirate, necessarily reflected the exigencies of the conquering effort, continued security and stability. In the interest of solidarity local leaders of the *jihād* and the interest groups that coalesced around them had to be duly compensated by positions in the top cadre of the administrative hierarchy. D. M. Last has shown that the distribution of jurisdiction over land in the Sokoto hinterland reflected the role played by the dominant Fulani families and local leaders of the *jihād*.[2] This was also true for the emirates. In virtually every emirate, political rivalries among local leaders of the *jihād* were beginning to emerge, even at the height of religious enthusiasm under the first emirs.

There was rivalry among the various clans of Fulani in Adamawa for leadership of the *jihād* from the beginning and, as

1. They had in the first place, been appointed by the Shaikh and accepted by their local communities on the strength of their learning and piety.
2. D. M. Last, *The Sokoto Caliphate*, pp. 94–6.

already mentioned, the Shaikh 'Uthmān had to intervene. After the death of Modibo Adam, some of his governors revolted against Emir Lawal's authority (*c*. 1847–72). The Fulani district of Rei set up its capital in the mountain fastnesses of Scholire, from where it obeyed or defied Sokoto and Yola as it found convenient.[3] Tibati not only followed the Rei example but proceeded to attack two other Adamawa districts, Ngaundere and Banyo. These revolts could not be brought under control by the Emir, Lawal, and remained to plague the reign of his successor, 'Umar Sanda (1872–91).

Adamawa's neighbouring emirate of Muri was originally founded by Buba Yero of Gombe, while the task of full establishment was accomplished by his brother, Hamman Ruwa.[4] The ambition of Buba Yero to maintain Muri succession in his own direct line led him into plotting the death of Hamman Ruwa and the latter's eldest son, Bose.[5] The Caliph Muḥammad Bello declared Muri independent of Gombe and settled the succession on Hamman Ruwa's line. Dissension between Hamman, son of Hamman Ruwa, who succeeded his father and Hamadu, Bose's son, dominated Muri politics until the ascension of Muḥammad Nya (*c*. 1874–95), under whom Muri was finally consolidated and even attempted to expand at the expense of the Tiv and the Jukun.[6]

The examples of Adamawa and Muri can be multiplied. In Nupe there was bitter rivalry between two sons of Dendo, 'Uthmān Zaki and Muḥammad Saba (Masaba). This rivalry was played out against the background of the discontent of the ancient Nupe dynasties whose rivalries the two brothers continued to exploit diplomatically to further their own ambitions.[7]

3. H. K. Strumpell, *A History of Adamawa*, p. 31; see also H. Barth, *Travels and Discoveries in North and Central Africa*, vol. iv, pp. 508–9. Dr Barth refers to Yola vassals like those of Ribago, Fali, Holma, Song, Mendif, Bogo, as over-mighty vassals, with a tendency to asserting their independence.
4. *Tabyīn amr Buba Yero*.
5. A. H. M. Kirk-Greene, *Adamawa Past and Present* (Oxford, 1960), p. 153; see also J. M. Fremantle: *Gazetteer of Muri Province*, p. 17.
6. Fremantle, *op. cit*., pp. 17–18, and Kirk-Greene, *op. cit*., p. 157.
7. The summary of 'Uthmān Zaki and Masaba rivalry and the political instability in Nupe from the 1830s to 1857 is based on *Tarīkh min bilād Bida*, p. 5 f.; E. G. M. Dupigny, *Gazetteer of Nupe Province*, p. 10 ff.; and A. Burdon, *Northern Nigeria, Notes on certain Tribes and Emirates*, pp. 52–4.

The rivalry and the wars it produced resulted in the revolt of the indigenous Nupe against the *ajẹlẹ* (resident agent of the ruler) system. All but the more popular *ajẹlẹs* were killed. Subsequently, Khalīl, Emir of Gwandu, intervened to restore peace, exiled Zaki to Birnin Kebbi and allowed Masaba to rule over Nupe in the former's stead. A subsequent revolt of Nupe elements, abetted by a general of Masaba (Maiyaki 'Umar), led to the exile of Masaba to Ilọrin and the return of Zaki to Nupeland. Not until the death of Zaki (1859) and the second reign of Masaba (1859–73) could Nupe be described as securely consolidated. It has been noted that essentially similar rivalry broke out between 'Abd al-Salām and Ṣọlagbẹru in Ilọrin, following Alimi's death. In Zaria, also, similar elements of rivalry were observable under Musa, the contestants being Yamusa, his chief collaborator, and Jaye, a Fulanin Zazzau collaborator.[8] Musa was in the circumstances compelled to make large concessions to Yamusa, who later succeeded him. The gradual growth of the claim of different Fulani dynasties in Zaria, the Mallawa, Bornawa and Sullebawa, further complicated the internal rivalries within Zaria emirate. This helped to weaken the state and enhanced Sokoto's control over its politics.

In Kano the Fulani clans of Modibawa, Sullebawa, Jobawa, Yolawa, Daneji and Dan Bazawa had combined along with other Muslims during the *jihād* to achieve victory.[9] The Shaikh 'Uthmān had resolved rivalries among these clans by his appointment of Suleiman b. Abū Hamman as emir on account of his piety and learning.[10] Nonetheless fresh and bitter rivalries broke out again on the succession of Ibrahim Dabo, *c.* 1819, which the new emir had to put down. Revolt centred around Dan Tunku, a prominent leader of the *jihād* in the Katsina Daura and Kano region in the early years. Muḥammad Bello settled the dispute by creating the separate emirate of Kazaure with Dan Tunku as emir.[11]

Rivalries such as the foregoing, it seems, created the need to balance appointments to high offices of state in the various

8. M. G. Smith, *Government in Zazzau*, pp. 146–8.
9. W. F. Gowers, *Gazetteer of Kano Province*, p. 11.
10. *Ibid.*, p. 12; and *I.M.* p. 104, Suleiman is described as al-Faqīh al-'Adil; see also *Tarikh Kano*, p. 96, and S. J. Hogben, *Muhammedan Emirates of Nigeria*, p. 76.
11. H. A. S. Johnston, *The Fulani Empire of Sokoto*, pp. 178–9.

emirates. Administration became increasingly complex as the century wore on, and increasing patronage directed at creating an ever-expanding clientele by rival groups became a vital factor in the contests for succession to the emirship. Thus after the first emirs, offices proliferated.[12] Most top-ranking offices appear to have changed hands with the succession of a new emir anxious to instal his own clients in key positions. This feature is probably best illustrated by the Kano example.[13] The degree of weakness necessarily caused by this type of political activity in each emirate cannot be assessed merely by whether or not it led to open violent clashes. Even non-violent internal rivalries could considerably weaken the internal solidarity of an emirate.

Moreover, the political problem in the emirates went beyond the juggling for position among the ruling class. Other factors, contingent on the revolution, made the situation more complex. As already mentioned, the local government of the emirates were replicas of the Sokoto model. This, except in a general sense, does not imply uniformity of administrative structure and practice throughout the Caliphate. Revolutions, including that of the *jihād*, do not create a vacuum which they then proceed to fill with entirely new concepts and practices. Hence the differing historical antecedents of each emirate as well as the varied circumstances attendant on its foundation, no doubt, produced a wide range of diversity, at least in details, in the nature of the administrative practices it evolved. Whereas the end of the government of an emirate was to institute the 'Islamic Way' it should not be imagined that the process of reconciling Islamic precepts of administration with the antecedent culture was not productive of different kinds and degrees of tension.

The rise of the Fulani élite from the position of a subject people to that of rulers in the emirates generally must have had a profound effect on the nature of political, social and other forms of relations with the different groups of the communities within each emirate. Added to the new tensions arising from this was that the *jihād* did result in a repatterning of the composition and distribution of population. Thus, for instance, large numbers of the Gobirawa, Katsinawa, Daurawa and Zazzawa Hausa emigrated from their homes to found new states elsewhere. V. N.

12. R. A. Adeleyẹ, 'The Sokoto Caliphate in the nineteenth century'.
13. *Tarīkh Kano*, see the reigns of 'Abdullāh and Muḥammad Bello; also below p. 99.

Low has shown that the emigration of Fulani, apparently in substantial numbers, from Bornu to the emirates of the eastern frontiers led to a steady rise of the percentage population of Fulani in those emirates in the course of the nineteenth century.[14] There was a steady influx of Fulani and perhaps Hausa Muslims into Nupe in the course of the protracted *jihād* there.[15] In the Iḷọrin–old Ọyọ region, southward emigration of population took place on a revolutionary scale while foreign elements came in to support the *jihād*. These events must have resulted in some measure of dislocation of existing political, social and economic systems as well as raise new and urgent problems, all of which increased the complexities of administration. The above are some of the factors which conditioned the evolution of new administrative structures and practices in the emirates within a general Islamic framework.

Ambitions for office and political rivalries in the nascent Caliphate may be seen as deviations from the religious ideals in which the *jihād* was conceived and on which the Caliphate was established. Aberrations from these ideals had been noted with disgust by ʿAbdullāh b. Fodiye as early as 1806–7 even among the Shaikh's community. His charges against the community included hypocrisy and preoccupation with seeking power and authority and other similar worldly vainglories.[16] Muḥammad Bello was in agreement with ʿAbdullāh on this point.[17] Be that as it may, rivalry for office was a normal product of the practical working out of the day-to-day administration. So long as there were offices to be filled it is to be expected that those who had contributed most to the *jihād* would feel entitled to lay claims to these offices. This was, no doubt, a fertile ground for dissension. The founding fathers of the emirates were not necessarily better than their successors in this regard.

There were also succession disputes to the Caliphate itself. The greatest threat to the Caliphate arising from such disputes was the ʿAbd al-Salām revolt. At the Shaikh's division of the

14. V. N. Low, 'The Border Emirates: a political history of three north-east Nigerian Emirates, *c.* 1800–1902' (unpublished Ph.D. thesis, U.C.L.A., 1968).

15. M. D. Mason, 'The Nupe kingdoms in the nineteenth century' (unpublished Ph.D. thesis Birmingham, 1970).

16. ʿAbdullāh b. Fodiye, *T.W.* pp. 121–2.

17. Last, *op. cit.*, p. 59, cited from Muḥammad Bello's *fī Aqwām al-Muhājirīn*.

emirates in *c.* 1812 between 'Abdullāh and Muḥammad Bello, 'Abd al-Salām had been given a district around Kware under the Gwandu section of the Caliphate.[18] He was dissatisfied, and his attempts to aggrandize himself by claiming control over other districts had to be curbed by 'Abdullāh. Over this affair, 'Abd al-Salām had attempted to revolt even during the Shaikh's lifetime but had deferred to the latter's authority.[19] As soon as the Shaikh died in 1817, 'Abd al-Salām, supported by 'people of his tribe', raised the standard of revolt against the Caliph, Muḥammad Bello. This revolt, preceded by a sharp exchange of letters[20] between the Caliph and 'Abd al-Salām, resulted in an armed clash. The revolt occupied Bello's attention until 1818 when he successfully crushed it. 'Abd al-Salām died from wounds sustained in battle.[21]

Muḥammad Bello's situation was further aggravated by 'Abdullāh's resentment at Bello's succession to the Caliphate.[22] However, the revolt of the Kebbawa, allied with emigrants from the followers of 'Abd al-Salām, and their threat to Gwandu provided the occasion for the reconciliation of 'Abdullāh with Bello. After defeating 'Abd al-Salām in 1818 Bello sent a force to 'Abdullāh with which the latter crushed the Kebbawa revolt. Thereafter 'Abdullāh accepted Bello's succession and paid the homage to him as *Amīr al-Mu'minīn*. Succession disputes to the emirship and other offices continued to be a feature of the political life of the emirates, while dispute even over succession to the Caliphate itself did not end with Muḥammad Bello.[23]

18. *Sard al-Kalām.*
19. *Ibid.*
20. See *ibid.* for letters exchanged between Muḥammad Bello and 'Abd al-Salām.
21. *Ibid.* See also *Tarīkh Sokoto*, in *Tadhkirat al-Nisian* by Al-hajj Sa'id, tr. C. E. J. Whitting (Kano, 1949), pp. 2–3.
22. Following the death of the Shaikh 'Uthmān b. Fodiye the Sokoto electors appointed Muḥammad Bello in his place. 'Abdullāh who, as the Shaikh's Chief Lieutenant and Chief Wazir expected to be elected was not only bypassed but the Sokoto gates were shut in his face; hence his resentment—see Burdon, *op. cit.*, p. 68 and Last, *op. cit.*, p. 64.
23. There were sharp succession disputes at Atiqu's succession in 1837 as Ali Jedo the *Amir al-Jaish* backed al-Bukhārī b. al-Shaikh 'Uthmān, see *Tarīkh Sokoto*, pp. 14–15. The appointment of the Caliph 'Alī (1842) was marked by even more disturbing disputes; also *Tarīkh Sokoto*, pp. 22–4.

THE ROLE OF THE CALIPH IN SETTLING EMIRATE SUCCESSION DISPUTES

Often, it seems, succession disputes, even when they resulted in open hostilities, were settled locally, as in the cases just discussed and, later on in the century (*c.* 1881), at the succession of the Emir ʿUthmān of Bauchi.[24] Sometimes, however, succession disputes in emirates did involve the Caliph as final arbiter. On a number of occasions, such arbitration produced strains between the Caliph's authority and the emirates concerned. Thus in 1873 and 1897 open rebellion against the Caliph's stand was narrowly avoided in succession disputes in Zaria.[25] About 1872 the succession of ʿUmar Sanda in Adamawa had been disputed by a certain Hamidu who sought and received the initial support of the Caliph.[26] The local electors set aside the Caliph's recommendation but apparently averted strained relations with Sokoto by explaining the grounds of their action to the Caliph—that succession in Adamawa had been fixed by Modibo Adam in his line in the order Lawal, ʿUmar Sanda and Zubeir.[27] The subsequent armed revolt of Hamidu was a localized affair, settled by his death soon after.

Two major revolts, the Bukhārī and Tukur[28] revolts, in Hadejia and Kano respectively, which successfully defied Sokoto authority, were the outcome of succession disputes. In *c.* 1848 Bukhārī b. Muḥammad Sambo, unfavoured son of the Emir of Hadejia, succeeded to the Hadejia throne on his father's death. It is suggested that he got his appointment ratified by presenting numerous gifts to the Wazīr of Sokoto, ʿAbd al-Qādir.[29] However, Bukhārī subsequently disobeyed the Wazīr when the latter invited him to answer complaints brought against him by his subjects. Bukhārī's refusal precipitated war between him and Sokoto. Bukhārī, in a protracted war in which he was strengthened by Bornu assistance, routed the combined army of Sokoto,

24. See, *Tarīkh ʿUmarāʾ Bauchi*, pp. 249–61; also *Labarun Hausawa da Makwabtansu*, vol. i, p. 50; and below, p. 91.
25. M. G. Smith, *op. cit.*, pp. 174–6, 193–4.
26. *Labarun Hausawa da Makwabtansu*, vol. ii, p. 104, 'Labarun Sarakunan Adamawa', tr. from Fulfulde.
27. *Ibid.*, the formula was La-U-Zu.
28. See below, p. 97 f. for the Tukur revolt.
29. *Tarīkh Sokoto*, pp. 27–8.

Katagum, Bauchi, Kano and Missau.[30] Subsequently, he killed off Aḥmad, the legitimate emir appointed by Sokoto to take his place. For the rest of his life (he died *c.* 1863, fighting the Bedde) Bukhārī defied Sokoto authority and ravaged the emirates close to Hadejia.[31]

The weakening effect of succession disputes on individual emirates and on the Caliphate is an important subject for further investigation. Although such disputes harboured no threat to disintegrate the Caliphate, their effect would seem to have been the undermining of the internal cohesion of the emirates and therefore consequently of their strength.

UNDIGESTED CONQUESTS

Easier to locate than individual or group ambitions within the Caliphate, and therefore easier to tackle though not necessarily to resolve, was the problem posed by peoples who, though conquered at the beginning of the *jihād*, subsequently revolted. The suppression of revolts in the early days of the emirates forms part of the protracted process of conquest. Indeed the revolts of the Kebbawa and Zamfarawa in the wake of the ʿAbd al-Salām revolt was symptomatic of what happened in several emirates after the death of the founders. In the southernmost emirates the question was more properly that of expansion against peoples who would not accept the new Muslim authority. Such was true of Nupe, Ilọrin, Adamawa, Zaria and Muri emirates.

In the case of Nupe in the early days, the problem of consolidation against recalcitrant elements was intimately tied up with the rivalry between Dendo's sons. Shortly before the return of ʿUthmān Zaki from Kebbi to Nupe in 1857, Masaba had to find refuge in Ilọrin. He had been forced to accept defeat at the hands of the indigenous Etsu Muʿadh, who led a civil war against him. Etsu Muʿadh ruled Nupe only for a brief period.[32] Towards the end of his life, Masaba had to face yet another major rebellion, this time of the Nupe of the Kaduna river banks. This rebellion,

30. *D.M.* ff. 49–50; *op. cit.*, Barth, vol. ii, p. 176.
31. Gowers, *op. cit.*, pp. 22–3.
32. *Tarīkh min bilād Bida*, pp. 6–9. Masaba's general, ʿUmar Mayaki, who had earlier aided Muʿadh, revolted against him and killed him in battle.

known as the Kpenti war, was only suppressed after 'Umar Majigi's forces, loyal to Masaba, had suffered many reverses.[33] The Nupe emirate was to evince more signs of underground resentment among the indigenous peoples during the rest of the nineteenth century, but by 1880 these were no longer a threat to effective rule by the Muslim–Fulani dynasty.

In Adamawa both under Modibo Adam and his successor, Lawal, the wars of consolidation against the numerous tribes continued. Mandara and Marghi, on the Bornu–Adamawa frontiers, were never really properly integrated with Adamawa. In *c.* 1852 Bagele, capital of the Batta, was captured, but the tribe was not thereby subdued.[34] Muslim raids into Batta territory were chronic for the rest of the nineteenth century. Dr Barth's picture of Adamawa in the mid-nineteenth century, as a kingdom in which the conquerors possessed only detached settlements with the intervening regions and mountainous terrains in the hands of heathens, aptly summarizes Adamawa's problems of consolidation.[35] Indeed, Adamawa was, as described to Dr Barth by the Emir Lawal's messenger, 'a fresh, unconsolidated conquest'.[36] Sanda (*c.* 1872–91) was mainly preoccupied with fighting against pagans.[37] Zubeir, Emir of Adamawa (1891–1901), is said to have been always either at war or preparing for one.[38]

Like Adamawa, recorded oral traditions of Gombe are in the main a catalogue of a chain of wars between the successive emirs and various heathen tribes.[39] Bauchi emirate, which had identical problems of defence and consolidation against recalcitrant pagan tribes, perhaps typifies in some measure the problems of these three emirates. The Dass[40] tribe, the Angas (of Pankshin Division), the Pyem of Gindiri district, the Yergam, the Montol, the Ankwe and many other tribes who had caused Ya'qūb, first

33. Dupigny, *op. cit.*, p. 17.
34. Strumpell, *op. cit.*, pp. 34–5 and Vicars-Boyle, 'Historical Notes on the Yola Fulani', p. 85.
35. Barth, *op. cit.*, vol. iv, p. 503.
36. *Ibid.*, p. 497.
37. *Labarun Hausawa da Makwabtansu*, vol. ii, p. 106 f.
38. *Ibid.*, p. 109.
39. See *Tabyīn amr Buba Yero*. Tribes in the Gongola bend, the Fali, Biu, Bolewa (Fika) Buhum (Muri) Tangale-Waja peoples, etc. were victims of Gombe raids.
40. *Tarīkh 'Umarā' Bauchi*, p. 41. It took Ya'qūb five years' struggle to subdue the Dass people in the first instance.

Emir of Bauchi, considerable anxiety and who had then been subdued with difficulty, grew restive again under Ibrāhīm b. Ya'qūb. The first preoccupation of Ibrāhīm was to subdue the revolted Angas and the Montol.[41] During the eighth year of his reign numerous subject populations are said to have risen in a revolt which must have caused him great anxiety.[42] Towards the end of his reign Ibrāhīm devoted his attention to religious matters. He built a *ribāṭ* at Rauta, near Garun Bauchi, where many students, mallams and Qur'ān readers were gathered.[43] It is not known whether or not the building of the *ribāṭ* at Rauta formed part of a more comprehensive defence policy.

In the Sokoto hinterland itself, Gobir, Zamfara and Kebbi, conquered early in the *jihād* but never effectively controlled, had allied with 'Abd al-Salām.[44] To this general rising was added the hostility of the Habe of Tessawa and Maradi who, with the Tamesgida Tuareg, allied with Gobir against Sokoto. Sokoto expeditions sent out annually against the allies, notably against Gobir, inflicted a crushing defeat on them in the dry season of 1820–21.[45] The Sarkin Gobir, Gomki, died in the battle. The first few years after the death of the Shaikh indicated what enemies and what combinations Sokoto would have to face for the rest of the century. In 1822–23, Muḥammad Bello decisively defeated Zamfara.[46] Gobir and Kebbi remained hostile but Kebbi was defeated in *c.* 1831 while Gobir suffered a serious defeat at the hands of Sokoto at the battle of Gawakuke in 1836.[47] The Caliph Muḥammad Bello succeeded in a few years in consolidating Sokoto conquests against the rebels.

Clapperton observed that by 1826 the revolts had been put down. The military capacity of Sokoto must have been taxed almost to its limits. During a reign of twenty years the Caliph, Muḥammad Bello, is said to have gone on forty-seven campaigns

41. *Ibid.*, pp. 159–61; pp. 194–5. Ibrahīm continued his struggle against the Dass to the end of his reign.
42. *Ibid.*, p. 162 f.
43. *Ibid.*, pp. 195, 221–2, 242.
44. Al-Ḥajj Sa'īd, *Tarīkh Sokoto*, p. 3; Last, *op. cit.*, p. 65 f.; *D.M.* f. 35; Zamfara and Kebbi revolted in the same year as Bello's succession.
45. *Ibid.*, f. 37. In the 1822–23 war the Kel-Geres allied with Zamfara but had been heavily defeated, see Barth, *op. cit.*, p. 355.
46. *D.M.* ff. 38, 41; and Y. Urvoy, *Histoire de populations du Soudan Central* (Paris, 1936), p. 282.
47. *D.M.* f. 41.

against Sokoto's enemies.[48] He and his successors also got from the emirates reinforcing contingents which were customarily sent to aid in the Sokoto annual *jihād* raids, or at Sokoto's demand. For all practical purposes, Gobir, Kebbi and the Katsina succession towns, became independent enemy states like Damagaram and Bornu, whose hostility Sokoto had to continue to face. This aspect of the Caliphate's problems now has to be considered.

THE OUTER FRONTIERS

(*a*) *The western and northern frontiers.* The problem of defending the Caliphate against its enemies on its outer frontiers was one which intimately and urgently concerned most of the emirates in varying degrees throughout the nineteenth century. The western and northern frontiers in the neighbourhoods of Gwandu, Sokoto and Katsina were perhaps the most vulnerable; certainly the most productive of relentless wars.

It will be recalled that Caliph Muḥammad Bello had succeeded in inflicting crushing defeats on the Caliphate's enemies on his frontiers one after the other. To give lasting security against enemy attacks he established *ribāṭs* on his frontiers with Kebbi and Gobir and in Zamfara as a defensive measure.[49]

A great measure of consolidation had been achieved under Muḥammad Bello. Kebbi was quiescent from 1831–49. However, both Gobir and Maradi, the former in particular, very soon recovered from their military humiliation at Gawakuke and were determined once more to challenge the might of the Sokoto Caliphate. To the west the successive Emirs of Gwandu, 'Abdullāh (d. *c.* 1828), Muḥammad Wani (1828–32) and Khalīl (1832–58), had also achieved a great measure of success in consolidating the early conquests. The Caliphate west of Gwandu was however burdened with a loosely defined and embarrassing frontier. Arewa, Zaberma Dendi, a large part of Gurma, including Liptako, and a small portion of Borgu had, according to Barth, come under the sway of Gwandu.[50] They were never

48. *Ibid.*
49. See Last, *op. cit.*, pp. 74–80. Muḥammad Bello's defence policy and the part played by *ribāṭs* in this have been dealt with by Dr Last; see also *D.M.*, f 42.
50. Barth, *op. cit.*, vol. iv, p. 203.

firmly held: ʿAbdullāh's numerous expeditions and those of his successors had not successfully subjugated these border territories.[51] Even when recalcitrant Kebbi was quiescent from 1831 to 1849 these half-subdued territories of Gwandu continued to be restive.

It has been suggested that the significance of the *jihād* among the Arewa and Zaberma was to substitute a single authority for a fragmented one under petty principalities.[52] These areas were controlled in some degree by a policy of exploiting political rivalries and trying to create a loyal clientele.[53] This policy of divide and rule had its disadvantages, in that it subsequently provided the strongest bond of united action among all the aggrieved parties. Only a leader was needed to precipitate a revolt. He was not to appear until 1849.

In the meantime, following the death of Muḥammad Bello in 1837, Gobir, Zamfara—once more in revolt—and Maradi were the immediate threats. The Caliph ʿAtīq (Atiqu) led several expeditions reinforced by contingents from the emirates against them and their Tuareg and Damagaram allies until his death in 1842.[54] By 1843 the new Sarki of Gobir had erected his capital at Chibiri (Tsibiri) and was prepared to be an even greater nuisance to Sokoto under the Caliph ʿAlī b. Muḥammad Bello (i.e. Aliyu Baba, 1842–59).

The revival of Maradi after Gawakuke was accompanied by an expansion of Maradawa raids on caliphal territories. Under successive *Sarakuna* of Maradi from 1844 to 1850 Maradawa raids on the emirates of Katsina, Kano, Daura and the Sokoto hinterland itself increased in frequency and intensity. Maradi raiding of the caliphal lands reached its peak under Dan Baskore (1850–73). His raids, going south as far as Kano, became a permanent feature of Maradi's relations with northern frontier emirates. Dan Baskore's son, Barmu (1873–77), is said to have overrun Kano territory and was for some time settled at Yan

51. Urvoy, *op. cit.*, pp. 100, 101.

52. Jean Perié et Michel Sellier, 'Histoire des populations du Cercle de Dosso' *Bulletin de l'IFAN*, vol. xii (1950), p. 1046

53. *Ibid.* According to Mr S. A. Balogun, a research student working on 'The Gwandu Emirates', the degree of political integration in this area was limited while Gwandu's control appears to have been greater than is commonly supposed.

54. For the Amīr al-Mu'minīn Atiqu's expeditions, see Last, *op. cit.*, pp. 81–3; and *D.M.* ff. 43, 44, 45.

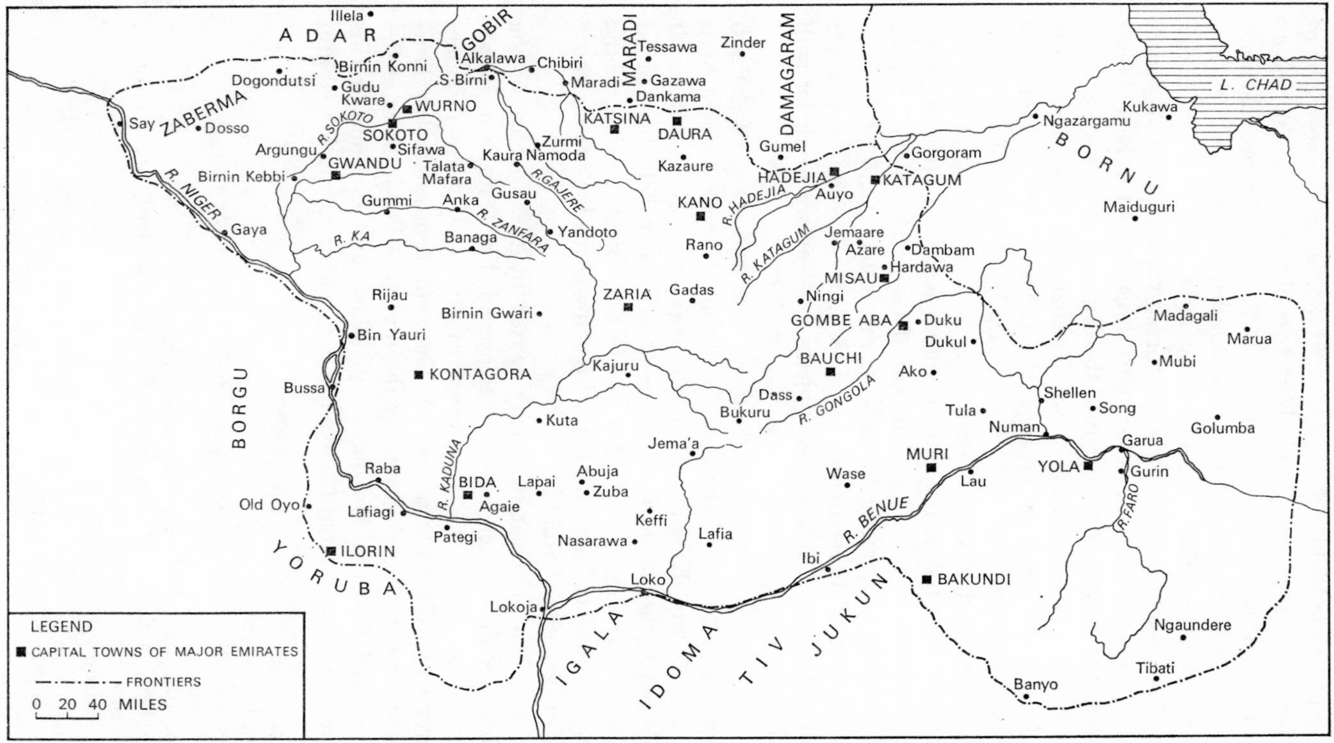

The Sokoto Caliphate: external frontiers

Gwarzo near Bichi.[55] Not until 1877–80, when the new king of Maradi, Mazoge, tried to establish friendly relations with Sokoto did hostilities abate. Furthermore Mazoge's rapprochement with Sokoto incurred Gobir's hostility towards Maradi.[56] The division within the ranks of the enemies of Sokoto which this implied, meant a reduction of the threat which Gobir and Maradi hitherto had posed to Sokoto. This threat ceased to be a serious danger to Sokoto for the rest of the century.

While Maradi raided Kano, Katsina and Daura from the 1840s to the reign of Mazoge, the Caliph ʿAlī was kept busy repelling Gobir's offensive in Zamfara.[57] In spite of the regular participation of the eastern emirates' contingents in the Caliph's resistance, the Sokoto forces were defeated in 1847–48[58] by the powerful combination of Gobir and Maradi forces. The latter were aided by Siddiq, the former Emir of Katsina who, having been deposed in 1844,[59] following complaints brought against him by his subjects, had thrown in his lot with Maradi.

In 1849 Kebbi revolted under the leadership of Yaʿqūb Nabame, the son of the King of Kebbi, Karar, who had been killed during Kebbi's defeat in 1831. The Kebbawa revolt opened with an attack on the *ribāṭ* of Silame held by Aḥmad al-Rifāʿī. In Arewa, Zaberma and Dendi, Daud, a prince of the ruling house of Zaberma, led the revolt and made common cause with Nabame of Kebbi.[60]

A feeling of great insecurity caused by the pressure of the forces of the Caliphate's enemies prevailed in Katsina in 1853[61] and even during the following year, 1854, Gobirawa raiders pressed hard on Wurno itself.[62] The road from Sokoto to Timbuktu was rendered unsafe by the revolts.[63] But in spite of the many-sided opposition, faced by Sokoto and Gwandu at this time, they had beaten Daud's forces in Zaberma and forced him

55. Urvoy, *op. cit.*, pp. 283, 284.
56. *Ibid.*, p. 291.
57. *D.M.* ff. 47, 48. Al-ḥajj Sa'id, *Tarīkh Sokoto*, p. 24 f.
58. *Ibid.*
59. Al-ḥajj Sa'id, *Tarīkh Sokoto*, p. 29.
60. Perié et Sellier, *op. cit.*, pp. 1046, 1047; and Barth, *op. cit.*, vol. iv, p. 165.
61. Barth, vol. iv, p. 164.
62. Barth, vol. v, p. 337.
63. Barth, vol. iv, p. 134.

to flee to Dendi by 1854.[64] By the time the Caliph 'Alī died in 1859 the atmosphere of hostility and revolt still persisted but there was no longer any vital threat to the Caliphate from the Kebbawa and their allied rebels.

The series of revolts by the states to the west of Sokoto and Gwandu against the Caliphate's authority, beginning from 1849, as well as the Bukhārī rebellion in Hadejia which was going on at the same time, paralysed the Caliphate's control over those places. The independence asserted at this time by Kebbi, Arewa, Zaberma and Dendi, was not to be reversed for the rest of the century. These territories had always chafed under Sokoto's or Gwandu's control as the case might be. Their breaking away from the Caliphate must be seen as the successful completion of an independence movement directed against a power which, from the early years of the *jihād*, they had never really accepted.

The more striking event at this time was the Bukhārī rebellion, which took place in an emirate under the direct and regular control of Sokoto. Even this petered out with the death of Bukhārī himself, *c.* 1864. These revolts produced such a seemingly chronic state of warfare that Dr Barth was led to the conclusion that they indicated that the Caliphate was crumbling.[65] But seen in their proper historical setting, these revolts formed a mere passing phase, a trying phase nevertheless, in Sokoto's perennial problem of consolidation during the first half of the nineteenth century.

The truce of Toga[66] (Lafiyar Toga), signed in 1867 between Kebbi and Sokoto, put an end to their mutual hostilities for eight years. By 1880, and for the rest of the century, Gobir as well as Maradi, both plagued with political rivalries and palace revolutions,[67] remained only a nuisance rather than a threat to the Caliphate.

(*b*) *The northern, north-eastern, eastern and Adamawa frontiers.* On these frontiers Bornu itself and its vassal, Damagaram, were

64. Barth, vol. v, p. 275.
65. Barth, vol. iv, pp. 154–5.
66. E. J. Arnett, *Gazetteer of Sokoto* (London, 1920), p. 12. The truce was made between 'Abdullāh Toga, Sarkin Kebbi (1863–80), and the Caliph, Aḥmad al-Rifā'ī (1867–73).
67. See Jean Perié, 'Notes historiques sur la région de Maradi', *Bulletin de l'IFAN*, i (1939), p. 383 f. for a description of the 'anarchy' which from about 1870 onwards beset Gobir and Maradi.

equally serious sources of threat to the Sokoto Caliphate. Bornu's hostility started with the unsuccessful attempt of the *jihād* against it.[68] In 1824–25 under Muḥammad al-Amīn al-Kānemī, Bornu launched a determined attack on Katagum and Hadejia emirates, both of which had been founded on Bornu territory.[69] The country was evacuated at the approach of Bornu army and Dankawa, Emir of Hadejia, fled. In 1826[70] El-Kānemī advanced with his forces to near Kano. His intention was to ally with Gobir and other enemies of Sokoto. Muḥammad Bello was at that time busy investing Konya and Magariya. El-Kānemī's forces were routed only a day's journey from Kano by a combination of the armies of several emirates brilliantly led by Ya'qūb of Bauchi. The march of Bornu westward, which might have proved fatal to the Sokoto Caliphate, was thus stopped. This expedition of El-Kānemī constituted the most serious threat of Bornu to the Caliphate throughout the nineteenth century.

From *c.* 1822 onwards, under the reign of Ibrāhīm b. Saliman, Damagaram raids were directed against Daura, Katsina and Kano.[71] The greatest Damagaram threat to Kano came during the reign of Tenimu b. Saliman (1851–84), contemporaneously with Dan Baskore of Maradi. Backed by a strong army, equipped with imported firearms and locally manufacted gunpowder,[72] he was the terror of not only Kano but also Hadejia, both of which he raided many times. Although he never subdued these emirates he was to them a nuisance that kept them on the alert and often at war.

After El-Kānemī's death (1837) Bornu–Sokoto relations were reduced to border clashes on Sokoto's eastern frontiers. Bornu remained a potential source of danger to the Caliphate. During the Bukhārī revolt, for instance, the Shaikh of Bornu's surreptitious granting of refuge and military aid to the rebel had contributed to the vehemence of the rebellion.[73] During the rebel-

68. One of the fullest accounts of the *jihād* against Bornu is to be found in Y. Urvoy, *Histoire de l'Empire du Bornou*, p. 99 f.
69. *Ibid.*, p. 107.
70. For a description of this battle, see R. Lander, *Captain Clapperton's Last Expedition to Africa* (London, 1830), vol. ii, pp. 37–48; and *Tarīkh 'Umarā' Bauchi*, pp. 121–31.
71. Tilho, *Documents Scientifiques de la Mission Tilho* (Paris, 1911), vol. ii, p. 441.
72. *Ibid.*, p. 445; Tenimu is said to have had 6000 guns and 40 cannon.
73. Barth, *op. cit.*, vol. ii, pp. 175, 176. The enmity between the Caliphate

lion, Kano lived in fear of a Bornu attack—a contingency which seemed imminent, seeing that the Wazir of Bornu was reported eager to attack Kano.[74] During the Bukhārī revolt the border hostilities between Jama'ari emirate and Bornu, and between Katagum-Hadejia and Bedde, all of which had become traditional, seem to have been[75] accentuated. Bukar (Bakr), Yerima of Bornu, also attacked Missau emirate in *c.* 1870.[76] He turned back only when the Shaikh 'Umar, anxious to avoid complications with Sokoto, recalled him. Without further disturbing the Sokoto emirates Bukar nevertheless settled close to them on the western marches of Bornu. It seems that towards the end of his life the Shaikh, 'Umar, relented in the Bornu traditional bellicosity towards the Sokoto Caliphate. Between 1877 and 1880 Bukar and the Emir of Katagum worked out a boundary agreement after border clashes between them. The Shaikh, 'Umar, urged this peaceful settlement on the Caliph Mu'adh with a promise not to break the treaty.[77]

The Adamawa–Bornu frontier was a fruitful source of disputes and clashes between the two states till late in the century. These disputes were still being vigorously prosecuted in 1851 when Dr Barth visited Adamawa.[78] In *c.* 1866 Yerima Bukar of Bornu was said to have made an unsuccessful raid into Adamawa.

(*c*) *Frontiers of expansion* (*Nupe–Ilọrin*). The southern frontiers, notably in Nupe and Ilọrin, were frontiers of expansion, unlike the western, northern, eastern and Adamawa frontiers which were perforce frontiers of defence for the Caliphate. The Bunu, Yagba, Owe, Ijumu, Akoko as far as Ikarẹ, Kukuruku, all to the south of the Niger, were the easy prey of Nupe cavalry men. These pagan areas, which were the object of Nupe annual raids, were governed in a perfunctory manner, districts being placed under agents (*ajẹlẹs*) charged with collecting tribute which often

and Bornu was expressed by the Wazir of Bornu's charge to Barth in 1853, not to visit Kano lest he should thereby incur the displeasure of the Shaikh.

74. *Ibid.*, vol. iii, p. 14.
75. J. M. Fremantle, 'History of Katagum Emirate', *J.A.S.* x (1910), pp. 403, 411, 414.
76. Tilho, *op. cit.*, vol. ii, p. 371.
77. From 'Umar b. Muḥammad al-Amīn al-Kānemī to Amīr al-Mu'minīn Mu'adh in A. D. H. Bivar, 'Arabic Documents of Northern Nigeria', *B.S.O.A.S.* xxii (1959), pp. 332, 333.
78. Barth, *op. cit.*, vol. ii, pp. 417, 491–4, 496.

took the form of contributions of freeborns of the subject people. The harshness of Nupe rule over the reluctant subject population led to frequent revolts against Nupe authority in the area south of the Niger. In addition Nupe had to compete with the Ibadan who, during the second half of the nineteenth century, began to push their conquest into the same area. On one occasion Bida forces had to face the Ibadan at Ikarẹ.[79]

In Ilọrin rivalries and intrigues between various Yoruba kings in the neighbourhood, culminating in many towns throwing off their allegiance to Ọyọ, provided Ilọrin with an opportunity for expansion which they did not miss.[80] Ọyọ (old Ọyọ)[81] fell to Ilọrin. Igbomina towns and Ikirun followed apace.[82] Southward expansion was halted only by the thick forest of Ilesha at the Polẹ war and later by a combination of the Oshogbo–Ibadan army which defeated the Ilọrin at Oshogbo in *c.* 1842. Under Emir Shittu, Ilọrin expanded eastwards. It seems that towns like Usi (near Ikọle), Ikọle itself, in Ekiti north, western Yagba, Awtun, Ẹrinmọpẹ, all came under some form of Ilọrin control. Under Emir Aliyu Ilọrin raids were said to have been carried as far as Igbiraland.[83] The consolidation of the Ilọrin conquests before 1880 was not hindered by any serious enemy challenge. Ilọrin was the centre of a Muslim political as well as religio-cultural expansion which spread beyond its political boundaries into the rest of Yorubaland to the south.

POCKET STATES WITHIN THE CALIPHATE

Within these outer frontiers of the Caliphate which we have just surveyed, it is not possible in the present state of our knowledge to demarcate with anything approaching accuracy the pocket states which did not form an integral part of the Caliphate. The tensions created by the incomplete subjugation of territories in Adamawa earlier in the century have been mentioned. So also has the opposition to Muslim rule by recalcitrant tribes of the Bauchi and Gombe domains. All these were sources of un-

79. Dupigny, *op. cit.*, pp. 15, 16, 17.
80. Rev. Samuel Johnson, *History of the Yorubas*, p. 210.
81. *Ibid.*, pp. 217, 218, 222.
82. *Ta'lif akhbār al-qurūn min 'Umarā' bilād Ilọrin.*
83. *Ibid.*

avoidable distraction to the Caliphate but by 1880 they were not threats to survival. At most they were barriers to desired expansion. Indeed raids into their territories also furnished slaves for sustaining the economy of the emirates.

Many of the heathen subjects of the emirates were, in effect, more like enemy states than subject peoples, while some were loosely integrated with the Caliphate. Yauri, for instance, is said to have been accepted with a *dhimmi* status, tributary to Gwandu quite early during the *jihād*.[84] There were, however, territories independent of the Caliphate. To the east of Yauri, for instance, were unsubjugated territories, the largest part of which was Gwariland. Not until about 1857 did the conquest of a large part of this territory begin under ʿUmar Nagwamatse, who subdued Minna, Yelwa, Kuta, Garun Gabas and Tegina in turn, and became the first emir and founder of Kontagora emirate.[85] The process of consolidation and conquest of this new emirate continued until the British occupation and was productive of many wars, and therefore of slaves, for which a certain notoriety was attached to its emir by the British conquerors. Even then not all Gwariland was subdued, or accepted Kontagora authority. The Ningawa of the Bauchi plateau furnished another example of the anxieties which pocket pagan states caused the Muslim emirates. They were a threat at least to the security of Kano, Bauchi, Gombe and Zaria, from the mid-1840s until the end of the century.

Ningi power originated in the expulsion of Mallam Hamza from Yar Sokwa in Kano territory by Usman Dabo for non-payment of *kharaj*.[86] With a number of mallams and followers Mallam Hamza first settled in Bauchi territory, with the Emir Ibrāhīm's permission. Later, following disagreements with their host people, Hamza and his party rebelled. After Hamza's death his community moved to Ningi, where they built a new capital. From this base under their successive rulers, Aḥmad, Abubakar and Dan Maji, the Ningi encouraged revolts among the subject

84. Barth, *op. cit.*, vol. iv, Appendix II, p. 545.
85. For the history of Kontagora emirate and its founding, see (*Tarihin Kontagora*) from Kontagora Divisional Office, tr. in the possession of E. J. Lannert; substance of the history also in Duff, *Gazetteer of Kontagora Province* (London, 1920).
86. *Labarun Hausawa da Makwabtansu*, vol. i, p. 51; for a detailed account of Ningi history and depredations against neighbouring emirates see *Tarīkh ʿUmarāʾ Bauchi*, pp. 161–91.

peoples of Bauchi and undertook predatory raids in Kano, Zaria and farther afield.[87] They were not subdued until the British occupation.

Up to 1880, in all emirates, including those founded in the early days of the *jihād*, the problem of consolidation against recalcitrant enemies remained a general one. By 1880 most of the more pressing dangers posed by the Caliphate's enemies had either disappeared or had become sufficiently reduced to enable the Caliphate to live with them without any serious apprehensions. These dangers, nonetheless, remained for the rest of the century sources of distraction to the various parts of the Caliphate, at least sufficiently disturbing to dictate vigilance in the defence arrangements of each emirate. Quite often these potential dangers did issue in physical conflict which kept the emirates preoccupied.

The picture that emerges from an assessment of the defence problems of the Caliphate and how far it could solve them is that from the point of view of military commitments the Caliphate continued to show features of a state in formation up to *c.* 1880. On the one hand it can be said that, militarily, the Caliphate does not seem to have been a powerful polity even during its heyday of religious zeal. On the other, the founding and the survival of each emirate against established dynasties indicates that each emirate must have been powerful militarily. As Dr Barth observed during his travels,[88] the total military strength of the Caliphate would have been imposing but for the fact that the distracted state of the emirates would not allow them to contribute their quota to a central force. This was true for the whole of the nineteenth century.

The arrangement whereby Sokoto or Gwandu could call upon the emirates for military aid did not amount to a centralization of defence policy, since it was not usual for other emirates to receive similar aid. In reality, therefore, a policy of centralized defence arrangement did not emerge in the Sokoto Caliphate. The lack of such an arrangement meant that the total striking force of the Caliphate remained a potential that could not be deployed at will against a common enemy. Yet, inauspicious as

87. *Tarīkh 'Umarā' Bauchi*, pp. 180, 181; see M. G. Smith, *op. cit.*, pp. 82, 101, for Ningi attacks on Zaria.

88. Barth, *op. cit.*, vol. iv, pp. 155, 156.

were the circumstances in which the emirates found themselves, the course of their history outlined above suggests that the Caliphate as a whole was by 1880 growing stronger *vis-à-vis* its enemies, many of whose hostilities had been stopped, reduced, or at least could be kept at bay whenever necessary.

Conflict within the Islamic community—the *Umma*—in one part of the Caliphate or the other, which appeared from time to time, was expressive of that basic contradiction between theory and practical reality involved in the attempt to establish an ideal way of life, such as the *sharī'a* in its purity represents, in a human society. While the *sharī'a*'s claim to absolute theoretical validity as the ideal way of life for Muslims *must* remain unchallenged, it is unlikely (even granted that this ideal could be fully comprehended) that any society could be found which would accept its application without demur. Moreover, in the case of the Sokoto Caliphate, as in revolutions generally, after the initial ardour, a natural balance was struck between the ideal and the practicable. In this light, personal rivalries, dynastic disputes and even rebellions such as those mentioned above, can be understood. This implied no radical change in the Islamic framework within which the Caliphate functioned and the bond of Islam which held its various parts together as a single polity.

Conflict within the Islamic community itself was one source of anxiety but not the most important with regard to the Caliphate's strength. Far more crucial was conflict with groups which, having been conquered, managed to set up again as independent states implacably hostile to the Caliphate throughout the century. Other enemy states constituted pockets of resistance which had either never been conquered or, if conquered, could not be firmly held thereafter. The attempts of these states to preserve their independence and attempts by Sokoto and the emirates to bring them under control were productive of many wars. When wars were not actually being fought or an uneasy truce concluded a state of chronic warfare prevailed.

In spite of the fact that many of the enemy states were Muslim the Caliphate waged *jihāds* against them, partly for reasons of self-preservation and partly for the expansion of *Dār al-Islām*. Since these states were opposed to the Caliphate, even if they were Muslim, the Caliphate would see them as *bughāt*—dissenters—against whom the *jihād* might be justifiably waged.

Others were of course polytheists against whom *jihād* must be waged by the Muslims. The existence of these groups and their recalcitrance produced a state of warfare which, seen in its right perspective, was a struggle between *Dār al-Islām* and *Dār al-ḥarb*. The groups comprising the *Dār al-ḥarb* were outside the Caliphate and wars fought against them were more in the nature of war against foreign states than against rebels. Constant war or constant readiness for defence on numerous frontiers constituted an element of built-in instability in the Caliphate's defence arrangements which persisted to the end of the century.

Chapter 4
The Caliphate: elements of stability and instability, 1880-1900

It has been shown that the basis of Sokoto authority and influence in the emirates lay in the fact that each emir owed his investiture to the Caliph or, in the emirates directly dependent on Gwandu, to the Emir of Gwandu. Every emir held his office at the pleasure of the Caliph or the Emir of Gwandu as the case might be, the condition of continued tenure of office being obedience to the overlord and a just and equitable government of the emirate. But the power of Sokoto or Gwandu to appoint or depose an emir was in reality not absolute. A just and equitable ruler who was at the same time obedient to his overlord could not be arbitrarily deposed, while in the question of appointment the overlord could not ordinarily bypass the choice of the local electoral council.

GWANDU–SOKOTO RELATIONS

Appointments and ultimate settlement of disputes about positions in the administration in Nupe emirate by Gwandu have been mentioned in the previous chapter. Gwandu's right to instal a new emir in Nupe held good to the end of the century, as witnessed by the investiture of Abubakar (Abū Bakr), the Emir of Nupe, by Gwandu officials in 1895.[1] The degree of Gwandu's control over its emirates must however be the subject of fuller study.[2] The relationship between the important emirate of Ilọrin with Gwandu in the second half of the nineteenth century is, for instance, at present obscure. Apart from the military support sent to Ilọrin in its fight against Ọyọ (the Eleduwẹ war *c.* 1837) no other evidence of direct Gwandu–Ilọrin relations thereafter has yet come to light. Presumably, in the matter of

1. R.H.B.E., S.101, vol. 18, Watts to R.N.C. 10 Nov. 1895. On visit to Bida during the Emir Abubakar's installation by Gwandu officials.
2. Mr S. A. Balogun is currently engaged in the study of this subject.

appointments, succession in Ilọrin was so smooth that Gwandu's role has escaped documentation.

But there is also evidence which suggests that Sokoto intervened in Ilọrin. Sokoto is said to have used its good offices to attempt a settlement of the Ilọrin–Ibadan wars in 1883–84.[3] It may well be that this attempt, reported by the *Lagos Observer*, was in fact made by the Emir of Gwandu but was attributed by the paper to the Caliph who was known to be the head of the Caliphate. But again in 1901 it was reported that the Caliph sent a messenger to Ilọrin to warn the Emir against cultivating friendly relations with the British.[4] This can, perhaps, be explained by the fact that even at the end of the century, in matters of great importance touching on the security of the Caliphate, Gwandu showed itself dependent on Sokoto. Thus, between 1888 and 1891, the people of Yabo, not far from Gwandu, were said to have joined in the rebellion of some unbelievers in their neighbourhood. Extant correspondence shows clearly that the Caliph gave specific instructions to the Emir of Gwandu regarding his role in crushing the rebellion. The steps taken by Gwandu were reported to Sokoto and the free men captured by Gwandu were duly forwarded to the Caliph.[5] 'Umar Bakatara, the Emir of Gwandu (1888–97), effectively and succinctly defined the relationship between himself and the Caliph when he wrote: 'I am the left hand, you are the right in the war against the rebels.'[6] The acknowledgement of Gwandu's subordination to Sokoto, as well as the evidence of co-operation between the two, are thus summarized. As further evidence of Gwandu's acknowledgement of Sokoto's overlordship 'Umar, the Emir of Gwandu, reported to Sokoto the steps he took to effect reconciliation between the Christians (the Royal Niger Company) and the emir of Nupe in *c.* 1896–98.[7]

In fact there were other instances when the Caliph issued instructions to Gwandu. As the Cazemajou expedition passed near Sokoto in 1898, the Caliph, 'Abd al-Raḥmān, gave instructions to the Emir of Gwandu to close the roads against them and prevent them from entering the Caliphate. The Emir of Gwandu

3. See below, p. 142.
4. See below, p. 225.
5. Corr. IX, nos. 1, 2, 3, 4.
6. Corr. IX, no. 4.
7. See below, p. 180.

wrote back to say 'we abide by your orders'.[8] In 1902, the Emir of Gwandu, Bayero, reported to the Caliph Attahiru (Al-Ṭāhir) on British military activities in Nupe.[9] All these indicate that, at least in matters of state security, supreme control rested with the Caliph. Perhaps the most explicit definition of the constitutional relations between Sokoto and Gwandu is one supplied by the Emir of Gwandu, 'Umar Bakatara, in 1895. In a letter he wrote to the German Emperor on the occasion of the visit of Dr Gruner's expedition,[10] he described himself as *Amīr aqālīm al-gharb al-Fallatiyya wa-'l-Sūdāniyya* (Emir of the Western Fulani and Sudanese provinces). There can thus be no doubt as to the subordinate position of Gwandu to Sokoto up to the fall of the Caliphate. However, this does not imply that there were no occasions of friction between the Caliphs and the emirs of Gwandu. Though the Caliphate remained one political entity in theory and practice, the unusually independent position of Gwandu meant that a dyarchy existed within it. Smooth relations would seem to have depended on the Caliphs' appreciation of, and reckoning with, this factor.

APPOINTMENT OF EMIRS

The procedure in matters of appointments in emirates directly dependent on Sokoto has been clearly described by D. M. Last.[11] It suffices here to note that while nomination rested with the local electors and Sokoto's role was usually one of confirmation and installation and the issue of a letter of appointment, in cases of dispute Sokoto's control was demonstrated to be usually real and final. Through intervention in succession disputes, Sokoto was able to acquire increasing control over the administration and distribution of offices in Zaria throughout the nineteenth century.[12] With the power to make appointments also went the power to depose—a power which Sokoto frequently exercised in Zaria and elsewhere in the second half of the nineteenth century.

8. Corr. IX, no. 110.
9. Corr. IX, no. 109.
10. See below, pp. 173–5.
11. D. M. Last, *The Sokoto Caliphate*, p. 180 ff.
12. M. G. Smith, *Government in Zazzau*, pp. 178–9. Zaria dates are taken from Last, 'Chronology', *op. cit.*

Thus in 1855, Sidi Abdulkadir ('Abd Al-Qādir) of Zaria was deposed on the order of the Caliph, 'Alī, and removed to Sokoto for acts of misgovernment and insubordination,[13] while in 1870 'Abdullāh was similarly deposed for disobeying the Caliph's order to withdraw from his attack on Keffi.[14]

Thenceforth Sokoto strained its power over appointments by appointing 'Abdullāh's successor, Abubakar, without any reference to the Zaria electors. The Caliph, Abū Bakr b. Bello (1873–77), reappointed 'Abdullāh as Emir of Zaria on Abubakar's death, on the ground that 'Abdullāh had in the first instance been dismissed without due processes of the law. For the practical purposes of administration, respect for the law must be supreme. By acting, as it appears, on this principle Abū Bakr had levied a telling criticism at the action of the Caliph, Aḥmad al-Rifā'ī. But in bypassing the local electors at the appointment of Abubakar the Caliph Aḥmad al-Rifā'ī, was merely adhering to the letter of the law, or rather the earliest traditions of the Caliphate, seeing that the first emirs at the inception of the *jihād* owed their appointments solely to the authority of the *Amīr al-mu'minīn*, while the tradition of having local electors was a later development which became stabilized only after the emirates had settled down to the problems of administration after the *jihād*. After the death of 'Abdullāh of Zaria (November/December 1878), the local electors of Zaria were required to send to the Caliph three nominees, indicating their order of preference. Final decision rested with Sokoto. The practice of sending the names of several candidates for the emirship for the Caliph's final choice antedated this period in some emirates, and may in fact have been quite general throughout the Caliphate.[15] Further, when eventually Sambo was chosen, he was given specific instruction as to whom to appoint to the three top-ranking offices of Madaki, Wombai and Galadima.[16]

This exercise of power was in fact not outside the legal competence of the Caliph, considering the fact that the government of each emirate was indeed his government, and local

13. M. G. Smith, *op. cit.*, pp. 163–4. Al-ḥajj Sa'īd, *Tarīkh sokoto* p. 36, the charges given here are oppression, illegal killings, dissipation of public funds and voluptuous living with strange women.
14. M. G. Smith, *op. cit.*, pp. 170–1.
15. R. A. Adeḷẹyẹ: 'The Sokoto Caliphate in the nineteenth century'.
16. M. G. Smith, *op. cit.*, pp. 178–9.

officials performed their functions as part of a hierarchy of authority with him at the apex. Conditions in Zaria had merely given Sokoto the opportunity to exercise powers that lay dormant in law under the force of tradition. Sambo was deposed in 1888 after the Zaria people had complained to the Caliph of his inability to defend his state against its enemies—the peoples of Ningi, Maradi and Abuja.[17]

The Zaria example shows that Sokoto's control of appointments in an emirate increased with the degree of rivalries and divisions within that emirate. Thus towards the end of the century, 1897, the Wazir, Bukhārī, was forced to abandon his choice for the Zaria emirship in the face of bitter opposition by the Bornawa, Katsinawa and Sullebawa dynasties of Zaria and their unanimous support for a rival candidate, Muḥammad Lawal (Kwassau). Besides this strong support, Kwassau threw into the bargain his '*Yan bindiga*', a well disciplined regiment equipped with firearms and loyal to Kwassau.[18] The Wazir appointed Kwassau. Obviously, Sokoto could not force an unwanted emir on the people. On this occasion, Sokoto had overplayed its hand.

The *Missau Chronicle* shows that successive Emirs of Missau were, after appointment, installed by the Wazir of Sokoto, or any other high official of Sokoto duly selected for the purpose. The power of deposition was exercised by Sokoto to remove the Emir, Usman ('Uthmān), for arbitrary dismissal of several office-holders to the great annoyance of the Missau people.[19] Also in Katsina, the Emir, Ṣiddīq, was deposed in 1843–44 by the Caliph, 'Alī (Aliyu Baba), for charges of oppression levied against him by his subjects.[20]

It seems also that where there was dispute over minor appointments, for instance of a district head, reference had to be made to Sokoto. Between 1886 and 1891, Musa, the Emir of Gwaram—a vassal of Kano—died while the Emir of Kano, Muḥammad Bello, was away on a visit to Sokoto. When he returned he appointed a man from Kano called Buji who was the late Emir's brother—

17. *Ibid.*, p. 187. Extant correspondence shows that Sambo appealed to the Caliph as a helpless man to help him raise his house. The Caliph replied granting him pardon: see Corr. VI, nos. 90 and 91. The pardon was, however, not followed by reinstatement in office.
18. M. G. Smith, *op. cit.*, p. 190.
19. *Chronicle of Missau*, *op. cit.*
20. Al-ḥajj Sa'īd, *Tarīkh Sokoto*, p. 25.

'as our custom, we take an agent of this town and instal him over another town'.[21] The people of Gwaram rejected Kano's nominee. Muḥammad Bello, apparently viewing the matter as beyond his power, applied to Sokoto for instructions. The Caliph, 'Umar, ruled that Buji should be deposed and the popular choice, Saliman b. Musa (son of the late Emir), appointed.[22] This was done. Later the people of Gwaram became dissatisfied with Saliman on account of his oppression over them and 'his wickedness and alliance with unbelievers'. They appealed to the Emir of Kano to depose him as indeed they deemed him deposed by the *sharīʿa*.[23] Again Kano decided to depose Saliman but informed Sokoto accordingly. As Muḥammad Bello said, 'because to untie is in your hand and it is not just ruling for me to instal an emir over them without waiting for your reply'.[24] Similarly between 1880 and 1891 Muḥammad Bello had reported his deposition of the governor of Dutsi to Sokoto.

When Haruna (Harūn), Sarkin Tambawel, died in 1902, there was a succession dispute between Saʿd, Haruna's brother and Aliyu, Haruna's son. Saʿd was supported by Sarkin Dogondaji who appealed to the Caliph, Attahiru, on behalf of Saʿd, mentioning that Saʿd was the popular choice of the people. Saʿd was subsequently appointed.[25]

The Caliph's control over the appointment of emirs and his power of arbitration in the appointment of other officials about which there was dispute remained unimpaired down to the overthrow of the Caliphate. It seems clear that regard for *maṣlaḥā* (public welfare), an important principle of Malikī law, not only guided but also constrained the Caliph in his intervention in the emirates. Installation of new emirs remained a function of Sokoto officials and was necessary to make a new appointment

21. Corr. VIII, no. 6: Muḥammad Bello, Emir of Kano, to Amīr al-mu'minīn 'Umar.
22. Corr. VIII, no. 7, from Muḥammad Bello to Amīr al-mu'minīn 'Umar.
23. Corr. VII, no. 55. Saliman was accused by the people of Gwaram of having sent 43 horses to Danyaya the chief of the Ningi.
24. Corr. I, no. 59; Corr. VII, no. 34.
25. Corr. IX, nos. 56–67. The importance of the power of the Caliph as final arbiter is illustrated by letter 64. From 'Alī b. Harūn to the Amīr al-mu'minīn in which 'Alī complained that Sarkin Yama had forged two letters purported to have been written by the Caliph and the Wazir authorising the appointment of Saʿd with the insignia of office.

legally valid. As late as 1896 the Wazir Muḥammad Bukhārī was sent to Katagum to instal Abdulkadiri (ʿAbd al-Qādir) as Emir of Katagum and to fill the vacancy left by him as ruler of Shira.[26] The emirates attached great importance to the Caliph's confirmation. In 1898 both the Emirs of Kano and Bauchi wrote to Amīr al-jaish ʿUmar b. Koiranga of Gombe, to congratulate him on his choice as Emir. Later, the Emir of Bauchi, ʿUmar, wrote to congratulate the new Emir for receiving the Caliph's confirmation of his appointment.[27]

The ultimate dependence of each Emir on Sokoto or Gwandu, as the case might be, for his appointment and continuance in office, was a guarantee of loyalty to his overlord and of equitable rule in his province. The importance of this factor to the unity and preservation of the Caliphate can hardly be overstressed. That Sokoto was the source of ultimate power and authority in the Caliphate gave a semblance of centralization to the government of the Caliphate. In theory this centralization was indeed real, but in practice, as long as an emir kept within the limits imposed by the constitution by fulfilling his obligations both to his overlord and his subjects, he remained virtually independent of control because by acting correctly he rendered intervention by Sokoto unnecessary.

Yet, no matter how independent an emir might seem in practice, his dependence on his overlord was more real than his independence. Even in times of settled government, he was still under an obligation to take instructions from his overlord and act on them. Through the supervision of the officials in Sokoto responsible for overseeing the affairs of the various emirates and from reports reaching Sokoto from these emirates, the Caliph and his Wazir could keep an eye on events in the provinces. The Caliphate's administration was thus far more closely centralized than is commonly imagined and the power and control of the Caliph over his emirates was never remote.

26. Corr. IX, no. 6. See J. M. Fremantle, *J.A.S.* x (1910), pp. 420–1, records that a sharp succession dispute broke out in Katagum in 1896 on Muḥammad al-Ḥajj's death between Abu Bakr, brother of Al-Ḥajj, and Abdulkadiri, son of Al-Ḥajj. Their supporters by analogy to recent events in Kano were referred to as Yusubawa and Tukurawa. The final settlement was Sokoto's, imposed by Bukhārī on the visit referred to in the above letter.

27. Corr. X, nos. 84, 87, 136.

VISITS AND TRIBUTE FROM THE EMIRS

The tie with Sokoto was acknowledged by the emirs in various ways. Each emir on appointment paid a visit to the Caliph and often more frequently. Even the Emirs of distant Adamawa made such visits.[28] M. G. Smith gives the impression that such visits to Sokoto were performed annually by the Emirs of Zaria.[29] In fact, the visit to the Caliph on the occasion of the annual gathering of all emirs known as the meeting of *Manya Sarakuna* (Big Chiefs) was obligatory on all emirs. Although an emir could send representatives under special circumstances, failure to attend in person was normally seriously viewed by the Caliph. An emir could also be summoned to Sokoto on the Caliph's specific order, as was the case with Sidi Abdulkadiri and ʿAbdullāh (both of Zaria) shortly before they were deposed. The *Missau Chronicle* records the summoning of all the emirs to meet the Caliph on several occasions. On one of these occasions the Caliph, ʿUmar (1881–91), angrily deprived Muḥammad Manga of his extra-territorial rights over the Bornu Fulani settled in other emirates outside Missau, because Manga sent a representative instead of attending in person. However, reconciliation was later effected between Muḥammad Manga and Caliph ʿUmar, through the good offices of the Emir of Bauchi, ʿUmar.[30]

Loyalty and subservience to Sokoto were also expressed by the payment of tribute. The revenue from the emirates to Sokoto, as revealed by the correspondence of the last two decades of the nineteenth century, were in the form of gifts. However, these gifts do not seem to have been as voluntarily given as D. M. Last suggests. They were usually referred to as 'well-known and covenanted gifts' (*al-Hadīyat al-maʿlūmat al-maʿhūdat*). The word *al-maʿlūmat* means 'covenanted' or 'agreed'. It is at least clear that these gifts had become so established by tradition that

28. See, for instance, below, p. 102, Zubeir's visit.
29. M. G. Smith, *op. cit.*, p. 74.
30. From Amīr al-mu'minīn, ʿUmar, to Usman (ʿUthmān), Emir of Bauchi; uncatalogued letter in University of Ibadan Library in a collection of letters from Bauchi translated by A. N. Skinner. In the same collection another letter (from Muḥammad, Emir of Muri, to Ibrāhīm, Emir of Bauchi), Muḥammad of Muri said he could not visit Ibrāhīm because he was going to Sokoto—'the journey which is a duty for all set over a people'.

non-payment would amount to a breach of obligation.[31] In a letter written between 1891 and 1900, Emir Abubakar of Katsina apologized for sending his tribute to Sokoto late due to war with Maradi, while in another letter from the Emir of Bauchi, ʿUmar, to Sokoto, ʿUmar apologized for sending his annual usual present of seventy slaves and ten bags of cloth late, and for inability to attend personally at the Sokoto court.[32]

According to M. G. Smith, the Wazir of Sokoto was responsible for the collection of the tribute which Zaria sent twice a year to Sokoto during *ʿId al-Fiṭr* and *ʿId al-Kabīr* and that the Wazir collected levies on grains for himself.[33] Again it is reported that tax was increased in Zaria on the orders of the Caliph, ʿAlī. The suggestion is that Sokoto demands on Zaria were rising during the century. Nonetheless, it was a usual practice to send voluntary gifts with letters, but these must not be confused with tribute.[34] Often, however, voluntary gifts amounted to much in value[35] and must therefore be reckoned with as a steady source of revenue for the Caliph.

Concerning the customary or covenanted tribute, Dr Barth records that he met the bearers of the Zaria and Kano tribute on their way to Sokoto in March 1853. Zaria's gift, he recorded,

31. Corr. VII, no. 51 (*c.* 1886–93). From Muḥammad Bello (Emir of Kano) to Wazir Muḥammad Bukhārī. Muḥammad Bello in answer to an order by the Wazir Bukhārī that he should pay higher tribute to him than he had already done wrote that Bukhārī ordered that he should increase his share of the tribute by 5 million (cowries) but that as they had not yet collected anything from the *Jizya* and *Kurdin Karofi* he could only send 2000 cowries. Earlier the Emir, Bello, had sent 10 million and 5 million cowries to the Caliph and Bukhārī respectively through the Sokoto messenger sent down with orders to collect the dues. Kano's 'gift' on this occasion cannot be viewed as voluntary. It is significant that Muḥammad Bello considers the Wazir's demand normal. In Corr. IX alone nos. 6, 7, 20, 25, 27, 38, 41, 71, 73, 76, 79, 89, 101, 103, 109, 112, 114, 115, 116, 117, 118, 122, 123, 124, record 'gifts' to Sokoto from the emirates.
32. Corr. IX, nos. 38, and 15, respectively.
33. M. G. Smith, *op. cit.*, p. 74.
34. *Ibid.*, p. 94.
35. Note Corr. IX, nos. 73, 89, ʿAbdullāh Bayero (Emir of Gwandu) to the Caliph Attahiru, *c.* 1902—early 1903 sent 1000 kolanuts on each occasion. No. 112, *c.* 1901–02, Zubeir, Emir of Yola sends 30 cows to Attahiru. This class of voluntary gifts was quite normal, and while they were well-known customs *ʿIdat Maʿrufat*, Corr. ix, no. 86, they differed from *al-hadīyat al-maʿlūmat al-maʿhūdat* which were tribute.

consisted of 2 million cowries, 500 tobes and 30 horses. That of Katsina was only 400,000 cowries. The improbably heavy tribute from Zaria seems to be an exaggeration, and we may presume that Dr Barth's claim that this heavy tribute was sent in from Zaria to Sokoto every second month was based on misinformation.[36] Adamu Jekada, at one time the trusted messenger and political informant of the Royal Niger Company whose services were inherited by the Lugard administration, reported in 1900 that Kano sent its imposed annual tribute to Sokoto, consisting of 100 fine horses, 60 of which were heavily laden with riches consisting of fine gowns and clothes.[37] This large Kano tribute to Sokoto reported by Adamu Jekada seems to agree with the large sums remitted by Muḥammad Bello to Sokoto.[38]

Booty obtained in war against unbelievers was usually one of the regular sources of revenue from the emirates to Sokoto. According to the orthodox Muslim concept on the division of the booty one-fifth (*khums*) should go to the Imām—i.e. the Caliph. After one of his battles with unbelievers Muḥammad al-ḥajj, Emir of Hadejia (1885–1906), sent three horses and three slaves to the Wazir Bukhārī,[39] 'as is well-known and covenanted (or agreed)'. It seems that the usual practice was to send part of the booty to Sokoto. There is no evidence that Muḥammad al-hajj's gift to Bukhārī represents the *khums* but as this gift was not specifically intended for the Caliph it may be presumed that the Caliph's share was also sent. The usual practice was to send a smaller gift to the Wazir alongside with the tribute sent to the Caliph. After a successful battle with the Ningi in which Muḥammad Bello of Kano captured about 500 slaves, he sent the *khums*, 100, to the Caliph 'Umar and 50 to other dignitaries of Sokoto. After another engagement with the Ningi he sent 90 slaves to the

36. Dr Barth, *Travels and Discoveries in North and Central Africa*, vol. iii, pp. 116, 127; cf. Corr. IV, no. 45, Zaria sends 20 slaves and 70 gowns. However, considering the large number of towns and districts which were dependent on Zaria, Barth's estimates may in fact not be far out. The frequency must, however, remain a matter of doubt.

37. Adamu Jekada to Lugard, N.A.K. KADKAPTORY, Box 45, item 26; Arabic letter book, no. 145, received 12th Jan., 1901.

38. See Corr. VII, no. 85 (*c.* 1886–91). Muḥammad Bello sends 10 million to the Caliph, 5000 to Wazir Bukhārī and 2000 to Dan Galadima; and (in letter 51) he sent 10 million cowries to the Caliph, and 5 million to the Wazir.

39. Corr. II, no. 3.

Caliph and 20 to other officials in Sokoto out of a total of about 500.[40]

It became customary for emirs to pay *kurdin sarauta* to the Caliph on accession to office. When an emir died or was deposed, it was usual to send one-third of his inheritance to the Caliph.[41] When the governor of Dutse (Dutsi) was deposed by the Emir of Kano, Muḥammad Bello, an inventory of his property was made. Materials for war such as horses, swords and guns were made over to the new governor. Of the eighty slaves owned by the late governor, forty were made over to the new governor. Muḥammad Bello kept twenty and twenty were sent to Sokoto—fifteen for the Caliph and five for the Wazir 'Abdullāh.[42] There is a hint that inheritance money (*irth*) may also have been taken by the state from some people other than officials. On the death of a native of Binji at Kano (*c.* 1883–91) the Caliph, 'Umar, ordered his inheritance to be sent to him. This Muḥammad Bello did promptly.[43] It is possible that the property of the man falls under inheritance of which the heir is not known, which is one of the seven sources of the state's revenue mentioned by 'Uthmān b. Fodiye in *Kitāb al-Farq* and *Bayān Wujūb al-hijra.*

The payment of tribute and sending of gifts by the emirates to Sokoto continued until the early years of the British occupation. In 1902 Lugard complained that in spite of the vigilance of the British officers, all the emirates, posed between fear of the Caliph and the British military forces, continued to send tribute to Sokoto surreptitiously. In April 1901 Wazir Bukhārī came to Zaria to collect the tribute and hurried away to escape capture or interference by the British officers there. The Wazir of Gwandu,

40. Corr. VII, no. 15 and Corr. VIII, no. 5.

41. Last, *op. cit.*, pp. 105–6; cf. *Missau Chronicle*: when an emir died the people of Missau, sent his horse, one of his concubines and his sword, to Sokoto. It is likely but not explicitly stated that more of the late Emir's possessions were sent to Sokoto on the arrival of Sokoto officials delegated to instal the new Emir. On the appointment of Muḥammad Manga, Galadima Abbās of Sokoto, sent down for the purpose, stayed three months in Missau because Manga would not send all the childless concubines of the late Emir to Sokoto.

42. Corr. VII, no. 34 (*c.* 1883–86). From Muḥammad Bello to Wazir 'Abdullāh.

43. Corr. VII, no. 28. From Muḥammad Bello to Amīr al-mu'minīn, 'Umar. Since Binji formed part of the Sokoto District the Caliph's order to Kano may have been given merely to protect the estate of a subject under Sokoto's direct jurisdiction.

on a tribute collecting round, was met by Burdon in Bida in 1901.[44] The continued payment of tribute by the emirates was a manifestation of their continued loyalty and vassalage to Sokoto.

SOKOTO ARBITRATION IN INTER- AND INTRA-EMIRATE DISPUTES

Another significant aspect of the organization of the Sokoto Caliphate which persisted to the end was that the emirates depended on Sokoto for settlement of disputes in their different localities. One of the minor spheres, but apparently one viewed seriously, in which resort was made to Sokoto from the emirates, was that of runaway slaves or the enslavement of people, who because they were Muslims or free-born, could not legally be enslaved. There were numerous appeals to the Caliph, both from high officials and on behalf of private citizens, for help through application of the law to effect restitution of absconded slaves.[45] In one case, an absconded slave, property of a subject of Haruna, Emir of Tambawel, was found to be in the possession of the Amīr al-mu'minīn, and application was made for his restitution.[46] The law regarding property in slaves was apparently no respecter of persons. There is a spate of letters from the Emir, ʿUmar of Bauchi to ʿUmar, Emir of Gombe, asking for restitution, in keeping with the law, of runaway slaves found in the possession of the latter's subjects.[47] The case of a Sokoto man who bought a free-born woman from Gombe territory and brought her to Kano furnishes an interesting illustration of the working of the *sharīʿa* with regard to the enslavement of free-born people and Sokoto's role in upholding it. The Emir of Kano, Aliyu Baba (ʿAlī al-kabīr) (1894–1903), confirmed the free status of the woman according to the *sharīʿa* and arrangements were made for the restitution of the money paid by the owner—the Sokoto

44. See below, p. 257.
45. For example, Corr. IX, nos. 5, 8, 44. Corr. I, nos. 5 and 7, Corr. IV, no. 8.
46. Corr. IX, no. 44, from Harūn to Wazir Bukhārī.
47. For example, Corr. X, nos. 82, 83, 120, 125, 158, 159, 164, 165, 166, 222, 225; also similar complaints from other neighbouring emirates to Gombe in *ibid.*, nos. 104, 115, 129, 148.

man.[48] Wazir Bukhārī, to whom Aliyu reported the case, confirmed the latter's judgment.[49]

Thus on the eve of the overthrow of the Caliphate a distinction was still being made between Unbelievers and Muslims in the matter of enslavement. It cannot be shown conclusively that illegitimate raids were not carried out by the emirates but the law which frowns on this was by no means a dead letter.[50] The Caliph exercised his authority to ensure conformity with the law of slavery in Islam. The legality of enslavement was apparently a lively issue in the Caliphate to the end of the nineteenth century. On one occasion when Ṣāliḥ, Emir of Missau (*c.* 1861–86), attacked some Kerikeri towns and conquered them, the Emir of Katagum, Muḥammad al-ḥajj, reported to Sokoto that the towns attacked were not pagan but Muslim. The Amīr al-mu'minīn ordered the Emir of Kano, 'Abdullāh, to send down people to the affected towns to verify the charge. Investigations proved that the conquered towns were pagan. Ṣāliḥ sent six of the captured slaves to Sokoto as proof of the pagan status of the towns he conquered.[51]

Although the emirates were all bound by a common tie of loyalty to the same overlord, maintained friendly relation with one another and usually co-operated against their common enemies, there were occasional disputes between them. In such disputes Sokoto's arbitration was usually decisive in restoring peace. Sokoto's intervention took the form of sending a delegation to investigate the dispute on the spot and thereafter making a ruling which would be binding on the disputants. Sometimes, as

48. Corr. X, no. 11 (1898–1902), from Aliyu, Emir of Kano, to 'Umar, Emir of Gombe.
49. Bukhārī to the Caliph, 'Umar, Corr. X, no. 33. Bukhārī said that 'the *sharī'a* disallowed her enslavement because she is free'. In Corr. III, no. 13, Haruna of Tambawel made an appeal to Bukhārī to declare a free woman who had been enslaved free. See also Corr. X, no. 77. Muḥammad Manga appealed to 'Umar of Gombe to free one of his subjects as she was a free-born who had been enslaved in Gombe.
50. See below, p. 90. The allegations made by Muḥammad Lawal, Emir of Zaria, against Ibrāhīm, Emir of Kontagora, show that the charges of raiding and capturing of Muslims as slaves were not completely unfounded.
51. *Chronicle of Missau*; also N.A.K. Bauchi prof., Acc. 311. *Historical notes on Azare district* (collected by Katagum District Officer, 1928). The evidence in these two sources are so similar that it may be presumed that they have a common origin.

in the revolt of Galadiman Ako discussed below, the negotiations were tortuous and protracted. A study of a number of inter- and intra-emirate disputes, other than those concerning slavery, will further illustrate Sokoto's role in minimizing the danger of internal disputes to the wellbeing and solidarity of the Caliphate.

In the period 1891–1900, there was a dispute, the circumstances of which are obscure, between Daura and Kazaure. The Amīr al-mu'minīn, 'Abd al-Raḥmān, sent Galadima 'Umar to arbitrate between the disputants.[52] Nearer to Sokoto, a land dispute between Sarkin Zamfara, 'Umar, and Sarkin Katsina (i.e. Sarkin Gusau), Muḥammad Gidado, over a town called Doko became so acute that an armed conflict between the two *Sarakuna* seemed likely. The case was submitted to the Caliph's arbitration. It seems clear from the surviving correspondence that the Caliph ruled in favour of Sarkin Zamfara, 'Umar. The Emir of Gusau persisted in professing his innocence but, in deference to the Caliph, desisted from the use of force even under provocation from 'Umar. Rather, he appealed to the Caliph, 'Abd al-Raḥmān, to institute an enquiry conducted by men of probity to clear him of the charges brought against him.[53]

In Zaria, during the reign of 'Uthmān Yero (1888–97) the wars of expansion of the Emir of Kontagora, Ibrāhīm Nagwamatse, impinged on Zaria territory. Kontagora forces conquered Bene, in western Zaria territory, intending to cross the Gurara river at Je're. 'Uthmān, probably too weak but also reluctant to attack a fellow Emir, appealed to Wazir Bukhārī as the proper person to judge and arbitrate.[54] The Kontagora attacks continued in 1899, at which time it appeared that Sokoto, after a recent rumpus with Zaria over the succession of Kwassau (1897) in which a revolt of Zaria was narrowly averted, seemed unenthusiastic to take action. The Caliph's appeals to Ibrāhīm were unheeded. When nothing happened until 1901 Muḥammad Lawal (Kwassau) was induced by Lugard's skilfully dropped hints to invite a British garrison to establish itself in Zaria.[55]

The emirates of the eastern marches of the Caliphate were

52. Corr. VIII, no. 30. Amīr al-mu'minīn 'Umar to Wazir Bukhārī.
53. Corr. IX, nos. 18, 19, 20, 21, 22. See Blackwell's note on the background to the dispute. H. F. Blackwell, *Occupation of Hausaland* (Lagos, 1927), pp. 24–5.
54. Corr. VI, no. 36; M. G. Smith, *op. cit.* p. 196.
55. See below, pp. 243–7.

noted for their unceasing raids against the numerous pagan communities which interspersed their territories. Gombe, Bauchi, and Missau oral traditions are filled with the anti-pagan military campaigns of their emirs.[56] The numerous letters about slaves written by ʿUmar of Bauchi to ʿUmar of Gombe, as noted above, within the short period of under four years (August 1898–1902), indicate the frequency and fruitfulness of expeditions against pagans.

Of all parts of the Caliphate the emirates of the eastern marches were perhaps the most fruitful grounds for inter-emirate disputes. The Emirs of Missau, Ṣāliḥ and Muḥammad Manga, were often mixed up in disputes either as principal actors or as helpers. Ṣāliḥ's aid to ʿUthmān, Emir of Bauchi, in *c.* 1881, was decisive in quelling the Khalīl rebellion—an attempt by the latter in league with pagans and *dhimmis* to seize the Bauchi throne which resulted in a devastating war and his death.[57] Muḥammad Manga, Ṣāliḥ's successor,[58] was involved in protracted hostilities with Katagum over the town of Isawa. Isawa was one of the many towns in the eastern emirates peopled by *Fulanin Bornu*, from which by an extraterritorial grant made to Muḥammad Manga, the first Emir of Missau, the Emirs of Missau collected *Jangali*. The right was withdrawn from Muḥammad Manga when soon after his accession to office in *c.* 1885, he refused to answer the summons to all emirs to meet the Caliph.[59] After he was pardoned, Isawa, with the encouragement and connivance of Sarkin Shira, Abdulkadiri (Emir of Katagum 1896–1902), refused to submit to Muḥammad Manga. Events soon led to a military clash in which Isawa was evacuated at the approach of M. Manga supported by the forces of Aliyu, Emir of Kano. The aftermath was a relentless hostility between Katagum and Missau emirates which looked like plunging the whole of Gudiri (Katagum, Hadejia and Missau emirates) in civil war. There was actual fighting and raiding between the forces of Katagum and Missau.[60]

The affair gave rise to much animated correspondence with

56. See *Missau Chronicle*, *Tarīkh ʿUmarāʾ Bauchi*, and *Tabyīn Amr Buba Yero*.
57. Maḥmūd b. Muḥammad Bello b. Aḥmad b. Idrīs al-Sudānī, *Tarīkh ʿUmarāʾ Bauchi*, p. 249 ff.; see also *Missau Chronicle*, and *History of Bauchi Emirates*, N.A.K. Bauchi prof., vol. ii, 690.
58. Ṣalīḥ was killed fighting against the pagans of Warje, see Corr. IV, no. 6, from Muḥammad al-ḥajj to Wazir Bukhārī.
59. *Missau Chronicle*.
60. Corr. IV, no. 15, from Muḥammad al-ḥajj to Wazir Bukhārī.

Sokoto from both emirates with accusations, counter-accusations and threats of war. Muḥammad Manga claimed he was merely insisting on his rights and that the Emir of Katagum was a rebel against the Caliph—a serious charge. The Emir of Katagum also accused Manga of being a rebel. The Isawa episode was only closed by Sokoto's ruling, consequent on which the Emir of Katagum, Muḥammad al-ḥajj, agreed to withdraw from the dispute.[61] Sarkin Isawa, Muḥammad Gidado, was subsequently lured into a trap by Muḥammad Manga and killed. Isawa returned to the allegiance of Missau.

Muḥammad Manga seemed to have thrown himself against virtually every neighbouring emir at one time or the other. Once, he complained bitterly to 'Umar, Emir of Bauchi, against the Emir of Kano for collecting *Zakat* in his territory—a matter he felt might force him to a reluctant war—yet on another occasion, as above, he sought and received much-needed help from Kano.[62]

The origins of the revolt of Galadiman Ako, which took place between 1899 and 1901[63] are still shrouded in mystery. The Galadima revolted against his Emir, 'Umar of Gombe. It seems clear from the surviving correspondence on the affair (on which this account is based) that this revolt, which caused Gombe considerable anxiety, might have been limited and brought under easy control but for the support the Galadima received from Muḥammad Manga, who moved his men to Ako. 'Umar also moved his forces to Tukulma near Ako.[64]

A situation capable of producing explosive consequences was thus created. That Muḥammad Manga and the Galadima were both considered as being in the wrong by the neighbouring emirs is certain. The letters of Sarkin Dallari, Muḥammad Wabi, Aliyu, Emir of Kano and Ibrāhīm, Sarkin Nafada, imply support for 'Umar.[65] 'Umar himself insisted that Muḥammad Manga was

61. *Missau Chronicle*. J. M. Fremantle, *J.A.S.*, vol. x, pp. 419–20. N.A.K. Bauchi prof., 690, vol. i; *History of Jemaari*; Corr. IV, nos. 4, 7, 15, 16, 39, 42.
62. Corr. IV, no. 37.
63. In December 1898 when Lt Bryan of the W.A.F.F. was travelling in Gombe emirate, the Emir and the Galadima Ako were still co-operating against Mallam Jibrīl Gaini.
64. Corr. X, no. 170.
65. Corr. X, nos. 216, 209, and 200 respectively. Cf. Last, *op. cit.*, p. 229. I can find no evidence to substantiate the claim that 'Umar had been unjust to the Galadima.

trying to impose the Galadiman Ako on him, but Muḥammad Manga pleaded that he had no intention of exciting disaffection between 'Umar and the Galadima but merely wanted 'Umar to give the Galadima his freedom. The men he moved to Ako, Muḥammad Manga claimed, were meant to stay with the Galadima, not to fight for him—and if the affair was still unsettled it was only because 'Umar would not return to Gombe with his men. 'Umar submitted the matter to 'Umar of Bauchi for arbitration. The latter was reluctant, to begin with, because he felt it was a matter for the Caliph's arbitration. He, however, entered into correspondence with Muḥammad Manga, the Galadima and 'Umar of Gombe. While he urged submission on the Galadima, he pressed 'Umar to move away from Tukulma to create a favourable atmosphere for fruitful negotiations. The efforts of the Emir of Bauchi, 'Umar, demonstrate a phenomenon, that was neither new nor unique, of co-operation between neighbouring emirs to settle their disputes and avert threats to state security.

The Ako affair was finally submitted to the Caliph, 'Abd al-Raḥmān, for arbitration. An official, Wali Shehu, was sent by the Caliph to investigate it and on his return to Sokoto both the Caliph and the Wazir wrote to Muḥammad Manga to withdraw from the affair and to the Galadiman Ako to go to Gombe to seek 'Umar's pardon. These instructions were passed on to Gombe for 'Umar's information, with instructions to accept the Galadima's request for pardon. Muḥammad Manga withdrew, the Galadiman Ako received his pardon and a situation which might easily have produced open hostilities was resolved by Sokoto's intervention.[66] Soon after the settlement Muḥammad Manga died. His successor, Aḥmad, wrote warm letters to 'Umar of Gombe in which he blamed his brother, Muḥammad Manga, for breaking the age-old friendship between their emirates in consideration of furthering his own personal passions.[67]

66. Corr. X, no. 61. From 'Umar of Gombe to the Amīr al-mu'minīn—reports going to Ako and pardoning the Galadima. The date is Friday 1st Rabi' al-awwāl which I reckon to be 29 June 1900—the only Friday in the years 1898–1901 which fell on the 1st.

67. The account of the Galadiman Ako revolt is reconstructed from a large number of letters. To avoid frequent citing of the same letter those used are cited here: Corr. X, nos. 2, 17, 18, 19, 29, 30, 31, 34, 35, 42, 61, 72, 80, 81, 86, 87, 97, 118, 137, 139, 140, 142, 143, 154, 155, 157, 160, 170, 172, 173, 174, 177, 200, 211, 216, 224.

In 1900 Sarkin Gwaram, a vassal of Bauchi, revolted. ʿUmar, the Emir of Bauchi, proceeded to suppress the revolt by force but for nine long months he had little success until he received help from Muḥammad Manga and the Emir of Jama'ari.[68] As in the Ako revolt, Sokoto intervened to effect reconciliation but apparently too late to prevent the execution of Sarkin Gwaram and the enslavement of several thousands of the inhabitants by Muḥammad Manga.[69] The chronicler of this revolt points out the legality of killing the revolted Sarki and the illegality of the enslavement of free-born.[70]

In the light of the instances cited above, there is no doubt that the emirs were not only loyal and obedient to Sokoto but that they looked up to the Caliph for leadership and direction in their affairs as well, especially in times of crisis. Moreover they needed and valued the Caliph's role as the final arbiter in their internal differences. These instances also illustrate an aspect of the tensions within the Caliphate.

REVOLTS AGAINST THE CALIPH'S AUTHORITY

That the Sokoto Caliphs could reckon on obedience and loyalty from their emirates is a measure of the justness and effectiveness of their rule. Obedience was not unconditional as the state was essentially nomocratic. While the lesser instruments of law enforcement like the ʿ*Umarā*' and their officials were duty-bound to discharge the authority delegated to them by the Caliph, the Caliph, as the supreme instrument of the enforcement of the law, was equally duty-bound to keep within the limits imposed on him by the law. If he was unjust or flouted usages sanctioned by custom, he risked forfeiting the obedience of his subjects. Revolts

68. *Tarīkh ʿUmarā' Bauchi*, pp. 273 ff.; see also *Missau Chronicle* and N.A.K. Bauchi prof., 690, vol. ii, *History of Bauchi*.
69. Corr. X, nos. 28 and 40. From Muḥammad Bukhārī to ʿUmar, Emir of Gombe and from Wali Shehu (Sokoto) to ʿUmar, Emir of Gombe respectively. See also uncatalogued letter in A. N. Skinner's translation of letters from Bauchi in Ibadan Library, the Caliph ʿAbd al-Raḥmān ordered ʿUmar of Bauchi to leave Gwaram and its Emir, return to his house and pardon the Emir of Gwaram.
70. *Tarīkh ʿUmarā' Bauchi*, pp. 274–5. The author records that about 9000 inhabitants were captured. This can be taken as indicating that the captured were numerous.

against the Caliph by any of the emirates throughout the nineteenth century were remarkably rare. Besides, none of the few that took place came near to upsetting the organization of the Caliphate. The Bukhārī rebellion which began in *c.* 1850 and raged for fifteen years is a case in point.[71]

The Bukhārī Revolt. According to Al-ḥajj Sa'īd, Bukhārī had prevailed on the Wazir, 'Abd al-Qādir b. Gidado, by large bribes to secure his appointment as emir. The point to emphasize is that, far from getting the support of other emirates, Bukhārī was virtually ostracized by them. Katagum, Zaria, Kano, Bauchi and some others sent contingents against him. However, the marshy terrain in which Bukhārī operated, coupled with active support given to him by the Shehu of Bornu, 'Umar, including a grant of political asylum at Yerimari and a promise of the governorship of Mashena, enabled the rebel to defy Sokoto authority. The revolt is significant here not only because it failed[72] but even more so because the isolation of Bukhārī and the combination of other emirates against him demonstrated the cohesion of the Caliphate. The Bukhārī rebellion shows further that as long as the Caliph exercised his authority justly he was assured of the unanimous support of his emirs. The Caliphate of 'Abd al-Raḥmān b. Atīq (March 1891 to November 1902) furnishes two contrasting illustrations of the practical operation of the principles mentioned here. These were the Mafara and the Tukur revolts.

The Mafara Revolt. The Mafara revolt was in certain respects similar to the Bukhārī rebellion. They were both clear cases of disobedience and the other emirates acknowledged the justice of the Caliph's cause. Their support was therefore readily given to the Caliph.

The occasion of the Talata Mafara revolt was, first the refusal of Sarkin Talata Mafara to come in person to pay homage as demanded by the newly appointed Caliph, 'Abd al-Raḥmān

71. For details of the revolt, see Barth, *op. cit.*, vol. ii, p. 175 f.; J. M. Fremantle in *J.A.S.* (1910), pp. 404, 412; Al-ḥajj Sa'īd, *op. cit.*, tr. Whitting, pp. 27–8 or tr. O. Houdas, in *Tadhkirat al-Nizian*, p. 346 f. See above, pp. 61–2.

72. It failed in the sense that it persisted as the revolt of one man rather than that of an emirate. It did not become a popular movement within the Caliphate against the Caliph.

(24 March 1891),[73] instead of sending his Galadima. His plea of illness was unacceptable to the Caliph. The other cause of the revolt was the refusal by Sarkin Talata Mafara to accept the arbitration of the Caliph in the dispute between him and Sarkin Burmi over Birnin Tudu which the Caliph awarded to Burmi. Mafara did not heed the Caliph's warning that disobedience to his order in the Birnin Tudu dispute would amount to rebellion. Mafara was supported by Sarkin Anka. The Caliph proclaimed both of them rebels. Letters were written to the emirates ordering them to desist from intercourse and trade with Mafara people, an order which seems to have been effective. The Sokoto mobilization and attacks on Talata Mafara, Anka and their collaborators was effective and completely successful. The strategy employed was encirclement of the rebels. The Sokoto forces spread devastation. Town after town fell to them until first Mafara, after deposing its Sarki, Buzu, and then Anka, both in dire straits, sued for peace which they got at a very high price. Their defeat was complete.

Mafara and Anka agreed to free all free-born taken captive, to deliver 1,000 slaves to the Caliph, to lose all their towns that were conquered during the revolt. The Sarkin Burmi was to have not only Birnin Tudu, but also Sabon Gari, Ruwanbori and Damre, while Maradun was to go to al-Ḥajj (Sarkin Rafi). The land of Zamma was divided into two—one half to Sarkin Mafara (Gumi), Laje, and the other to Ali, Sarkin Donko. All those who benefited territorially had fought actively in the war. Further, all runaway slaves were to be returned to the Caliph and all pagan customs, like pouring dust on the head, were to stop. The revolt thus ended, the Caliph informed the eastern emirs that they could resume normal relations with Talata Mafara and Anka.

The outcome of the Mafara revolt demonstrates not only the

73. The date is based on a reckoning with the date in *Ḍabṭ al-multaqaṭāt*, f. 60, which puts the date as Wednesday 13th of Sha'ban.
For details of the military arrangements and engagements see *Ḍabṭ al-multaqaṭāt*, ff. 61–2. My account of the Mafara revolt is based mainly on Wazir Junaidu's *Ḍabṭ al-multaqaṭāt*, ff. 60–4. There is a close similarity between this account and D. M. Last's (*op. cit.*, pp. 131–3) based mainly on Bukhārī's *Rauḍ al-rayahīn* which Wazir Junaidu copied word for word as he did with Bukhārī's *Kitāb fi ma jarā bainī wa bain Amīr Hadejia wa Yūsuf*: the *Ḍabṭ's* account is identical with a separate copy of the *Kitāb fī ma jarā* in N.A.K. KADCAPTORY, Box 2, item 30.

risk a disobedient emir ran but also the effectiveness of Sokoto's control over its emirs so long as it had right and justice on its side. The planning and swift execution of a brilliant military strategy which ensured success was made possible by the proximity of Mafara and Anka to Sokoto. A revolt in a distant emirate such as Adamawa could not have been so easily crushed. Indeed, the farther a territory was from Sokoto the more did the Caliph have to depend on the local rulers or leaders because the less easy it became for him to exercise direct control.

The Revolt of Yūsuf. The Yūsuf revolt of Kano in 1893 illustrates a contrasting picture of another aspect of the control machinery of the Caliph. After a long reign of twenty-seven years[74] (*c.* 1855–83), the Emir of Kano, ʿAbdullāh, died at Karofi on his way to meet the Caliph, ʿUmar, at Kaura Namoda. The origins of the Yūsuf revolt (commonly referred to as the Tukur revolt) can be traced to the problem of succession created by the sudden death of ʿAbdullāh. The subsequent negotiations of the Kanawa with Sokoto, which seem to have been traditional in Kano after the death of an emir, revealed that the Caliph played a decisive role in the appointment of the Emirs of Kano. On ʿAbdullāh's death, Kano presented to Sokoto four candidates, Dan Lawal, Aḥmad Mai Danda, Yūsuf and Muḥammad Bello. Dan Lawal, the most senior of the candidates was ailing seriously, and died a few days later. Indeed the real contest was between Yūsuf, whom the Caliph preferred, and Muḥammad Bello. Aḥmad had little chance because he was the most junior contestant.

Although Muḥammad Bello was not, strictly speaking, the favourite of the Wazir ʿAbdullāh of Sokoto the latter allowed a personal grudge against Yūsuf to influence his action. He pressed his disapproval on the Caliph by exhortation and by demanding that if Yūsuf became Emir of Kano the Caliph should take Kano away from his (the Wazir's) supervision. This was a virtual ultimatum if not blackmail. Wazir ʿAbdullāh's pique against Yūsuf dated back to the Makama ʿAli's revolt in Zaria at the appointment of ʿAbdullāh (*c.* 1873) as Emir of Zaria. A force from Kano under Yūsuf was present at the settlement. Yūsuf is said to have insulted the Wazir publicly on that occasion. Yūsuf having once (at ʿAbdullāh's death), come so close to becoming the

74. *Tarīkh Kano*, p. 109.

Emir, was baulked of success. The memory of this episode must have rankled deeply in his mind.[75] Having thus very narrowly missed his chance he, together with his brothers, ʿAbdullāh's sons, must have felt certain of his succession when Muḥammad Bello died in November 1893.[76]

The occasion of Muḥammad Bello's death was opportune; the Wazir was in Kano intending to go to Hadejia, presumably on one of his routine tours of his emirates. There was a premonition of trouble in Kano among the *Masu Sarauta* who therefore urged Bukhārī to make an urgent settlement of the succession. Both Bukhārī and the Kano electors are said to have recommended Yūsuf for appointment. It seems certain also that popular support was on the side of Yūsuf.[77] It is related that the slaves of Tukur's palace used to say ' "*Mutun biyar sun kada mutun dari; watau yayan Bello sun kada na Abdullah*" ' (' "Five people have overcome one hundred people; that is, the sons of M. Bello have overcome those of Abdullah" ').[78] Apprehensive of impending dispute, Bukhārī summoned Yūsuf to mollify him. He urged upon him to accept whatever God might ordain for him through the decision of the Caliph and reassured him of the popular support he enjoyed in Kano.[79] The Wazir referred to the Caliph. The Caliph ordered that Tukur, the son of Muḥammad Bello, be appointed Emir.[80]

Torn between obedience to the Caliph (but unflinching in this obedience) and fear of what action Yūsuf might take, the *Masu Sarauta* of Kano advised Bukhārī to instal Tukur by night.

75. The account of the succession of Muḥammad Bello is based on an Edgar notebook, *Labarin Kano*, photocopy in Ibadan 8 OY5. Other major sources consulted on the revolt are *Tarīkh Kano*, Ibadan 82/165 al-Wazir Muḥammad Bukhārī. *Kitāb fī ma jarā bainī wa bain Amīr Hadejia wa Yūsuf*, N.A.K. KADCAPTORY, Box 2, item 30, *Kano ta Dabo Cigari* by Abubakar Dokaji (Zaria, 1958) and various correspondence.
76. British consul at Tripoli to C.O., F.O. 101/85 of 18 July 1895. Information concerning Muḥammad Bello's death contained in a letter dated Kano 28 February 1895 from a Tripoli merchant. See D. M. Last, *op. cit.*, p. 135, note 88.
77. *Labarun Hausawa*, vol. ii, p. 66; *Littafin Tarihin Kano*, being the Kano Chronicle expanded to include the reigns of Emirs after Muḥammad Bello. See also Edgar, *Tatsuniyoyi*, vol. i, p. 187.
78. *Labarun Hausawa*, vol. ii, p. 66.
79. Edgar, *op. cit.*, p. 4.
80. Wazir Bukhārī, *Kitāb fī mā jarā bainī wa bain Amīr Hadejia wa Yūsuf.*

Installation was carried out accordingly in virtual secrecy, without the usual beating of drums and trumpeting.[81]

Presumably, as Last points out, the choice of Tukur by the Caliph sprang from the close ties between the Caliph and Tukur's father, Muḥammad Bello. Muḥammad Bello had during his lifetime ingratiated himself with the Caliph by means of the large gifts he remitted to Sokoto. In addition Tukur had given valuable support to the Caliph in his 1891 Argungu campaign.[82]

The reign of Muḥammad Bello had been characterized by depositions of the officials who served ʿAbdullāh and the replacement of many of them by his own sons. Tukur was appointed Galadima, other sons like Zakariya became Dan Turaki, Chiroma Musa was expelled to Bauchi and his place was taken by Abubakar—another son of Muḥammad Bello. The Galadima, Ibrāhīm, was dismissed; so was the Ma'ji, Maiganga, in favour of Mallam Kazaure.[83] The exclusion of ʿAbdullāh's sons from office under Muḥammad Bello, an otherwise normal practice, must have predisposed them to feeling completely disillusioned when Yūsuf was for the second time cheated of what they considered his right.

The Wazir broke the news of Tukur's appointment to Yūsuf who initially maintained a dignified restraint. Nevertheless, the impending crisis could no longer be staved off since the sons of ʿAbdullāh vehemently urged Yūsuf to take extreme action, such as sacking the palace and killing Tukur. A devout Muslim, anxious not to appear a rebel against Sokoto by fighting within Kano city while the Wazir was there (an action which he probably knew would spoil his case), Yūsuf as yet refused to fight.[84] Moreover, besides the sense of wrong and desire for revenge, time was needed to consolidate an army capable of sustaining an effective revolt. Meanwhile Yūsuf, in agreement with his brothers, quit Kano and established himself at Takai.[85]

81. Edgar, *Labarin Kano*, p. 5.
82. D. M. Last, *op. cit.*, pp. 134–6; see also F. Edgar, *Litafi na Tatsuniyoyi na Hausa* (Belfast, 1911), vol. i, pp. 187, 188. On p. 187 Wazir Bukhārī is quoted as saying to Tukur '*Sarkin Musulmi ya che a ba ka sarauta domin ka taimake shi yakin Argungu*'. See also Abubakar Dokaji, *op. cit.*, p. 61.
83. *Tarīkh Kano*, Ibadan 82/165, p. 110.
84. Edgar, *Labarin Kano*, p. 6.
85. Bukhārī, *Kitāb fī ma jarā*; also Goldie to F.O., F.O. 83/134 of 20 April 1894, Goldie reports the emigration of Yūsuf with a large following from Kano, and that the Caliph ordered him to return to Kano.

The Caliph, 'Abd al-Raḥmān, by appointing Tukur against the popular wish had exceeded the bounds of discretion, but for him there could be no going back. He formally delegated authority to the Wazir, Bukhārī, to settle the revolt of Yūsuf.[86] Bukhārī promptly took steps to isolate Yūsuf by despatching letters to the various emirates. A letter from him to 'Uthmān (Yero), the Emir of Zaria, commanded all the subjects of the Emir by their allegiance to the *'Uthmaniyya* (the regime established by the Shaikh), to prohibit communications between them and Yūsuf either by correspondence or otherwise.[87] Similar letters were presumably despatched to other emirates. Replies (probably to the above-mentioned circular letter) from Katagum, Missau, and a certain Sarkin Rafi, expressed support for the Amīr al-mu'minīn's decision. Muḥammad Manga of Missau and Muḥammad al-ḥajj of Katagum prayed that God might guide Yūsuf and his brothers to the truth.[88]

Bukhārī, unable to stop Yūsuf's devastations in the suburbs, appealed to the Emir of Hadejia (Muḥammad b. Harūn) to intervene in order to bring to an end the increasing violence of the activities of Yūsuf and his men.[89] But it is significant that no emir seemed to have made any serious move to rally round Tukur in order to uphold the Caliph's command. Placid compliance and pious wishes for a change of heart on the part of the rebels was the maximum assistance voluntarily offered by the majority of the emirs. While it was easy to fight in support of the Caliph when his cause was decidedly just, the risk of rising in arms against his authority by allying with rebels against him (no matter how justified the rebellion) seems to have been considered too great to be worth taking. In this light only can the practical neutrality of most emirates in the Tukur affair be explained.[90]

At the same time, the Emir of Hadejia came near to collaborating actively with Yūsuf, but a verbal demand that Wazir Bukhārī should depose Tukur and appoint Yūsuf Emir of Kano was the farthest limit he could go. Since Sarkin Hadejia's chiefs and

86. Corr. IX, no. 24, Caliph 'Abd al-Raḥmān, to Bukhārī.
87. Corr. VI, no. 100.
88. Corr. VIII, no. 71; IV, no. 20; III, no. 9, respectively.
89. Corr. II, no. 11.
90. The Emir of Kontagora 'Umar (Nagwamatse) b. Ibrāhīm is said to have refused to fight against Yūsuf on the ground that he could not fight against a fellow Muslim. See D. M. Last, *op. cit.*, p. 135.

followers were in open disagreement with his point of view and Bukhārī was adamant in his protestations, that he had merely carried out the orders of the Caliph as he was in duty bound to do, the colloquy ended in the Emir of Hadejia supporting Tukur.[91]

Yūsuf, unable to obtain overt assistance from the emirates, fell back on traditional enemies of the Caliphate. Gumel, vassal of Bornu, and the Ningi sent powerful contingents.[92] Thus Yūsuf and the Ningi, against whom he had fought relentlessly when he was Galadima, became allies of convenience.[93] The rebel forces spread devastation in all directions. Their troops headed towards Kano pursued by a Hadejia force which had to turn back having failed to head them off.[94] In another engagement, the Hadejia army was routed. This was enough to convince the Emir of Hadejia, never enthusiastic in Tukur's cause, to withdraw and return home. Wazir Bukhārī, apparently dissatisfied with the whole affair, went to Zaria but was ordered back to Kano by the Caliph, to see the Yūsuf affair to its end. A great famine coupled with water shortage raged in Kano at this time on account of the protracted wars. The Wazir was allowed to return to Sokoto after Yūsuf had entered Kano, sacked it and ousted Tukur.[95] A few weeks later news of a heavy defeat, inflicted by Yūsuf on one of Tukur's largest forces, compelled the Wazir to summon the forces of the emirates (people of the east) but before his messenger reached Kano, Yūsuf had become ill and died at Garko.[96]

Soon after Yūsuf's death his brother, Aliyu Baba, who succeeded him, entered and pillaged Kano with his forces on 23 September 1894.[97] The Tukur partisans were expelled, but

91. Muḥammad Bukhārī, *Kitāb fī ma jarā'*.
92. Edgar, *Labarin Kano*, p. 7.
93. For Yūsuf's wars against Ningi, see *Tarīkh Kano*, p. 105.
94. *Kitāb fī ma jarā*.
95. F.O. 101/85, Br. Consul at Tripoli to F.O., 10 July 1895. Letter from Kano already cited. According to this letter, Yūsuf's forces entered Kano on 23 June 1894. The letter also reports the great famine in Kano.
96. Corr. VII, no. 2. From Aliyu Baba to Amīr al-mu'minīn 'Abd al-Raḥmān; gives the date of Yūsuf's death as during *Muharram*. Letter in F.O. 101/85 of 18 July 1895 makes it clear that Yūsuf died in 1894. Yūsuf must have died between 5 July and 3 August.
97. Corr. VII, no. 2. Aliyu Baba informed the Caliph of Yūsuf's death and of his having been chosen to succeed him. Aliyu pledged loyalty to the Caliph.

merchants from Tripoli and Ghadames were untouched. Tukur sought refuge in Katsina territory. The position of the Wazir was very delicate, the more so as the Caliph refused to have anything to do with Aliyu Baba's peace delegations. So long as Tukur was still alive there was really no other course open to the Caliph; the war had to go on. But the problem of organizing the Tukur resistance and recouping its depleted strength—a duty for the Wazir—was easier stated than solved.

The Wazir summoned the eastern forces. The Katsina forces were camped on the borders of Kano and the Wazir came with Zamfara forces to Fawa. It does not seem that any other emirates actually sent troops. The Emir of Katsina, who seemed to have supported Tukur merely to avoid disobeying the Wazir, seized the opportunity of a threatened attack by Maradi on his territory to excuse himself. It was in his best interest so to do, seeing that his forces had been routed by Aliyu Baba's army. The Emir of Adamawa, returning from Sokoto, seemed by his movement to have been mainly concerned with avoiding involvement in the war. Finally in March 1895, Aliyu Baba's forces captured and killed Tukur. The Emir of Adamawa, Zubeir, advised reconciliation with Kano, already in Aliyu's hands.

Tukur's death paved the way for a settlement. The messengers of Aliyu Baba were now received by the Caliph, his apologies were accepted and he was granted pardon. Arrangements were made for Tukur's partisans to return to Kano safely and the Wazir wrote to all emirs to notify them that the Caliph had pardoned Aliyu.[98] The crisis was over.

The failure of Sokoto to suppress Yūsuf's revolt demonstrates the powerlessness of the Caliph to enforce a whim considered unpopular and unjust by the emirates. To succeed in Kano he needed active military aid from the emirates. This he failed to get. The Yūsuf revolt succeeded because the Caliph's cause won no deep sympathies or support and by their do-nothing attitude, or half-hearted military assistance at the best, the emirates tacitly supported Yūsuf.

It has been necessary to dwell at length on the revolt of Yūsuf because, apart from the strict question of the legality of the Caliph's exercise of his authority involved, it was a constitutional

98. M. Bukhārī, *Kitāb fī ma jarā*. Also, F.O. 83/1379. Goldie to F.O. 27 May 1895, reports that the Caliph had definitely recognized Aliyu Baba as the Emir of Kano.

crisis which shows up in bold relief important aspects of the machinery of government of the Caliphate at work. Some of these aspects are self-evident. Attention must, however, be drawn to the procedure employed in choosing a new emir, the way the Wazir performed his functions in the emirates and his ultimate subservience to the Caliph, the loyalty of the emirates to the Caliph as demonstrated by their unwillingness to aid Yūsuf, no matter how just his cause might have been, and the priority given by each emirate to its own internal interests as shown by the roles of the Emirs of Katsina and Hadejia.

The Mahdist movements and revolts. The foregoing account of the occasions and the nature of Sokoto's control over the emirates indicates how the Caliphate was organized as well as the internal strains within it. Like any state the Caliphate had its own administrative problems to face, but its peculiar machinery of government was capable of holding the state together. Throughout its existence, the Caliphate was administered against a background of pressing problems of defence and security the nature of which has been discussed in a previous chapter. These problems tended to weaken the cohesion of the Caliphate because each emirate was usually preoccupied with meeting its own peculiar defence needs.

The failure of the Caliphate's attempt effectively to crush the rebellious repercussions produced within its frontiers by the Mahdist revolt of the Eastern Sudan (1881–98), aptly illustrates the weakness of its defence arrangements particularly that aspect of it which involved organization of the defence of distant emirates from Sokoto. This failure underlined the lack of an effective centrally controlled military machinery which could operate in times of crisis.

Another aspect of the Mahdist movement within the Caliphate is that the following it could muster even in the face of Sokoto's official disapproval indicates the strong adherence of many to the idea of the Mahdī. The cause of the Eastern Sudan Mahdī, because it was championed within the Caliphate by Ḥayat b. Sa'īd b. Muḥammad Bello b. 'Uthmān b. Fodiye (Ḥayatu), a rebel of the Shaikh's family, was one of rebellion against the Caliph. The movement was also an indication of an under-current of religious zeal within the Caliphate which foreign invasion by unbelievers was later to bring more forcefully into the open.

The Mahdist uprising in the Eastern Sudan affected the Sokoto Caliphate not only through Rābiḥ b. Faḍlallāh's threat which will be discussed below but also through the activities of Ḥayat b. Sa'īd and the response to him by Mallam Jibrīl Gaini.

Expectation of the Mahdī in the Caliphate was at least as old as the Caliphate itself. 'Uthmān b. Fodiye wrote many books on the Expected Mahdī.[99] As early as *c.* 1805, he had warned his *Amīrs* of the nearness of the Mahdī's appearance and predicted that his *jihād* would continue till his advent.[100] It is also on record that he ('Uthmān b. Fodiye) believed that Muḥammad Bello, his son, would be one of the lieutenants of the Mahdī.[101] In view of the strong tradition of the expectation of the Mahdī in the Caliphate, it is puzzling to note that the Mahdī of the Eastern Sudan found not sympathy but hostility among the authorities of the Sokoto Caliphate.[102] The Mahdī nevertheless found a devoted supporter in Ḥayat b. Sa'īd.

Ḥayat b. Sa'īd left Sokoto and made for the east sometime after 1873. The cause of his departure has been ascribed to dissatisfaction with the succession to the Caliphate. Be that as it may, it is fairly certain that he left as a result of a dispute of some sort.[103] He was well received in Bauchi as well as in Adamawa,

99. See *Infāq al-Maisūr*, pp. 104–5. See 'Sifofin Shehu', Introduction by F. H. El-Masri, and R. A. Adeleye, in *Research Bulletin of the Centre of Arabic Documentation*, vol. ii, no. 1 (Jan. 1966), pp. 7–13.
100. *Infāq al-Maisūr*, p. 105.
101. See *Wa'z* in Fulfulde by Muḥammad Dikko who claims to have been told by the Shaikh himself. The poem, property of Al-Hajj Boyi in Sokoto, is on microfilm at the C.A.D., Ibadan, No. 235. I am very grateful to Ibrahim Mukoshy of the Centre for locating and translating this document for me.
102. The Amīr al-mu'minīn 'Umar's refusal of requested assistance from the Mahdī, Muḥammad b. 'Abdullāh, has been attributed to unwillingness to help a rebel against the authority of the Sultan of Constantinople—see *West Africa*, 6 March 1920. It seems clear, however, that the Caliphate authorities considered the Mahdī as a pretender. See Corr. IV, no. 25, Muḥammad Manga to Caliph 'Umar in which Ḥayat's religion is described as 'a religion of lies and falsehood'.
103. Mr K. Post told me on the authority of Sa'īd b. Ḥayat b. Sa'īd that Ḥayat left Sokoto as a result of his disappointment when Abubakar b. Bello succeeded to the Caliphate. While this may be true it is unlikely however that he expected to succeed while his father Sa'īd and his uncle Mu'adh were still alive.

where Sanda was the Emir. The avowed purpose of his journey was that he was going to Mecca.[104]

What emerges from the *Labarin Ḥayatu* and the account of H. K. Strumpell,[105] the chronicler of his exploits in Adamawa, is that Ḥayat subsequently settled in Balda, in Marua district, where he very soon gained a large following and cleverly exploited the political rivalries which plagued the district to erect himself as a major power. He was in fact a rebel thenceforth against Yola authority, but was in the meantime protected from attack because of the respect accorded to him as a descendant of the Shaikh 'Uthmān. He (Ḥayat) subsequently ravaged and dominated Marua territory.

It seems that the call of the Mahdī reached Ḥayat in Adamawa. His support for Mahdism was unfeigned. The letters exchanged between him and the Mahdī in the cause of Mahdism were passionate. In his letter of invitation, the Mahdī took great pains to prove that he was the Expected Mahdī and with many pious exhortations backed by relevant quotations from the Qur'ān and *Hadīth* he urged on Ḥayat and his people the obligation of *hijra* to meet him. Ḥayat had been a keen expectant of the Mahdī. He had written a poem in praise of him while his father had written another one which, with tears in his eyes, he had urged his son, Ḥayat, to commit to memory. Ḥayat, who called the Mahdī the Prophet's descendant,[106] did not doubt his genuineness. He said that he had pledged his devotion, allegiance and assistance to the Mahdī even before his appearance.

On receipt of the Mahdī's call, Ḥayat wrote to his father Sa'īd, to the *Amīr al-mu'minīn*, 'Umar, to Maryam bt. Al-Shaikh 'Uthmān b. Fodiye and to his own daughter, to the Sokoto community and to the emirates, exhorting them to emigrate.[107] He pointed out that he was already on his way and could not

104. *Labarin Ḥayatu* in Edgar notebook (see p. 98, n. 75 above); H. K. Strumpell, *A History of Adamawa*, pp. 37–41, gives a detailed account of the adventures of Ḥayat in Adamawa.

105. Strumpell, *op. cit.*, pp. 37–42.

106. The Mahdī must be a descendant of the Prophet, his father's name and his own name must coincide with the name of the Prophet's father ('Abdullāh) and the Prophet's (Muḥammad).

107. According to the *Missau Chronicle*, Ḥayat wrote not only to emirs but to religious leaders among the 'Ulamā'. He pointed out to them that the Mahdī had appeared and he who would not emigrate with him was to be regarded as *al-Dajjal* (the anti-Christ).

wait for his people but merely prayed that they too would follow after him.[108] These letters must have been written between 1881 and 1885.

Ḥayat may have abandoned his migration to the east on the death of the Mahdī in 1885. He nevertheless continued to believe in the Mahdī, who had appointed him as his Khalīfa in the Western Sudan. Some of his main collaborators were Yūsuf Babikīr al-Mandarawī and Muḥammad al-Amīn al-Mallawī.[109] His appeal won sufficient adherents to constitute a source of anxiety for the Caliphate. One of the earliest to heed Ḥayat's call was a mallam of Dutsin Gadawur called Liman Yamusa, who gathered a large following *c.* 1882–83 and set out to emigrate with them to meet the Mahdī. This movement was forcibly stopped by the Emirs of Missau and Hadejia, Muḥammad Ṣāliḥ and Haruna respectively, acting on the orders of the Amīr al-mu'minīn. Yamusa was captured and sent to Sokoto.[110]

Mahdism in the emirates survived this check and a number of other setbacks. In his lifetime Shehu Bukar, who had apparently toyed with the idea of embracing Mahdism, turned sharply against it and broke off friendly relations with Ḥayat. Babikīr al-Mandarawī had caused disturbances in Mandara while Ḥayat's troops had suffered a serious reverse there. Shehu Bukar therefore asked Ḥayat to desist from following the Mahdī and from attacking his subjects, the Mandarawa.[111] Although official opposition to the cause of Mahdism in both the Caliphate

108. Evidence of Ḥayat's belief in the Mahdī and his relationship with the Mahdī, Muḥammad b. ʿAbdullāh, is to be found in *Al-Khitābāt al-mutabādalāt bain al-Imām al-Mahdī wa al-Shaikh Hayatu*, Khartoum, 1962, pp. 1–10. Three letters, two from the Mahdī to Ḥayat and one from Ḥayat to the Mahdī, are included. After receiving the Mahdī's invitation, Ḥayat wrote a book on Mahdism. *Miftāh al-Khairāt wa mazīd al-barakat li 'l-dhākirīn Allāh kathiran wa 'l-dhạkirāt*, Ibadan 82/384.

109. N.A.K. KADCAPTORY, Box 38, file no. 10, Yūsuf Babikīr al-Mandarawī to Khalifa ʿAbdullāh, *c.* 1898.

110. *Missau Chronicle* and *History of Bauchi Emirate*, N.A.K. Bauchi prof., 690, vol. i.

111. *Ibid.* See also letter from Ḥayat to Shaikh Ibrāhīm, Ibadan 82/229. The reign of Shaikh Ibrāhīm 1884–85, fixes the date of his letter. In it, Ḥayat enumerates a number of people who came to him intending to emigrate with him. These were a certain Al-Ḥajj Ibrāhīm, the sons of a certain Idrīs and of Musa with their followers (probably Liman Yamusa) Ibrahim's eldest son actually reached the Mahdī, another son went to join the Sanussi at Jaghbub.

and Bornu was strong, its threat to security and stability increased.

From about 1888, from his base at Balda, which legend associated with the Mahdī's appearance, with Yūsuf Babikīr and Muḥammad al-Amīn, Ḥayat fought against the neighbouring territories but (according to the evidence of Yūsuf Babikīr) without much success. Nevertheless his power was a major threat to Adamawa emirate. The Caliph declared him an outlaw to be fought as an infidel. Several expeditions led by Amoa b. Manṣūr b. Adam Modibo failed to subdue him. A determined effort led by the Emir of Yola, Zubeir, to conquer him early in 1893, resulted in the rout of the Emir's forces in which many Yola notables, including the learned ʿAlī b. Adam Modibo, were killed.[112] Later in the year, Ḥayat and his followers left to meet Rābiḥ Faḍlallāh and made a compact of mutual co-operation with him.

The inability of Sokoto to organize an effective resistance to crush Ḥayat demonstrates its weakness to oversee the defence of the Caliphate in areas far away from the more powerful and more northerly emirates. Besides, Adamawa emirate, surrounded and interspersed by warring pagan tribes, had too much to cope with to be able to organize and sustain effective action. The rest of Ḥayat's story forms part of the story of Rābiḥ Faḍlallāh.

Ḥayat's Mahdist propaganda gave birth to Mallam Jibrīl Gaini's movement. The revolt which arose from this movement became a serious threat to the Caliphate. For many years the Jibrīl rebellion spread devastation and fear in the eastern marches, particularly in Gombe emirate.

After the Emir of Missau, Muḥammad Manga, had turned down Ḥayat's letter to embrace Mahdism, Ḥayat sent flags to a famous mallam called Jibrīl (variously known as Jibrīl Gaini or Mallam Zai) in the town of Zai in Katagum, and to a certain Ḥajj Gurdi (probably Al-Ḥajj Ibrāhīm mentioned above) and Musa Didari, ordering them to begin trouble in the land of Gombe.[113] Jibrīl subsequently established himself in Burmi, with a large following which was at the same time a resolute

112. Corr. I, no. 49, Letter to Wazir Bakhārī (name of sender undecipherable). Ali was at this time governor of Mubi. Lt. Mizon, A.N.S.O.M. Mission 7, *Dossier Mizon*, 'Carnets de routes'.

113. Corr. IV, no. 24, from Muḥammad Manga to Amīr al-Mu'minīn 'Umar. This appears to have been written at the beginning of the Jibrīl revolt as Manga mentions in the letter that the mallams commissioned by Ḥayat had started trouble in Gombe and he was

fighting force. Zailani, the Emir of Gombe, died in 1888 from wounds sustained during his attack on Burmi. Jibrīl ravaged Gombe territory and caused panic there, and in neighbouring emirates like Bauchi, Hadejia, Katagum and Missau who all sent pressing appeals to Sokoto.[114] The *Amīr al-Mu'minīn* appointed 'Umar, Emir of Bauchi, to organize the forces of the threatened emirates to fight Jibrīl. An attack by the combined army of these emirates inflicted a crushing defeat on Jibrīl at Bajoga during the reign of Ḥasan of Gombe (1888–95), as a result of which Jibrīl sued for peace. Having been granted a peace compact, he broke it and started his raids again, just when the Emir of Bauchi had virtually completed arrangements to send his messengers with those of Jibrīl to the *Amīr al-Mu'minīn* to effect final settlement. Jibrīl subsequently defeated the combined armies of Gombe, Bauchi and Missau, laying many towns in ruins.

During his recruiting tour in 1898 Captain Lynch of the West African Frontier Force bore witness to Jibrīl's ravages, evident in the ruins of a large number of villages and the desertion of many. Both the Emir of Gombe and Galadiman Ako were anxious that Captain Lynch should help them wipe out Mallam Jibrīl's forces but the conditions under which Lynch would offer help were unacceptable to Gombe even in its dire necessity.[115] Jibrīl's power was not broken until 1902, and the momentum of the force he represented largely accounts for the stubborn resistance the British had to face in Burmi in 1903.

The challenge to the Caliphate from the Mahdist movement is significant in two main ways. That the movement was able to

proceeding against them. If the trouble had been long started there would be no necessity to report its beginning. Muḥammad Manga began his reign in 1885. According to *Tabyīn Amr Buba Yero*, Zailani, Emir of Gombe, was killed fighting against Jibrīl at Burmi. The Jibrīl rebellion must have started after 1885, and probably in 1888 when Zailani died.

114. The account of the Jibrīl revolt is based on the following: Corr. II, nos. 16, 21, 30, 34, 35; Corr. IV, nos. 24, 25, 40, 43; Corr. V, no. 19; Corr. IX, no. 81; Corr. X, no. 217. *Tabyīn Amr Buba Yero; History of Bauchi Emirate; History of Gombe Emirate*, both in N.A.K. Bauchi prof., 690, vol. ii. Report by Capt. Lynch on his Recruiting tour of Bauchi and Gombe in C.O. 446/4, 18 December 1898, and 'Bornu Report' by T. N. L. Morland in N.A.K., S.N.P. 15, no. 18, 1902.

115. Capt. Lynch: Report on a Recruiting tour, C.O. 446/4, 18 December 1898.

rally enough adherents to set at naught the disapprobation of the Caliph and his emirs and defy the striking power of the combined emirates of the east for about fifteen years is indicative of how deep the traditional expectation of the Mahdī was in the minds of many and what 'fanaticism' the cause evoked. Bima hill, south of Jibrīl's base at Burmi, was by tradition associated with miracles and the appearance of the Mahdī. But perhaps more significant is that the measure of success gained by Jibrīl's forces underlines a weakness intrinsic in the Caliphate's defence arrangements. In this respect revolts arising from the Mahdist movement, in particular that of Jibrīl, cannot be considered in isolation. They raise the important question of Sokoto's inability to organize and control the defence of the Caliphate as a whole.

The military preoccupation of the emirates. The exercise of Sokoto control and general supervision of the emirates as studied in this chapter can be divided into two spheres: control over administrative and constitutional arrangements and intervention to resolve problems of defence and security. In the first sphere the evidence is conclusive that Sokoto's control over administrative and constitutional matters were strict matters of policy. In this aspect obedience to the Caliph's ruling was usually sufficient to settle disputes. But to topple a recalcitrant and powerful rebel like Jibrīl it was necessary to organize a sustained war effort and stronger forces against him than the local emirates could muster. Jibrīl's army, practically a professional fighting force, became stronger and stronger.

Co-operation between neighbouring emirates in times of crisis against a common enemy like Jibrīl was traditional in the Caliphate. For instance, Kano, Zaria, Bauchi, Gombe, Missau and Hadejia are known to have co-operated against the Ningi from time to time during the nineteenth century. Sokoto was not capable of effectively arranging for the defence of its emirates. As the emirates were usually individually capable of defending themselves, the system proved adequate for their nineteenth-century defence needs. The rulers never had need to face an enemy whose aim was to conquer the whole Caliphate or the greater part of it (with the possible exception of Muḥammad Al-Amīn Al-Kānemī, 1824–26). The marked localism imposed on each emirate by its defence problems was a barrier to effective centralism.

From the military point of view the fact that most of the emirates were preoccupied with annual raids against their traditional enemies meant that, without adequate notice, they could not afford to send out a force outside their emirates which would leave their home fronts exposed to enemies most anxious to seize such an opportunity. By way of conclusion, we must take a brief look at the type of such preoccupations within the various emirates.

In the southern emirates like Ilọrin, Nupe, Zaria and Adamawa, there were internal conflicts. In Ilọrin, during the 1890s, the intrigues of Balogun Alanamu and Adamu, which made a figurehead of the Emir, meant that the emirate had enough troubles on its hands,[116] while its long wars with the Yoruba states to the south meant that the Baloguns' rivalries were carried out in a state exhausted by war.[117] In Nupe the dispossessed Etsu families remained intransigent. Discontent was latent and found expression in Etsu Gana's co-operation with the British in the 1897 'Sudan Campaign'.[118] In both Nupe and Ilọrin the wars with the British in 1897 had left the two emirates crippled. Thenceforth, the British presence, never far away since their victory in 1897, was like an incubus, the dread of which had to be kept constantly in mind in any contemplation of reorganizing their destroyed military power. Hardly able to help themselves, Ilọrin and Nupe were after 1897 not in a position to aid other emirates.

The problems of Zaria were those of a far-flung state whose subdivisions, Keffi, Kwotto, Jema'an Dororo and others, were too independent, though militarily weak. During the reign of Sambo, Keffi and Kwotto went to war. Far away Adamawa was faced with the problem of interspersion of hostile pagan states which it had endeavoured, but failed, to digest throughout the nineteenth century. In Adamawa, as well as the emirates of the eastern marches, the activities of Ḥayat and his agents served but as introduction to the greater panic into which they were thrown by daily expectation of the descent of Rābiḥ on them—a contingency which had seemed impending since Rābiḥ's advent to Bornu in 1893 and which assumed greater and greater validity, until by 1897–98 the panic had escalated into a general commo-

116. See below, pp. 185–8.
117. See Johnson: *History of Yorubas*, p. 46 ff., *passim*.
118. See below, p. 182

tion.[119] Until Rābiḥ died, and this did not happen until 1900, fear of him remained an awesome preoccupation.

To the wave of fear spread by Rābiḥ in the eastern marches must be added the preoccupation of continued raids into the Kerikeri country especially from Missau. For Gombe and Bauchi, the problem of their traditional enemies (the multifarious pagan communities whom, like Adamawa, they had failed to digest during the course of the century) was yet to be finally resolved.[120]

Kano, Zaria, and Bauchi shared the fear of disturbing incursions into their territories from Ningi. Ningi raids of Zaria territory had been a determinant in the events which resulted in the deposition of Muḥammad Sambo of Zaria in 1888. In Kano, in the later years of the 1870s, an army led by Yūsuf, then Galadiman Kano, had put such a check on Ningi power that the Ningawa sued for an armistice. But during the reigns of Muḥammad Bello and ʿAbdullāh in Kano, and of Harūna (Harūn) and Dan Yaya in Ningi, hostilities involving reversals in the fortunes of war broke out again between Ningi and Kano.[121] The struggles were ultimately resolved in Kano's favour.

119. See below, pp. 177–8.

120. See *Missau Chronicle*, for the wars of Muḥammad Manga. According to the *Tabyīn Amr Buba Yero*, the Emirs of Gombe Ḥasan (*c.* 1888–1895) and Tukur (1895–98) could not afford to send out contingents to Sokoto as Zailani had done before them. For Bauchi, see *Tarīkh ʿUmarāʾ Buachi*; see also N.A.K. Bauchi prof., no. 311, *Historical notes on Azare District*. For similar notes on Gombe, Bauchi and Ningis, see N.A.K. Bauchi prof., no. 690, vols i and ii.

121. For an account of Ningi engagements with Kano, Zaria and in particular with Bauchi—under Dan Maji, Harūn Dan. Maji, and Dan Yaya see *Tarīkh ʿUmarāʾ Bauchi*, pp. 180–90: Ningi wars with Kano.
See *Tarīkh Kano*, Ibadan 82/165. Yūsuf defeated Dan Maji. Corr. VII, no. 61. From ʿAbdullāh, Emir of Kano (*c.* 1855–83) to Wazir (Sokoto) Ibrahim—seems to refer to Yūsuf's victory. The Ningawa asked Wazir Ibrahīm for a peace compact (*Amāna*) and pledged submission to the Caliphate. A similar letter is Yūsuf to Ibrāhīm Corr. VII, no. 62.
Between 1886 and 1891, the compact was broken. The Caliph ʿUmar ordered the Emir of Kano to fight the Ningis. Corr. VII, no. 13. Haruna of Ningi pleaded persistently for a peace compact. Two battles were fought between Kano and Ningi (1886–91) in which Kano was victorious. See Corr. VII, nos. 5, 15. Dan Yaya (ʿUthmān b. Harūn) pleaded once again for a peace compact see Corr. VII, no. 123.

The traditional Maradawa hostilities against emirates of the Caliphate were a different matter. The improved relations with the Caliphate noticeable in the late 1870s were reversed in the 1890s, when Dan Barahiya of Maradi raided as far as Zaria. More potent an enemy than Maradi to Katsina, Daura, Kano as well as Hadejia was Damagaram whose forces made regular incursions into these emirates in the late 1890s. A Damagaram raid into Kano territory had proved fatal for Kano in *c.* 1898. Even though Kano retaliated shortly after, a defensive posture against Damagaram was imposed on the Northern emirates of Kano, Katsina, Daura and Hadejia during the last and critical few years of the nineteenth century.[122]

Last's studies show that in Sokoto itself, the Gobir threat was generally contained or at least rendered indeterminate, since the creation of Sabon Birni (between 1859 and 1866) in opposition to Tsibiri, to the end of the century.[123] The Gobir-Maradi alliance broke down in the last two decades of the century. At the end of the century Gobir's hostility could not be ignored by Sokoto, but it was only a nuisance.

The survival even in weakened forms of the problem of fighting traditional enemies by different parts of the Caliphate must be reckoned with as a factor which could vitiate, or at least seriously limit, the strength of the forces that the Caliphate could rally against a common foe even when the other difficulties of mobilization are discounted.

Quite often, the fall of a state can be rightly ascribed to disintegration and decline of various kinds within it. It is, how-

122. Tilho, *Documents scientifiques de la Mission Tilho*, vol. ii, p. 444 ff. From the reign of Tenimu of Zinder, attacks on Kano, Daura, Hadejia from Zinder became usual (Tilho, pp. 451–2). Late in 1898 Aḥmad Emir of Zinder raided Gazawa. Aliyu of Kano successfully retaliated. Corr. X, no. 12, Aliyu to 'Umar of Gombe, seems to refer to this battle because Aliyu writes of his victory as a reversal of the 'unfortunate news'.

Tilho, p. 450 records the coming of Aḥmad of Zinder to Malikawa. The details of his movements are recorded in Corr. VII, no. 36. M. Bello (d. 1891) to Bukhārī pre-dated the 1898 battle. Kano-Zinder hostilities seem to have been continuous in the 1890s. Corr. II, no. 2, Hadejia to Sokoto and Corr. IX, no. 86, Hadejia to Sokoto report the inability of Hadejia to despatch a messenger to Sokoto since the enemy of Hadejia the Emir of Zinder had resolved on raiding Hadejia.

123. Tilho, vol. ii, p. 477. Last, *op. cit.*, p. 116.

ever, clear that the Sokoto Caliphate in 1900 exhibited no such features in any marked form. Its machinery of government, far from having become rusty, was in good working order. Rather than look for elements of decay to explain the fall, the historian must direct his attention to the fact that the Caliphate was caught in the strong current of a historical movement (the European imperial expansion in Africa) the source of which was outside its awareness, not to speak of its control. It had to grapple with forces the nature and the dimensions of which it was not in a position fully to comprehend. This was of the last consequence in determining the course and manner of the destruction of the Caliphate. Superimposed therefore on the problems of defence against its traditional enemies, which the Caliphate could cope with, albeit with considerable inconvenience, was this new and bigger problem of infiltration and encirclement by foreign enemies—the agents of European imperial expansion. These were the last enemies of the Caliphate and they were to bring about its collapse as a political entity.

Part II
Relations with Europeans during the Scramble Era

Chapter 5
Era of trade and treaties 1879-1894

During the first half of the nineteenth century contacts between the Caliphate and Europeans were few and infrequent. These contacts were established by European travellers, practically all of whom were British citizens or other nationals sponsored by the British government. Consequently when the scramble for territories in Africa began British influence was, among European nations, dominant in the Caliphate. Relations between the Caliphate and Europeans during this period of sporadic contacts were mainly commercial.

British commercial establishments began with the founding of the Inland Commercial Company in 1833 and the expedition which that company sent to the Niger–Benue confluence in that year.[1] The venture was pioneered by McGregor Laird, with the assistance of the British government. Thenceforth British enterprise within the Caliphate was confined to the Niger–Benue waterways. Nupe emirate became the main base of British activities. The details of these activities are, however, outside the scope of this study.[2]

The period of intensive and regularized trading by the British opened with the expedition led by Dr Baikie in 1857. Between 1857 and 1859 Lokoja was made the centre of British activities. By 1867 British interest had become so firmly established that the British government appointed a consul at Lokoja. Although the consulate was withdrawn in 1869,[3] British trading groups continued to flourish and to advance British interests along the waterways. During the 1860s a firm friendship was built up by the British with Masaba, the Emir of Bida. A number of British

1. For an account of this venture see C. C. Ifemesia, 'British Enterprise on the Niger, 1830–69', unpublished Ph.D. thesis (London, 1959), p. 218 f.
2. Ifemesia, *op. cit.*, *passim*, for a full account.
3. *Ibid.*, pp. 463–99. Detailed account of Baikie's work on the Niger.

expeditions visited Bida in the 1860s.[4] In 1862 and 1863 respectively the West African Company Ltd and the Company of African Merchants trading to the Upper Niger, were founded.[5] By 1871 Holland Jacques and Company, the Miller Brothers, and several other traders had entered the Niger trade.[6]

The commercial relations thus opened up were of mutual advantage to the Africans and the Europeans. Apart from ordinary merchandise, textiles, utensils of various types, trinkets and other articles, the Emir of Nupe concentrated on the purchase of firearms and ammunition for strengthening his army. The European traders purchased shea butter, cotton, antimony, cowhide and other skins in exchange.[7] In 1874 the West Africa Company started purchasing ivory at 'Bomasha'.[8]

In 1877 Bishop Ajayi Crowther reported that British friendship with Bida, Gwandu and Sokoto had grown as had the volume of trade on the Niger–Benue rivers.[9] At Egga (in 1876) 46 tons of ivory were collected and whereas only five cases of shea butter were collected in 1857, in 1876 the figure had risen to 2000 cases. Instead of the earlier ships which carried 80–100 cases, the ships employed in the Niger trade by 1876 could carry from 400 to 600 cases.[10]

The Benue river was not neglected. In 1879 a Church Missionary Society's exploratory mission led by Ashcroft and accompanied by Flegel ascended the Benue as far as Garua and sent

4. *Proceedings of the Royal Geographical Society*, vii (1863), p. 67, Record of Lt. Lefroy's visit to Masaba in September 1862; see also vol. viii (1864), pp. 53–4 f., for record of Commodore Wilmot's visit to Bida in December 1863 in H.M.S. *Rattlesnake*.
5. Ifemesia, *op. cit.*, p. 459.
6. J. E. Flint, *Sir George Goldie and the Making of Nigeria* (London, 1960), pp. 26–30. For a study of early British commercial activities see pp. 9–33 and Ifemesia, *op. cit.*, *passim*. In 1876, the 'Central African Company' (i.e. Holland Jacques under a new name) began trading on the Benue, *Proc. R.G.S.* new series, xiii (1891), pp. 449–77.
7. Letter from Masaba to McKoskry, a trader based in Lagos. He was acting British Consul in Lagos in May 1861 and acting Governor in August of the same year. Ibadan 82/372 photocopy: The original of this letter is in the Library of the McGill University, Canada.
8. Claude Macdonald, 'Exploration of the Benue and its northern tributary, the Kebbi', *Proc. R.G.S.* new series, xiii (1891), p. 450.
9. Bishop Ajayi Crowther, 'Notes on the Niger', *Proc. R.G.S.*, xxi (1877), pp. 479–98.
10. *Ibid.*

gifts to the Emir of Yola.[11] The expedition was followed up in subsequent years by the founding of trading stations by European traders.

From 1860 the development of European trade on the Niger–Benue rivers was characterized by the proliferation of British companies engaged in cut-throat competition which by the 1870s had degenerated into a commercial war of mutual attrition. This competition was brought to an end by the amalgamation of the English companies in 1879 under the inspiration and leadership of George Taubman Goldie to form the United African Company.[12]

The appearance of this new combine on the scene marked the beginning of a new phase in the relations between Europeans and the Caliphate. The new company, formed as it was in the age of the scramble, was immediately engaged, though unofficially, in promoting British imperial interests against the rivalry of France and Germany. This phase was also characterized by European attempts to establish treaty relations with the Caliphate, aimed at establishing European political control over it. Beyond simple commercial relations there was, however, a basic polarity of attitude and interest thenceforth between the Caliphate and the Europeans. Rather than diminish, the gulf between the two sides progressively widened in subsequent years until it ended in military clash during the opening years of this century.

The Caliphate's attitude to Europeans remained basically the same throughout the nineteenth century. While trade with them was welcomed, often enthusiastically,[13] and their friendship accepted for that reason, any indication that the Europeans wished to engage in political activities prejudicial to the sove-

11. E. Hutchinson, 'Ascent up the river Benue in August 1879; with, remarks on the Shari and Benue', *Proc. R.G.S.*, new series, ii (1880), p. 295.
12. For details of the amalgamation see Flint, *op. cit.*, pp. 26–33.
13. Clapperton on his first journey obtained letters of introduction to several potentates of the Western Sudan. Translations of these letters are to be found in Major Denham, *Narrative of Travels and discoveries in North and Central Africa in the years 1822, 1823 and 1824* (London, 1826), Appendices III–VII; among the letters were two from the Shaikh al-Amīn al-Kānemī to Ibrahim Dabo, Emir of Kano, and to the Caliph Muḥammad Bello. Muḥammad Bello gave Clapperton a letter of introduction to the Emir of Yauri.

reignty of the state was met with vehement resistance. Thus, while in 1824 Hugh Clapperton was warmly welcomed in Sokoto, where the Caliph, Muḥammad Bello, gave him a commercial agreement which, if implemented, would have put Sokoto–British commercial relations on a firm footing,[14] he encountered a severe opposition from the same Caliph during his second visit to Sokoto in 1826–27. Clapperton's visit had started off with a warm welcome followed by hopeful discussions on trade and by the agreement of the Caliph to accept a British consul in Sokoto. But once he was suspected of being friendly with Bornu (Sokoto's inveterate enemy) and of having the intention of aiding that state with firearms, Sokoto's friendship changed into hostility.[15]

Even when they did not engage in political or quasi-political activities, Europeans were the object of a deep-seated suspicion throughout the century. Clapperton recorded that he was regarded as a spy in Sokoto and that it was the common talk of the town that Europeans intended to take Hausaland as they had taken India.[16] This suspicion was reflected even in the commercial agreements which the Caliph granted to visiting explorers (like Clapperton and Dr Barth) before the scramble. The commercial concession which Muḥammad Bello granted to Clapperton in 1824[17] was a guarantee of security given by one sovereign to the subjects of another. The treaty between the Caliph ʿAlī (Aliyu Baba), and Dr Barth (on behalf of the Queen of England) in 1853 was similar to the 1824 Treaty. The Caliph avoided giving any but commercial concessions.

An aspect of these concessions was that they were, in effect, official *amāns* (safe conducts) given for an indefinite period, placing the British citizens in the Caliphate under the Caliph's protection. Under this arrangement, which is in accordance with

14. *Ibid.*, Appendix II: Muḥammad Bello to George IV, 18 April 1824.
15. R. Lander, *Record of Captain Clapperton's Last Voyage to Africa* (1830), vol. i, pp. 225 f., 251–2, and A. Adu Boahen, *Britain, the Sahara and the Western Sudan 1778–1861* (Oxford, 1964), pp. 80–3. This book gives a detailed appraisal of the British penetration of the Western Sudan including the Sokoto Caliphate during the period it covers.
16. Lander, *op. cit.*, vol. i, pp. 89–90, 94.
17. H. Clapperton, *Journal of a second expedition into the interior of Africa* (London, 1829), p. 275.

the *sharī'a*, the *musta'min*, though a *ḥarbī*, might reside in *Dār al-Islām* and carry on his normal business.[18]

Another aspect of the Sokoto–British 'Treaties' of the pre-scramble period is that the granting of the *amān* for an indefinite period implies the conferment of *dhimmī* status on the *musta'min*, because, strictly speaking, *amāns* can only be granted for short durations while grants made to *dhimmis* are for an indefinite period. However, even though the Europeans were the inferior partner (as people seeking and receiving protection) in these 'treaties', they were not specifically put under the obligation of paying *jizya* to the Caliph, which as *dhimmis* they should have done. The treaties of the scramble period included stipulations for the payment of subsidies which can only be regarded as *jizya*.

Dr Barth's treaty of 1853 with Sokoto illustrates the kind of treaty relations Sokoto was prepared to enter into with Europeans (*Nasara*—Christians). The treaty was more explicit than Clapperton's. Barth had left Great Britain, it seems, with a general model treaty which he was to sign with Western Sudan potentates.[19] The clauses of these treaties, which were eventually presented to these rulers, were carefully set out in the treaty which the Shaikh 'Umar of Bornu concluded with Barth on 3 September 1852.[20] Instead of the Shaikh of Bornu and the Caliph of Sokoto signing Dr Barth's draft, as many African rulers are said or known to have done later on in the century with draft treaties presented to them by agents of European imperialism, they wrote out sealed documents containing what they were prepared to grant. By its clarity and explicitness the Bornu treaty is a useful model with which that of Sokoto may usefully be compared.

The Bornu treaty stated clearly that the requests of the British government could only be granted in so far as the *sharī'a* permitted. It allowed the British unrestricted commercial enterprise in things permitted by the *sharī'a*, but not in copies of the Qur'ān

18. M. Khadduri, *War and Peace in the Law of Islam* (Baltimore, 1965), pp. 163–8, for a concise account of the regulations regarding the granting of *amān* and the obligations and rights of the *musta'min*. The protection given to *dhimmis* cannot be revoked.
19. Boahen, *op. cit.*, p. 186.
20. F.O. 93/17/1 original Arabic text; see tr. in Appendix I; the draft treaty was written in Bornu on 5 August 1851, 7th Shawāl 1267 A.H. It was apparently finally concluded on 3 September 1852; see Boahen, *op. cit.*, p. 205.

and slaves which were forbidden. It stated clearly that Bornu would not give preferential treatment to one European nation over another so long as they were all 'Christians', since the *sharīʿa* lays down a set covenant of protection which Muslims could conclude with Christians. Bornu was prepared to accept a British consul but would not put itself under his influence ('heed his words'). The consul would be treated as the *sharīʿa* enjoins, 'because it would not be proper for us to exceed its limits'.

The Sokoto 'treaty' is brief and, on the surface, less explicit than the Bornu treaty.[21] It granted unrestricted commercial enterprise in things permitted by the *sharīʿa* and protection of the merchants from injustice. The Qur'ān, which the English were not likely to trade in, was not specifically mentioned as forbidden, but slaves were. Considering the fact that the clauses presented by Barth to Bornu and Sokoto were probably identical, the silence of the Sokoto treaty on most of the other clauses in the Bornu treaty is significant. The suggestion is that the Caliph of Sokoto was interested mainly in a simple commercial relationship in consonance with the *sharīʿa*, but he was unwilling to commit himself on questions such as 'preferential treatment' and establishment of a British consulate in Sokoto as these might undermine the Caliphate's sovereignty. He, however, insisted that if any of the English merchants died his property would be subjected to the canonical 10 per cent tax (*irth*) and the rest could be claimed by the nearest British consular agent.[22]

The attitude of Sokoto, like that of Bornu, was one of caution against possible designs by Europeans against the sovereignty of the state. Sokoto adhered to the stipulations of Islam which permitted the *Dār al-Islām* to engage in trade with *ḥarbīs* coming to them and to conclude strictly commercial treaties with them.[23] It was an explicit aspect of the policy of the Caliphate that, legally, political concessions prejudicial to the Caliph's

21. F.O. 93/97/1, 2 May 1853, Sokoto Arabic original (see Appendix II for translation). The Emir of Gwandu also gave Dr Barth a guarantee of security for British merchants, Boahen, *op. cit.*, p. 187.
22. If a *Musta'min* dies while he is in *Dār al-Islām*, the *amān* granted to him was valid for his property which could therefore be taken out. See Khadduri, *op. cit.*, p. 168.
23. *Ibid.*, pp. 223–30. The Maliki jurists permit *ḥarbīs* to come into *Dār al-Islām* for trade but not Muslims going into *Dār al-ḥarb* for the same purpose.

sovereignty could not be granted to Europeans, whom they classified as Christians. Further, the Christians must accept the position of protected peoples under the Caliphate.

The attitude and policy of the Caliphate, which remained unchanged throughout the century, later constituted a major obstacle to the realization of European imperial ambitions in it. Effectively, the contest between the rulers of the Caliphate, anxious to preserve their independence, and the European powers, bent on acquiring political control over them, began in earnest with the opening (about 1879) of the scramble among European powers for possession of the Caliphate.

THE GENESIS OF EUROPEAN RIVALRY ON THE NIGER–BENUE WATERWAYS: 1879–84

With the formation of the United African Company in 1879 rivalry between British firms ended and rivalry between agents and representatives of Britain, France and Germany supervened. The new European interests, because they were in national rivalry, proved irreconcilable. The traders of each of these nations vied with one another to obtain concessions from the African rulers in order to enable them to acquire a dominant control of the market. The contest in the early years was mainly between the English and the French and was most intense in Nupe. The competition for the favour of African rulers became a factor in the local politics which the ruler could exploit to consolidate and enhance his own strength.

The consequence of this interaction was the gradual increase, often not immediately perceptible to the Africans, of European power of intervention and acquisition of political influence.

French commercial activities on the Upper Niger began in 1878 when Comte de Semellé of Comte de Semellé et Cie visited Lokoja and the Benue.[24] In 1880, de Semellé's company amalgamated with Hutchet Deprez et Cie to form the Compagnie Française de l'Afrique Equatoriale.[25] De Semellé visited the

24. C.M.S. G3/A3/01, T. C. John, Report of Lokoja Station, year ending 30 Sept. 1880. On this occasion de Semellé had tried but failed to reach Yola overland from Bida.
25. A.N.S.E., Afrique 86, Mattei au Ministre des Affaires Etrangères 11 May 1883.

Upper Niger again in June 1880, where he obtained the permission of 'Umar, Emir of Nupe, for the French to trade freely in his territory.[26] In 1880 the French had trading stations in Gbebe, Lokoja, Egga, Shonga and Raba along the Niger, and in Loko and Demsa on the Benue.[27] The English had a few trading posts in Nupe territory and one in Loko. In 1882 another French company, the Compagnie de Sénégal et de la Côte Occidentale d'Afrique, appeared on the Niger and started doing a prosperous trade.[28]

From the beginning the French companies assumed the role of agents of the French government for the realization of French imperial ambition in Africa. After a lull in French expansionist activities from North Africa from 1870–79, the French began to send expeditions through North Africa to the interior. A plan worked out in 1875 for a trans-Saharan railway was seriously taken in hand in 1879. The French minister for Public Works, created the Commission Supérieur du Trans-Saharien.[29] The railway was to be pushed to Senegal to tap the resources of that region more effectively. The plan was never executed. The White Fathers from their base in Ghadames, in response to the call of Cardinal Lavigérie, sought to convert Muslims to Christianity until a series of massacres between 1876 and 1881 put a stop to their proselytizing activities.[30] The idea of creating a French block of territories, comprising French North African and West African possessions with an addition of the Central Sudan, the Chad and the Niger–Benue basins, was rapidly gaining ground.

French activities on the Niger–Benue formed an essential part of the French imperial programme in Africa. Following the death of Comte de Semellé in 1882, Antoine Mattei, who succeeded him as the agent-general of the Compagnie Française de

26. C.M.S. G3/A3/01, T. C. John, Report, 30 Sept. 1880.
27. A.N.S.E., Afrique 57. Comte de Semellé à Monsieur L'Amiral Commandant en chef de la division navale de l'Atlantique du sud, 20 Sept. 1880, enclosed in Ministre de la Marine au Ministre des Affaires Etrangères of the same date.
28. For progress report on the company see Dumas (directeur) au Ministre des affaires d' outre-mer in A.N.S.O.M., Afrique 6, File 34d; Ministre des affaires d'outre-mer au Ministre des Affaires Etrangères, 18 June 1883.
29. Henri Blet, *France d'outre-mer* (Paris, 1950), pp. 124, 125.
30. *Ibid.*

l'Afrique Equatoriale, appealed to the French President, Gambetta, for government support, which was promptly given. Mattei was appointed French Consul-General of the Niger–Benue basins.[31] The political programme of the French companies ruled out reconciliation between them and the English company; furthermore, it underlined the fact that for Europeans to control the market they had to embark on acquiring political influence in the territories of the African rulers.

From 1880 German commercial groups also began to develop an ambition for political control over the Niger–Benue basins. In that year, the African Society was formed by a German colonial association. It sponsored Flegel on a mission to Sokoto. He travelled from Raba to Sokoto and back (18 October 1880 to 16 April 1881) through Mokwa, Bokani, Kontagora emirate, Yauri and Raha (on the Kebbi river) to Sokoto, and returned through Sabon Birni, Kebbi, Jega and Gwandu.[32] Flegel claimed to have been given a letter of recommendation from the Caliph 'to all good Muslims in Africa and the subjects of his vast empire'.[33] Towards the end of 1881, the German flag was hoisted on the Benue by Flegel for the first time.[34] Flegel's single-handed effort on behalf of Germany constituted no serious challenge to the British and the French. In February 1882 he was forced to leave Loko (but not the Benue) in sad circumstances, leaving half his property behind. Other European ivory traders there had harried him out.[35] In the same year he was refused entry into Yola.[36]

Faced with the French challenge the United African Company remustered its strength and embarked on an effort to exterminate the French companies. In 1881 it was reconstituted under the new name of the National African Company and its capital was increased to £1 million. Its objective was first, to acquire political influence with the African rulers and then to use this as a means for achieving the ultimate purpose of developing its

31. Jean Darcy, *France et L'Angleterre, cent années de rivalité coloniale en Afrique* (Paris, 1904), p. 238.
32. C.M.S. G3/A3/01 1881b. Sketch of a journey from Raba to Sokoto.
33. Eduard Flegel, *Vom Niger-Benue: Briefes aus Afrika: Von Eduard Karl Flegel* (Leipzig, 1890), p. 34. I am grateful to Professor Karl Hoffman for translation of extracts from this book.
34. Flegel, *op. cit.*, p. 40, Flegel to Karl, 7 Dec. 1881.
35. Flegel, *op. cit.*, p. 66, Flegel to Karl, 9 Feb. 1882.
36. Mockler-Ferryman, *British Nigeria* (London, 1902), pp. 158–9.

commerce.[37] By underselling and paying higher prices for African products, the N.A.C. exerted itself to the utmost to force the French companies to withdraw from the Niger trade or to be absorbed into the N.A.C.[38]

The British and the French vied with each other to ingratiate themselves with the African rulers by establishing post after post in their territories, plying them with gifts,[39] seeking treaty relations with them and finally by giving them military aid or promising to do so whenever necessary. European favours to African rulers were aimed at securing a trade monopoly. This led to increasing European attempts to control African territories politically. Such attempts resulted in conflict between Europeans and Africans. The latter were as consistently unwilling to lose any aspect of their sovereignty to foreigners as the former were bent on seizing it.

European trade was of great advantage to the Africans as it gave them easy access to much-desired European goods and increased their wealth and military power. Far from appearing dangerous to the Africans the European presence was seen as a source of strength the harmlessness of which they could always guarantee. As the Europeans were few their excesses, if any, could be easily controlled. The Emir ʿUmar of Nupe, for instance, derived great benefit from the Anglo–French rivalry in 1882 when a serious revolt broke out in his domains.

The revolt[40] was caused by the refusal of the Emir to abandon his attempt, which had proved a signal failure, to suppress the revolt of the Akoko.[41] The devotion of the Emir to what appeared to be a lost cause excited discontent among his generals who thereupon revolted. They summoned Etsu Baba (a descendant

37. R.H.B.E., S.85: T. Goldie, 'Concise history of the Royal Niger Company—1870–1887'.
38. For a full study of this subject see Flint, *op. cit.*, p. 34 ff.
39. A.N.S.O.M., Afrique 6, File 134d. Mattei au Ministre des Affaires Etrangères, 5 Nov. 1883.
40. The account of this revolt is based on C.M.S. G3/A3/01: no. 129 Report, 1 Sept. 1883; Johnson to A. Crowther, 2 Feb. 1882, no. 80—2 March 1882—Report, 19 March 1882; no. 128, 2 April 1882; and Rev. C. Paul, Report on Upper Niger, 24 Sept. 1882, which may be consulted for details which cannot be appropriately given here.
41. For many years Nupe Emirs had been extending their power over the region south of the Niger. The Akoko are a Yoruba-speaking 'tribe' whose chief town is Ikarẹ.

of a pre-*jihād* Nupe dynasty) then living in exile at Yauri, to lead them. Although this rebellion was crushed by the Emir's forces, the Kede, who were traditionally opposed to the Fulani dynasty, seized the opportunity to revolt.

The Kede were in a strong position to resist the Emir because they controlled the Nupe canoe traffic on the Niger. They blockaded the Niger between Raba and Egga and thus effectively cut off the Emir's forces to the south of the river. Thereafter they sent emissaries throughout Nupeland to incite the people to rebellion. They seized Egga and compelled the Rogan (the Emir's representative there) to support them. Shonga, Kippo and Katcha were destroyed. The Emir proved incapable of crushing the revolt until he got the military support of the European firms. The Kede revolt was finally crushed by an allied force of the Emir's troops and those of the British and French companies.

In other ways the rulers of the Niger–Benue banks benefited from the Anglo–French rivalry. Because the N.A.C. lavishly distributed gifts to these rulers, the French were compelled to do the same.[42] This, however, did not induce these rulers to show any marked preference for one European national over the other. They saw themselves as, and were indeed, the protectors of the Europeans trading in their territories, while the latter had to content themselves with this subordinate position.

'Umar, the Emir of Nupe (d. June 1882)[43] had, by a written permission, given the French and the English equal rights to trade freely in his territory.[44] This right was renewed by 'Umar's successor, Mālik (Maliki).[45] In October 1882 the new Emir, acting under pressure from the N.A.C., withdrew this permission temporarily from the French and only restored it in September 1883 in response to Mattei's pleading. Mattei promised Maliki that the French would restrict themselves to commerce. In return for this kind gesture, Mattei presented to

42. A.N.S.O.M., Afrique 6, file 34d, 5 Nov. 1882, Mattei au Ministre des Affaires Etrangères, and A.N.S.E., Afrique 86, Mattei au Ministre des Affaires Etrangères, 29 June 1883, contains an inventory of gifts distributed by Mattei on the Niger–Benue. See encl. in Ministre des Affaires Etrangères au Ministre des Colonies, 18 June 1883.
43. C.M.S. G3/A3/01, no. 128, Johnson to Rev. R. Lang 6 Sept. 1882.
44. A.N.S.E., Afrique 86, encl. 2, "Umar to his friends, the French' in Mattei au Ministre des Affaires Etrangères, 11 May 1883.
45. *Ibid.*, encl. 3, Maliki to Mattei.

the Emir 201 rifles, 200 barrels of powder and 200 pieces of cloth.[46]

By 1882 the French had realized that the English were too well established on the Niger to be dislodged by them. They therefore concentrated their attention on the Benue river. They reckoned that their establishment on the Benue would be a first step towards expansion to the Chad basin: 'Une semblable politique habilement suivie assurait à nos négotiants la route du lac Chad et de riches marchés de l'Adamawa et du Bornou.'[47]

Mattei was already pursuing such a policy and it was not completely abandoned until the 1890s. He concluded a treaty with Loko in August 1882[48] and obtained the permission of the Emir of Jibu to start a French station at Ibi (a flourishing ivory market) in September 1883.[49] The Ibi concession was a simple permission to the French to trade there under the Emir of Jibu's protection. A month after the French established themselves at Ibi the Emir of Jibu gave a similar permission to the N.A.C. to start a trading station there as well.[50] Mattei's treaty with Loko, though more elaborate, granted no more than the concession given to the French by the Emir of Jibu. The Emir of Loko, Aḥmad, stated explicitly that he would be the protector of Frenchmen who came to trade and promised to secure justice for them always. In return the French were to pay him an annual tribute.

To get rid of the French the N.A.C. set out to make the French companies either amalgamate under the British flag or sell to them (the N.A.C.) their assets. But since French national sentiment and ambition ruled out amalgamation, the N.A.C. concentrated their attention on a rapid expansion programme designed to squeeze out their competitors. New stations were therefore opened in areas hitherto cut off from European trade[51]

46. A.N.S.O.M., Afrique 6, file 34d (copy), Mattei au Ministre des Affaires Etrangères, 11 May 1883.
47. A.N.S.E., Afrique 86, Ministre de la Marine au Ministre des Affaires Etrangères, 25 Jan. 1883.
48. A.N.S.O.M., Afrique 6, file 34d, Mattei au Ministre des Affaires Etrangères, 11 May 1883, encl.
49. *Ibid.* See also A.N.S.E., Afrique 86, encl. Arabic original of Emir of Jibu's reply written on Mattei's letter to Jibu.
50. *Ibid.*
51. R.H.B.E., Africa S.85, vol. i, T. Goldie, 'Concise History of the R.N.C. 1879–1887'.

and subsidies were scattered broadcast among African rulers. Thus European activities expanded rapidly on the Niger–Benue rivers up to 1884. Soon the French companies had had enough. They sold out to the N.A.C. on 31 October 1884.[52]

In the African–European relations on the Niger–Benue which grew up rapidly between 1879 and 1884 as a result of the Anglo-French rivalry the African rulers as protectors of the Europeans were the superior partners in an arrangement from which they (the African rulers) derived great economic profit. The Europeans were, and continued to be regarded by the African rulers as, their protégés. The Africans were not aware of the dimensions of the threat to their sovereignty which lay in the logic of their new relationship with Europeans. They, indeed, could not be aware of it because, in reality, the threat to the sovereignty of African states during the European scramble lay not in the activities of Europeans on the spot but in the logic of the politics of European imperialism and rivalry which made possession of political control the prerequisite for control of the African market or sometimes even for access to it. As yet the danger of European imperial conquest in the Senegal–Niger area, from which the Caliphate was to take warning, had not loomed large and the Europeans within the Caliphate had not as yet, proved contumacious.

In the final analysis the treaties which Europeans signed with the African rulers had no relevance to eventual loss of the sovereignty of African states to Europeans except in so far as they determined which particular European nation was to take over which particular African state. The preconquest treaties of the Sokoto Caliphate with Europeans did not, in fact, especially from the African viewpoint, pose the question of European political control which was for them quite out of the question. Albeit, the treaties deserve attention because they provided the excuse for the presence of Europeans within the Caliphate as well as explaining and largely justifying the African resistance to increasing European encroachment on their independence.

The antithesis between European desires, as understood by the Africans, and their treaties with the Caliph and his emirs, remained a source of increasing conflict between the two parties in various parts of the Caliphate up to the final destruction of the Caliphate. The extra-treaty claims to the exercise of political

52. *Ibid.* See Flint, *op. cit.*, pp. 67–8.

control made by Europeans which produced these conflicts were seen by the Caliph and his emirs as departures from treaty engagements. They did not and could not as yet realize that the European attitude was an aspect of a general policy aimed at eventual assumption of European political control of the whole Caliphate. Realization of the real import of the commercial relationship with Europeans was not grasped until almost on the eve of European wars of conquest. Even in individual emirates the full danger posed by Europeans to their independence was not realized until the British conquest of Nupe and Iḷorin in 1897. This was because, until then, the riverain emirates which were in direct contact with Europeans had found it easy to check European excesses with firmness. Besides, direct, close and continuous contact between Europeans and the emirates away from the river banks did not come until the actual wars of European conquest by the French and the British.

The above considerations have to be borne in mind in seeking to understand the Caliphate's attitude to European penetration during the last two decades of the nineteenth century. The rest of this chapter will be devoted to an examination of African resistance to Europeans within the context of their treaty relations. In this connection, only by a regional appraisal of European–African relations in the Caliphate can the details and the tempo of the mounting tension between the two parties and the implications for the Caliphate fully be grasped.

EUROPEAN TREATY RELATIONS WITH THE RIVERAIN EMIRATES, GWANDU AND SOKOTO, 1885–94

With the disappearance of the French companies from the Niger–Benue in 1884, the N.A.C. became the dominant European traders there although its monopoly was consistently challenged by German traders as well as by traders based in Liverpool, African merchants from Freetown, Lagos and Brass, and, from 1890, by the French.

The numerous treaties signed with the territories on the banks of the Niger–Benue between 1884 and 1885 were largely with 'pagan' villages and towns and only a few were concluded with towns and villages properly within the Caliphate.[53] With regard

53. For copies of these treaties see F.O. 2/167.

to these treaties no more need be said than that they were aimed at creating an atmosphere of peace and security in order to promote trade. Conflicts soon arose not only with 'pagan' settlements but also with the emirates on the Niger–Benue banks as a result of the opposing views between the Africans and the N.A.C. as to the real import of the treaties. The N.A.C. claimed that their treaties conferred rights of sovereignty on them while the Africans denied signing away their sovereignty.

The conflicting interpretations of the treaties arose largely from the N.A.C.'s desire to assume more and more effective control over the areas in which they traded. The role played by the interpreters of these treaties also contributed substantially to the misunderstandings between the Africans and the N.A.C.

The task of interpreting the treaties to the African signatories was not an easy one, involving, as it did, a competent command of the English language and precise understanding of legal terms such as 'cession of territory', 'sovereignty', and 'Protectorate' as well as ability to render them in the African languages in which the concepts might not exist. As the interpreters were of the low-ranking level of the N.A.C.'s staff, it may be assumed that their knowledge of English was not profound. In addition, being themselves alien speakers of the African languages into which they interpreted, the interpreters faced the difficulty of translating from a language imperfectly understood to another which they probably understood even less. The versions of the treaties conveyed to the African rulers would appear to have been substantially different from the English originals.[54]

N.A.C. TREATIES WITH SOKOTO AND GWANDU, 1885

The policy of the N.A.C. from its foundation was to advance gradually from the coast to the interior.[55] The company hoped to establish direct relations with Sokoto[56] although it took no step in this direction until 1885. In 1882 the company decided on avoiding collision with the emirates through pursuing a too-forward policy because it rated their military power very high. However, immediately after the Berlin West African Conference

54. For the different treaty forms used by the N.A.C., see F.O. 2/167.
55. F.O. 84/2266, Goldie to F.O., 18 June 1892.
56. R.H.B.E., Africa, S.85, vol. i, 'Concise History of R.N.C.'

of 1884–85, the company was compelled to establish direct relations with the Caliph and the Emir of Gwandu in order to stultify German efforts then being actively directed towards signing a treaty with Sokoto.

Flegel was once again despatched to Sokoto to sign a treaty on behalf of Germany.[57] The N.A.C. therefore sent Thomson post-haste to Sokoto (at a cost of £500)[58] on a similar mission. Thomson's instructions were to obtain treaties from Sokoto and Gwandu which would grant to the British the complete monopoly of the foreign trade of their territories.[59] The N.A.C. envisaged that other Europeans to whom it granted permits would be free to trade in the Caliphate. The treaties were reported duly signed with Sokoto and Gwandu on 1 and 13 June 1885 respectively.[60]

By these treaties Sokoto and Gwandu are said to have transferred to the N.A.C. their 'entire rights to the country on both sides of the rivers Benue and Kwarra (Niger) for a distance of ten hours' journey inland or such other distance as they may desire from each bank of both rivers throughout their dominions'. In addition the N.A.C. or its successors were to have sole right among foreigners to trade and to mine minerals, while Sokoto and Gwandu were to have communications with other foreigners only through them. In return the Caliph and the Emir of Gwandu were to receive annually, 3000 and 2000 bags of cowries respectively from the company.

Otherwise, the treaties were much along the same lines as the early capitulation treaties signed by European powers with the Ottoman Empire.[61] Apart from a grant of free commercial enterprise, the Caliphate delegated to the N.A.C. its power of jurisdiction over foreigners. The company was, in return, to pay

57. Mockler-Ferryman, *British Nigeria*, p. 158.
58. Cost recorded by Lugard in his diaries. R.H.B.E., Africa, S.95: entry for 20 Sept. 1894.
59. See J. Thomson, 'Sketch of a journey from the Niger to Sokoto', *Journal of the Manchester Geographical Society*, ii (1886), pp. 1–18.
60. There is no detailed account of the Thomson expedition because Thomson claimed that he lost his papers. The R.N.C. was also very secretive about the details of the expedition. For copies of the Treaties, see F.O. 84/1749, encl. in Hewett to F.O., 9 Jan. 1886. Hewett described the treaties as 'agreements called treaties'.
61. M. Khadduri and H. J. Liebesny, ed., *Law in the Middle East* (Washington, 1965), vol. i, p. 312 ff. for a discussion of the content and history of capitulation treaties from the eleventh to the nineteenth century.

jizya (called subsidy), to the Caliph and the Emir of Gwandu for these rights—a confirmation of the company's subordination to the Caliphate.

In the absence of the originals of these treaties, in particular the Arabic versions, it is difficult to be categorical on the meaning of 'entire rights'. But within the context of the treaties, it does not seem to mean more than 'entire rights' over foreign trade. Nothing in the previous or subsequent attitude of the Sokoto Caliphs to Europeans suggests a disposition on their part to grant more than commercial rights. It seems likely therefore that the Arabic originals did not include 'entire rights' or were at least substantially different from the extant copies of the English version.

In 1890, at the height of the Anglo-French rivalry in the Niger–Benue basin, both Goldie and Lord Aberdare claimed that Thomson's treaties conferred on the N.A.C. sovereign rights to a distance of three days journey on either side of the Benue and the middle Niger and certain commercial privileges over the whole of the Caliphate.[62] However, Aberdare underlined the fact that communications between the company and Sokoto 'in those days' were limited and the company 'did not then think it prudent to propose a more ambitious treaty'.[63]

What Aberdare meant by 'a more ambitious treaty' is obscure, but possibly it refers to a treaty which granted sovereign rights, involving the company's control of the Caliphate's relations with other European powers and nationals, over the whole Caliphate. The question is whether or not the Caliph granted such rights, not to speak of rights of intervention in the internal affairs of the Caliphate to the N.A.C. over any part of the Caliphate, no matter how limited the extent. There are grave doubts concerning the exact terms of Thomson's treaties. The R.N.C. was very secretive about them. In 1886 Goldie warned Hewett, then British Consul in the Niger Delta, to keep the terms of the treaties secret.[64] The draft of a lecture read by Thomson before the Manchester Geographical Society in the same year was edited by the N.A.C. to expunge his assertion that 'not one half of the territories supposed to be under British protection are

62. F.O. 84/2087, Goldie to F.O., 'Précis on the Niger basin', 24 July 1890; and Lord Aberdare, speech delivered to annual meeting of the R.N.C. 29 July 1890.
63. Aberdare's speech.
64. F.O. 84/1749, Hewett to F.O., 9 Jan. 1886.

really secured by treaties, the remaining interspersed territories are therefore still open to annexation by foreign nations whose cupidity it would be impolitic to arouse'.[65]

According to a view ascribed to P. L. Monteil, who visited Sokoto in 1891, Thomson had sought to buy land from the Caliph but was told that the law forbade the sale of land to Christians.[66] Although the same source claimed that Monteil could not find a copy of the treaty at Sokoto, there is no doubt that some sort of concession was given to Thomson. These concessions seem to have been merely commercial.

It is unlikely that Thomson signed a treaty with Gwandu. Whereas the Sokoto treaty was said to have been sealed, there were no signatures on the one with Gwandu. Instead of signatures there is a statement 'duly executed in Arabic by the government of Gwandu',[67] at the end of the treaty. Furthermore it is inconceivable that the Emir of Gwandu could have signed a treaty giving away land on the banks of the Niger and Benue when he must have known that he had no territories on the Benue.

In view of these doubts the views of El-Ḥajj Maḥmūd Sherif, an Egyptian who, according to Lt. Mizon, had spent two and a half years in the service of the N.A.C. and who accompanied Thomson to Sokoto,[68] may represent more faithfully what happened to Thomson at Sokoto and Gwandu. According to Sherif, the Caliph would not sign the already written draft treaty which Thomson presented but authorized a permit granting commercial privileges to be written in Arabic. According to Sherif, the draft in Arabic initially granted that the Company would have 'power to trade' but the Caliph had the word 'permission' substituted for 'power'. At Gwandu only a verbal promise according the same rights as Sokoto had done was given. This would explain why the British version of the Gwandu treaty bore no signatures.

The subsequent policy of the N.A.C. (the company became

65. F.O. 84/1780, N.A.C. to F.O., 19 Jan. 1886. The clear meaning of the quotation is, however, that the 1885 British treaties left the greater part of the Caliphate outside British protection.
66. Darcy, *op. cit.*, p. 246.
67. See F.O. 84/1749, Hewett to F.O., 19 Jan. 1886, copy of treaty enclosed. Since Gwandu had no seal like Sokoto it is to be expected that Thomson would have insisted on signatures.
68. A.N.S.O.M., Afrique 3, file 16b, Mizon au sous-secrétaire d'Etat de la Marine et aux Colonies, 12 May 1893.

the Royal Niger Company Chartered and Limited in 1886 on receipt of a royal charter) was one of great caution with regard to the emirates of the Caliphate. In 1886 the R.N.C. laid it down that it would, as much as possible, avoid fighting and conquering any of the Muslim provinces of the 'Foulah Empire' because it feared that any success in that direction might be dearly bought if, as seemed likely, it aroused the hostility of the other provinces and shut the door against European penetration before the company could muster the necessary force to hold its own against the onslaught of Muslim 'fanaticism'.[69] The company envisaged that it would eventually be in a position to levy a force of 10,000 Sikh troops to march on the capital of the Caliphate.[70] The R.N.C. therefore early realized that it could only take possession of the Caliphate by force. This realization, apparently born of experience, does not suggest that in 1885 the company dealt with a state willing to sign away its sovereignty.

Far more important, perhaps, than all the doubts raised by the Thomson treaties and others was that the attitude of the Caliph and his emirs to Europeans in subsequent years shows clearly that they believed that all they had granted the British company were strictly commercial privileges. It has been necessary to examine the Thomson treaties closely because the R.N.C. took the view that these constituted its title deeds to the Caliphate. In 1895 Goldie claimed that only the Sokoto treaties[71] had any intrinsic value. All the others, Gwandu's included, he regarded as having no more value than to serve as a mere insurance policy to counter the claims of foreign rivals who might assert that any of the emirates fell outside the Caliphate.[72] By this assertion, no treaty signed with any emir which purported to grant more than did the Sokoto treaties could be valid.

69. R.H.B.E., S.58 (Private and confidential), Goldie to R.N.C. 24 November 1896.
70. *Ibid.* It is instructive to note the large estimate of troops deemed necessary to conquer the Caliphate before the introduction of the Maxim gun. The Maxim gun was invented in 1885.
71. i.e. treaties of 1890 and 1894 which were meant to confirm the 1885 Treaty.
72. F.O. 83/1380, Goldie's speech to the annual meeting of the R.N.C., 19 July 1895; see also F.O. 27/3160, R.N.C. Akassa to R.N.C. London, 8 July 1893; comments on R.N.C. treaty with Yola, extract enclosed in R.N.C. to F.O., 17 July 1893; also *ibid.*, R.N.C. to F.O., 15 June 1893, again on Yola treaty of May 1893.

The 1885 treaty with Sokoto did not lead to any remarkable increase in European contact with the hinterland emirates (i.e. emirates away from the Niger–Benue banks). Such contacts remained mainly sporadic until the overthrow of the Caliphate. Furthermore, relations of the emirates with Europeans were, after 1885, characterized by increasing friction. The riverain emirates were the most active centres of conflict. For Sokoto and the emirates of the interior, the fear of Europeans remained remote until the mid-1890s.

NUPE–N.A.C. RELATIONS, 1885–94

Until 1885 the Emir of Bida had refused to sign a treaty with the N.A.C., in spite of the latter's entreaties. The company was, moreover, facing competition from a German company (Hoenigsberg and Sons), Lander & Co. (an English company) and African merchants mainly from Lagos and Sierra Leone who the N.A.C. feared might use their influence with the chiefs to make them averse to signing treaties with the N.A.C.[73] In March 1885 David McIntosh at last succeeded in concluding a formal treaty with Maliki, the Emir of Bida. By this treaty the Emir gave the N.A.C. 'entire charge of all trading interests in the country; all foreigners in the country wishing to have the right to trade therein must obtain permission to do so from the N.A.C. Ltd'.[74] The company was also granted the sole right to mine. On their part, the N.A.C. 'agree and bind themselves to allow anyone who wishes to trade full liberty; always provided it shall be on equitable terms and according to British laws'. The company further paid 800 bags of cowries and promised to pay an annual subsidy to the Emir.

Although this treaty did not grant full monopoly rights of trade to the company it proceeded to behave in the ensuing years not only as if it did but also as if Nupe had conferred on it the right to exercise political control. The R.N.C. (as the N.A.C. became from 1886) harassed other foreign traders in Nupe and exercised the right of levying duties on them. It also took the view that consequent on the treaty, Nupe had become a British protectorate.

73. F.O. 84/1749, Hewett to F.O., 19 Jan. 1886.
74. F.O. 84/1749, Hewett to F.O., 19 Jan. 1886, encl. I, copy of the treaty of 19 March 1885 with Nupe; see also F.O. 2/167, Treaty no. 322.

The interpretation put on the 1885 treaty by the Emir of Nupe and his attitude to the question of cession of his rights to foreigners came out clearly during the interview which Claude Macdonald (sent out in 1889 by the British government to investigate R.N.C.'s activities on the Niger–Benue) had with him on 15 September 1889. On that occasion events in Nupe between 1885 and 1887 were reviewed. After the 1885 treaty had been retranslated into Hausa, both the Emir and his chief official, the Ndegi, agreed that they understood it and that Nupe was subordinate to Gwandu. Macdonald then read to them the preamble of the Gwandu Treaty of 1885, upon which the Emir asked Macdonald, in astonishment, what, in his opinion, the people of Lagos as British subjects would think if, without consulting them, the Queen of England handed them over to the French. The Emir would not believe that the Emir of Gwandu could have transferred Nupe to the British without consulting him. Failing to see any reasonableness in Gwandu's alleged action, the Emir further asked Macdonald whether even if the Queen of England were tired of ruling she would hand over her Empire to perfect strangers.[75]

The Emir, Maliki, concluded that the alleged Gwandu treaty was a fake. To Macdonald's further enquiry as to what the Emir thought he was receiving a huge subsidy from the R.N.C. for, the Emir assured him that the best way to find out would be to ask the company. The Ndegi, however, explained that the company's tribute was for the jurisdiction granted them over all foreigners and the right to mine in Nupe. On the right to levy duties, the Ndegi explained that this was a right the company could exercise south of Lokoja but not north of it.[76]

The Macdonald–Nupe discussions arose from Nupe–R.N.C. relations which had been deteriorating seriously from the signing of the 1885 treaty until it issued in a crisis in 1887. During the latter year, the Emir discovered that the R.N.C. was levying duties on traders at Egga. The strong-arm methods employed by the company against foreign traders had compelled four trading companies (Herr Hoenigsberg & Sons, John Lander & Co. Hutton & Osborne, and Sant Anna) to withdraw from Nupe.[77] Hoenigsberg lodged a complaint both with the German government

75. F.O. 84/2109, Macdonald's Report, ch. 3; Flint, pp. 140–1.
76. *Ibid.*
77. Flint, *op. cit.*, pp. 114–15.

and the Emir of Nupe to the effect that he had paid heavy duties to the company and to the Rogan at Egga to trade freely.[78] In November 1887 the Emir sent for Mr W. Wallace, the R.N.C. agent, and to all merchants to report at Bida.[79] The R.N.C. party consisted of Wallace, Robinson (their agent at Egga) and Vierra, their African agent.

On 13 November 1887 the Emir addressed a public assembly of all European merchants and their agents in Nupe. With his executioner standing by his side, the Emir, in a towering rage, declared that all must leave his country. He expressed surprise to note that Robinson had left Egga for Wunangi without his permission and remarked that it was well for him that he came back as he had sent a party to catch him or kill him if he attempted to escape. He demanded to know from Robinson the meaning of the notices outside the Egga factory of the company and if it was true, as he had been informed, that it signified that the company had taken over his country. He ordered that the symbols be brought to him at once. Furthermore, the Emir required Robinson to explain why the R.N.C. collected duties and on whose authority. Finally, with the Ndegi prostrating before him to assuage his mounting rage, the Emir ordered that all duties already collected be sent to him immediately.[80] He declared that thenceforward all, without exception, were free to trade in his territory, subject to payment of duties to him, and that he had never ceded any territory either to the British or to anybody else.[81] On the morning of the 14th, Wallace hurriedly despatched Vierra to Egga to bring the notices and the flag for the Emir's inspection and raised the annual tribute payable to him from £400 to £2000.[82]

Thereafter the R.N.C. shifted its centre of activity to Lokoja, a district under the supervision of a prince of Nupe. By using the

78. F.O. 84/2109, Count Hatzfeldt's memo. to F.O., 27 Jan. 1888 enclosed in the Macdonald report.
79. F.O. 84/2109, Macdonald Report, ch. 4: an account of the meeting of 13 Nov. 1887 at Bida from Wallace's diary taken in evidence before Sir James Marshall at the Asaba court. See also Flint's account and analysis, *op. cit.*, pp. 114–15.
80. *Ibid.*
81. F.O. 84/1874, memo by merchants and traders at Egga to F.O., 17 Nov. 1887.
82. F.O. 84/2109, Macdonald Report, ch. 4, extracts from Wallace's diary. Flint, *op. cit.*, p. 115.

troops to prevent the agents of the prince from collecting tribute and slaves, in 1889, the R.N.C. once again provoked the anger of the Nupe chiefs who saw in the company's interference, an attempt to undermine their economic position and a first step towards depriving them of their land. Hostilities between the chiefs (who mounted an offensive) and the company were only narrowly averted in 1890.[83]

The Emir, taking the cue from his chiefs, became decidedly hostile to the R.N.C. It was probably as a result of this hostility that in 1890 he sent emissaries to Lokoja to welcome Mizon, who was on his way to Muri and Yola at the head of a French expedition, to ask if and where he would like to establish his factory in Nupeland.[84] The Emir, Maliki, thus gave further expression to his open market policy declared in 1887. It seems also that he saw in Mizon a possible ally whom he could use against the R.N.C. As Nupe–R.N.C. relations continued to deteriorate the Emir apparently wished more and more to have a firm European ally against the R.N.C. Thus when Mizon came on his second expedition (1892–93) he once again wrote to the explorer offering to renew his friendship with the French. The Emir wrote: 'I am your friend and so is Abubakar, the Yerima.'[85]

The Emir's need for such an alliance is understandable in the light of the breach between him and the R.N.C. in 1890–92, a breach which negotiation had failed to heal. Mizon learnt from the envoys that Maliki had told the R.N.C. to evacuate its forces from Lokoja and to desist from exercising justice over natives of Nupe.[86] A Nupe–R.N.C. war had seemed imminent at the end of 1891.

The R.N.C., anxious to avoid war, had sent a delegation, comprising Goldie and the Earl of Scarbrough, to Bida,[87] where they arrived on 24 January 1892. They were armed with a letter from Queen Victoria to Maliki expressing satisfaction at improved relations between Nupe and the company and 'covering our meaning that he (Maliki) is under our protection . . .

83. For an account of this crisis see Flint, *op. cit.*, pp. 234–5.
84. A.N.S.O.M., Afrique 3, file 16b. Mizon au sous-secrétaire d'Etat aux Colonies, 12 May 1893.
85. *Ibid.*, encl., translation of Maliki to Mizon, 1892.
86. A.N.S.O.M., Afrique 3, file 16b, Mizon au sous-secrétaire d'Etat aux Colonies, 12 May 1893.
87. F.O. 84/2245, Goldie to Salisbury: 'Report on Nupe visit', 24 March 1892; also Flint, *op. cit.*, p. 235.

yet not incompatible with his possible assertion of independence.'[88]

On their arrival Goldie and Scarbrough discovered that the R.N.C. stations were being threatened with destruction. In a speech delivered in open court Goldie assured the Emir that the company's officials had been warned to stop interfering with slavery in Nupe. They promised that the R.N.C. would adhere to the 1885 treaty and that it had no intention whatsoever of taking over Nupe territory. After this appropriately placatory introduction, Goldie, as if he was anxious to provoke the Emir, threatened that if Maliki broke the treaty Nupe would be blockaded and its trade with the Christians (Europeans) would be diverted to Adamawa, Bauchi, Borgu, Zaria and other places, and that Nupe raids into pagan areas under R.N.C. jurisdiction would mean war.

It was an apology that carried a sting in its tail but it was, in reality, mere bluff. The R.N.C. did not have the necessary force to back up the threat. Goldie, criticizing the forward action of the company's officials in the Lokoja district, stressed that the company had no military force to back up such action without denuding the rest of the 'R.N.C. territory'.[89] This was in spite of the fact that the company's forces had been more than doubled after the 1887 fracas with Emir Maliki.[90] In reply to Goldie's speech, Maliki said that his views were identical with the company's. He publicly refuted the fears of his chiefs that he intended to give out his land to the Europeans. The Emir's attitude, as evidenced by this reply, was surprisingly submissive. For some reason, he seemed to have felt unequal to the task of calling Goldie's bluff. Could this have been owing to consideration for possible loss of the profits accruing to him from Nupe–R.N.C. trade as well as the obviously superior river power of the company or some internal political problems? Be that as it may, Maliki's appeal to Mizon later in 1892 is understandable in the light of the retreat he had had to beat before Goldie's threat.

Following Goldie's visit tension between Nupe and the R.N.C.

88. F.O. 84/2179, minute by Anderson on R.N.C. to F.O., 26 Nov. 1892. For quotation see Flint, *op. cit.*, p. 235.
89. F.O. 84/2245, Goldie to Salisbury, Report on Nupe visit, 24 March 1892.
90. F.O. 84/2171, Goldie to F.O., 'Hoenigsberg and the R.N.C.', 20 July 1891.

eased. Nupe's forces were withdrawn from the region south-west of Lokoja. The period of calm was, however, short. Goldie had not expected more. After the visit he had reached the conclusion that war between the R.N.C. and Nupe lay in the logic of events.[91] The company's policy thenceforth was to play for time until it was strong enough to face Nupe in battle.

In 1889 Nupe's military strength had been estimated at 1000 horsemen and 3500 footmen (*Danganas*). Besides there were many chiefs with powerful contingents of retinues and the Emir could in times of need count on help from neighbouring emirates. Nassarawa had given him such help in the past.[92] The Nupe army was well armed with trade guns, spears (seven feet long, solid iron and used solely for thrusting), bows and arrows and double-edged swords with Solingen blades.[93]

By July 1893 there was fresh evidence of Nupe's hardening attitude to the company,[94] but the company had no answer other than conciliation and patience. The Emir was master in Nupe, and so far he had proved capable of effectively curbing the excesses of the Europeans. So far as Nupe was concerned the problem of European penetration was a local one: a nuisance which it seemed could always be controlled at need.

THE R.N.C. AND LAGOS GOVERNMENT'S RELATION WITH ILỌRIN, 1885–94

In spite of the fact that the N.A.C. signed a treaty with Ilọrin on 18 April 1885, its agents rarely found their way there.[95] Ilọrin had traditionally traded with Lagos and the coast. By the treaty of 1885 with the N.A.C. the Emir and chiefs of Ilọrin are said to have accepted the protectorate and the British flag offered to

91. R.H.B.E., Africa, S.58, Memo. on Nupe campaign (1897) by Goldie.
92. F.O. 84/2109, Military Report on Nupe by Capt. Ferryman, Macdonald's Secretary on his visit to the Niger and Benue.
93. *Ibid.*
94. R.H.B.E., Africa, S.85, vol. i, Proceedings of R.N.C. general meeting of 13 July 1893.
95. F.O. 84/1239, C.O. to F.O., 5 May 1893; also F.O. 84/1940, Macdonald's report on his visit to Ilọrin (Conf. Print), encl. no. 3: Report by Rev. C. Paul who accompanied Macdonald to Ilọrin. On their journey from Ilọrin to Ọffa, it became clear that the people had never seen a white man previous to that occasion.

them by the N.A.C.[96] Ilọrin was to govern itself according to its own laws and customs while it ceded to the N.A.C. the right to govern all foreigners and the power to exclude foreign traders from the emirate as they saw fit.

When Macdonald visited Ilọrin in 1889, however, Aliyu (ʿAlī), the Emir asserted that he did not, by the 1885 treaty, put himself under the protection of the company or the British flag.[97] His treaty, he said, was a commercial agreement which gave the N.A.C. monopoly of trade and mining rights. Moses, the interpreter of the 1885 treaty, confirmed Aliyu's view of the treaty and assured Macdonald that nothing was mentioned to Ilọrin about protection of the company or the British flag. He also confirmed Aliyu's claim that he did not actually sign the treaty although it had his blessing. Even though the Imām is said to have signed for Ilọrin, there is an 'X' mark on the surviving copy purported to have been made by the Emir.[98] Yet available evidence indicates that the Emir could write.[99] The R.N.C.'s influence was, in fact, next to nothing in Ilọrin.

On the other hand, after 1885 the British government at Lagos had its eyes on Ilọrin, with which its diplomatic intervention in the protracted Yoruba wars[100] had brought it into contact. Various attempts at ending these wars had failed. An attempt made by the Caliph, ʿUmar, of Sokoto in 1883 to negotiate a settlement between Ilọrin and Ibadan through the agency of Emir Maliki of Nupe had proved abortive because neither Karara, the Ilọrin general, nor Ashubiaro (Latosa), the Arẹ of Ibadan, would entertain the idea of returning home without the glory of a major victory.[101]

In his turn, Macdonald endeavoured to negotiate peace between Ilọrin and Ibadan. This time Ilọrin wanted peace, but then the Emir would not accept the peace proposals drawn up by

96. F.O. 84/1940, Macdonald's Report (Conf. Print) no. 33, encl. no. I.
97. F.O. 84/1940, Macdonald's Report on Ilọrin.
98. *Ibid.*, encl. no. I.
99. It is said that he was unwilling to sign for fear that the Europeans would do something with his name harmful to him and his emirate.
100. For an account of these wars, see S. Johnson, *History of the Yorubas* (5th edn, London, 1960), pp. 413 ff., J. F. Ade Ajayi, *Yoruba Warfare in the Nineteenth century* (London, 1964) and S. A. Akintoye, 'The Ekiti Parapo and the Kiriji War' (unpublished Ph.D. thesis, Ibadan, 1966).
101. *The Lagos Observer*, July and August 1883.

Macdonald. Rather, he ordered his Imām to draw up, in Arabic, an undertaking similar to, though not identical with, Macdonald's proposals and sign it. The negotiations broke down because the Emir refused to sign even the document drawn up by his Imām in spite of Macdonald's insistent urging.[102]

It was through the good offices of Governor Carter of Lagos that a peace settlement was made between Ibadan and Ilọrin in March 1893.[103] The Emir, Aliyu, told Governor Carter that he had no treaty with the R.N.C. and that he considered himself perfectly independent.[104]

However, there is a copy extant, in English, of a treaty allegedly concluded between the R.N.C. and Ilọrin on 9 August 1890 by which Ilọrin confirmed the treaty of 1885 and undertook to accept the protection of the British flag whenever called upon to do so.[105]

There is nothing to explain the sudden change in Ilọrin's attitude from refusal to sign away its sovereignty in 1885 to a willingness to do so in 1890 at the request of the company. The subsequent attitude of Ilọrin to the R.N.C. and white men in general contradicts the letter and the spirit of the 1890 treaty. The question that arises is whether the treaty was forged or whether, once again, it was not properly explained to Ilọrin. That the treaty was not signed by anybody in Ilọrin—not even the Imām[106]—renders it highly probable that it was forged. The fact was that, treaty or no treaty, the R.N.C. had no influence in Ilọrin.

With regard to the government of Lagos, once the 1893 peace settlement was concluded, the Emir of Ilọrin made manifest his hostility to any attempt by Europeans to interfere in his emirate. He claimed that the Lagos government had included within its territory a portion of his emirate. After an initial show of willingness by Ilọrin to co-operate with him, Captain Bower who was deputed by the Lagos government to settle the Ilọrin boundary,

102. F.O. 83/1238, Carter to the Marquis of Ripon, Tel. 21 March 1893.
103. For correspondence on the settlement see F.O. 84/1238, Carter to the Marquis of Ripon, Tel. 21 March 1893 and same to same, 18 Feb. 1893.
104. F.O. 83/1239, Carter to C.O., encl. 28 March 1893 in C.O. to F.O., 5 April 1893.
105. Macdonald Report on Ilọrin F.O. 84/1940.
106. In place of signatures the treaty ended with the statement, 'duly executed in Arabic by the Ilọrin government'.

was given a decidedly hostile reception. The Emir, Aliyu, refused to correspond with Bower and wrote to Carter to inform him that he would not allow any Europeans in his town.[107]

Thenceforth the deterioration of Iḷọrin's attitude was aggravated by the example of Nupe's hostility to the R.N.C. In 1894 there were reports that hostilities would soon commence between Nupe and the company. The R.N.C. had felt compelled by the imminence of war to withdraw from its Egga and Jebba stations.[108]

What Iḷọrin opposed was European encroachment on its independence or its territory and not European trade. This is evidenced by the fact that even when the Emir was showing hostility to the Lagos government in 1894 he not only welcomed F. D. Lugard, who claimed to be travelling solely for the purpose of peaceful trade, but he also gave him a letter of introduction to the King of Kishi in which he stressed that Lugard had come only for trade and had no intention of plundering or perpetrating any mischief.[109]

TRADE AND CONFLICT ON THE BENUE, 1884–94

On the Benue river, the attitude of the Africans to European penetration was similar to that which obtained on the Niger. As on the Niger, many treaties had been signed by the N.A.C. on the Benue between 1884 and 1885. In 1889, when Macdonald visited the Benue on his investigations, the interpreters of several of the treaties sent in affidavits sworn before the Chief Justice of Lagos which showed that in no case were the African signatories of those treaties made to understand that they were giving up their country to Europeans. Macdonald elicited from many of the actual signatories the view that they had neither sold their country nor given it to the N.A.C. Although they confessed to being under the protection of the company this, in their view, meant simply that the company would give them military protection against aggressive enemies. Talking of the signing away of sovereign rights with special reference to Muslim emirates,

107. R.H.B.E., Africa, S.95, Lugard's Diaries, entry for 8 December 1894.
108. *Ibid.*
109. R.H.B.E., Scarbrough Papers Africa S.101, vol. xviii, Translation of Emir of Iḷọrin, Moma, son of ʿAbd al-Salām's letter to Kishi (n.d.).

Macdonald came to the conclusion that: 'In Mohammedan countries, this would under existing circumstances be quite impossible and could only follow on conquest . . . and amongst the majority of the pagan tribes, if not impossible certainly most inadvisable.'[110]

With the more important emirates and Muslim districts of the Benue, as on the Niger, the N.A.C. and other Europeans failed to acquire sovereign rights. According to existing copies of the N.A.C. treaties with Bakundi, Lafia and Gashaka, the Muslim rulers of those places accepted the protection of the company and even ceded their territories to it with 'sovereignty rights'.[111] The English versions were apparently different from what was conveyed to these rulers. In the case of Bakundi as noted by J. E. Flint, the interpreter confessed to Macdonald in 1889 that he did not make the king understand that he had ceded his country to the company:

> Conscientiously [he said] I cannot say that I made the king understand that he had ceded his country to the company. I made him understand that he gave over the whole of his territory to the company for trading purposes; that nobody else could trade in his country without the permission of the company, that all Europeans should be under the jurisdiction of the company, but I was not aware that 'ceding' meant giving over rights of government and I dare not have made this suggestion to him as he would not have listened to it for a minute.[112]

This declaration apparently applied to many another treaty.

The N.A.C.'s treaty with Muri is typical of treaties signed with the more important Muslim rulers on the Benue banks.[113] According to the preamble, the aim of this treaty was to put an end to the disputes between various European traders and foreigners and between these and the natives. The N.A.C. was to have control over all foreigners and the foreign trade of Muri. But it was to have no rights to the land and in all its actions it was to understand that it was acting on behalf of the Emir of Muri,

110. F.O. 84/2109, Macdonald Report, ch. 2, 'Notes on the Benue'.
111. F.O. 2/167: Treaties nos. 310 of 27 March 1885, 307 of 16 Dec. 1885, 318 of 1885 for Bakundi, Lafia, and Gashaka respectively; see also copy of Bakundi treaty in F.O. 93/6/13 and Macdonald Report on Benue, *loc. cit.*, Bakundi is said to have signed away its sovereignty for £33.16*s*.3*d*.
112. F.O. 84/2109, Macdonald Report, ch. 2, 'Notes on the Benue'. See also Flint, *op. cit.*, p. 139 for quotation.
113. F.O. 2/167, Treaty no. 321.

under whose protection it was. For these privileges and the Emir's protection the N.A.C. paid 500 bags of cowries on the spot and agreed to paying an annual tribute of 160 bags of cowries. Nassarawa, Keffi and Bauchi had similar treaties with the N.A.C. by which they granted commercial privileges to it with the clear understanding that the company was under their protection.[114]

However, as on the Niger so also on the Benue, the N.A.C.'s attempts to exercise sovereign powers resulted in conflicts with the native rulers. The emirates of Muri and Adamawa were the major centres of the most intense European activities and conflicts with the native rulers.

MURI, 1884–93

From 1884 relations between the Emir of Muri and the N.A.C. deteriorated consistently until in 1891 the company was expelled. Late in 1884 the N.A.C. attacked and burnt Jibu (a Muri town), killing many of its inhabitants[115] for the reason that the ruler had refused to hand over a runaway culprit who had killed one of the company's servants at Ibi. The Emir of Muri is said to have come to Ibi with his troops and ordered the N.A.C. to evacuate his territory for wantonly encroaching on his authority by attempting to exercise judicial powers in his territory. The company was allowed to remain only when it promised always to refer all complaints to the Emir instead of taking the law into its own hands. Nevertheless the R.N.C. attacked Jibu again in 1888, thus further worsening relations with the Emir of Muri.[116]

Finally in 1891 Jibu was once more sacked by the R.N.C., whereupon the Emir of Muri ordered the company to quit his territory and the company's factories at Kunini and Lau were

114. F.O. 93/6/11, Treaty with Nassarawa 25 Oct. 1884; and F.O. 2/167, Treaty no. 316 of 1 April 1888 and Keffi Treaty of 22 May 1885 in the same volume.

115. A.N.S.O.M., Afrique 3, file 16b; Mizon au sous-secrétaire d'Etat aux Colonies, 11 Jan. 1893, extract of entry in his diary for 19 Nov. 1892, enclosed in Mizon Reports of 14 Oct. 1893. R.N.C. attacks on Jibu are also recorded in J. M. Fremantle, *Gazetteer of Muri Province* (London, 1922), p. 8.

116. *Ibid.*, Mizon's report.

closed on his orders.[117] The company thereafter retired to Ibi where it had a military garrison. Following on these events the R.N.C. lodged a complaint against the Emir of Muri with the Caliph at Sokoto, in which it alleged that the Emir had looted its stores and closed the trade routes. The Caliph, while not condoning the sack of Jibu by the R.N.C., ordered the Emir of Muri to return goods seized from the company's factories.[118] The Caliph reminded the Emir of Muri of the obligation of a Muslim ruler to his protected (*dhimmi*) subjects. He wrote: 'When foreigners settle in Muslim land by permission it is contrary to honesty to plunder their factories and the duty of a Muslim prince is to favour their trade and not to close the road against them.'[119]

In 1891 Lt. de Vaisseau Mizon led a French expedition to the Benue. On that occasion he had passed through Muri, but his scheduled destination and the centre of his activities was Adamawa. His first expedition is discussed below in connection with Anglo-French rivalry in Adamawa.[120] With regard to Muri the arrival there of Mizon in October 1892[121] on a second expedition to the Benue compelled the R.N.C. to intensify its efforts to effect reconciliation with the Emir of Muri. In November 1892 an R.N.C. peace delegation arrived in Muri but was put off by the Emir, who merely promised that he would think about its proposition.[122]

Relying on Mizon as a counterpoise against the R.N.C., the Emir of Muri became decidedly intransigent towards the British Company. For Mizon, anxious to promote French influence on the Benue, the impasse between Muri and the R.N.C. was most opportune. In addition, the Emir of Muri saw in Mizon a welcome helper against the nearby village of Kwana which had been a source of constant anxiety for Muri since the founding of the emirate. During the first year of his reign, Muḥammad Abubakar Nya, the reigning Emir of Muri had, with Bauchi's aid, attacked

117. *Ibid.* See also A. H. M. Kirk-Greene, *J.H.S.N.*, i, no. 3 (1958), p. 235.
118. Mizon au sous-secrétaire d'Etat, 11 Jan. 1893.
119. *Ibid.* Translation of Caliph's letter (1892) enclosed, being extract from entries in Mizon's diaries, for 22 and 23 Dec. 1892.
120. See below, pp. 152–3.
121. A.N.S.O.M., Afrique 3, file 14, Mizon au sous-secrétaire d'Etat aux Colonies, 18 Nov. 1893.
122. *Ibid.*

Kwana but had failed to take it. In 1891 Kwana had closed the trade routes leading to Bauchi and the hinterland of the Caliphate. This closure was wrongly blamed on Muri by the R.N.C. When Mizon arrived in Muri, the Emir had attacked Kwana three times without avail over a period of eighteen months.[123]

Mizon came in good time to show his friendship and that of the government of France to Muri by aiding the Emir in his attack on Kwana which took place on Christmas day 1892.[124] Previous to the attack Mizon had concluded a protectorate treaty with Muri on 22 November. Under a French Protectorate, Mizon explained, the independence of Muri would remain intact, their laws and customs would not be interfered with, all traders coming to Muri must be under the control of the French but they were, nonetheless, to obey the laws of Muri and the French must submit grievances to the Emir for settlement. France undertook by the terms of the treaty to furnish the Emir with arms sufficient to maintain a police force and for ensuring the security of the trade routes. The Emir was to accept a French Resident in Muri. Mizon delivered thirty guns and twenty revolvers to the Emir and trained his soldiers to use them as well as to use the Snider rifles which the R.N.C. had at one time given to the Emir.[125]

With the aid of Mizon's men and the newly trained Muri troops, Kwana was sacked in the ensuing battle. Many prisoners were captured and enslaved. Five envoys from Sokoto are said to have been present at, and participated in, the taking of Kwana.[126]

In the meantime Mizon had opened two French trading posts at Mainarawa and at a place he called Menardville in Muri territory. He established what he called 'protectorat français du Soudan' over Muri emirate which for six months maintained a

123. *Ibid.*

124. *Ibid.*, contains a detailed report on the destruction of Kwana covering the preparations for war in Muri previous to and especially from the 23 to 27 Dec.—two days after the battle. See also Description of battle of Kwana in F.O. 83/1240 by Dr Ward (member of Mizon's expedition), encl. I in R.N.C. to F.O. 25 May 1893.

125. A.N.S.O.M., Afrique 3, file 16b, Mizon au sous-secrétaire d'Etat aux Colonies, Mizon Report of 18 October 1893 entry for 22 and 23 Nov. 1892. For the terms of the treaty, see A.N.S.O.M., Afrique 3, file 14, Mizon au sous-secrétaire, 18 Nov. 1893.

126. *Ibid.*

monopoly against other Europeans wanting to trade in Muri.[127] It was not surprising that the Caliph apparently supported the Muri attack on Kwana since this would be war against unbelievers—a perennial preoccupation of the emirates against enemy states.

Although Mizon's methods were not always above board (as evidenced by the accusations brought against him by Dr Ward and Vaughan,[128] his colleagues on the expedition), he had succeeded in holding the Emir of Muri in deep gratitude to France. The Emir did not fail to draw the contrast between Mizon who gave positive help to 'Muslims against infidels' and the R.N.C. whom he (the Emir) said had misrepresented him to the world as 'a raider and plunderer'. Mizon's actions in aid of the Emir were clearly to the advantage of Muri and met the kind of hopes which African rulers cherished in their relations with Europeans—a friend to augment their military power. In return Mizon got what he wanted—a free hand to control Muri's trade with Europeans.

The co-operation between Muri and Mizon was brought to an end by the R.N.C. who, left with no alternative in its efforts to expel the French from the Benue, declared a blockade of Muri in July 1893.[129] The recall of Mizon followed a few months later.

ADAMAWA

The Emirs of Adamawa had been consistently averse to entering into formal relations with Europeans throughout the century. In 1852 Barth had been summarily turned back from Yola by the Emir, Lawal, who demanded that the traveller must obtain

127. *Ibid.*
128. F.O. 83/1240. The evidence of Dr Ward, Vaughan and Mr Nebout, encl. 1 in R.N.C. to F.O., no. 62, 25 May 1893; cf. Flint, *op. cit.*, pp. 174–7. While it must be conceded that Mizon exaggerated in parts, it seems from his detailed records, that he did not run his ship aground deliberately. The evidence of Ward and Vaughan, the first of whom accused him of being ambitious, seem coloured. Whereas they decry his methods they do not deny his achievements: A.N.S.O.M., Afrique 3, file 16b, Mizon au sous-secrétaire, 14 Oct. 1893, for Mizon's detailed report.
129. A.N.S.O.M., Afrique 3, file 14, Mizon au sous-secrétaire, 18 Nov. 1893, p. 58; Mizon received a letter from the R.N.C. dated Ibi 14 July 1893 announcing the blockade of Muri.

permission to visit him from the Caliph.[130] In 1880 a C.M.S. Mission was refused entry into Yola.[131]

In 1882 and 1884 William Wallace of the N.A.C. was turned back from Yola.[132] Again in 1886 Sanda, the Emir of Adamawa, not only refused to grant audience to Wallace but he also returned his gifts sent through a servant of the R.N.C. The R.N.C. complained to the Caliph who thereupon advised the Emir of Yola to allow the English to trade in Adamawa, but a reply in the affirmative was not received by the R.N.C. from the Emir until his death in 1891.[133] According to Macdonald who visited the Benue in 1889, although the R.N.C.'s stations extended as far as Ribago (in Adamawa) their treaties did not cover a like expanse of territory. At Ribago there was no treaty, owing to the hostility of the Emir of Yola.[134] In Yola itself the R.N.C.'s footing, confined for a short while from 1886 entirely to a trading hulk (the *Emily Waters*) moored to the banks, was precarious in the extreme.[135]

Flegel, after an initial rebuff in 1882, had a precarious sojourn in Yola until he was harried out of the Benue by the N.A.C. in 1885.[136] Dr Zintgraff, representing the interests of the German colonial society (with particular interest in Adamawa) visited Yola in 1888 but was peremptorily sent away.[137] In 1889, when Macdonald came on his mission of investigation, the Emir of Yola bluntly refused to welcome him. From 1890, however, a new turn in European rivalry, between the British, French and

130. Barth, *Travels and Discoveries in North and Central Africa* (London, 1857), vol. ii, pp. 496–7.
131. Mockler-Ferryman, *British Nigeria*, p. 158.
132. *Ibid.*, p. 159, Wallace met with initial success but was later ordered away.
133. Mockler-Ferryman, *Up the Niger* (London, 1892), p. 91. On being shown Thomson's treaty of 1885 with Sokoto, the Emir, Sanda, agreed he was a vassal of the Caliph but said the treaty did not refer to him.
134. F.O. 84/2109, Macdonald Report, Ch. 2, 'Notes on the Benue'. Macdonald emphasizes the intransigence of the Emir of Yola as the main factor responsible for the inability of the R.N.C. to conclude treaties in Adamawa.
135. Story of R.N.C. in Yola told to Mizon by his host there—see A.N.S.O.M., Afrique 3, file 15a, Report for 27 August 1891.
136. F.O. 84/1781, F.O. to Goldie, 2 Nov. 1885. Flegel died soon after.
137. F.O. 84/1940, Macdonald to F.O., no. 29 of 9 Sept. 1889; Zintgraff arrived in Yola in July 1889.

Germans over territories in the Benue and Chad basins, enabled Adamawa to see the grim implications of European penetration even more clearly and to readjust its policy to meet the situation. In 1886 the British and the Germans had signed a convention[138] by which Britain conceded to Germany the eastern portion of Adamawa beyond Garua. The British aim in so doing was to create a buffer between their sphere of influence and that of the French. To prevent French infiltration into areas in which Britain had interest she concluded the Say–Barua line agreement with France in August 1890.[139] The details and consequences of these agreements are outside the scope of this study. Suffice it here to mention that they did not bring Anglo–French–German rivalry to an end. The increasing tempo of this rivalry over Adamawa territory posed a new and urgent challenge to the Emir from 1890.

The execution of the French plan to join the North African territories with her western and equatorial African possessions in an unbroken block was now vigorously taken in hand. To realize this plan, possession of the eastern part of Adamawa, Baghirmi and the Shari basin was essential for France. In 1890 M. Cholet, coming from the Congo on behalf of the French government, had reached the 4th latitude by way of the Sangha. In the same year another French expedition under Crampel was fast approaching the Chad basin by way of the Mbangi.[140] In 1891 yet another French expedition, under Col. Monteil, left France to reconnoitre the Say–Barua line.

The Mizon expeditions (1890–92 and 1892–93) to the Benue river were part of the larger French plan to win the Congo, Benue and Chad basins. These expeditions produced a heated Anglo–French–German rivalry over Adamawa. From 1890 to 1893, numerous European expeditions from the contesting countries visited Adamawa, all seeking concessions from the Emir and his

138. Hertslet, *Map of Africa by Treaties* (London, 1909), vol. iii, p. 880; also R.H.B.E., S.85, vol. i, Proceedings of Ordinary General Meeting (R.N.C.) 12 July 1894. See also Flint, *op. cit.*, pp. 164–8.

139. For full text of treaty see Hertslet, *op. cit.*, vol. ii, pp. 738–9. For a fuller discussion, see Flint, pp. 164–8.

140. A.N.S.O.M., Afrique 6, 82c. French Ambassador in London, to French Minister for Foreign Affairs, 17 Dec. 1890, encl., tr. of article in *The Times*, 'The International race for Lake Chad', 17 Dec. 1890. The French plan was said to have included a railway line from Algeria to Brazzaville.

subordinate rulers. The policy of Adamawa in the face of the stream of European travellers (accompanied by numerous armed escorts and carriers) was one of firmness mixed with judicious exploitation of the rivalry between the various European nationals by playing one against another, to keep all at arms' length and thereby maintain Adamawa's sovereignty intact. Whenever circumstances forced the hand of the Emir he granted concessions to Europeans, always ensuring that his sovereign rights were preserved.

Zubeir, Sanda's successor as Emir, was less intransigent to the R.N.C. at the beginning of his reign. On his accession in 1891 he allowed the company to keep an African agent in Yola to trade from a hulk, but not to build factories on land. Later in the same year Zubeir is said to have withdrawn this concession because he considered that the company had encroached on his judicial authority by arresting its own agent for beating his wife to death and taking him away to Asaba to be condemned by the Company's court. To Zubeir, since the offence had been committed in his territory, judgment was exclusively within his competence.[141] He therefore forbade the company to have even wooding (i.e. fuelling) stations within his territory, let alone trading stations.

The Mizon expedition, promoted by leading colonial associations in France which were anxious to assert French commercial supremacy in the Benue–Congo basins, had left France on 10 August 1890 and reached Adamawa in August 1891.[142] Mizon's aim was to conclude a treaty with the Emir of Yola. 'Une convention avec l' Adamawa', he wrote, 'fermera aux Anglais et aux Allemands la route de l'intérieur de l'Afrique, du Bagirmi et du Ouaday, et même du Bornou.'[143]

The Emir of Yola, who had had previous information of Mizon's approach, was hostile to the explorer when the latter met him in council on 21 August 1891.[144] Mizon, the Emir claimed,

141. A.N.S.O.M., Afrique 3, file 14, Mizon au sous-secrétaire d'Etat aux Colonies, 18 Nov. 1893. The African agent was nicknamed 'Mai Tumbi' (i.e. man with a pouch).

142. *Ibid.* Mizon was sponsored by 'Société Française du Haut Benito' and a body under Count D'Arenberg which later became 'Comité de l'Afrique Française'.

143. A.N.S.O.M., Afrique 3, file 15a, Mizon au sous-secrétaire d'Etat aux Colonies, Yola, 1 Sept. 1891.

144. *Ibid.* Mizon Report, entry for 20 and 21 August 1891.

had come as the ally of Ḥayat b. Saʿīd, his bitterest enemy.[145] Muḥammad Meckham, an Algerian who accompanied Mizon, was made to swear ten times on the Qur'ān that he was a Muslim.[146] However, after a long debate, the Emir agreed to allow the French to trade in Yola on condition that they paid 10 per cent duties but he would not allow them to build factories on land because, as Mizon quoted him as saying: 'Si aujourd'hui il accorde une mesure de terre, demain on lui prendra l'Adamawa entier et qu' on y emmènera des soldats comme les Anglais ont fait à Lukodja à Ibi et chez les Zchehou.'[147]

The Emir of Yola grasped the full implications which contact with Europeans could have for his sovereignty. When finally he agreed to conclude a treaty with France after Arabs in Yola (successfully lobbied by Muḥammad Meckham and Al-ḥajj Maḥmūd Sherif, an Egyptian on the expedition) had pleaded for Mizon, the Emir was willing to sign only a commercial agreement.[148] Even then he postponed actual signature until Mizon must have returned to France and come back to Yola well equipped to fulfil the clauses of the commercial treaty. Mizon left Yola on 14 December 1891 and returned to France on 19 June 1892, having come by way of the Sangha and the Congo. He was to return to Yola again in 1893.

Meanwhile Yola continued her traditional policy of hostility to Europeans. In 1891 a German traveller, Lt. Morgan, coming from the Cameroons, had been attacked at Tibati on the orders of the Emir of Yola.[149] In April 1892 another explorer, Forneau, had attempted to reach Yola from the south but, owing to the hostile appearance of his expedition, he was attacked at night near Ngaundere.[150]

Anti-European feelings were mounting in Adamawa. In 1892 the hulk *René Caillé*, which Mizon had left at Yola, was attacked by the populace.[151] The Emir of Ngaundere, vassal of Yola,

145. *Ibid.* Mizon's reception by the Emir was initially decidedly hostile. The Emir refused to accept Mizon's gifts. The Fulani of Yola were also hostile. For Ḥayat see above, p. 104f.
146. *Ibid.*
147. *Ibid.* Meeting of Friday 21 August 1891 between Mizon and Emir of Yola in Council.
148. *Ibid.* Mizon Report, entry for 23 August 1891.
149. *Ibid.*
150. A.N.S.O.M., Afrique 3, 16b, Mizon to a friend, 10 March 1893.
151. A.N.S.O.M., Afrique 6, file 106g, 'Notes on Mizon's reports and

closed the route to the south and wrote to the Emir of Yola, blaming him for showing the road to one Christian who had shown it to others. De Maistre's expedition which came to Garua in February 1893, with a party of 150 soldiers and a host of carriers advancing in regular military formation had all the appearances of an invading army.[152] De Maistre hurried through Yola when the Emir was away from the town. This annoyed the Emir.

With this influx of European expeditions into Adamawa the Emir of Yola seems to have despaired of help from the French, whom by 1893 he had cause to fear by reason of their activities in Ngaundere and Tibati and possibly because of Mizon's activities in Muri. At the same time it must have been clear to him that he could not foil the designs of Europeans on his state single-handed. He therefore turned in desperation to the R.N.C. who, though traditionally his enemy, now appeared to him as the least dangerous of the European influences which were threatening to engulf his emirate.[153] In February 1893 he sent an autograph letter to 'Mai Gashi' (Wallace) appealing to the R.N.C. for protection. By this letter the whole of Adamawa was to be protected by the R.N.C. 'You are to see it [Adamawa] protected from all quarrel that may come into cause by any other powers and . . . you are allowed to build houses in any place you may think fit for your business not allowing any foreigners to come in without your consent.'[154]

However, dependence on the R.N.C. in the moment of danger did not mean a willingness on the part of the Emir to tie himself too formally to the company. Thus when Spink, an agent of the R.N.C., appeared in Yola in 1893 to sign a formal treaty with the Emir, he was not only coldly received but it was only by adroit persuasion that he was able to make the reluctant Emir sign the R.N.C.'s treaty.[155] After the treaty was signed Zubeir, anxious

their conclusions', 17 June 1893; in Ribot to Casimir Périer, 24 December 1893.

152. A. H. M. Kirk-Greene, *Adamawa Past and Present*, pp. 36–7.

153. See F.O. 27/3160, R.N.C. to F.O., 15 June 1893, the R.N.C. surmised that Zubeir must have appealed to them out of fear.

154. *Ibid.*, translation of autograph letter from Zubeir, Emir of Yola to 'Mai Gashi' (Hausa, meaning man with moustache—Mr Wallace); see quotation also in Flint, *op. cit.*, p. 177.

155. F.O. 27/3161, R.N.C. to F.O., 7 Sept. 1893, encl. Spink's report on his visit to Emir of Yola dated 30 May 1893, for the negotiations

to obviate any disruptive social, economic and political influences that the European presence might bring, outlined the conditions which must govern the operation of the new treaty. He insisted that the R.N.C. must not permit their employees to meddle with Adamawa women and those of them who stole must be punished. Runaway slaves must not be employed by the company and on no account must the company interfere with the religious principles of Islam. Further, Christianity must not be preached in Adamawa as white men were doing in Nupe.[156]

In the months subsequent to the signing of the treaty with the R.N.C.[157] a definite departure from Yola's traditional policy of keeping Europeans at arms' length is discernible. The stream of Europeans flowing into Adamawa seems to have convinced the Emir that the new phenomenon was something to be reckoned with, a potent force of change which had to be controlled. As a means of putting up with what had become unavoidable, Zubeir veered from his temporizing attitude (which had led to his invitation to the R.N.C. in February 1893) to one of an open door policy. He welcomed desirable European concession-seekers but tied them down to formal agreements which, while not conceding political rights, would prevent any single European power from becoming dominant in Adamawa.

Meanwhile Mizon had returned to the Benue at the head of an elaborately planned expedition. He had two steamers: the *Mosca* for scientific purposes and the *Sgt Mallamine*, the latter equipped by a group of French industrialists who had pooled together several hundred thousands of francs-worth of goods.[158] Although the expedition was described as peaceful it carried 150 rifles,

between Zubeir and Spink. For a fuller discussion, see Flint, *op. cit.*, p. 178.

156. *Ibid.*

157. F.O. 2/167, Treaty no. 343, 7 May 1893. The terms set out in this copy touching cession of territory 'full jurisdiction of every kind' and sole mining rights and recognition of the R.N.C. as 'authorized government of my territory' contradict Spink's report of his interview with Zubeir and the conditions the latter laid down for a treaty.

158. A.N.S.O.M., Afrique 3, file 16a, Letter of instructions to Mizon; Jamais, sous-secrétaire d'Etat aux Colonies à Mizon, 2 August 1892; also Afrique 3, file 14, Mizon au sous-secrétaire, 18 Nov. 1893. The government of France also contributed money to the Mizon Mission; see F.O. 83/1240, R.N.C. to F.O., no. 62, encl. 1, 25 May 1893; Goldie to F.O., see also Flint, p. 173.

100 revolvers, besides the personal possession of the 100 members including 25 armed escorts and 3 cannon for the defence of the expedition.[159] Previous to the 1890s in Adamawa an expedition so well armed would not have been allowed to enter. Yet, in being thus armed, the Mizon expedition was typical of European expeditions which visited Yola in 1892–93. Within those two years the number of expeditions which streamed into Adamawa from Europe had heightened the Emir's feeling of insecurity. His open-door policy just mentioned, however, meant that in practice he was not only more cautious in dealing with them, but also that he became even more firm than ever before. He tightened up his security measures. No strangers were allowed to enter Adamawa without his specific permission.[160]

In pursuance of his new open-door policy, it appears, the Emir signed the provisional treaty of 1891 with France and sent to inform Mizon of it while the latter was still in Muri in June 1893.[161] Similarly the Emir welcomed von Stetten to Adamawa in July 1893 and gave him permission for all Germans to trade in his territory.[162] Stetten, however, testified that it would need considerable force to extract a protectorate treaty from the Emir.[163]

Mizon arrived in Yola on 19 August 1893 and on the 25th the final arrangements for the French treaty with Yola were completed.[164] By the terms of the treaty, French merchants who were to establish themselves in Adamawa were to refrain from exporting grain from the country; they were to pay an impost of 10 per cent on all their transactions; and on no account were they to entertain Adamawa women on board their vessels. The French in return promised to supply the Emir with arms, and with

159. *Ibid.*
160. A.N.S.O.M., Afrique 3, 16b, Mizon to a friend, 10 March 1893.
161. A.N.S.O.M., Afrique 3, file 14, Mizon Report, enclosed in Mizon au député sous-secrétaire, 18 Nov. 1893.
162. For an account of von Stetten's expedition and activities see Tr. in *Bulletin du Comité de l'Afrique Française*, July 1895. 'Renseignements Coloniaux', Supplementary bulletin no. 3 of 1895, culled from *Deutsches Kolonial Zeitung* of 15 March and 1 April 1895.
163. *Ibid.*
164. A.N.S.O.M., Afrique 3, file 14, Mizon au député sous-secrétaire 18 Nov. 1893. Mizon Report: Mizon informed Mr Wallace and Von Uechtritz, both then in Yola, of the signature of the treaty, see also Afrique 6, file 115c, Casimir Périer to Lord Dufferin, for the letters exchanged, 9 Feb. 1894.

personnel to train his men in their use.[165] At a crowded gathering on 26 August Mizon introduced Chambredier and Senegalese instructors and presented the arms and ammunition to the Emir. The French party to be resident in Yola consisted of Muḥammad Meckham, to act as French Resident in Yola, Maḥmūd Sherif, two corporals and six Senegalese *tirailleurs* (sharp-shooters) with subalterns and auxiliaries. The French military post was set up a short distance from the Emir's palace.[166]

From Adamawa's point of view the treaty with France was advantageous because it in no way implied French supremacy over other Europeans. Nonetheless, the potential danger to Adamawa's sovereignty which the Emir's acceptance of the nucleus of a military post could mean, must not be ignored. However, such a danger, if it in fact existed, was to be rendered of no account by R.N.C.'s hostility to the French. In the week which followed the conclusion of the treaty, a motley gathering of European nationals assembled in Yola. Wallace of the R.N.C. had been there before Mizon. On 31 August, von Uechtritz and Dr Passarge arrived, to the great surprise of the Emir, who wondered why another German expedition followed so closely on the heels of von Stetten, who had left Yola on 22 August.[167] The Uechtritz–Passarge expedition was nevertheless welcomed to Yola.

At a meeting on 7 September with all the Europeans in Yola and his councillors, Zubeir explained that he had not ceded sovereignty rights to any Europeans but had merely allowed all to trade.[168] Wallace declined to attend another meeting which was held on the 13th with the Emir. He was prevented from carrying out a threat to attack the *Sgt Mallamine* by the Emir, who warned that such an action would be considered by him as a hostile act towards himself.[169]

165. A.N.S.O.M., Afrique 3, file 14, Mizon au député sous-secrétaire 18 Nov. 1893, Report.
166. A.N.S.O.M., Afrique 3, file 14, Mizon au député sous-secrétaire, Report, 18 Nov. 1893.
167. *Ibid.*, entry for 31 August (extract from his diary), Mizon recorded that Zubeir feared that the numerous escorts of the expedition would have hostile designs against his territory; also A. H. M. Kirk-Greene, 'Von Uechtritz's expedition to Adamawa 1893', *J.H.S.N.*, I, no. 2 (1957), pp. 91–2.
168. *Ibid.*
169. A.N.S.O.M., Afrique 6, file 115c, Casimir Périer to Lord Dufferin, 9 Feb. 1894.

Mizon left Yola on 22 September. No sooner had he left than Wallace seized the *Sgt Mallamine*, giving the Emir to understand that he was acting on instructions from the French government. The two French trading stations in Muri had meanwhile been seized by the R.N.C. At Lokoja Mizon's ship, the *Mosca*, was also seized by the R.N.C. Almost before Mizon had quit the Niger territories the R.N.C. had destroyed the foundations of French influence which he had laid on the Benue.[170] In the first place it was the R.N.C. working through the British Foreign Office who had, through a devious diplomacy in which lying was freely employed, constrained the French government to recall Mizon from the Benue.[171] After Mizon's departure the R.N.C. went to work with a vigilant will. According to the Governor of Dahomey, by bribing the Emir and his councillors, by cajoling and intimidating members of the French post at Yola and by other underhand means, the R.N.C. succeeded in persuading the Emir of Yola to agree to repatriate the French Resident, Muḥammad Meckham, in October 1895.[172]

So far as controlling the Europeans in his territory was concerned, the Emir of Yola had been remarkably successful. But the real forces which were to decide the future of his emirate lay beyond his control. No sooner had the R.N.C. signed the 1893 treaty with the Emir than it entered into an agreement with Germany, by which both countries divided Adamawa between themselves, seven-eighths of it going to Germany, with the German boundary coming very close to Yola.[173] The provisions of the Anglo–German treaty by which the signatories promised to maintain the allegiance of the subjects of their respective spheres to the Emir of Yola and at the same time to prevent chiefs in one sphere meddling in the affairs of the other were, to say the least, impractical and hypocritical. This Anglo–German partition sealed the fate of Adamawa.

. . .

170. *Ibid.*, for R.N.C. attack on the remnants of the Mizon expedition at Yola.

171. F.O. 27/3160, R.N.C. to F.O., 24 June 1893, 28 June 1893, 4, 5 and 17 July 1893, Goldie to Curie and 6 July 1893, for efforts of the R.N.C. to get Mizon recalled from the Benue.

172. A.N.S.O.M., Afrique 3, file 16e, Gouverneur du Dahomey au sous-secrétaire d'Etat aux Colonies, 23 Oct. 1895.

173. For full text see Hertslet, *op. cit.*, vol. iii, p. 914 f.; for a discussion of the treaty, see Flint, *op. cit.*, pp. 179–84.

In the period before 1900 it was external forces of this nature that mattered more in the history of the European takeover of the Sokoto Caliphate than immediate threat from Europeans on the spot. What the history of the Caliphate's nineteenth-century contact with Europeans illustrates is the consistent jealous regard of the rulers for their independence and their confidence (borne out by experience) that they could always keep the intruding Europeans within their proper bounds.

SOKOTO–R.N.C. RELATIONS, 1890–94

From 1890 the position of the R.N.C. was being seriously challenged by the French on the Benue. Furthermore, the nature of concessions granted it by Sokoto had become the subject of much animated controversy and doubt in the chancelleries of France and Germany. It therefore became essential for the company to obtain more far-reaching concessions from Sokoto than the Thomson treaty of 1885 gave it. This necessity was made even more urgent by the conflicting interpretations of the Say–Barua line agreement of 5 August 1890.

It appears, however, that the R.N.C. did not feel confident of being able to secure the concessions from Sokoto that would finally validate its claims to the Caliphate. It was alleged by Mizon that Sokoto had refused the annual tribute sent by the R.N.C. for 1890–91.[174] Early in 1890 the company, as Flint aptly remarks,[175] took the unusual step of sending an African political agent instead of a high-ranking European official (as would be expected), to Sokoto with the important assignment of concluding a new treaty with the Caliph, which would put its (R.N.C.) claims beyond doubt.

At Wurno on 1 April, the Wazir, Muḥammad Bukhārī, conveyed to Mr A. King, the R.N.C.'s political agent, the Caliph's order that he must leave Wurno the following day.[176] This was

174. Allegation made by Mizon on information collected from a man who claimed to have received a letter to that effect from the Emir of Bida, see Afrique 3, 16b, Mizon Report, entry 14 Oct. for Loko.
175. Flint, *op. cit.*, p. 162.
176. N.A.K. LOKOPROF, L.O.K. file 22, R.N.C. Court Record Book; King's Evidence before W. P. Hewby, District Agent, in David King versus Richard E. Stevens, a steward who served under King during the Sokoto expedition, 24 July 1890.

after King had waited there patiently but fruitlessly for ten days. Two hours before the expulsion order, the Wazir had expressed disgust at the behaviour of members of King's mission towards Wurno women.[177] He was allowed however to go to Gwandu. Most of his carriers refused to go to Gwandu with him on account of reports which reached them that the road to Gwandu was closed because it was fraught with danger.[178]

King alleged that he concluded a treaty with Gwandu on 7 April, by which the Emir granted to the company monopoly rights of trade and 'full and complete power and jurisdiction' over all foreigners in his domains. King returned to Sokoto where, he claimed, he concluded with the Caliph a treaty identical with that of Gwandu.[179]

The King treaties of 1890 were clearly forgeries.[180] It is difficult to believe that after having been summarily expelled from Wurno, King returned there and within a couple of days concluded with the Caliph a treaty which he had earlier failed to obtain in ten days. The untoward circumstances which faced the mission at Wurno and the fact that English versions of the treaty indicate that it did not bear the Caliph's seal must be seen as confirmation that King did not sign any treaty there. Even the ordinary letters emanating from the Sokoto court all bore the Caliph's seal. It was their authenticating mark. The Gwandu Treaty also bore no Gwandu signatures.

It was clear that Sokoto would not grant to Europeans any but commercial concessions excluding monopoly rights. Col. Monteil who arrived in Sokoto on 18 October 1891 could only obtain from the Caliph commercial concessions which allowed French traders to enter the Caliphate as protected persons.[181] Monteil reported that the R.N.C. had no treaty with Sokoto beyond a mere commercial grant. Besides this assertion by Monteil, the R.N.C. was harassed by Mizon in Adamawa and Muri and it was also faced with the refusal of the Emirs of those places to give it preferential treatment. In addition the company had to reckon

177. *Ibid.*
178. *Ibid.*
179. F.O. 84/2171, copy of English version of the Sokoto Treaty of 1890, identical with Gwandu treaty; see also Flint, *op. cit.*, pp. 162–3.
180. See Flint, *op. cit.*, p. 163, for identical view.
181. A.N.S.O.M., Traités 12, p. 17, for copy of the French version, Monteil's treaty, ratified by the French government decree of 1 March 1895.

with the hostility of Nupe. In view of these facts the R.N.C.'s claims to the Caliphate were shown in a very poor light in Europe.

The easiest way out for the Company was to show the originals of its treaties to the unbelieving French and German governments, to persuade them to call off their rivalry with the British over the Caliphate. Such a step was never taken; in all probability because an exhibition of the originals might have done greater harm still to British claims.

To obtain a formal statement from the Caliph on what transpired between him and Monteil as well as an assurance that he did not deny the 'validity of his treaties with us' the R.N.C. despatched Wallace to Sokoto in February 1894.[182] Wallace was also to obtain from Sokoto and Gwandu properly attested documents as to the real extent of the Caliphate.[183] The R.N.C. was taking no chances. The Wallace expedition was armed with a letter of introduction to the Caliph in imitation of Monteil who had carried similar letters from the President of France to Sokoto.

Wallace returned with two identical treaties dated 26 June and 4 July 1894, purported to have been signed with Sokoto and Gwandu respectively.[184] By these treaties Sokoto and Gwandu were alleged to have confirmed their 1885 and even 1890 treaties with the R.N.C.! Apart from 'rights in perpetuity' over all foreigners and the right of 'just taxation', the R.N.C. was purported to have been granted all mining rights, but not monopoly of trade. Sokoto and Gwandu were alleged to have acknowledged that the Company was acting on behalf of the Queen of England. Gwandu was reported to have claimed that Ilọrin and the country of Gurma, extending as far as Liptako, belonged to him while Sokoto allegedly claimed influence as far north as 'Air and Asben'. It will be noted that Gurma had since the mid-century ceased to be effectively held by Gwandu, while Air and Asben refer to the same country and Sokoto would clearly have known this.

182. F.O. 83/1243, Immediate, Goldie to F.O., 18 Nov. 1893; also note (dated 18 Nov. 1893) to above letter, Goldie stressing the urgency of the situation wrote 'France and time wait for no man'.
183. F.O. 83/1244, Goldie to F.O., 28 Dec. 1893.
184. Hertslet, vol. i, p. 155 for copy of Wallace's treaty with Gwandu. The Sokoto treaty is not included in Hertslet's collection.

Exactly what transpired between Wallace, the Caliph and the Emir of Gwandu may never be known, but there are strong grounds for entertaining the most serious doubts about the authenticity of the treaty. From the literal translation of the Arabic original made by Charles Wells of Cambridge University in 1898, it is deducible that the treaty did not emanate from the Sokoto Chancery. Contrary to the bold hand of the Sokoto official scribe of the period, Wells complained of the illegibility of the characters, which seem to have been tiny.[185] It is suspicious that Wallace, charged with obtaining well-attested documents, came away with a treaty with Sokoto which did not bear the Caliph's seal. Extant copies of the English translation of this treaty indicate only that they bore Arabic signatures of people whose names are not mentioned.[186] Furthermore, the hostile attitude of Sokoto to foreign powers by 1894[187] would explain the Caliph's unwillingness to accept an R.N.C. treaty involving any far-reaching commitments.

The doubts surrounding the authenticity of the 1894 treaties were as good as confirmed by Goldie at the death of Wallace in 1924. In discussing proposals for writing Wallace's biography for the *Dictionary of National Biography*, Goldie had suggested that Wallace's trip to Sokoto and Gwandu in 1894 was the most important event to mention in his honour. 'I cannot,' Goldie wrote, 'think of any other incident to mention, more worthy of Wallace's real work.'[188] But in the end Goldie wrote Wallace's biography without any mention of the 1894 Sokoto mission because, as he said: 'On consideration, I have not been able to refer to Wallace's visit to Sokoto and Gwandu—a fiasco, the only one we had during 20 years of work. The story is a long and complicated one.'[189]

185. C.O. 537/16, C. Wells to C.O., 11 March 1898, the 'b' of what Wells guessed was Asben, he said, could hardly be deciphered under a microscope!
186. It was by the Caliph's seal and not by signatures that Sokoto documents were authenticated. Flint, *op. cit.*, p. 220, mentions that the R.N.C. claimed that the treaty bore the Caliph's seal. However, no reference is made to any Seal in Charles Wells's translation from the Arabic. If the treaty was sealed, then the Arabic signatures would have been unnecessary.
187. See below, p. 165 ff.
188. R.H.B.E., Africa S.101, Goldie to Scarborough, 3 Dec. 1924.
189. R.H.B.E., Africa S.101, Goldie to Scarborough, 28 Dec. 1924.

Goldie's revelation not only suggests that Wallace failed to obtain the alleged treaties from Sokoto but also that in all probability he did not receive a good welcome there.[190] Indeed, owing probably to the increasing number of visiting Europeans now coming from all sides and their obvious desire to interfere in the affairs of the territories of the Caliphate, the traditional suspicion of Europeans entertained by Sokoto and its emirates changed into active resentment and greater vigilance to have the minimum contact with them. The Caliphate was prepared to have intercourse with foreigners provided they knew their place and confined themselves to trade.

The period 1880–94 witnessed a growth in European establishments within the Caliphate, especially on the Niger–Benue banks. The growth of commerce which went side by side with increasing European trading establishments was of doubtless advantage to the African rulers to whom it brought rich profits. Even though European interference, or desire to interfere, in the government of the African communities was increasing, it appears that the African rulers did not usually deem it necessary to expel them. In this connection it must be noted that for the emirates arbitrarily to expel the Europeans would be cutting off the nose to spite the face. They depended on these Europeans for supply of firearms and ammunition, which they needed badly to deal with problems of military insecurity (discussed in the previous chapters) occasioned by the hostility of pocket enemy states within their frontiers. In fact, there was no need to. With the Muslim emirates such as Ilọrin, Nupe, Muri and Adamawa whenever Europeans exceeded their bounds or essayed to do so, it had not been too difficult to check their excesses either by direct threat of using force or by exploiting the intra-European rivalry.

Another important factor in this era of trade and treaties, and one which remained substantially unchanged up to the fall of the Caliphate, was the fact that as each emirate had entered into treaty relations unilaterally with Europeans, the problems which arose from the relations were seen by each as peculiar to itself

190. F.O. 83/1380, Extract from Goldie's speech to R.N.C. annual meeting, 19 July 1895. Goldie stated that Wallace was also expected to settle 'some questions that had arisen regarding Nupe, Adamawa, Muri and Zaria'.

and therefore treated in isolation from the others in the same way as each had handled its defence and security problems throughout the century.

Beyond granting to Europeans permission to trade the Caliph did not evolve an elaborate policy towards them. This was not called for, in any case, because the European traders were few and their activities were confined almost exclusively to the Niger–Benue waterways. Over the greater part of the Caliphate Europeans had never been seen until the conquest. The problem raised by contact with Europeans did not become general until their wars of conquest. Although suspect, up to 1894 they were not seen as being sufficiently powerful to constitute an obvious insurmountable danger to the Caliphate.

Even on the Niger–Benue, the R.N.C. (the most powerful European group) had in 1889 a constabulary of only five English officers, two African officers, two sergeant-majors, fifteen sergeants, sixteen corporals and 380 privates; 150 soldiers were stationed in Lokoja and 50 at Ibi.[191] With this weak force the R.N.C. was not in a position, nor did it ever attempt, to resort to force against the Muslim emirates, with the exception of Jibu in Muri. The company's activities in Jibu had led to its expulsion from Muri territory (1891), except for its military post at Ibi.

In most European trading stations along the Niger–Benue, African agents from the lower rungs of the company's service were in charge. The widespread presence of trading stations did not indicate a similar distribution of European personnel. In all, during the period 1880–94, the rulers of the Caliphate in regular contact with Europeans had proved themselves masters in their own house against European interference. It had usually been possible to keep conflict short of armed clash because the Europeans had set themselves to avoid war. The R.N.C. policy, as stated by Goldie, aptly sums up the factor that staved off war. He wrote: 'We have by subsidies, diplomacy, and timely exhibition of force deferred the day of conflict with the Felattah power and we shall continue this policy as long as possible.'[192]

191. F.O. 84/2109, Macdonald Report, Ch. 6.
192. F.O. 83/1239, Goldie to Anderson, 4 May 1893.

Chapter 6
Encirclement, diplomacy and hostility, 1894-1899

The last decade of the nineteenth century, part of which is discussed in this chapter, may be described as 'a decade of troubles' for the Sokoto Caliphate. True, the Caliphate had been thoroughly consolidated long before then. But, as already shown, the problem of security against traditional enemies both within and without its external frontiers, though no longer a problem of survival, was still a factor to be constantly reckoned with. The Caliphate of 'Abd al-Raḥmān (1891–1902) was beset with several problems of internal security. In this connection the fierce war with Kebbi in 1891, the Mafara and the Tukur revolts, the activities of Ḥayat in Adamawa and of Jibrīl Gaini in the Bauchi–Gombe region, Kwassau's succession in Zaria in 1897 and the Galadiman Ako revolt will be readily recalled. Although these problems, with the exception of the Jibrīl Gaini revolt, were successfully resolved, their existence meant that they, rather than the threat of foreign invasion, constituted the urgent problems facing the Caliphate.

A handful of European traders in the riverain regions of the Niger–Benue waterways, a small garrison of the R.N.C. Constabulary at Lokoja and Ibi respectively, and occasional European visitors to Sokoto and Gwandu requesting commercial concessions—these were, no doubt, seen as people to be closely watched; a potential but not an immediate source of danger.

Indeed, the French wars with Dahomey, German activities on the Togo coast and the French conquest of Segu, may have sent strange stories along the trade routes. These events were probably disturbing to the Caliphate, but as they took place far away from it they could not have been considered an immediate threat. Furthermore, even before the 1890s, the Caliphate, connected with the outside Muslim world by the trans-Saharan caravan routes used by foreign merchants and native pilgrims alike, must have known about European colonization of Muslim countries in North Africa and in the Eastern Sudan. This knowledge had not produced a feeling of immediate danger in the Caliphate. But the Caliphate had clearly taken warning from these events; hence the resistance of its rulers, so far, to European treaties aimed at acquisition of sovereignty powers.

However, as the Europeans began to penetrate inland from their coastal and river bases with an increase in the number and frequency of expeditions sent by them into the interior in the 1890s, apprehension occasioned by reports of their activities in neighbouring states counselled increasing vigilance and firmness on the part of the Caliph and his emirs in dealing with those of them who actually entered the Caliphate. With the mounting tension between Europeans and Nupe from 1890 and the influx of European expeditions into Yola from that year, the foreign threat, though not yet a matter of life and death for the Caliphate, had become a serious factor.

It must be noted that up to 1894, and indeed thereafter, the initiative in the Caliphate–European relations rested with the Europeans. The role of the Caliph and his emirs was limited to reacting to moves by Europeans as the latter gradually, and from place to place, pursued their ambition to deprive the Caliphate of its sovereignty. In this respect, increasing vigilance, characterized more than ever before by extreme caution but greater firmness, can be observed in the attitude of the Caliph and his emirs to European infiltration from about 1894. The traditional suspicion in which Europeans had hitherto been held changed thereafter into an open distrust and mounting hostility to their penetration.

The genesis of this change can be seen in the hardening attitude of Nupe, Ilọrin, Muri and Adamawa, discussed in the previous chapter. It is also clear from what can be inferred from the reception which one may reasonably suspect was accorded to the R.N.C. treaty-signing mission to Sokoto and Gwandu in 1890 and 1894 that the Caliph and the Emir of Gwandu had become disenchanted, at least with the R.N.C., if not with all Europeans. As the 1890s wore on the threat of European invasion of the Caliphate became more and more real.

No doubt the cause of the change in attitude to Europeans within the Caliphate is to be found, as hinted above, partly in the increased vehemence with which rivalry over the Caliphate and its neighbouring territories, between the British, French and Germans, was prosecuted on the spot in the years after 1890. The

Yola example well illustrates this phenomenon. Further, the area of conflict between Europeans was from 1890 no longer confined to the Niger–Benue waterways.

Consequent on the conclusion of the Say–Barua line agreement in 1890, and the conflicting interpretations put on it by the British and the French, the area to the north and south of the line became the subject of animated dispute between the two nations. This dispute was marked by the sending out of several expeditions from both nations to the Niger bend, the countries immediately to the north of Sokoto, the northern frontier emirates of the Caliphate and the Chad region. Germany, whose efforts had hitherto been directed towards establishing a strong hold on the hinterland of the Cameroons as far as the Chad, also challenged British claims to the Gwandu emirates in a bid to expand to the interior from her base in Togo.

Direct confrontation between the numerous expeditions of the contesting powers within the Caliphate or close to its frontiers served to deepen the traditional suspicion with which Europeans were regarded. It was not only the increasing number of these expeditions that excited the suspicion as well as the fear and open hostility of the local populations, but also the fact that these expeditions no longer comprised just one or two Europeans and a few carriers but a military escort as well and, consequently, more numerous carriers. From about 1894 the European expeditions approached the Caliphate from all directions.

The rulers of the Caliphate were, of course, ignorant of the various treaties by which the Western Sudan and other parts of Africa had been divided into spheres of influence among European powers. Thus they could not have known that by the Say–Barua line agreement of 1890, the Sokoto Caliphate had been assigned to the British. Moreover, the inter-European rivalry over the Caliphate subsequent to this agreement did not give the impression that the Caliphate had only one European power to deal with as an enemy. From about 1894 most frontier emirates had become aware of the approach of European expeditions. While this fact and the fear of external aggression arising therefrom may not have generated a common feeling of encirclement, there can be no doubting the practical consequence for the Caliphate as a whole: it was being gradually surrounded by European powers.

The attitude of the Caliph and his emirs was thenceforth

conditioned, or in fact determined, by the threat of European rivalries within or close to their domains. An aspect of such rivalries was that each European power involved stepped up its efforts to ingratiate itself more thoroughly with African rulers through treaty relations as a means of guaranteeing its respective territorial claims against the challenge of the other interested powers. This in turn aggravated the disputes among the different European nationals within and close to the Caliphate, and encouraged hostility among the African rulers to European penetration of their territories.

The European scramble for the Caliphate was at its fiercest between 1894 and 1899. In these circumstances, there developed a highly tangled and many-sided diplomatic situation, with a logic and a dynamic of its own, which determined the policies and the varying tactics of not only the European contestants but also of the Caliph and his emirs. Each of the parties involved shifted its diplomatic position, often with unpredictable rapidity, according to whether or not it understood the objectives behind the actions of the other contestants. Events on one frontier of the Caliphate produced repercussions on the others. Each participant group had to keep a watchful eye on events on all frontiers to enable it to revise its policies and intensify its efforts in pursuit of the desired objectives. Of all the groups caught up in this struggle, the Caliphate, by reason of its inability to gain knowledge of the inter-European diplomacy attendant on the situation, was the least capable of appraising the events happening around it in such a way as to maximize its chances of success. Though now extremely suspicious and cautious, it showed hostility or 'friendship' according to its judgment as to which Europeans seemed, at any particular time, the most imminent source of danger. This judgment was not always correct.

The already difficult diplomatic situation in which the Caliphate found itself by 1894 was further complicated by two other factors which rendered its encirclement more apparent and served to exacerbate its antagonism to all intruding foreign powers. The French conquest of Segu (1890–91)[1] and some of the repercussions of that event confirmed existing fears of European penetration, while the advent of Rābiḥ Faḍlallāh to Bornu in 1893 from the Eastern Sudan distracted the full attention which

1. See B. O. Ọlọruntimẹhin, 'The Segu Tukulor Empire: 1848–1893' (unpublished Ph.D. thesis, University of Ibadan, 1966), ch. 8.

the Caliph and many emirs might have paid to the European threat. It was the interaction between all the foregoing factors, from one frontier of the Caliphate to another, that paralysed whatever potential the Caliphate possessed to deal, perhaps in a different way, with the European invasion to which it ultimately succumbed during the first few years of the present century. Only through a chronological rather than an episodic treatment can these interactions be brought out. In this connection, three phases 1894–95, 1895–97 and 1897–99, can be discerned.

UNSETTLING NEWS, 1894–95

By 1894 news of the conquest of the Segu–Tukulor Empire as well as the eastward advance of French troops from Segu had been confirmed in the Sokoto Caliphate. At the same time, Bornu lay prostrate at the feet of Rābiḥ Faḍlallāh. Between 1894 and 1895 French and British expeditions were engaged in such a fierce rivalry over Borgu in a manner that could not have failed to attract the uneasy attention of neighbouring emirates. Never before had the Caliphate received such potent warnings of foreign invasion.

Following the overthrow of the Tukulor Empire by the French, its Caliph, Amīr al-mu'minīn Aḥmad b. Shaikh 'Umar b. Sa'īd, fled eastwards with a large party, his intention being to go to Mecca.[2] The pursuit of the fugitive party by French troops caused fear among the local populations along their routes. In 1893 the people of Timbuktu were so frightened that they sent a delegation to the Sultan of Morocco complaining about French troops.[3]

No doubt the party of Amīr al-mu'minīn Aḥmad spread the news of the danger which French penetration carried with it.[4]

2. A.N.S.O.M., Soudan I, files 1c and 5a; for French pursuit of Aḥmad b. Shaikh 'Umar. For his intention to go to Mecca, see N.A.K. KAD-CAPTORY, Box 43, item 7; photocopy of Biography of Aḥmad b. Shaikh 'Umar b. Sa'īd, by an anonymous *Ṭālib* collected by Viellard in Macina in 1942.
3. *Bulletin du Comité de l'Afrique Française*, April 1894, p. 23.
4. Besides Aḥmad's biography *loc. cit.*, which gives the route of flight, see Jean Perié and Michel Sellier, 'Histoire des populations du Cercle de Dosso', *Bulletin de l'IFAN*, xii (1950), pp. 1016–72, for a description of Aḥmad's flight.

The news may have reached Sokoto earlier than 1894, but in that year the messengers of Aḥmad b. Shaikh ʿUmar actually arrived at Sokoto.[5] Aḥmad's party was then established in the region of Say, where they constituted a barrier to European penetration. On their way back from their visit to Sokoto in 1894, Wallace and his companion, Tead, had wanted to go to Say but their canoemen refused to go so far because, as they said, some 'fanatics' driven from Masina by the French (Aḥmad and his followers) were in Say and had vowed to kill any white man they saw.[6] The overthrow of Aḥmad's empire and his flight was an object lesson to the peoples of the West-Central Sudan as to what could be the ultimate result of their relations with Europeans.

From about December 1893 Rābiḥ Faḍlallāh began the conquest of Bornu. Originally in the service of Zubeir Pasha in the Eastern Sudan, he had fought against Romolo Gessi, commander of Egyptian forces in the Sudan. In 1878 Gessi had planned to lure the remnants of Zubeir's army into a trap with a view to exterminate them. But Rābiḥ had escaped the treachery with a body of Negro troops loyal to him. Thereafter he had fought his way, building up the strength and the discipline of his army at the same time, through Dār-Sila, Dār-Runga, Wadai, Dār-Kuti and Baghirmi, conquering the latter place in 1893. His troops, well equipped with firearms, were efficiently drilled. Having been implicated in the massacre of a French expedition led by Crampel in 1891, he had usefully augmented his supply of arms and ammunition from the expedition's stock.[7] In addition he forced six captured members of the expedition to help train his army.[8] Rābiḥ became stronger and stronger as he advanced westwards.[9]

5. F.O. 2/118, Diary of a journey from Cairo to Lokoja, *c.* 1893–95 by Sherif Hassan (messenger of the Egyptian government).
6. R.H.B.E., Africa S.95, Lugard Diaries, p. 26, 29 Aug. 1894.
7. F.O. 101/86, Jago to F.O., 10 April 1896, encl. Statement by Ḥajj Arfan (who had lived in Dikwa from 1891–95). Rābiḥ is said to have seized 150 martini rifles from the Crampel expedition. On the whole, it was estimated that Rābiḥ had about 370 Martini and Winchester rifles, and 2500 double-barrelled fowling pieces, besides numerous swords. See also E. Gentil, *La Chute de l'Empire de Rabeh* (Paris, 1902). Gentil recorded that Rābiḥ inherited 300 rifles from the Crampel expedition.
8. F.O. 101/86, Jago to F.O., 10 April 1896, encl. statement by Ḥajj Arfan.
9. For an account of Rābiḥ's movements from the Sudan to Bornu see (i) William Everett, 'A Short History of Rābiḥ Zubeir' (Secret), C.O. 537/11 Africa, no. 2, 19 Dec. 1898, written for the I.D.W.O.;

In 1893 he had a formidable army at his disposal, with a dazzling record of victories behind it.

Rābiḥ's army was further reinforced by forces under Ḥayat b. Saʿīd who, on hearing of his approach, had left Adamawa with his lieutenants, Yūsuf Babikīr al-Mandarawī and Muḥammad al-Amīn al-Mallawī, to meet him at Logone.[10] Ḥayat and his men joined Rābiḥ because they learnt that he was a Madhist.[11] The activities of Ḥayat and his supporters had already alienated the Sokoto Caliphate and Bornu who had both rejected the Mahdī's invitation to follow him.[12]

Not only therefore did the league between Ḥayat and Rābiḥ mark out the latter as an enemy of the Caliphate but his continued conquests in Bornu showed clearly that he was to be dreaded. Although he had acknowledged the Mahdī of the Eastern Sudan, fought under a Mahdist flag and clothed his soldiers in Mahdist dress,[13] he eschewed any formal relations with the *Khalīfa* (successor) of the Eastern Sudan Mahdī.[14] His alliance with Ḥayat from 1893 raised the whole question of the legitimacy of the Sokoto Caliphate which was openly hostile to the Eastern Sudan Mahdī and his followers. The Caliphate must have viewed the Rābiḥ–Ḥayat alliance with particular apprehension.

The rapid conquest of Bornu, the sack of Kukawa,[15] followed by political upheaval involving first the flight of Hashimi (the Shehu of Bornu) to Zinder and then by his assassination and the execution shortly afterwards on Rābiḥ's orders of Kiari, his successor, created panic in the Caliphate and neighbouring

(ii) N.A.K. KADCAPTORY, Box 77, *Labarin Rabeh* in ʿ*ajami* Hausa script —anonymous; (iii) M. Gaudefroy-Demonbynes: *Rabeh et les Arabes du Chari* (Paris, 1905).

10. N.A.K. KADCAPTORY, Box 38, item 10, Yūsuf Babikir al-Mandarawī to *Khalīfa* ʿAbdullāh (*c.* 1898).
11. N.A.K. KADCAPTORY, Yūsuf Babikir to *Khalīfa* ʿAbdullāh; also F.O. 101/84, 19 July 1898, *loc. cit.*, Alvarez to F.O., Africa no. 5, encl. translation of an Arabic letter from Waday.
12. See above, pp. 104, 106–7; also Muḥammad al-Ḥajj and S. Biobaku, 'The Sudanese Mahdiyya and the Niger-Chad Region', in I. M. Lewis, ed., *Islam in Tropical Africa* (Oxford, 1966), p. 435.
13. C.O. 537/11, William Everett, *op. cit.*, p. 7, statement by Ḥajj Arfan.
14. Muḥammad al-Ḥajj and Biobaku, p. 434.
15. F.O. 101/84, Africa no. 7, Alvarez to F.O., 3 April 1894. Rābiḥ's first victory against Muḥammad Tahir, Shehu Hashimi's general, seems to have taken place in Dec. 1893.

countries. Rābiḥ was reported to have sent threatening messages in 1894 demanding submission to himself from the Emir of Katagum and the Sultan of Zinder.[16] During the same year, the air was thick with rumours that Rābiḥ intended to march on Kano. In fact Baron von Uechtritz and Dr Passarge, coming from Adamawa to the Chad region early in 1894, were forced to turn back by rumours that the Mahdist had taken Kano and Sokoto.[17]

What should be stressed from all the foregoing is not the correctness or otherwise of the rumours but the psychological fear which agitated parts of the Caliphate as a result of the nearness of Rābiḥ. To the threat posed by foreign invaders was added the Caliphate's preoccupation with the Tukur revolt of 1893–95.[18] From about 1894 the erstwhile friendly, if guarded, trust accorded to outsiders was evaporating fast and was being replaced by hostility and unwillingness to negotiate.

The details and diplomatic exchanges in the course of the Anglo–French rivalry in the Niger-bend and Borgu are of no direct relevance to this study. The number of European expeditions accompanied by large numbers of armed escorts and carriers was, however, of direct significance to the African populations of those regions and their neighbours who must have viewed them with uneasiness. Whereas for the Caliph and his emirs the rape of Segu by the French was an event which took place relatively far away, the frequent visits, in large numbers, of French and other European expeditions to the Niger-bend and Borgu on the frontiers of the Caliphate must have caused them considerable anxiety.

Besides the famous 'race to Nikki' between Major F. D. Lugard on behalf of the British, and Capt. DeCœur, sent by the French government, in 1894,[19] numerous expeditions, mainly French, followed hot on their footsteps. Alby reached Nikki only a few days after DeCœur. In December 1894 Ballot, the French governor of Dahomey, travelled extensively in Borgu, going as

16. F.O. 2/118, Sherif Hassan's diary. According to Sherif Hassan the Emir of Zinder sent Rābiḥ's messengers back with loads of valued gifts to placate Rābiḥ.
17. F.O. 83/1131. Report by Major Ewart (of I.D.W.O.) of interview with Uechtritz and Passarge, 4 May 1894.
18. See above, p. 97 f.
19. See Margery Perham, *Lugard: The Years of Adventure* (London, 1956), pp. 491 ff. For a different view see J. E. Flint, *Sir George Goldie and the Making of Nigeria* (Oxford, 1960), pp. 222–30.

far as Bussa.[20] From late 1894 to early 1895 Lts. Vergoz and Baud, Frenchmen, came as far as Dendi via Say.

The Anglo–French rivalry in the Niger-bend reached its peak in 1895, with the arrival of Lt. Toutée in Borgu. His instructions were to extend French relations with the populations of the middle Niger 'principalement dans les régions où les efforts de nos voisins Anglais et Allemands tendrent à nous devancer'.[21] He signed a treaty with Yauri on 6 January 1895 and with many places along the Niger banks. Opposite an R.N.C. trading post at Bajibo (in Nupeland) he established a French post—Fort D'Arenberg. Toutée left behind him twenty-five soldiers to hold fort D'Arenberg against British opposition.[22]

Besides arousing the fears and mistrust of the local populations, the Anglo–French confrontation in Borgu and north-western Nupe had the effect of compelling the R.N.C. to assert its claims to the Sokoto Caliphate more effectively by adopting a forward policy from 1895 to 1897. The rivalry set off a chain reaction. Both the Caliphate and the French reacted positively to R.N.C. forward policy while this counter-reaction in turn determined British policy to the Caliphate after 1897.

In the meantime, in 1895, a German expedition under Dr Gruner did actually reach Gwandu and attempted to sign a treaty with the Emir. Above all others, this expedition, armed with 90 carbines and 27,000 rounds of ammunition, was bound to frighten the local populations and was a warning of the hostile intentions of Europeans towards them.[23] Starting from Lome on

20. A.N.S.O.M., Afrique 6, file 133, 'Notes sur la délimitation du Niger' by Binger, being a summary of French expeditions to the middle Niger; also file 133b, 'Etude sur les missions Européennes dans la boucle du Niger et sur les négotiations rélatives au partage', by Camille Guy.
21. A.N.S.O.M., Soudan 3, file 2, Ministre de Colonies to Capt. Toutée, 17 Nov. 1894, 'Instructions politiques'.
22. Camille Guy, 'Etude sur les missions Européennes . . .' *loc. cit.*
23. My account of Gruner's expedition is based mainly on W. Markov and P. Sebald 'The Treaty between Germany and the Sultan of Gwandu', *J.H.S.N.* iv, no. 1 (1967), pp. 141–53. The article is based on documents from the former German Imperial Colonial Office and the German Society documents in the Central archives at Potsdam (head RKA). The route and account of rivalry between the Dr Gruner and DeCœur expeditions can be followed in *Bulletin du Comité*, July 1895, p. 21 (culled from the Gazette of Cologne), and translation of extracts from *Nord Deutsche Zeitung* of 8 Oct. 1895, in A.N.S.O.M., Afrique 6, file 127a.

27 November 1894, it reached Gwandu (via Bikini, Boti, Karimama, Say, Illo) in April 1895. It obtained written declarations in Arabic from the towns mentioned, either by persuasion or by military demonstration, to the effect that they were tributary to Gwandu. According to the expedition ʿUmar Bakatara, the Emir of Gwandu, signed the proposed treaty (previously drafted in Germany) after due consultation with his council and after several words in the treaty, which had been drawn up in Arabic, had been explained to the satisfaction of his Qāḍī.

Markov and Sebald have shown convincingly that the Arabic signatures on the Gwandu treaty were forged. Far from signing the German treaty, the Emir of Gwandu had written a letter to the German Emperor on the back of the German treaty, in which he stated emphatically that he would not sign a treaty with Germany as demanded. 'We shall make no compact with you about anything because what you say cannot be possible between us and you.'[24] In the letter the Emir warned that German traders entering his territory after receiving his letter would not be granted safe conduct (*amān*). After an emphatic statement, that Germans who persisted in entering Gwandu territories would be doing so at their own risk, the letter ends tersely with a reiteration of the Emir's refusal to sign a treaty and an oath that he would abide by what he had written.

The proposed German treaty had asked for permission to trade and for Gwandu to treat with foreign nations with the consent of the German government. Germany promised to protect Gwandu against all its enemies, keep a representative with the Emir as a token of friendship but not to interfere in Gwandu's internal affairs.[25] The treaty demanded no more than R.N.C.'s professed treaties with Sokoto and Gwandu. The Emir's outright rejection of all the clauses and the terse manner in which he did so reflect his firm determination to ward off European infiltration. It seems that the Gruner expedition was considered as the *avant garde* of the same European forces which had overthrown the empire of Amīr al-mu'minīn Aḥmad of Segu.[26]

24. Markov and Sebald, *loc. cit.*, Appendix, photocopy of Emir of Gwandu's letter. The Emir of Gwandu referred to himself in this letter as *Amīr aqalīm al-gharb al-Fallatiyya wa'l-Sudānīyya*.
25. *Ibid.*
26. R.H.B.E., Africa S.101, vol. 18, Walter Watts to R.N.C. 10 Nov. 1895. Watts had been told in Bida by messengers of the Emir of Gwandu who came for the installation of the Emir of Bida, Abubakar,

The hostile military demonstrations with which Gruner blazed his way from Togo to Gwandu could only have strengthened this impression. In Sokoto and Gwandu Europeans in general were by 1895 discredited as friends. They were, in addition, dreaded. This period was clearly one of emergency for the Caliphate.

Fully aware of the attitude of Sokoto and Gwandu, the R.N.C. adopted a policy of soft-pedalling towards them after 1894, while at the same time it was secretly preparing hard for a military showdown with Nupe and Iḷorin. Thus, among foreign powers which encircled the Caliphate, the R.N.C. presented an appearance of being the least likely to attack the Caliphate. Considering themselves surrounded by enemies, Sokoto and Gwandu, though suspicious of the R.N.C., accepted its proffered friendship.

As evidence of R.N.C.'s friendship towards Sokoto, Wallace seized the occasion of the Akassa raid of 1895 to write a conciliatory letter to Muḥammad Bukhārī,[27] the Wazir of Sokoto, in which he apologized for his company's delay in sending their tribute for that year. He blamed the Akassa raiders, whom he described as unbelievers (*kufār*), for this delay. There was a deliberate desire, evident in the letter, to emphasize the fact that the R.N.C., by fighting the Akassa people, was engaged in a battle against infidels. It seems that Wallace intended to point out to Sokoto the contrast between the R.N.C., warring against infidels, and the French, Germans and even Rābiḥ who were fighting against Muslims. Wallace seems to have been anxious to convince the Caliph by these skilfully dropped hints that the R.N.C. was the only real friend of the Caliphate. Wallace's move on this occasion may have been dictated by a realization on his part that friendly relations with Sokoto were becoming increasingly difficult to maintain.

However, the company's successful diplomacy in this respect was shortlived. The European rivalry in West Africa was soon to force it into open hostility with the Caliphate. Events on the Caliphate's frontiers during 1895–97 demonstrated beyond any doubt the enmity of the Europeans and Rābiḥ towards the Caliphate as well as the imminent danger that it might succumb to their machinations.

· · ·

in October 1895, that Dr Gruner and his party were taken as a French mission to Gwandu.

27. Corr. VIII, no. 1, Wallace to al-Wazīr, Muḥammad Bukhārī, 1895.

1897, THE YEAR OF DILEMMA FOR THE CALIPHATE

In 1897 the Sokoto Caliphate found itself in a crippling dilemma caused by the threat of conquest by Rābiḥ and the conquest of Nupe and Ilọrin by the Royal Niger Company. The Caliph's sovereignty and the integrity of his domains seemed to be in danger of destruction. The development of the events which culminated in the crisis of 1897 was clearly noticeable from 1895, when Rābiḥ's threat appeared the most imminent.

Rābiḥ's desire to expand westwards from Bornu arose from his anxiety to find new markets and new sources for supply of necessities, in particular for replenishing his stock of arms and ammunition. Bornu's trade with North Africa had been destroyed by Rābiḥ's conquest, particularly the sack of Kukawa during which many merchants lost their lives and property.[28] The principal caravan route from Murzuk to Bornu was closed to traffic from 1893 to 1895.[29] Thomas Holt, an English trader who was in Kano in 1895, reported that Rābiḥ, obviously wishing to find a secure base from which to trade, wanted to establish himself at Missau by negotiation with the Emir.[30] The R.N.C. in Ibi, during the same year, had sure evidence of Rābiḥ's efforts to push down the Gongola–Benue valleys.[31] Early in 1895, there were rumours again that Rābiḥ intended to march on Zinder and Kano. Rumours of his advance westwards, or of his intention to do so, whether true or false, made the eastern emirates of the Caliphate anxious and frightened. Rābiḥ's drummers are said to have made popular the saying, 'conquer Bornu and then comes Kano'.[32] Kano, a throbbing commercial centre in the Western Sudan, was an obvious attraction to Rābiḥ.

To prevent Rābiḥ coming west, Sokoto, in the characteristic way it had dealt with crises in the Caliphate throughout the century, did no more than send instructions to the eastern

28. F.O. 101/84, Africa no. 3, British Consul General at Tripoli (news received) to F.O., 12 April 1894.
29. F.O. 101/84, Africa no. 2, Jago to F.O., 15 April 1895.
30. F.O. 101/84, Africa no. 4, Jago to F.O., 2 May 1896, encl. Thomas Holt to Jago, 22 May 1895.
31. F.O. 83/1443, R.N.C. to F.O., 18 May 1896; also F.O. 2/118, same to same 31 Oct. 1895, 'Report on Rābiḥ's movements'.
32. J. M. Fremantle, 'A history of the region comprising the Katagum division of Kano province', *J.A.S.*, xi (1911), p. 64.

emirates to prohibit trade with Rābiḥ.[33] In 1895, it is said, Rābiḥ requested trade with Kano from the Emir, Aliyu, with a threat that if he refused he (Rābiḥ) would attack Kano. Aliyu advised Rābiḥ to negotiate directly with the Caliph.[34]

In 1896 merchants in Kawar (Bilma) accepted an invitation from Rābiḥ to come to Bornu but, owing apparently to persistent rumours that he was advancing westwards, they remained in Kano until they were sure the road to Bornu was safe.[35] It seems definite that once the rains cleared in 1896 Rābiḥ's troops started to advance westwards.[36] Late in 1896 it was reported that Kano received fresh instructions from the Caliph to prohibit trade with Bornu and to kill merchants coming from there.[37] The state of increasing hostility between the Caliphate and Rābiḥ is reflected in reports that a large caravan from Bornu was attacked by Kano people who killed its merchants and seized their goods and that Zinder was getting prepared to resist an expected march by Rābiḥ on it.[38]

Sometime in late 1896 or early 1897, Rābiḥ's troops, under the command of Shaikh Dab, attacked and sacked Bedde.[39] The Emir of Bedde, Maiduna, and his people fled to Hadejia for refuge.[40] This event spread panic and confusion through the emirates of Missau, Katagum and Hadejia.[41]

33. F.O. 101/84, Africa no. 2, Jago to F.O., 15 April 1895.
34. A.N.S.O.M., Afrique 4, file 36c, French Consul at Tripoli to Ministre des Affaires Etrangères, 20 Jan. 1897, enclosed in Ministre des Affaires Etrangères au Ministre des Colonies of 24 May 1897. Information collected from a Tripolitanian merchant, Bedjeb el-Kodja, who left Kano about 15 May 1896.
35. F.O. 101/86, Africa no. 8, Jago to F.O., 8 July 1896.
36. F.O. 101/86, Jago to F.O., 5 Sept. 1896, reports of merchants going from Kano to Bornu.
37. F.O. 101/86, Africa no. 11, Jago to F.O., 17 Dec. 1896, information by a courier who had arrived in Ghat about 7 Dec. 1896. It seems that with the commencement of the dry season 1896–97, Rābiḥ's troops began their advance westwards from Bornu.
38. F.O. 101/86, Africa no. 12, Jago to F.O., 29 Dec. 1896.
39. Corr. IX, no. 96, Muḥammad Manga b. Ṣalīh, Emir of Missau, to Emir of Kano Aliyu Baba; no. 93, Wazir of Katagum Sa'īd to Emir of Kano Aliyu Baba; no. 94, Emir of Hadejia Muḥammad b. Harūn to al-Wazir Muḥammad Bukhārī; also H. R. Palmer, *Gazetteer of Bornu Province* (Lagos, 1927), p. 41.
40. Corr. IX, no. 95, Emir Aḥmad of Gumel to Aliyu Baba; no. 97, Emir of Hadejia Muḥammad b. Harūn to Aliyu Baba.
41. Corr. IX, nos. 92, 94, 95, 96, 97, Emir of Kano; no. 94 reports that 'The people of the East are much agitated with terrible fear'. No. 95

Missau, not knowing where the conquering army would go next, could do nothing but panic.[42] The wave of fear spread fast through the eastern emirates. Soon it was known that Rābiḥ's troops intended to go to Gamawa (an important market town in Katagum emirate) and then to Badeiri, in Hadejia emirate, from where, according to Hadejia's spies, they would march on Kano either through Katagum or Hadejia or via Damagaram.[43] Rābiḥ's troops pressed westwards until they were only one day's journey from Katagum territory.[44]

So far there is no available evidence that the emirates which were immediately threatened took any positive steps to organize a joint defence against their enemy. Rather they sent frantic letters of appeal to Kano and Sokoto to warn them and to request them to take measures to prevent the '*Uthmāniyya* land (i.e. the Caliphate) succumbing to Rābiḥ, 'the traitor, liar and deceiver', the enemy of all the faithful.[45] The threatened emirates resorted to prayer and admonished Kano and Sokoto to leave everything aside and do the same.[46] The Emir of Gumel (independent since Rābiḥ's conquest of Bornu) appealed in panic to Kano and Sokoto, while in the meantime he gathered his '*ulamā*' to pray to God.[47]

The eastern emirates were overwhelmed and demoralized by their estimate of Rābiḥ's military power.[48] His great victories and reports of his army reaching them seem to have convinced the emirates that they could not face Rābiḥ in battle. On this occasion, their prayers were heard! Rābiḥ's troops were forced to turn back eastwards to meet a French expedition advancing towards Bornu from the south.[49] At the same time that the Caliphate was facing this predicament on its eastern frontiers, the R.N.C.

reports that the Emir of Hadejia took counsel with his people whether to fight or to flee.

42. Corr. IX, no. 96.
43. Corr. IX, nos. 94 and 97.
44. Corr. IX, no. 93.
45. Corr. IX, no. 96.
46. Corr. IV, no. 93 (Katagum) and no. 94 (Hadejia).
47. Corr. IX, no. 95.
48. Corr. IX, no. 97 (Hadejia to Kano): 'I tell you that between us and Rābiḥ there is none with power over him except Allah.'
49. W. Everett, 'A Short History of Rabeh Zubeir', *loc. cit.*; see also C.O. 446/1 Officer commanding W.A.F.F. at Jebba to C.O., 21 May 1898, encl. no. 2, in minute no. 120 to Wingfield, 21 May 1898.

was busy conquering Nupe and Ilọrin on the southern frontiers.

The conquest of Nupe, 1897. The success of Goldie's peace mission to the Emir of Nupe in 1892 was short-lived. As early as 1893 the R.N.C. had had fresh evidence of Nupe's hardening hostility to them.[50] By 1895 Nupe's attitude was menacing.[51] During this year the Emir was perturbed by the Anglo–French rivalry in Borgu and the north-western part of his territory.[52] The R.N.C., anxious to secure Nupe's favour, associated itself with the resentment felt by the Borgu and Nupe people at the establishment of a French military post at Bajibo. The French, finding their position untenable, withdrew from Fort D'Arenberg in September 1895.

The Emir of Nupe was pleased to see the French go. In October 1895 the new Emir of Nupe, Abubakar, promised to keep Nupe agreements with the R.N.C. and thanked the company for its assistance in seeing to it that the French evacuated his territory.[53] Early in 1896, however, the R.N.C. provoked Nupe hostility by establishing military posts at Leaba, Jebba and Bajibo.[54] The company was at this time being pushed, against its better judgment, by the British government and public opinion, to pursue a forward policy in Nupe and the Caliphate generally, as a proof that it could defend British interests against the French menace.[55] A forward policy, however, implied interference with Nupe's sovereignty. Nupe viewed the new military posts of Leaba, Jebba and Bajibo as a clear violation of its territory, contrary to existing agreements between him and the R.N.C. Thenceforth war became imminent. Both sides only needed time to mobilize their forces.

In the meantime the Emir of Nupe took prompt measures to

50. R.H.B.E., Africa S.85, vol. 1. Proceedings of R.N.C. general meeting, 13 July 1893.
51. R.H.B.E., Africa S.58, memo on Nupe Campaign written in 1896 by Goldie.
52. Flint, *op. cit.*, pp. 216 ff. It was thought probable in 1895 that the kings of Bussa and Kiama might join with Nupe to expel the French from Fort D'Arenberg.
53. R.H.B.E., Africa S.101, vol. 18, Walter Watts to R.N.C.
54. R.H.B.E., Africa S.58, conf. memo, Goldie to R.N.C. Council, 24 Nov. 1896.
55. Flint, *op. cit.*, pp. 231–2.

protect his territory and to force the R.N.C. to evacuate it without fighting. He attempted to starve out the new military post by ordering Nupe canoemen (carriers of the whole traffic between Lokoja and Bajibo) not to take provisions to the posts of Leaba and Bajibo.[56] The canoemen obeyed but since he was as yet unprepared for war, the Emir withdrew the order following a counter-threat from the R.N.C. Preparations went on apace in Bida. Ilọrin and Bussa were invited to participate in a joint effort with Nupe to break the power of the Christians.[57] Bussa was hesitant and finally declined; Bida's counsel was weighed seriously in Ilọrin.

In order to paralyse the company, the Emir, Abubakar, commanded all their Nupe African pilots working on ships and launches between Lokoja and Jebba to leave the company's service. They did. In June 1896 Nupe forces captured an R.N.C. constabulary force of forty-five men with their rifles and one Gardiner machine-gun.[58] Nupe and the R.N.C. had never before come so close to war.

Meanwhile reports of the situation in Nupe had reached Gwandu and Sokoto. An appeal for peaceful settlement made by Gwandu (and reported by the Emir to Sokoto) to both Nupe and the R.N.C. came too late.[59] Perhaps Gwandu and Sokoto, being in a better position to appraise the forces that threatened the Caliphate, were anxious that peace be preserved on at least one frontier. To them the British, who had up to 1896 shown no overt hostility to the Caliphate, still seemed possible friends. Besides, in 1896 it was Nupe, and not the R.N.C., that seemed to be showing aggression. The R.N.C. was, however, merely waiting for the rains of 1896 to clear to march on Bida.

The R.N.C. plan of campaign was excellently laid. Its main object was to crush a section of the Nupe forces (estimated at 12,000 including 1000 mounted) then under the Makun south of the Niger, blockade the Niger from Lokoja to Jebba in order to prevent a junction between the Makun and the Nupe home

56. Conf. memo, Goldie to R.N.C. Council, 24 Nov. 1896, *loc. cit.*
57. *Ibid.*
58. *Ibid.*; also Flint, *op. cit.*, p. 240.
59. Corr. IX, no. 111 'Umar b. Khalīl (Bakatara), Emir of Gwandu, to Amīr al-mu'minīn 'Abd al-Raḥmān. 'Umar reported that he had written to the Emir of Bida to seek reconciliation 'between us and the Christians' and keep 'our compact' with them unless they broke it and started war. He also wrote to the company in a similar vein.

forces, and cut him off from retreating to ally with Iḷorin forces. Nupe, thus isolated, would be easily dealt with. For the execution of this plan Egbom (fifty miles above Egga on the Niger) was made a new military base supplied with requisite equipment and provisions sufficient to enable the company's soldiers to make a dash there from Lokoja unburdened by heavy packs.[60] From Egbom a dash was to be made to the Makun's camp near Kabba, care having been taken to head off his retreat to Iḷorin by the company's troops who would thus compel him to move towards Lokoja where he would face the company's contingent stationed there to await him.[61]

Electric searchlights and heavy machine-guns that could be easily dismantled for easy transportation, and incendiary rockets for firing thatched roofs, were specially designed for the campaign.[62] A patrol flotilla (consisting of thirteen steamers, including two steam launches and an armed hulk carrying necessary stores) under the command of Wallace was to carry out the planned blockade. The steamers were well armed with Nordenfeldt quick-firing shell-guns and Gardiner machine-guns. Also in the steamers were armed riflemen at the ready.[63]

The Emir, Abubakar, who had received information from Lagos about the company's plans, countered with his own strategy. Half the forces of the Makun were instantly recalled to Bida with the intention that the other half and the forces in Nupe would make a pincer movement on the company's base at Lokoja.[64] Reinforcements, estimated at 10,000 men, from neighbouring districts of Nupe were obtained. For some unknown reason the projected alliance with Iḷorin did not materialize.

In December 1896 Goldie, then in Lokoja, directed his diplomatic efforts towards Gwandu and Sokoto by writing to them to explain that the company had been pushed to the necessity of attacking Nupe because of numerous unredressed outrages committed by the Emir against the company. The

60. R.H.B.E., Africa S.58, Goldie to R.N.C. Council, 25 Nov. 1896.
61. F.O. 83/1443, R.N.C. to F.O., 17 April 1896.
62. R.H.B.E., Africa S.58, Goldie to R.N.C., 25 Nov. 1896, and Flint, *op. cit.*, p. 248.
63. C.O. 147/124, Goldie to the Earl of Scarborough, Report on the Niger–Sudan Campaign, 6 March 1897.
64. *Ibid.*

letters to Gwandu and Sokoto were designed to reach the recipients before news of the war but too late for them to aid Bida should they be so disposed.[65] On the Nupe front, Goldie, by means of letters, piled pressure on the Makun to make him defect. But to Goldie's promises (including making him the Emir of Nupe) the Makun replied offering to arrange an amicable settlement between the company and the Emir. For the rest his loyalty was unshaken. He failed to keep three successive appointments with Goldie.[66]

Nupe's planned strategy was not successful. R.N.C. troops reached Kabba on 13 January, only to discover that the Nupe war camp at Ogidi (now eight miles by road from Kabba) had been deserted the previous day.[67] The Makun had fled towards Yagba district, on his way back to Nupe. On the 14th Goldie proclaimed to a gathering of chiefs in Kabba that their districts were free from Nupe tyranny. The Kabba column and the main body of the R.N.C. force which had left Lokoja since 6 January, assembled at Egbom on the 22nd. Wallace's blockade had been completely successful in preventing the remnants of the Makun's forces crossing to Bida. The Kede people had also been won over by Wallace to aid his blockade efforts. He had also won over Etsu Idris Gana, a descendant of one of Nupe's pre-*jihād* dynasties in Bida.[68]

The initiative, and the power of guns, with ability to use them efficiently, were on the side of the company. Numbers, grim determination and courage were the most distinguishing qualities of the Nupe army. The R.N.C. party consisted of 32 Europeans, 507 African rank and file and was armed with one 12-pounder and one 9-pounder Whitworth guns, twelve 9-pounder guns, five 7-pounder mountain guns, five .45 Maxim automatic

65. *Ibid.*
66. *Ibid.*; see R.H.B.E., Africa S.101, vol. 18, Watts to R.N.C. Council, 10 Nov. 1895. In his negotiations with the Makun, Muḥammad, Goldie depended on W. Watt's claim that he had made an unsuccessful bid for the throne at the death of Maliki in 1895.
67. My account of the Bida campaign is based principally on reports of the campaign by Major Alfred J. Arnold enclosed in C.O. 147/124 Goldie to the Earl of Scarbrough, 6 March 1897, two articles in *The Times* of London of 29 March and 2 April 1897, by a special correspondent on the campaign; Seymour Vandeleur *Campaigning in the Nile and Upper Niger* (London, 1898), and Flint, *op. cit.*
68. Dupigny, p. 43.

machine-guns, Snider rifles for the troops plus ample stores of ammunition. Nupe forces, estimated at 30,000 foot and 1000 mounted, were armed with Snider and Remington rifles, flint-locks, spears and swords.

Open battle began on 26 January. Nupe's advance guards charged the R.N.C. troops intrepidly in the face of heavy firing from the Maxim guns. 'Every inch of ground was disputed' as the R.N.C. force advanced. In spite of great execution done among them by the Whitworth guns the Nupe charged relentlessly until dusk against a background of beating of drums, blowing of horns and the enthusiastic roar of the crowd behind them. The R.N.C. troops, surrounded on all sides, would have been annihilated but for the inaccurate marksmanship of the Nupe. Shots, fired too high into the air, whistled threateningly but harmlessly over the square of the company's army.

Even so the company's troops were compelled to retreat at dusk, hotly pursued by the Nupe army. At this point poor strategy baulked Nupe of victory. Instead of making a dash to capture the British camp with its arms and ammunition, the Nupe army concentrated on harassing their enemies. In fact the Nupe army was by now demoralized. The Emir and the Lapeni (a high-ranking chief) were wounded while the Lapai and Agaie contingents withdrew consequent on the death of their generals.

The British-led army, which had suffered light casualties—Lt. A. C. Thomson, killed in a reconnoitring expedition, and four African soldiers wounded—advanced resolutely on Bida the following morning under cover of their heavy firing. Shell after shell was poured into Bida until by 4 p.m., four companies of the R.N.C. force entered the town and fired the houses with incendiary rockets. The Nupe army, still fighting bravely, was at last scattered. On the 28th Bida was occupied. The Emir had fled to Kontagora. The British flag fluttered over his palace, where Goldie had taken up residence.

While the R.N.C. casualties were only eight killed and nine Africans wounded, Bida casualties were estimated at 600–1000 killed and wounded. Ammunition seized in Bida included 10 pieces of artillery, 350 rifles, guns and pistols, 550 barrels of gun-powder and 2500 cartridges of various types. Nupe had fallen to superior arms and accurate marksmanship. Goldie commented: 'Our own highly trained force with thirty Europeans would have been annihilated at Bida, if it had not been for the field guns.'[69]

For some days Goldie had no one to sign a peace treaty with until the Makun, under pressure from his mother, gave himself up. At Kosoji Goldie concluded a treaty with him according to which he was recognized as Emir of northern Nupe, bound to follow such directions as the representatives of the R.N.C. might give him from time to time. The Makun recognized the company as governor of Nupe and their right to govern south-west Nupe direct and such parts of the north-west bank of the Niger for a distance of three miles inland, as they might desire.[70]

On the whole, the company's victory settled little in Nupe. A loyal general had been coerced into assuming the role of emir. The role played by Makun Muḥammad as intermediary between the Emir and Goldie on this occasion and later (1900–01)[71] between Lugard and the Emir leaves us in no doubt about his loyalty to the legitimate Emir. While it is fascinating to detect a passive traitor in the Makun there is no evidence to support such a claim. He appears as a statesman who shrank from extremes in the face of cold realities. If he was ambitious to become the Emir his refusal to meet Goldie on three different occasions and the fact that pressure had to be put on him to accept the emirship after the flight of Abubakar must be seen as going beyond the wiles of an astute schemer. He seems to have been unprepared to assume the emirship if, as in the situation, it involved flouting traditional Nupe usages. That he was next in line of succession after Abubakar does not mean that he would necessarily be prone to playing the traitor. Meanwhile resentment rankled underneath. Although the R.N.C. victory was irrefutable proof of its power to the British government and public, it could not set up so much as the skeleton of an administration in Nupe territory. The fugitive Emir soon returned and the Makun returned power to him. Nupe was living to fight another day.

· · ·

69. R.H.B.E., Africa S.58, Goldie to C.O., 19 July 1897.
70. F.O. 2/167, Treaty no. 398, text of Treaty of Kosoji.
71. See below, pp. 226–7. The whole tone of Flint's appraisal of the Makun amounts to saying that he was 'a passive traitor', see Flint, p. 249. Yet he remarks that Goldie was out to 'make sure that his loyalty to the Emir was tested'.

The fall of Iḷọrin, 1897. The R.N.C. undertook the conquest of Iḷọrin in 1897, under pressure from the British government at Lagos applied through the British Colonial Office.[72] Although the company claimed Iḷọrin, it had no regular contact with it. The hostility of Iḷọrin to Lagos after the settlement of the Yoruba wars in 1893 will be recalled. Dissatisfaction with Bower's boundary arrangements after the peace settlement lay at the root of Iḷọrin's bitterness. In mid-September 1895,[73] Moma, the Emir of Iḷọrin (1891–95), was killed in a plot organized by his generals who deprecated his softness towards the Lagos government. Alegẹ, used by the baloguns to get rid of his brother, the Emir, was pushed aside and Suleiman, a weak character and a suitable tool in the hands of the baloguns, was made Emir.

Earlier in 1895 the powerful baloguns had had further cause to feel increasingly hostile to the Lagos government because it had organized the expulsion of Iḷọrin Ajẹlẹs (Residents) from Awtun (Ọtun) Ishan, Aiyede and Ikọle.[74] In November 1895 the new Emir of Iḷọrin warned Denton, the acting Colonial Secretary in Lagos, that if he sent messengers to Iḷọrin they would be killed. Iḷọrin sent emissaries to all neighbouring Yoruba towns, requesting them to have nothing to do with white men and to combine to expel them.[75] In the meantime Yūsuf, a Lagos trader, was put in irons in Iḷọrin.

The R.N.C. concentrated on cultivating the feeling in Iḷọrin that it was a friend. The new Emir received a congratulatory letter from the Agent-General, Watts, to which he replied effusively in October 1895.[76] Least expecting danger to come to him from the Company, the Emir embarked on a belligerent policy towards the Lagos government. British troops stationed at Odo Ọtin were attacked by Iḷọrin soldiers in the early morning of 31 March 1896. Although the Iḷọrin were repulsed with heavy

72. The pressure put on the R.N.C. by the Lagos government and the British Colonial Office has been treated in detail by Flint, *op. cit.*, pp. 236–40.
73. F.O. 83/1386, Denton to C.O., 5 Nov. 1895, *Ta'lif Akhbār al-qurūn min 'Umarā' bilād Iḷọrin*; the account here of the *Ta'lif Akhbār* passes silently over the details of the affair.
74. K. V. Elphinstone, *Gazetteer of Iḷọrin* (London, 1921), pp. 18–19. By 1896 these towns had stopped paying tribute to Iḷọrin.
75. F.O. 83/2264, Denton to C.O., 20 Nov. 1895, encl. 1, R. L. Bower to Denton, 5 Nov. 1895.
76. R.H.B.E., Africa S.101, vol. 18, W. Watts to R.N.C., 10 Nov. 1895.

casualties (over fifty killed)[77] they attacked the reinforced Odo Ọtin contingent again on 2 April but without success.[78]

The R.N.C. had done nothing to help Ilọrin. When Goldie was in Jebba in 1896 the Emir, Suleiman, sent an urgent entreaty to him to tell him that he could not guarantee the safety of any white man in Ilọrin.[79] Goldie's messenger, Omoru ('Umar), whom he sent to the Emir after receiving the message, was directed to Balogun Alanamu as the real holder of power. The latter assured 'Umar that the R.N.C., unlike Captain Bower who after the peace settlement of 1893 had, by deceitful friendship, 'stolen' Ibadan and Ọyọ lands, was Ilọrin's friend.[80] But Ilọrin's reliance on the R.N.C. was misplaced. As early as 1895 Goldie had agreed in principle to break Ilọrin in order to put an end to its hostility to the Lagos government.[81] Faced with R.N.C.'s suspicious silence, Ilọrin had turned to Bida after the Odo Ọtin skirmishes.[82]

Ilọrin was ill-prepared to face the R.N.C. For years it had been engaged in a relentless war against Ibadan. This war must have seriously limited its chances of buying firearms from the coast. In this respect, Nupe was more favourably placed to buy arms direct from European traders. The palace revolution of 1895 had further weakened Ilọrin shortly after the Yoruba wars. Just before the R.N.C. attack, it suffered yet another military setback. In January its army under the baloguns, Alanamu, Adamu, Ajikọbi and a warrior nicknamed Gata Koko had suffered a crushing defeat at Ẹrinmọpẹ at the hands of British forces in which Balogun Adamu and about 150 Ilọrin soldiers were killed.[83] Nevertheless early in February the Emir Suleiman rejected Goldie's request that Ilọrin should submit peacefully.[84] On

77. Reconstructed from F.O. 83/1443: C.O. to F.O., 14 April 1896, encl. 1, Tel. Carter to Chamberlain (received 5 April); and F.O. 83/1444, C.O. to F.O., 27 May 1896, encls. 1 and 2, Carter to C.O.
78. F.O. 83/1443, R.N.C. to F.O., 18 April 1896, encl.
79. F.O. 83/1443, R.N.C. to F.O., 17 April 1896.
80. *Ibid.*, R.N.C. to F.O., 24 April 1896; encl. Omoru's report on his visit to Ilọrin.
81. F.O. 83/1443, R.N.C. to F.O., 17 April 1896.
82. *The Times*, London, cutting (n.d.) in R.H.B.E., Africa S.60, Reuter's interview with Capt. Bower. Bower got his information through his spies.
83. F.O. 83/1525, Denton to C.O., 8 Feb. 1897.
84. A. J. Arnold's report on the Niger–Sudan campaign, *loc. cit.* The Ilọrin campaign, as reconstructed here, is based on Arnold's report;

15 February R.N.C. forces, which had left Jebba on the 10th, were camped at the river Asa in front of Iḷọrin. The Emir refused to parley.

The Iḷọrin army, estimated at 8000–10,000 with about 800 mounted, appeared armed with rifles, muzzle-loading guns, swords and spears. Their intrepid charge against the R.N.C.'s square, often reaching to within less than 150 yards of it, exposed them to the destructive effect of the 7-pounder guns which did great execution among them. Fighting, suspended at noon on the 15th, was resumed early on the 16th. The R.N.C.'s force crossed the river Asa and with Maxim gunfire it drove the inhabitants to shelter within the walls. Shell fire poured into the city started a conflagration. At 3 p.m. the enemy entered the city and Goldie installed himself in the palace, in front of which the 'British flag' was soon after hoisted.

Iḷọrin suffered heavy casualties. Of horsemen alone, 200 were estimated killed while only a few among the R.N.C.'s force, including one European, were wounded. Iḷọrin, by reason of its weak force, was doomed from the beginning. Like the Nupe the Iḷọrin army also suffered from poor marksmanship.

The emirs and the baloguns fled to distant villages and did not give themselves up until the 18th. In the interval Goldie had feverishly sought out the pre-*jihād* dynasty and opened negotiations with its leaders. At the same time he carried on negotiations, through emissaries, with the fugitive Emir.[85] On the 18th, he concluded a treaty similar to that of Kosoji with the Emir and his four baloguns (Alanamu, Salu, Ajikọbi and Suberu).[86] Iḷọrin also undertook to accept the boundary with Lagos, as the company might direct.

Iḷọrin lost the war, lost her sovereignty (at least *de jure*) but as in Nupe, the R.N.C. victory settled little. The R.N.C.'s force left Iḷọrin on 19 February and no semblance of administration was established there by the company thereafter. This failure of the R.N.C. to administer Iḷọrin and Nupe after their conquest was, in a broader perspective, to the company's diplomatic advantage since it kept the door open for possibilities of reopening friendly

and F.O. 83/1525, Denton to C.O., 22 Feb. 1897, encl. Goldie to Denton; 'Report on Iḷọrin Campaign', 18 Feb. 1897.

85. *Ibid.* Goldie's report to Denton.

86. *Ibid.*, text of Treaty in F.O. 2/167, no. 399.

relations, which would otherwise have been blocked, with Sokoto and Gwandu.

Aftermath of the Nupe–Ilọrin conquest. Even though the conquest of Nupe and Ilọrin settled little, it had more than local significance. The neighbouring emirates, who saw it as an example of the frightful fate that could easily overtake them at the hands of European infidels, were stricken with awe. For the Caliph and the Emir of Gwandu, the British, no less than the French and Rābiḥ, confirmed themselves as enemies. But with the imminent descent of Rābiḥ's troops on the eastern emirates and the arrival at about the same time of the fugitive Amīr al-Mu'minīn Aḥmad of Segu and his entourage in Sokoto, bringing, no doubt, horrifying stories of French atrocities,[87] the Caliphate, hemmed in by three hostile forces, was in no position to strike a blow against any of its adversaries. For Sokoto and its emirates 1897 was, perhaps, the most anxious year in their history to date. For the Caliphate to mount an offensive against the R.N.C. was out of the question.

The Caliph and the Emir of Gwandu were bitter against the British. The former despatched instructions to all the emirs to close the roads leading to their emirates to European penetration (a traditional strategy of warfare in the Caliphate) and wage the *jihād* against them.[88] In a message to Yola the Caliph 'Abd al-Raḥmān wrote: 'You have seen what the company has done to Bida and Ilọrin, my territories. You are not to allow the company to remain in any part of the country where you have jurisdiction.'[89] But it was local particularism, rather than considerations for the Caliphate as a unit, that prevailed. Just as each emirate had fended for its own defence all through the century, in this moment of common danger, individual rulers allowed themselves to be guided by considerations of practical common sense as they saw it. Many emirs, afraid of the R.N.C.'s power, are said to have handed in the Caliph's letter to the R.N.C.[90]

87. Biography of Amīr al-Mu'minīn Aḥmad b. Shaikh 'Umar b. Sa'īd, *loc. cit.*
88. *Lagos Weekly Record*, 20 Feb. 1898; also C.O. 537/15 (Secret); no. 318, encl. (Confidential and Immediate) Goldie to Bertie, 2 March 1898.
89. A. H. M. Kirk-Greene, *Adamawa Past and Present* (Oxford, 1960), p. 51.
90. C.O. 537/15 (Secret) no. 318, encl. (Confidential and Immediate) Goldie to Bertie, 2 March 1898.

Faced with an excruciating dilemma, the Caliph and the Emir of Gwandu nonetheless remained hostile. They adamantly refused the Company's tribute 'with many carefully veiled threats'.[91] The Caliph declared that he did not recognize the R.N.C. conquests.[92] The basis for mutual trust and confidence between the Caliph and the R.N.C. was destroyed. However, subsequent events induced the Caliph to respond to R.N.C.'s diplomatic wooing after 1897 and to accept, albeit with mistrust, the Nupe–Ilọrin campaign as a breach between 'friends' which would not be repeated.

A suitable atmosphere for the R.N.C. to reopen negotiations with the Caliph was provided by French activities. The French, who had prior information of the R.N.C.'s intended campaign in Bida and Ilọrin,[93] feared that success would mean unprecedented British expansion in the West-Central Sudan which would vitiate French colonial ambition in Africa. There was also the fear that such expansion would eventually engulf the Caliphate and bring the British into contact with Rābiḥ in Bornu with the unsavoury result that the extensive domains of that conqueror would fall to the British. For France this would mean a loss of Bornu, the Chad and Shari regions—all of them crucial to the French African colonial programme. The middle Niger and Rābiḥ's possessions, therefore, became the two urgent objectives of the French.[94]

During late 1896 and January 1897 respectively, Lts Baud and Bretonnet were sent to Borgu to establish military posts on the right bank of the Niger. By the end of 1897 French military posts were established from Liptako to Say and down to Bussa. There were posts in Yagha, Botu, Karimama, Illo and Gomba[95]—all close to Gwandu territories. At the same time French soldiers in Borgu were estimated at about 800.[96] By adopting a similar policy, the British forced the French to reopen boundary

91. *Ibid.*
92. F.O. 83/1539, Goldie to C.O., 20 Dec. 1897.
93. Flint, *op. cit.*, pp. 241–2.
94. For details of Anglo-French rivalry on the middle-Niger and the diplomacy behind it (1897–98) see Perham, *The Years of Adventure*, pp. 623 ff., and Flint, *op. cit.*, ch. 12.
95. C.O. 537/13, Gosselin to F.O., Report of second meeting of the Anglo-French Boundary Commission, sitting in Paris, 3 Nov. 1897.
96. C.O. 537/11 (Secret), Ag. Director, Major Barker (I.D.W.O.) to C.O., 22 Jan. 1898.

negotiations between the two powers. These were not completed until 14 June 1898.[97]

In the meantime Sokoto and Gwandu, with cause to fear both the French and the British, were powerless to pursue a forward policy against either of them. Events played into the hands of the R.N.C. Despite numerous conciliatory letters written to Sokoto and Gwandu, confessed Goldie, their resentment as well as that of their emirs had not abated by the end of 1897. The company received letters couched in violent language from the Emir of Gwandu.[98] The company therefore seized on the French threat, apparently now made evident by their presence (as it were, at the Caliph's doorsteps) to strengthen its policy of conciliation by posing as the defender of the Caliphate against the French.

The time was propitious for the R.N.C. Sokoto was beginning to feel the pinch of French expansion. Goldie recognized that the Caliph was 'thoroughly well alive to the movements and intentions of the French, whom he dreads far more than he dreads us'.[99] Goldie, therefore concentrated on nursing Sokoto's fears. He wrote:

> I am persistently pouring in to him by letter the principle which we have urged upon him for the past seven years; that the French advance means more military conquest and dispossession of native rulers, whereas the Company means only British suzerainty, jurisdiction over all non-natives or cases in which non-natives are concerned and the expansion of commerce, which he greatly desires.[100]

In one such letter[101] the conquest of Bida and Ilọrin is defended. Proof of the company's sincerity and its determination not to seize the Caliph's lands was shown by the fact that no British administration was set up in the two emirates, nor were soldiers stationed in them after overwhelming victories. The French, who had conquered Algeria and driven out its king just as they had done to Segu, whose fugitive ruler was even then with the Caliph at Sokoto, were the real enemies of Islam. In contrast, the

97. Text of delimitation convention in Hertslet, *Map of Africa by Treaties*, vol. ii, pp. 785 f.
98. C.O. 445/4, W.A.F.F. Expeditions, W.A.F.F. to C.O., 5 Jan. 1898, encl. Goldie to Lugard, 20 Dec. 1897.
99. *Ibid.*, encl. Goldie to Lugard, 21 Dec. 1897, copy of the same letter also in C.O. 147/127.
100. *Ibid.*
101. N.A.K. KADCAPTORY, G.O.K.1/1/1, Box 45, R.N.C. to Amīr al-Mu'minīn (draft), 28 Dec. 1897.

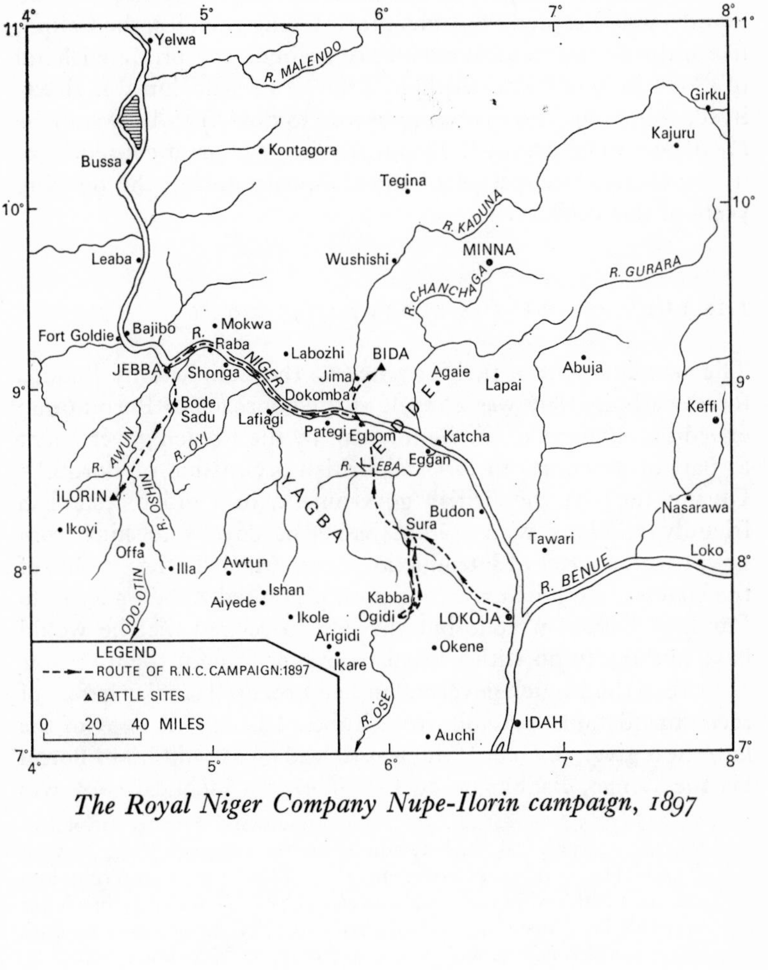

The Royal Niger Company Nupe-Ilorin campaign, 1897

Queen of England protected the Muslims of India against the French.

By means of such conciliatory moves the R.N.C. won Sokoto–Gwandu response. Early in 1898 the company's tribute to Sokoto and Gwandu which had been persistently refused for ten months was accepted.[102] Amidst threatening enemies, the Caliph, like a drowning man, momentarily grabbed the proffered hand of a treacherous friend. Although the new friendship was short-lived, from 1898 the French appeared to Sokoto and Gwandu as *the* danger to be dreaded. This was a factor of great consequence in the British occupation of the Caliphate during the opening years of this century.

THE LULL BEFORE THE STORM, 1897–99

The abandonment of their advance on the Caliphate by Rābiḥ's forces early in 1897 was a result of the approach to Bornu of an expedition under Col. E. Gentil, sent by the French government as part of its efforts to forestall British occupation of Bornu.[103] During 1893–94 the British government, in a bid to establish friendly relations with Rābiḥ, had sent envoys to him from Egypt with a letter of introduction from Zubeir Pasha.[104] One of the envoys, ʿAbdullāh al-Morghamī, presented Zubeir's letter to Rābiḥ at Dikwa in 1894 but the latter declared that he would have nothing to do with Christians except to fight them.[105]

In 1896 the French government had procured similar letters of recommendations to Rābiḥ from Zubeir Pasha.[106] A copy of the letter was given to Gentil who was to lead an expedition to Bornu via the Congo, Baghirmi and the Shari. An identical copy was

102. C.O. 537/15 (Secret) no. 318, Correspondence on negotiations in Paris, 2 March 1898, encl. Goldie to Bertie, 1 March 1898.
103. F.O. 2/118, Arthur Hardage to F.O. The idea of entering into relations with Rābiḥ had been first raised by Evelyn Baring in a letter he wrote (13 June 1891) to Lord Salisbury. Nothing was done until 1893; see also *ibid.* Zubeir Pasha to Rābiḥ, 24 Nov. 1893.
104. *Ibid.*, Zubeir Pasha to Rābiḥ, 24 Nov. 1893.
105. *Ibid.* Also Sherif Hassan, eye-witness account of Rābiḥ's reaction to Zubeir's messengers. Diary (Arabic), pp. 6–7.
106. A.N.S.O.M., Afrique 4, file 36c; tr. of Al-Zubeir ʿAbd al-Raḥmān Pasha to Rābiḥ, 28 Shawāl 1314 A.H. (1 April 1897) enclosed in Ministre des affaires Etrangères au Ministre des Colonies, 17 April 1897.

given to Captain Marius Gabriel Cazemajou who was in command of another expedition, with the objectives of reconnoitring the Say–Barrua line and visiting Rābiḥ, with whom the French hoped to be able to sign a protectorate treaty.[107] It was in order to repel the Gentil expedition that Rābiḥ's troops hastened back from the west, abandoning their apparent intention to invade the Caliphate. By a stroke of irony, Anglo–French rivalry had, it appears, spared the Caliphate from an attack by Rābiḥ's forces. French advance from the Congo towards the Shari and the Lake Chad regions kept Rābiḥ permanently away from the Caliphate. He was killed in battle by the French at Kusseri on 22 April 1900.

From 1897 Rābiḥ appeared as an ally of the Caliphate. Early in 1898 he had fallen out with Ḥayat. A battle ensued between his son, Faḍlallāh, and Ḥayat (aided by men from Jibrīl Gaini) in which Ḥayat was killed.[108] The killing of Ḥayat, added to the fact that Rābiḥ was fighting against Europeans—both enemies of the Caliphate—must have strengthened the impression that Rābiḥ was an indirect ally of Sokoto. The Caliph is said to have stated, 'behold I have another vassal, Rābiḥ has joined me'.[109]

Sometime between 1898 and 1900 Rābiḥ's envoys to Sokoto, sent to negotiate trading relations with Bornu, were peacefully received by the Emir of Katagum and sent on their way to Zaria,[110] where the Wazir of Sokoto, Muḥammad Bukhārī, was at that time. The latter referred the envoys to Sokoto.[111] Although

107. A.N.S.O.M., Afrique 3, file 25 'Instructions Politiques' Ministre des Colonies to Capt. Cazemajou, 22 Feb. 1897. Also Commandant Chailley, 'La Mission du Haut-Soudan et le drame de Zinder', *Bull. IFAN*, Série B, xvi (1953), p. 251.
108. N.A.K. KADCAPTORY, Box 38, item 10, Yūsuf Babikīr to *Khalīfa* 'Abdullāh contains an account of the fight between Ḥayat aided by men from Mallam Jibrīl Gaini and Rābiḥ's troops under his son Faḍlallāh b. Rābiḥ; also C.O. 446/5, Goldie to F.O., 21 March 1899 refers to the battle 'last year' between Ḥayat and Rābiḥ's troops, and F.O. 101/88, Africa no. 5, Alvarez (Benghazi) to F.O., 19 July 1898. The battle took place early in 1898.
109. N.A.K. KADCAPTORY, G.O.K.1/1/1 Box 45, draft letter, R.N.C. to Amīr al-Mu'minīn. Reference is made to the Caliph's boast that he had an ally in Rābiḥ; also Kirk-Greene, *op. cit.*, p. 51, source not indicated.
110. Corr. IX, no. 98, Emir of Katagum 'Abd al-Qādīr b. Muḥammad al-Ḥajj to Amīr al-Mu'minīn 'Abd al-Raḥmān.
111. Corr. IX, no. 99, Al-Wazīr Muḥammad Bukhārī to Amīr al-mu'minīn 'Abd al-Raḥmān.

the letters of both the Emir of Katagum and Bukhārī are coldly formal the mere fact that Rābiḥ's messengers were accepted at all indicates that hostility between the Caliph and Rābiḥ had subsided after 1897. Rābiḥ's activities on the Adamawa frontier in 1897 were probably unknown to Sokoto.

THE EXPEDITION OF CAPTAIN MARIUS GABRIEL CAZEMAJOU, 1898

On 15 January 1898 the expedition of Captain Cazemajou, having come via Dahomey through Say and Karimama, arrived in Argungu. On the 19th he signed a protectorate treaty with the Emir, who had earlier written to him requesting his help against the Caliph, ʿAbd al-Raḥmān.[112]

The size of the expedition, which consisted of Cazemajou, Olive and Badie Diara—interpreters—one corporal, one sergeant and 350 carriers, caused fear among the local populations.[113] The Segu community of Amīr al-Mu'minīn Aḥmad (d. 16 December 1897) was seized with such panic that they hurriedly exhumed Aḥmad's body and reburied it in another grave lest the Europeans should desecrate it.[114] Their panic must have contributed to the fear of Sokoto people. The Caliph, ʿAbd al-Raḥmān, seems to have feared an invasion. At a place called Gamashe, close to Sokoto, Cazemajou received an order from the Caliph to turn back and not to enter Sokoto.[115] Again, at Gande, north of Gamashe, Cazemajou received yet another order from the Caliph to turn back. After three days of negotiations with Sokoto emissaries—coming and going with numerous escorts—the expedition

112. *Bulletin du Comité*, Feb. 1900, 'Journal de route du Capitaine Cazemajou', entry for 17 Jan. 1898. An account of the expedition is contained in the 'Journal de route', Tome 10, Feb. 1900, pp. 42–7; March 1900, pp. 89–91; May 1900, pp. 172–4. For text of treaty with Argungu see A.N.S.O.M., Afrique 3, file 25, Cazemajou à Ministre des Colonies, 19 Jan. 1898.

113. Chailley, *loc. cit.*, pp. 252–3.

114. Biography of Amīr al-mu'minīn Aḥmad b. Shaikh ʿUmar b. Saʿīd *loc. cit.* After Aḥmad's death, his community moved from Maikuluki to a new village which they named Dār es-Salām. When they moved east to Gombe-Nafata region they again exhumed Aḥmad's body and carried it with them. Aḥmad was succeeded as Amīr al-mu'minīn by his son Bashīr.

115. Captain Cazemajou: 'Journal de route', March 1900.

was at last allowed to proceed via Birnin Konni to the north of Sokoto.[116] From Konni the expedition went to Tsibiri (Chibiri) and Zinder assisted by a guide provided by the Marafa of Sokoto, Muḥammad Maiturare, who had earlier pleaded with the Caliph to give Cazemajou transit permission.[117]

The expedition learned that the Caliph had assembled horsemen from Sokoto and its neighbourhood with the intention of attacking them. He had, however, been dissuaded from his resolve by the representation of his councillors that the expedition was a peaceful one desiring only to pass through his territory on its way to the East.[118] On 5 May 1898 Cazemajou and Olive were killed at Zinder. It has been claimed that the killings were inspired by messengers who had arrived in Zinder from Sokoto.[119]

With the departure of Cazemajou the Caliph felt relieved. He wrote to inform the Emir of Gwandu of the departure of the expedition to Birnin Konni. The Emir of Gwandu in his reply also expressed relief. He wrote: 'Praise be to God and thanks to Him for averting their war and dispelling their guile. We saw your warning and your order concerning hindering them from entering the land of Islam and preventing them from coming to you. We stand by this.'[120]

A BRITISH RESIDENT FOR SOKOTO, 1898

The Caliph's hostility to the Cazemajou expedition and his fear of it were seen by the R.N.C. as an excellent opportunity to ingratiate themselves further with him. In reality the British feared that the French might successfully ally with Sokoto against them. To prevent the growth of French power in Borgu as well as on the frontiers of the Caliphate, the British West African

116. A.N.S.O.M., Afrique 3, file 25, Capt. Chanoine au Ministre des Colonies, 16 Oct. 1898, forwarding account by Samba Traore, one of the survivors of the Cazemajou expedition.
117. A.N.S.O.M., Afrique 3, file 25, from Muḥammad (Maiturare) Marafa to *Amīr al-Jaish al-naṣrānī* (Captain of the Christian army).
118. Cazemajou 'Journal de route', May 1900.
119. A.N.S.O.M., Afrique 3, file 25, Capt. Chanoine à Ministre des Colonies, 16 Oct. 1898, Samba Traore's account.
120. Corr. IX, no. 110, 'Umar b. Khalīl (Emir of Gwandu) to Amīr al-mu'minīn 'Abd al-Raḥmān.

Frontier Force was hurriedly organized between September and October 1897. The officers of the 1st battalion arrived at Lokoja on 29 December 1897,[121] while other officers and three companies forming the 2nd battalion embarked from Liverpool in February 1898.[122] Backed by this force, which could keep the French occupied in Borgu, the British tried to use the excuse of Cazemajou's presence to establish military posts on the north bank of the Niger, and, if possible, closer still to Sokoto and Gwandu. This was part of a plan of gradual penetration of the Caliphate preparatory to its effective occupation.

To achieve its aim, the R.N.C. presented itself to Sokoto as a friend anxious to defend the Caliphate against French encroachment. On 20 February Goldie cabled instructions to Wallace to send 400 soldiers to Jega (near Sokoto) to assist the Caliph against Cazemajou. An express message saying 'Queen determined defend his Empire' was to be sent ahead to the Caliph.[123] The Caliph wrote to thank the company for its assistance and advice.

The R.N.C. expedition, commanded by Major Arnold, left Jebba on 15 March 1898 and reached Yelwa (in Yauri Emirate) on 1 April.[124] There they learnt that the Cazemajou expedition had gone north of Sokoto territory since February. The main body of the expedition therefore returned. A force of one European officer and twenty soldiers was left to garrison Yelwa while another force comprising two European officers, forty soldiers and a Resident designate, left for Sokoto.

At Jega, on 7 May, the expedition received the Caliph's order, conveyed by the Emir of Kontagora at the head of a large force of cavalry (estimated at 7000), to turn back or be attacked. The expedition returned to Yelwa to reinforce the garrison there.

121. C.O. 4455/6, report on organization of 1st battalion W.A.F.F., 14 March 1899. See Flint, *op. cit.*, p. 275 f., and Perham, *Years of Adventure*, pp. 634–42 for fuller discussion of the reasons behind the formation of W.A.F.F.

122. C.O. 445/6, regimental records of 2nd battalion, W.A.F.F. no. 02/739 of 1 March 1899, encl. 'State of W.A.F.F.', Feb. 1899.

123. C.O. 537/14, West Africa (Secret), no. 295, Goldie to C.O., 23 March 1898, forwarding copy of telegram to Wallace of 20 March 1898.

124. Account of 'Sokoto expedition' is reconstructed from C.O. 446/1, Diary, Frontier operations, May and June 1898 (p. 362). Lugard, to C.O., 20 April 1898; Butler to Wingfield, 13 June 1898, and encl.; Goldie to C.O., May 1898, reporting 'turn back' order. Lugard to C.O., Tel. 26 May 1898 received 30 May, and R.H.B.E., Africa S.95, Lugard Diaries, 17, 27, 28, 29 May and 6 June 1898.

From Yelwa, the British Resident designate wrote to the Caliph to inform him that, by his action, he had declared himself an enemy of the R.N.C. The Caliph sent a defiant reply, stating clearly that he would fight the Christians. Thereafter the Yelwa garrison of the R.N.C. troops was repeatedly ordered by the Caliph to withdraw and was frequently threatened.

The over-enthusiastic plan of the R.N.C. to 'assist' the Caliph completely misfired. Thenceforth and up to the occupation of the Caliphate British relations with Sokoto broke down beyond repair. Meanwhile the conclusion of the Anglo–French delimitation convention in Paris on 14 June 1898 gave the English a free hand to deal with Sokoto without fear of French machinations. However, the plan to instal a British Resident in Sokoto was abandoned. Earlier in 1898 several British military posts (W.A.F.F.) had been established in Borgu. In August a new post was founded at Illo.

The Caliph and the Emirs of Gwandu, Yauri and Kontagora did not look favourably on the Illo and Yelwa posts. The latter had to be withdrawn, while an attempt on 25 September, believed to have been instigated by the Emirs of Yauri and Kontagora, to burn the Illo post led to skirmishes between the local population and W.A.F.F. troops. During the first half of October, following the capture of the headman of an island called Helo (near Illo) by W.A.F.F. soldiers, who complained that his people had refused to supply them with canoes and provisions, the local population fell on a contingent of British troops. All the members of the contingent, Lt. Keating, Corporal Galt and fourteen African soldiers, were killed.[125] The W.A.F.F. troops could not attack the Emirs of Yauri and Kontagora because they feared that Sokoto and Gwandu would come to their aid.[126] The Helo island incident in which the British suffered comparatively one of the heaviest casualties they were to sustain in Northern Nigeria, though a blow to British prestige, did not lead to a W.A.F.F. attack on the Emirs believed responsible for it.[127] From 1898 to the overthrow of the Caliphate the British confined their activities to the riverain emirates of the Niger–Benue and contented themselves with sending African political agents and

125. C.O. 446/1, Tel. Willcocks to C.O., 15 Oct. 1898 (report of Keating's death); also Tel. Willcocks to C.O., 17 Oct. 1898.

126. *Ibid.*, Tel. C.O. to Willcocks, 18 Oct. 1898.

127. C.O. 446/1, Tel. no. 67, Willcocks to C.O., 27 Oct. 1898.

letters to Sokoto and Gwandu as they had done during the era of trade and treaties.

R.N.C. RELATIONS WITH THE RIVERAIN EMIRATES UP TO 1899

Nupe and Ilọrin. After the conquest of 1897 Nupe was restive. The situation caused the R.N.C. so much anxiety that the agent-general, Flint, encouraged the Kede people to revolt. He made a military demonstration before Bida shortly after the conquest and threatened to clear the Fulani, whom he believed to be the source of all the trouble, out of Nupe.[128] Resentment in Nupe was for the time being driven underground.

Early in 1898 the Makun, Muḥammad, the loyal general of the deposed Emir whom the R.N.C. had installed as Emir (an act of usurpation of Gwandu's prerogative rights) gave way before Abubakar, the legitimate Emir, when the latter returned to claim back his throne.[129] Rather than show resentment or rancour the Makun interceded with Wallace when he visited Bida in 1899 to recognize the Emir, Abubakar.[130] The R.N.C. accepted the *fait accompli*, despite the fact that in June 1898 Bida had joined hands with the Emirs of Lapai and Agaie who had resumed raiding Jebba and Lokoja areas as they had been wont to do before the R.N.C. conquest. A W.A.F.F. force under the command of Col. Pilcher had broken the confederate camp of Bida, Agaie and Lapai at Gulu in June 1898. Lapai itself was bombarded and sacked.[131] In spite of the presence of W.A.F.F. troops, Nupe remained sullen thereafter.

In Ilọrin, once the R.N.C. troops left the town after the 1897

128. R.H.B.E., Africa S.58, Goldie to F.O., 11 Oct. 1897.
129. Flint, *op. cit.*, p. 298, suggests August 1897. This is unlikely to be correct. In the draft letter to Sokoto of 28 Dec. 1897 (*loc. cit.*) Goldie complained to the Caliph about those who wanted to reinstate Abubakar. That the Makun was holding southern Nupe territory (present-day Kabba Division) at this time, as Flint claims, is unlikely to be true. Oral traditions in this area date the end of Nupe domination to the Ogidi battle of 1897.
130. C.O. 446/8, Tel. Lugard to C.O., 17 Oct. 1899, report of Wallace's cordial reception at Bida.
131. F.O. 83/1614, report of Lapai expedition, encl. Lugard to F.O., 31 July 1898, in F.O. ot C.O., 6 Oct. 1898.

conquest, hostility against Europeans broke out again. Since the only R.N.C. representative in the town was a powerless African clerk, Ilọrin felt free to give expression to its anti-European feelings. These feelings had been further exacerbated by the construction of a telegraph line through Ilọrin territory.[132] This was seen as evidence of the intention of Europeans to settle down permanently. Ilọrin subjects were forbidden to assist in the construction of the telegraph line under pain of severe punishment. In August 1898 the Emir intensified his raids, once more resumed, against territory claimed by the Lagos government, because the Governor of Lagos laid claim to Illa.[133]

In September 1898 the W.A.F.F. garrison at Jebba under Lt-Col. Willcocks, anxious to stop the threats reaching them from the Emir of Ilọrin and the latter's raids into Lagos territory, sent a corporal and some soldiers to deliver a letter of warning to the Emir. At the Emir's court, the letter was thrown on the ground by an attendant while the Emir threatened the messengers, whom he described as traitors and 'bastard Yorubas', with death, should they return to the town. They were turned out of the town with ignominy.[134]

On 28 September messengers from Willcocks, comprising a European officer, Somerset, and fifty soldiers, arrived in Ilọrin with a second letter, this time threatening the Emir with attack. The Emir refused, in open Durbar, to receive the letter, despite the fact that it was accompanied by another letter from the R.N.C.'s agent-general. Somerset remained in Ilọrin, issuing to the Emir, numerous warnings, which were completely ignored. He swallowed the contempt and the indignities which the Ilọrin authorities heaped on him and his escort. The road to Ogbomọshọ was closed and by 7 and 8 October Ilọrin seriously contemplated war. Even when Willcocks' letter was eventually opened during the second week of October its contents were ignored. On the 21st the Emir and Council resolved that food should not be taken to the W.A.F.F. contingent and that any of their soldiers or carriers found in town might be killed.[135]

132. C.O. 446/1, Somerset to Oliver, 22 Oct. 1898.
133. *Ibid.*, Willcocks to C.O., 21 Sept. 1898.
134. *Ibid.*, Tel. Willcocks to C.O., 30 Sept. 1898.
135. *Ibid.*, Somerset to Oliver, 22 Oct. 1898, and Somerset to Willcocks, 7 Nov. 1898, report on 'Mission to Ilọrin' enclosed in Willcocks to C.O.

Thereafter members of the escort found wandering were freely attacked, insulted and taunted by the townspeople.

About 27 October Watts of the R.N.C. arrived in Ilọrin. Earlier, he had rejected Willcocks' request that the R.N.C. should attack the town.[136] At this time the R.N.C. officials on the spot, knowing of the impending revocation of the Company's charter, seem to have indulged in putting obstacles in the way of the W.A.F.F. whom they saw as the undeserving beneficiaries from their (R.N.C.) labours. In any case they stopped spending money on political administration. In Ilọrin Watts, who had gone out of his way to pose as a friend, was warmly received. He worked out a settlement between Somerset and the Emir. The Emir was to pay a fine of £50 and to apologize to Somerset.[137] However, Ilọrin's repentance was rendered doubtful by an offer made by Watts to pay the fine with an R.N.C. cheque. Somerset left the city on 31 October. An R.N.C. force of one officer and fifty soldiers was left there.

The Emir accepted the R.N.C. contingent because he regarded it as a protecting force rather than as an enemy. He was grateful to Watts for the departure of Somerset. He described Watts as a man 'who loves and who improves the affairs of Muslims', and promised to take care of the R.N.C. garrison.[138] The Emir felt the need for a protector and, in his ignorance, he believed he had found one in the R.N.C. The basic hostility of the Emir and people of Ilọrin continued until long after the formal military occupation of the town in 1900.

Muri and Adamawa. The evacuation of the French post from Yola in 1895 brought to an end any hope of continued French support which Muri and Adamawa might have entertained. The advent of Rābiḥ to Bornu and his alliance with Ḥayat, an enemy of the Caliphate and of Adamawa in particular, threw Muri and Adamawa back on R.N.C. support. The latter had for some years desisted from hostile acts against either of the emirates. In 1894 the Emir, Zubeir, had detained British emissaries to Rābiḥ for

136. C.O. 446/1, Willocks to C.O., no. J/2380, 18 Oct. 1898.
137. C.O. 446/1, Willcocks to C.O., encl. Somerset to Willcocks 'Mission to Ilọrin', 7 Nov. 1898; also N.A.K. S.N.P. 15/11 Willcocks to C.O. 31 Oct. 1898.
138. N.A.K. KADCAPTORY, Box 46, file 6, Emir of Ilọrin Suleiman b. Al-Amīr Aliyu to the honoured master Mr Watts.

six months in Yola.[139] It will be recalled that in 1895 it was clear that Rābiḥ had intended to push his way down the Gongola–Benue valleys. The fear of Rābiḥ further served to induce Yola and Muri to accept conciliatory moves from the R.N.C.

In June 1895 the Emir of Muri, for years the inveterate enemy of the R.N.C., welcomed W. P. Hewby (the company's district agent in Yola) and signed a treaty with him.[140] It is evident from the Emir's insistence that trade would only be resumed on the understanding that the R.N.C. would do what he thought was good, avoid that which he considered bad and engage in no double dealing; that he was anxious only for resumption of simple friendly relations.

The company was not as pliable as the Emir of Muri had hoped, but his death in June 1896 would seem to have prevented an eruption of the old Muri hostility to the company. The new Emir, perhaps compelled by the apparently more serious fear of Rābiḥ or some other European interloper, signed a new treaty with the R.N.C. in 1897. This was despite the fact that since before the death of the late Emir the company had refused to recognize the authority of Muri west of the Donga river. Fear of the company's military might seems also to have been a factor in Muri's soft attitude. On receipt of instructions from Sokoto in November 1898,[141] asking the Emir to expel Europeans from his territories, he is said to have vacillated between his allegiance to the Caliph and fear of losing the company's support.[142] He did not expel the Europeans. His ultimate acceptance of them leaves no doubt that he was following the law of necessity as he could discern it.

Before the British occupation of the Caliphate Muri seems to have been on reasonably tolerable terms with the British. None of the many R.N.C. expeditions to the neighbouring territories,

139. Collection of al-Wazīr Junaidu, present Wazir of Sokoto: Adamu Jekada (political agent of R.N.C., native of Kano) to al-Wazīr Bukhārī. Adamu explained that the messengers at Yola were not Christians but Arabs going to Rābiḥ with a message. The Emir of Yola detained them for six months until R.N.C. officials came to plead with the Emir. He refused. They (the messengers) turned back and finally went to Bornu via Ibi.
140. Kirk-Greene, *op. cit.*, pp. 45–6, quoting from W. P. Hewby's diary of his visit; also J. Fremantle, *Gazetteer of Muri Province*, pp. 15–16.
141. Fremantle, *Gazetteer of Muri Province*, p. 6.
142. Kirk-Greene, *op. cit.*, p. 47, quoting Hewby.

such as those which conquered Wase and Suntai in 1898, was directed against Muri. The latter expedition (Suntai, September 1898) was in fact in aid of the Emir of Bakundi.[143]

For similar reasons as Muri's, the attitude of the Emir of Yola towards the R.N.C. after 1895 softened. Towards the end of 1896 he allowed the company for the first time ever to build stores and warehouses on his territory.[144] In 1897 there were rumours that Rābiḥ and Ḥayat had sent their troops south to Marua.[145] The Emir of Yola readily signed a treaty with the R.N.C. in August of that same year.[146] It is not known what reply the Emir gave to the Caliph's instructions, which he received later in the year, to expel Europeans from his territory following their conquest of Bida and Ilọrin, but the R.N.C. stations in Adamawa were not evacuated. It is probable that Rābiḥ's skirmishes with the French in the Shari region—not far from his territory—kept him friendly with the R.N.C., whose agents probably missed no opportunity of impressing upon him the valuable asset he would find in the company if he was attacked.

In 1898 the Germans began the effective conquest of the part of Adamawa which had fallen to them by the Anglo–German treaty of 1893. In April 1899 a German expedition under Capt. von Kamptz conquered Tibati and entered into friendly relations with Ngaundere (both in Adamawa). In August of the same year, von Kamptz found it necessary to reconquer Tibati.[147] As the Emir of Yola was most probably ignorant of the Anglo–German agreement of 1893, German conquest of his territory would presumably have strengthened his reliance on the R.N.C. which showed no sign of hostility towards his territory. Until the British conquest in 1901 the Germans, not the British, may have seemed to the Emir the obvious evil to be dreaded.

Bauchi and Gombe. Away from the Benue valley, the emirates of Bauchi and Gombe, which were visited by two W.A.F.F.

143. For detailed description of the R.N.C. campaigns on the Benue see R.N.C. military expeditions 1886–99, in Military Museum, Zaria, no. 1602; also Fremantle, *Gazetteer of Muri*, pp. 8–14.
144. Kirk-Greene, *op. cit.*, p. 44.
145. *Ibid.*, p. 49, Records of a severe defeat of Zubeir Emir of Yola at the hands of a Rābiḥ-Ḥayat expedition.
146. Text of treaty in F.O. 2/167, Treaty no. 406, 25 Aug. 1897.
147. C.O. 446/5, F. Lascalles to Salisbury, 4 Oct. 1899, summary of article in *North German Gazette* of 3 Oct. 1899.

recruiting expeditions in 1898, did not show overt hostility to Europeans (of whom the vast majority of the local populations were ignorant) but they were undoubtedly sullen. The first expedition, led by Lt. Bryan, carried a friendly letter to the Emir of Bauchi from W. P. Hewby. On 14 July 1898, when the expedition reached Bauchi, the Emir told Bryan that the request to travel through his country to recruit people under a strange power was unusual. Although he could not give any active assistance, he said that he would not hinder people from enlisting provided slaves were not recruited. In actual fact he actively discouraged people from enlisting. Behind the diplomatic ruse of the permission granted, his hint, carefully dropped to the expedition, that a three days' stay would be considered sufficiently long, reveals what his real attitude was. Furthermore, although the Emir, commenting verbally on Hewby's letter, said he would be very happy to receive officers who might visit his country, he told Hewby bluntly in his written reply, that no more white men must visit his country.[148]

The hostility of Bauchi people was apparent to the expedition. The Emir sent them away with sweet words but exerted himself in undermining their recruiting efforts. At Gombe the Emir and Galadiman Ako were desirous for Bryan's assistance against Mallam Jibrīl Gaini, then at Burmi. As the expedition would not give such assistance nothing tangible resulted from the negotiations.[149]

A second W.A.F.F. recruiting expedition under Captain Lynch[150] agreed to assist Gombe against Mallam Jibrīl but only in return for 300 recruits. The initially enthusiastic welcome accorded Lynch changed to coldness. The new Emir, 'Umar, informed Lynch that Islam would not permit him to force his subjects to join his troops. In the evening of 24 October, it

148. C.O. 446/4, Willcocks to C.O., 10 Feb. 1899, encl. 1, Bryan's report on recruiting expeditions to Bauchi under Lts Bryan and MacNaghten (from Ibi on 15 June 1898 and back to Ibi on 15 September). Hewby was Company's agent at Ibi.

149. *Ibid.*, the Emir of Gombe 'Abd al-Qādir must have died in late June or early July 1898. According to Lt. Bryan, he received an invitation from the Emir on 30 June but on 14 July Lt. MacNaghten, whom Bryan asked to go to Gombe, received news of the Emir's death.

150. C.O. 446/4, Wallace to C.O., 3 Feb. 1899, encl. 1, reporting tour of Capt. Lynch in the Benue District (28 Sept. to Dec. 1898) by Capt. N. M. Lynch, 18 Dec. 1898.

became clear that negotiations had broken down when the Emir sent orders to Lynch to pay the price of the corporal he had with him because he was an absconded slave of the Ajia (Treasurer) of Gombe. Lynch observed that the 'fanatical hatred of white men among the ruling classes apart, the poorer folks felt ashamed to be seen in white men's following'.[151] This raises the question whether in fact the bulk of the British African soldiers (in effect, mercenaries) were not of slave origin.

By the end of 1899 consciousness and fear of imminent conquest at the hands of Europeans were widespread in the Caliphate. The will to resist attack was nowhere lacking, nor was it seriously in danger of being foiled by internal divisive forces within the emirates. The hatred of the prospect of rule by unbelievers overrode all other considerations. No one was more aware of this fact than Goldie who, commenting on the difference between the culture of Christian-Europeans and Muslims in particular (who looked down with contempt on the Europeans as *kafirs*), made the following remarks about the people of the Sokoto Caliphate:

> However it may be in other parts of the world, it is certain that the populations of Nigeria [i.e. Northern Nigeria] whether Mohammedan or pagan entertain entirely different views of life from those entertained in this country and they would rather be misgoverned by their own people, than be governed by the very best of our officials.[152]

One thing that emerges from this chapter is that conscious and resentful of the imminence of European conquest as the emirates of the Caliphate were, the forms their reactions to European penetration and activities took were determined not just by hatred for Europeans as unbelievers but mainly (and this implies no contradiction) by the immediate interests of each particular emirate. It must be noted also that by 1899 the pressure of the European advance was already closely felt by the Caliphate and tension between it and the Europeans had mounted so high that it seemed obvious that settlement would only be brought about by force.

The Caliph, it is clear, had an overall policy. But even his orders to the emirates, like the one asking them to close the roads

151. *Ibid.*
152. R.H.B.E., Africa S.58, interviews with Goldie taken down in short-hand by Darwin, 15 March 1899.

and wage *jihād* against foreigners, were given within the framework of the defence of particular areas by the emirates directly affected. The central authority of the Caliphate, though strained to some extent by the new problems, was functioning well. Even an outside observer like Goldie knew it. In December 1897 he had stressed the fact that the Caliph's power was the major obstacle to European assertion of sovereignty and that even though the British might have nothing to fear from his military power 'his power as *Khalifa* is very great'.[153]

A committee appointed by the British government in 1898 (the Niger Committee) to look into the problems of effective occupation of 'Northern Nigeria' recommended that since the Caliphate could not be taken by 'a general coup-de-main, . . . it should be done gradually, each Emir being taken in turn'.[154]

The policy of piecemeal occupation, which the British thereafter followed scrupulously, was particularly suited to conquering the Caliphate. By the end of 1899 the breach between the Caliph and the R.N.C. was complete. Earlier in that year the Caliph and the Emir of Gwandu had refused the R.N.C. tribute many times before they accepted it at last and then only grudgingly.[155] Sometime in 1899 or in early 1900 the Caliph broke off diplomatic relations with the R.N.C. He wrote:

> To the Royal Niger Company Ltd., greetings. . . . That you may know that we have received your letter and we understand your words. But, as for us, our Lord is Allāh . . ., our creator and our possessor. We take whatever our prophet, Muḥammad, upon him be peace, brought to us. We shall not change it for anything until our end. Do not send to us after this.[156]

From 1899 until the proclamation of F. D. Lugard, the British High Commissioner for Northern Nigeria, was sent to Sokoto there appears to have been no communication between the Caliph

153. C.O. 445/4, Goldie to Lugard, 20 Dec. 1897.
154. R.H.B.E., Africa S.58, Report of Niger Committee, 4 August 1898.
155. C.O. 446/30, Lugard to C.O., 23 Jan. 1903.
156. N.A.K. KADCAPTORY, G.O.K.1/1/2, Box 45, Amīr al-Mu'minīn 'Abd al-Raḥmān to the Royal Niger Company Ltd (see Appendix III). This letter was received by the Lugard administration. Since this administration did not inherit any paper from the R.N.C. it seems that the letter was written in late 1899 (and reached Lokoja after 1 Jan. 1900) or early in 1900 before the receipt of Lugard's proclamation in Sokoto.

and the British. The R.N.C. Charter was revoked 'by warrant under the Queen's sign Manual' of 28 December 1899.[157] Since 1897, when it had become clear that the Company was in no position effectively to bear the 'Empire's burdens' in the Caliphate against the onslaught of France and Germany, the British government had been giving consideration to the revocation of its charter.

A factor which was important in the British occupation of the Caliphate was that even though there was hostility against Europeans in general, it seems to have been expected that conquest and establishment of infidel rule would most likely come from the French. By not establishing their rule over Nupe and Ilọrin after 1897, the R.N.C. did not appear anxious to seize the sovereignty of the Caliphate. From 1898 they had withdrawn to the Niger–Benue valleys and, already on the eve of the revocation of their Charter, they showed no overt intention of conquering again or of establishing their rule. By contrast, Sokoto, Gwandu and the emirates on the northern frontiers were more preoccupied with fear of French violence and conquests on their boundaries. Unaware that by agreement between Britain and France the Caliphate had been allotted to Britain, the French danger loomed larger in their eyes than ever before in the years 1899–1901. The attitude of the emirates on the northern frontiers to the French aptly illustrates the local particularism in defence matters within the Caliphate.

THE EMIRATES ON THE NORTHERN FRONTIERS AND THE FRENCH 1899

In 1899 the French government sent out Captains Voulet and Chanoine on a survey expedition of the Anglo–French boundary from Say to Barrua.[158] The expedition, whose original escort of 270 had been increased by 400 more by Voulet and Chanoine, besides 200 women and 800 carriers, resembled a force of occupation more than a survey party. Naturally, it spread panic

157. F.O. 93/6/22, for original of the warrant of revocation; see Flint, *op. cit.*, pp. 295–312 for a full discussion of the revocation.
158. A.N.S.O.M., Afrique 3, file 376, 'Instructions Politiques', to the Voulet-Chanoine expedition, Ministre des Affaires Etrangères au Ministre des Colonies, 25 July 1898.

before it among the local populations.[159] Sokoto, from information sent in by Modibo, the Emir of Say, knew of the approach of the expedition.

The Voulet–Chanoine expedition met far greater opposition from the inhabitants along their route than it had expected.[160] Yet such were the violent acts of the expedition that people fled several towns on its route. It burnt several towns. At its approach the chiefs of Arewa towns and Chibiri submitted and offered gifts.[161] From Matankari, which was deserted in panic, Voulet and Chanoine sent detachments in all directions. Sabon Birni was evacuated. The terror spread to Sokoto. The Caliph, ʿAbd al-Raḥmān, went to Wurno from Sokoto, presumably with an army, on hearing of the expedition's approach to his northern boundaries. The expedition left by night (26 May 1899) on hearing of the Caliph's movements, but not before it had burnt two towns in Sokoto territory.[162] The Caliph wrote to inform the Emir of Gombe (this might well have been a general circular to the Emirs) and thanked God for instilling fear into the heart of the Christians.[163]

The leader of another French expedition, Klobb, sent to investigate reports of the Voulet–Chanoine atrocities, was murdered on the orders of Voulet and Chanoine, who were in turn killed by their own soldiers on 16 July 1899. The remnants of the Klobb expedition led by Lt. Pallier, assisted by Joalland and Maynier, marched towards Zinder. At Tirmeni, near Zinder, the Zinder army was routed on 30 July and on 15 September the fugitive Emir was caught and killed by the French.[164] In July Agades fell to another French expedition led by Foureau and

159. *Ibid.*, file 38b, Military minutes, Ministre des affaires d'outre-mer 15 Oct. 1900; for an account of the expedition see Jean Perie and Michel Sellier, 'Histoire des populations du cercle de Dosso', *Bulletin de l'IFAN*, xii (1950), pp. 1016–72.
160. A.N.S.O.M., Afrique 3, file 37b, Voulet au Ministre des Colonies, report from Chibiri, 1 March 1899.
161. Perié and Sellier, *loc. cit.*
162. Corr. X, no. 27, Amīr al-Mu'minīn ʿAbd al-Raḥmān to Amīr al-Jaish, ʿUmar b. al-Amīr Koiranga, 15th Muḥarram, Friday. The only 15th Muḥarram which was a Friday during the years towards the end of the nineteenth century fell on 26 May 1899 (1377 A.H.).
163. *Ibid.*
164. Battle of Tirmeni can be followed in Perié and Sellier, *loc. cit.* Gabriel Hanotaux and Martineau, *Histoire des Colonies Françaises* (Paris, 1931), vol. iv, pp. 241–52.

Lamy, also going to the Chad. By the end of 1899 the French had become the rulers of the territories immediately to the north of the Caliphate.

The French conquests created panic in the emirates of the northern frontiers. During the subjugation of Tessawa by Lamy from November to December 1899, the Emir of Katsina, frightened by the French approach to Gazawa, sent envoys to them, with gifts of 10 horses, 10,000 kolanuts, 300 skins of *Filālī* (goat skins) and a load of tobacco, to plead for peace.[165] He was assured that Katsina would not be attacked unless he showed aggression. In return he promised free passage through his territory and protection to all French travellers who might come. The Emir of Kano, at a safer distance than Katsina, sent a congratulatory message to the French on the conquest of Zinder,[166] his mortal enemy. Daura, Kazaure and Hadejia promised to furnish the French with whatever they needed but begged that the latter should not compromise their relations with the Caliph.[167] A French official observing the situation in these emirates remarked 'ils paraissent craindre à la fois leur souverain et notre puissance'.[168]

The British threat had receded to the background before the French. In any case it was not the immediate problem of the northern frontier emirates who fixed their gaze on the French in whose activities they perceived danger to themselves. Even in the southern emirates the departure of a large British force to Ashanti early in 1900 reduced any fears of attack by the British, since it imposed a policy of military inaction on the new Lugard administration.

The Caliph, in the same way as his emirs, offered 'friendship' to the French to ward them off. For instance, he allowed the Emir of Birnin Konni to offer services to them to facilitate their passage. The French were, however, aware that despite his show of friendship the Caliph was not well disposed either to them or to the British, but was contented, in the circumstances, to work underground against them.[169]

165. A.N.S.O.M., Afrique 3, file 42b, Lamy à M. le Ministre des Colonies, 5 Jan. 1900.
166. *Ibid.*
167. A.N.S.O.M., Soudan 4, file 9, Capitaine Moll au Gouverneur Général, 'Situation politique', 1 Jan. 1901.
168. *Ibid.*
169. *Ibid.*

Local particularism apart, the apparent encirclement of the Caliphate by hostile foreigners must have rendered the prospect of combination of the emirates against them (even assuming it was ever contemplated) more difficult still. The position of the Caliph and indeed of the whole Caliphate was aptly summed up by Captain Moll, the Commandant of the French post at Zinder in 1901: 'The progress of European conquest to the West, North and East as much as to the South of his territories has also contributed not a little to the weakening of his power.'[170]

170. *Ibid.*

Part III
Overthrow of the Caliphate

Chapter 7
The fall of the Southern emirates Bauchi and Gombe, 1900-1902

CHANGING RELATIONS BETWEEN THE CALIPHATE AND THE BRITISH

The first day of this century witnessed a decisive change in British policy towards the Sokoto Caliphate. On that day the British administration of 'Northern Nigeria' was formally inaugurated at Lokoja by F. D. Lugard. The British had thus, at least by implication, abandoned their policy, hitherto directed towards establishing amicable relations with the Caliphate as a means of exercising an informal sway over it for a definite commitment to the establishment of formal rule either through peaceful negotiation or by force if necessary. Since the earlier peace policy had failed under the R.N.C., the coming of Lugard (as head of the new administration) must be seen as tantamount to a tacit expression of British willingness to overthrow the Caliphate by conquest.[1]

In the final analysis it must be admitted, even at the risk of following the 'ifs' of history, that the issue involved was not whether the Caliphate would be overthrown or not. Britain had the military power to do this. Even though Lugard was not implacably committed to a policy of war, war was implicit in the situation since the complete failure of R.N.C.'s policy of peaceful negotiation. Nevertheless Lugard did not abandon diplomacy completely, because he had a faint hope that it might succeed. To understand the course of the overthrow, and why it took that particular course, the whole stirring episode must be seen against the background of the history of the Caliphate as analysed in the preceding chapters.

Our appraisal of the establishment and organization of the

1. The British government was unwilling to make the large financial outlay which a military confrontation would involve. Nonetheless, a military confrontation could clearly not be avoided if the British administration of Northern Nigeria was to become effective.

Caliphate demonstrates its continued unity down to the eve of its overthrow. The question arises why this unity was apparently not shown among the emirates in their resistance to European conquest. Crucial to the answer is the nature of the unity. In the system which operated, it will be recalled that each emirate owed direct allegiance to the Caliph, who was the symbol and the bond of unity. The emirates were united from the top and the Caliph exercised his control over each of them separately.

Each emir exercised delegated authority of general import from the Caliph (*imarat al-tafwīḍ ʿalā al-ʿumūm*), as opposed to mere executive authority (*imarat al-tanfīdh*). Consequently each emirate enjoyed a high degree of autonomy (within the Islamic framework) in its day-to-day affairs. This arrangement emphasized the development of a high degree of particularism in the emirates. Held together by common ideals of Islam which had brought them together in the first instance, and by common allegiance to one Imām (the Caliph), the emirates were in the words of D. M. Last, 'microcosms of the Sokoto model'. Within this framework they had common general interests, shared a mutual sympathy and a common identity as members of one *Umma*. Localism was therefore not contradictory to unity.

As earlier noted, provincialism was best expressed in the sphere of defence, with which this study is immediately concerned. It was a distinctly marked feature of the manner in which the Caliphate was established, and it was thereafter perpetuated by the continued preoccupation of each emirate, albeit in a much attenuated degree by the end of the century, with maintaining or expanding its territory against the opposition of local enemies. True enough, emirates often looked up to, and depended on, the Caliph for guidance in facing their defence problems. But it seems that the Caliph's assistance was usually not expected to take the form of direct military aid. At best it amounted to giving instructions to neighbouring emirates to unite against a particular enemy.

The military threat to any particular emirate engaged the concern of the Caliph, but the defence of each emirate and its frontiers was the direct responsibility of the Emir. Hence ʿUthmān b. Fodiye stressed this duty in his letter of appointment to Yaʿqūb b. Daṭi (first Emir of Bauchi), and towards the end of the nineteenth century Muḥammad Sambo, Emir of Zaria (1878–88), was deposed for inability to defend his emirate. On the eastern frontiers military incursions from Bornu, after 1826 when they ceased to be aimed at a general invasion of the Caliphate, were a problem to be dealt with by the emirates there, including Adamawa, which shared a disputed boundary with Bornu. Even though Jibrīl Gaini established a state within the state in Burmi and for many years defied the combined effort of the neighbouring emirates, the latter were, in terms of military aid, left alone with the problem. The permanent threat of the Ningi to neighbouring emirates, from the mid-century to the end, was the exclusive concern of those emirates. Even Ḥayat b. Saʿīd, who espoused a cause to which the Caliph was decidedly antagonistic, was left to Adamawa (which suffered from his military exploits) to deal with. In the same manner as the above examples, Damagaram was the special incubus of Katsina, Daura, Hadejia and Kano at different times, just as Maradi attacks on Katsina were the latter's peculiar problem. Far away on the south-western frontiers, Ilọrin's military involvement in the Yoruba wars went on as if the rest of the Caliphate was unconcerned.

In fact, the emirates as a whole had hardly any occasion for taking common action in defence matters, and one can scarcely point to any event which brought representatives from all of them together at the same time and place. The occasions which brought peoples from a large number of emirates together were the participations of the eastern emirates in the Caliph's annual *razzias* or in wars to which he summoned them. The Gwandu emirates did not attend the annual gathering. The establishment of a central standing army, which could have ruled out the necessity of the Caliph's annual summonses to the emirates to send contingents, would have greatly increased the Caliphate's military effectiveness, and no doubt altered the course of its history. However, for the Caliphate, it was not an age of large professional or standing armies.

During times of mutual defence crises a common feeling and urge to act together was discernible among emirates which felt threatened by a common danger. Examples of inter-emirate co-operation for defence and offence are not lacking. The urge to combine when confronted with the threat of conquest by foreigners can be seen in the projected Ilọrin–Nupe–Bussa alliance in 1896–97 before the fall of the first two. Similarly the emirates immediately threatened by the reported approach of

Rābiḥ's troops showed by their appeals to Kano and Sokoto a disposition to, and at least a groping after, a policy of combined resistance.

The Caliph and the Emir of Gwandu, who both had responsibility for other emirates, appear to have been aware of the encirclement of the Caliphate by hostile forces towards the end of the century and had also acted with general consideration for the emirates as a whole in their relations with Europeans throughout the century. However, the same provincialism which characterized many aspects of government in the emirates was revealed in their relations with foreigners. They had not only entered unilaterally into relations with Europeans but had dealt in a similarly unilateral fashion with the conflict which arose from those relations. This was not without some qualifications. So long as the foreign engagements of the emirates did not, from their standpoint, go beyond simple commercial agreements, the Caliph's intervention was unnecessary. However, it is clear from the last two chapters that once these agreements provoked conflicts of a political nature, involving disputes about cession of sovereignty, the Caliphs and the Emirs of Gwandu often intervened by sending pertinent instructions to their emirs. Again, this was perfectly in tune with the tradition in the Caliphate. Whereas policy regarding overall security was the Caliph's concern, actual implementation of requisite measures through war had always been the responsibility of the particular emirate or group of emirates immediately threatened. Thus in terms of military involvement, even though the British conquest of Bida and Ilọrin caused much fear among the emirates, it was essentially a Nupe–Ilọrin affair, just as the threat from Rābiḥ's troops was the affair of the emirates immediately threatened. It must be noted that before the end of the nineteenth century there was never any obvious general threat to the whole Caliphate which might have invoked a general combination of all emirates. This observation does not in any way suggest that if such a state of emergency arose lack of a precedent would automatically rule out a general combination.

Yet it is clear that even if the state of emergency created by the threat of foreign invasion had made obvious the necessity of concerted action by all emirates as a departure from custom, the impression that the Caliphate was encircled by hostile forces was enough to vitiate efforts in that direction. As it was not known in the Caliphate that among Europeans the real source of danger were the British, reason called for vigilance on all frontiers. It is not surprising therefore that, to meet the unprecedented threat, the Caliph resorted to traditional methods which were hopelessly inadequate.

It will be recalled that the Caliph's instructions to the emirates after the British conquest of Bida and Iḷọrin were not to call them to take joint action but to ask for vigilance on the part of each emir in repelling European invasion of his territory by closing the roads to their advance and waging the *jihād* against them. Similarly Kano and the emirates east of it were instructed to close the road to Rābiḥ's troops; in the west Gwandu was to do the same to the Cazemajou expedition. When, in 1901, Faḍlallāh b. Rābiḥ was negotiating an alliance with the British and came as far as Gombe's frontiers, the Caliph instructed the Emir to halt his advance.[2] Likewise in a letter (probably written after 1900) the Caliph, ʿAbd al-Raḥmān, instructed the Emir, ʿUmar, of Gombe 'in the name of God, the Prophet and our Shaikh the *mujāddīd*, ʿUthmān b. Fodiye, to exercise great watchfulness over your towns and be on the look out for news of the Christians',[3] and to see to it that there should be no division among his people. This letter may well have been a circular to all emirs. So far, there is no way of telling whether the Caliph's adherence to the traditional security measures of the Caliphate was owing to his inability to formulate a new policy to meet changed circumstances or to a realization on his part that the new circumstances did not permit the adoption of any other policy.

Quite apart from the foregoing considerations, there were other factors which put the Caliphate at a disadvantage *vis-à-vis* the Europeans. The European threat was not just new, it was also extremely baffling. With regard, for instance, to the joint annual expeditions with Sokoto, the participating emirates used to have notification in advance, since the enemies were known long beforehand. Mobilization of the Caliphate's forces therefore raised no pressing problems. Even in the event of a sudden outbreak of war, the weapons of the opposing sides were similar, as were their methods of warfare. Since wars involved the use of few, if any, firearms (used with insufficient skill, as revealed during the wars with Europeans) battles were usually protracted,

2. See below, p. 238, n. 79.
3. Corr. X, no. 4.

often entailed long sieges and were more often than not inconclusive. It was therefore possible, if found necessary, for emirates distant from the theatre of a war to participate in it before the campaign ended.

In contrast, when dealing with Europeans the emirates were confronted with new problems of superior battle tactics as well as superior arms and skill in using them. Success or failure in battle was consequently decided in a few hours and sometimes within minutes. In the circumstances of the long distances involved there was little possibility of a quick general mobilization of the Caliphate's forces or even of the forces of a few emirates.

The invading Europeans also differed in another vital respect from the enemies the emirates were accustomed to dealing with. Whereas the latters' territories were accessible and visible targets for offence and retaliation the European countries were beyond reach. Admittedly the British invading army had a headquarters within the Caliphate. But since this was a military camp with war as its trade, and because Europeans were regarded with awe on account of their military power, they could not be harmed in the same way as traditional enemies. Besides, the British, with a standing army, were in a position to vitiate moves by the emirates to combine—a process which was bound to be slow. Even though the Caliphate's greatest chance of success in battle against the British lay in united resistance, in actual fact each emirate had to fend for itself.

In addition to the nineteenth-century antecedents of the Caliphate, the course and manner of its overthrow must also be seen against the background of the circumstances of its British invaders. As already mentioned, on 28 December 1899 the Charter of the R.N.C. was revoked and its claims to administer the territories of the Caliphate were transferred to the British government.[4] F. D. Lugard was appointed to head the administration of 'Northern Nigeria'. Earlier in the month he had been promoted to the rank of Brigadier-General to befit his status as High Commissioner. Lugard arrived at Lokoja on 31 December and on the following day, the new administration was inaugurated in an impressive ceremony.[5] The Caliphate had thus, in British Law, become a British Protectorate. This was however

4. F.O. 93/6/22, original of Revocation of R.N.C. Charter 'By warrant under the Queen's sign manual'.

5. Perham, *Years of Authority*, pp. 24–6.

no more than a claim yet to be made good. And Lugard was duly appreciative of the odds against his administration.

It is clear from R.N.C. relations with the emirates that the former had done little more than prevent other European powers from acquiring territories in the Caliphate. It will be recalled that after 1897 the R.N.C. was unable to establish an administration either in Ilọrin or in Nupe. The W.A.F.F. had its headquarters at Jebba, with detachments in Illo, Ashigiri (near Nikki), Bussa, and Yelwa, a garrison in Lokoja and detachments in the Benue region at Akwanaji, Ibi and Abinsi.[6] With the exception of Lokoja, Jebba, Yelwa and Ibi, the military posts of the company were outside the Caliphate. All were designed to control the Niger–Benue waterways. The military posts did not therefore represent any obviously immediate threat to the Caliphate. This is not to say that the Caliphate did not see the writing on the wall. The total strength of the W.A.F.F. when fully recruited was limited to two battalions of infantry, one battalion of mounted infantry and a small battery, amounting in all to 2288, including 212 European officers.[7]

Before 1900 the British had begun to tackle the problem of communication. By the end of 1899 a telegraph line from Lokoja to Jebba had been completed, while Lokoja was already linked with Lagos.[8] Thus the new administration could ask for reinforcements from Lagos without undue delay if it found itself in difficulties. In 1900 the telegraph line along the Benue from Lokoja was already under way. With regard to actual occupation of territory, however, even the seemingly modest claim,[9] that on Lugard's assumption of office only one-tenth of the 'Protectorate' showed any sign of organized British control, is an exaggeration.

Lugard had a small force to make the necessary fresh start. Out of this 1200 troops under Col. Willcocks were despatched to help in the Ashanti war in May 1900.[10] The W.A.F.F. apparently did not find recruitment easy, nor could it rely on the recruits it had in hand until they had been tried in battle. Lugard viewed the

6. C.O. 446/9, F. D. Lugard to C.O., 23 April 1900.
7. N.A.K., S.N.P.1/2, no. 3, C.O. to Treasury, 29 Jan. 1900. *Northern Nigeria Gazette*, 31 March 1900 (for details on personnel), *Military Report on Nigeria*, vol. i (1939), p. 36 f. and *Northern Nigeria Blue Book*, 1900, p. 1.
8. N.A.K., S.N.P.15/7, Major Festing's Report, Nov. 1899.
9. Perham, *Years of Authority*, p. 39.
10. C.O. 446/10, Tel. Lugard to C.O., Jebba, 17 June 1900.

rank and file with great suspicion on account of his fear of Muslim 'fanaticism'. He laid it down that officers must treat their Muslim rank and file with suspicion, especially as he believed that there were attempts from the emirates to suborn the troops. He also instructed officers to watch the rank and file closely in order to ensure that Yoruba Muslims, for some unspecified reason, were not recruited, and to confine Muslim elements to Hausas. Above all, Hausa-speaking pagans were to be preferred. Officers were instructed to spare no efforts in showing the Muslim rank and file that European rule over Muslims was not unusual. Mosques were to be built for the troops and mallams employed to look after their welfare, but ardent and at the same time intelligent mallams were to be regarded as distinct security risks.[11] The Lugard administration endeavoured to be cautious in order to avoid outbreak of Muslim 'fanaticism' not only within its own army but in the emirates. Although the study of Lugard's administration is outside the scope of this study, it is pertinent to remark that fear of an eruption of 'Muslim fanaticism' influenced his actions not only during the wars of conquest but also in his administrative policy thereafter.

To face his new task, Lugard did not inherit any records from the R.N.C. to guide him. Hence, although he intended to make continued payment of the old R.N.C. tribute to the emirs and the Caliph an essential part of his policy of conciliation, he did not know to which rulers tribute was to be paid and what were the exact amounts.[12] Most of the Caliphate's interior, including the names of some important towns, was unknown to the new administration.[13] Its task therefore appeared formidable.

The apparent weakness of the Lugard administration did not immediately handicap it. In fact, in a sense, it was of some advantage. The closest sources of danger to the British—Nupe and Ilọrin—had learned through hard experience the unwisdom of daring the European power. The seemingly peaceful attitude imposed on the British while their troops were away in Ashanti, as already mentioned, helped to strengthen the impression

11. N.A.K., S.N.P.15/1, no. 34, 14 June 1900.
12. N.A.K., S.N.P.7/2, no. 12, Lugard to C.O., 2 Feb. 1901.
13. N.A.K. KADCAPTORY, G.O.K.1/1/15, Abadie to H.C., 13 March 1902. As late as March 1902 Lugard was asking where Katagum and Hadejia were; see encl. Private Secretary to the H.C. to Abadie, 3 March 1902.

among the interior emirates that the French, and not the British, were to be feared.

Lugard embarked on establishing good relations with the Caliphate by sending out to the Caliph and the emirs, Arabic translations of his proclamation of 1 January 1900,[14] announcing the change in the administration. In the first paragraph it is stated that the R.N.C. had ruled over the 'territories of the Niger',[15] and the impression is given that the change of administration was made because the R.N.C. had imposed itself on the African states by use of force. Although the facts are distorted and the R.N.C. had never ruled any considerable part of the Caliphate the implication that the new administration was intended to be different from the displaced R.N.C. is obvious. Granted the unlikely premise that 'territories of the Niger' would be intelligible to Sokoto, the rights over the Caliphate which the proclamation by implication credited to the R.N.C. were completely unfounded in the light of the realities of R.N.C.–Caliphate relations and treaties. By its contents alone, particularly the breach of treaties implicit in it, the proclamation could hardly have been better framed to arouse the fear and the hostility of its recipients. Neither the R.N.C. nor their heir would be considered by the Caliph and his emirs to have any right to make such pronouncements over any part of the Caliphate.

The language of the translation, an extreme example of literal translation from English, is woefully inelegant, ungrammatical and misleading. The proclamation was certainly not in the spirit of the policy of caution which Lugard wanted to pursue. Alder Burdon, one of Lugard's Residents, appropriately summed up the implications of the bad translation when he wrote: 'To a highly educated man like Audu [he meant ʿAbd al-Raḥmān, the Caliph] the illiterate character of the letter would induce a feeling of contempt for its reputed author, while its ungrammatical unintelligibility could not help but cause a feeling of fear.'[16] On reading the proclamation, the Caliph is reported to have said: 'No letter ever brought fear like this one, I'll read no more letters

14. N.A.K. KADCAPTORY, Box 45, item 26, Arabic Letter Book, no. 1 (see Appendix IV).

15. It is not possible to say categorically that 'territories of the Niger' as used in the proclamation refers to the Lower Niger. Rather it appears to refer to territories bordering on the Niger—hence at least part of the Sokoto Caliphate.

16. N.A.K., S.N.P.7/3/40 (Conf.), Burdon to H.C., 7 April 1902.

from white men!'[17] A fundamental factor in the situation was that the conflict of interest between the Caliph and the British left room for neither mutual sympathetic understanding nor for compromise.

Sokoto and Gwandu's reaction to the proclamation confirmed their implacable hostility to the new administration and its pretensions. Kiari, Lugard's messenger to Sokoto, was told on arrival there to bring no more white men's letters. He was hastily conducted out of the town with an assurance, popularly echoed in Sokoto, that they would have nothing to do with the white men.[18] Babando, the messenger to Gwandu, was told that there could be no reply after white men had seized Gwandu territories.[19] Thus the first move in Lugard's diplomacy was a failure. His contact with Sokoto and Gwandu thereafter remained difficult and inconsequential until the fall of Sokoto.

The policy of piece-meal occupation recommended by the Niger Committee in 1898 was faithfully pursued by Lugard. For reasons already discussed, it provoked no unified military resistance in the Caliphate. The fall of each emirate was therefore, in the main, its peculiar history. Even though there are similarities in the process of the occupation of various emirates, for each of them it was in many ways a peculiar event. There are, besides, important variations from one emirate to another, depending on the particular circumstances of each. For these reasons and for a clear understanding of what actually happened, it is necessary to examine, as far as possible, the occupation of each emirate separately.

ILỌRIN, KONTAGORA AND NUPE

From the beginning the ultimate aim of the British was the occupation of Sokoto. The occupation of Ilọrin, Kontagora and Bida (the first emirates to fall) was part of a general British

17. *Ibid.*
18. N.A.K. KADCAPTORY, G.O.K.1/1/5, Box 45, Resident, Kabba to H.C., 23 Jan. 1901. The Caliph assured Kiari that he was ready to fight the white man. In March 1901 Wallace was still trying to send fresh copies of the proclamation to Sokoto and Gwandu; see *ibid.*, Wallace to H.C., 14 March 1901.
19. N.A.K. KADCAPTORY, G.O.K.1/1/7, Box 45, Assist. Resident, Middle Niger to H.C.

programme of gradual advance towards Sokoto, just as the occupation of Adamawa, Bauchi and Gombe was a prelude to British penetration of Bornu, which they also desired to occupy before the French could forestall them there. Nupe and Ilọrin had been weakened by the defeat of 1897. Lugard's administration was in consequence suitably placed not only to feel secure at Lokoja but also to turn to good advantage the fear of the white men in those emirates. At the same time the unabated hostility of these emirates and their neighbours, even if it was latent, was proved by its expression following the departure of Lugard's troops to Ashanti. Ilọrin surged with discontent while Bida and Kontagora engaged in numerous skirmishes with troops of a W.A.F.F. survey expedition sent into the Kaduna river region. These preliminary skirmishes ended in the final fall of Nupe and Kontagora, which fall in turn facilitated the stationing of a W.A.F.F. garrison in Zaria.

It will be recalled that Ilọrin politics during the closing years of the nineteenth century witnessed an increase in the power of the baloguns and the degeneration of the Emir to a mere puppet.[20] The support given by the white men (the R.N.C.) to the Emir to buttress his waning power divided authority in the emirate by widening the gap between the Emir and his baloguns. The baloguns, who enjoyed popular following, became naturally identified with opposition to the influence of the white man, while the Emir became his creature. In fact Ilọrin was ill-placed to resist outside attack. The resistance to British occupation in the emirate took the form of simmering discontent and unrest which rendered the position of the British very precarious down to 1903. However, no fresh war was fought before the establishment of British rule.

The Emir, Suleiman, appreciative of the boost to his power which he could derive from British backing, accepted Lugard's proclamation with gratitude, expressed in two letters couched in terms of abject dependence.[21] But the first two Residents, Carnegie and Dwyer, from their assessment of the hostility of the baloguns and the people realized that their safety and that of the British administration in Ilọrin depended strictly on their supporting the Emir at all costs. The baloguns (led by Balogun

20. See above, pp. 185–7.
21. N.A.K. KADCAPTORY, Box 45, item 26, Arabic Letter Book, nos. 10 and 25, from the Emir Suleiman to Governor Lugard.

Alanamu), anxious to deny the British any pretext for attacking Iḷọrin, maintained a judicious appearance of friendship, even though it was clear they were bent on ridding the town of white men. Carnegie, well aware of the seething unrest, recommended the stationing of a W.A.F.F. detachment in the town in July 1900.[22]

The unrest in Iḷọrin increased during the second half of 1900. Crimes were rampant, the gulf between the Emir and his baloguns widened, and the former completely depended on the British to free himself from their incubus. Knowledge of the departure of the troops to Ashanti heightened the tension. There were rumours that W.A.F.F. troops had left Jebba and it was hoped that Bida would defeat the British and thus give Iḷọrin the opportunity to drive them out with ease.[23] In response to Carnegie's recommendation and his report on the 'hostile spirit' of Iḷọrin, Lugard sent a force of one N.C.O. and thirty men there in July, but warned the Resident to avoid any action that might provoke open hostility.[24] By August it was clear that anti-British feelings in Iḷọrin, by now much aggravated, were extremely widespread. The masses were willing to answer Bida's call for aid, even in defiance of their Emir, who turned down the request. Their resolution was foiled only by the conviction that the Emir in league with the British was too powerful for them. The outlying districts of Iḷọrin simply neglected the Emir's orders. The baloguns waxed stronger. In September, by which time it appears the detachment had been withdrawn, Lugard instructed Dwyer, British Resident in Iḷọrin, to accumulate strong enough evidence to warrant the deportation of Balogun Alanamu, the worst offender, whom apparently the British did not feel strong enough to remove summarily. After his unsuccessful attempt in league with Balogun Ajikọbi to throw the Resident and ten civil police out of the town in September, Alanamu bade his time. The situation in Iḷọrin remained precarious until 1903, although British conquest of other emirates had a profound effect on the elements of opposition. In January 1903 'Umar, the deposed and

22. N.A.K., S.N.P.15/11, David Carnegie to H.C., Report, July 1900.
23. *Ibid.*, Resident to H.C., 31 July 1900.
24. N.A.K., S.N.P.15/11, Lugard to Dwyer, 18 July 1900. It seems the detachment was soon withdrawn since in August Lugard wrote against the stationing of a detachment in Iḷọrin, fearing this might lead to a showdown.

exiled Emir of Bauchi, was brought to Iḷọrin[25]—a salutary demonstration of the futility of resisting British power.

Because of the unrest in Ilọrin a contingent of W.A.F.F. from Lagos had arrived there on 4 January, causing great anxiety by its march through the town. A few days later, a messenger brought a letter from the Caliph, urging Ilọrin to create disturbance to divert attention from Sokoto.[26] The Emir read the letter to the public, as was customary. Faced with the difficult choice of either maintaining his obligatory loyalty to the Caliph or appearing disloyal to the British, and therefore forfeiting the basis of his power in Ilọrin, the Emir sent the messenger to the Resident and rejected the gift of a horse which accompanied the Sokoto letter. The Resident's investigations convinced him that the Emir had so acted towards Sokoto because he did not wish to do anything which the British might consider hostile as 'every day shows more clearly how futile it would be'. In the same month the Emir was presented with his staff of office by Dwyer, the Resident.[27]

Fear of British reprisal facilitated occupation of Ilọrin without fighting. Even so, as late as 1903 the British were yet to be accepted. The Emir testified to the Resident in May 1903 that the white men had not a single friend in Ilọrin and that he himself would have been murdered long before then but for the Resident's support.[28] The subtle but passive form of resistance in Ilọrin was typical of the attitude of other emirates over and above whatever military resistance they could put up. For the British administration it was a more virulent form of opposition than military confrontation which they could deal with. Commenting on the danger and vehemence of underground resistance in Ilọrin (which had not died down by 1903) Dwyer wrote: 'I am obliged to confess that at one time I was afraid that my first appointment under your excellency would have been a failure and that I would have been forced to report my inability to keep the town in order or even remain in Ilọrin.'[29]

In Nupe and Kontagora the relations with the British were

25. N.A.K. ILORINPROF 1/1, Dwyer, Report no. 6, January 1903.
26. R.H.B.E., S.64, Report on Ilọrin Province (n.d.).
27. *Ibid.*, N.A.K. ILORINPROF, Dwyer, Report no. 6, January 1903.
28. *Ibid.*, E. C. Watson, May/June Report, 1903.
29. N.A.K., S.N.P.15/11, Dwyer to H.C., 31 August 1900, Monthly Report.

characterized by open collision leading finally to British military occupation. The hostility of both emirates took the form of attempts to eliminate the British from their military posts. The defeat of 1897 had a sobering effect on Nupe's hostility to the white man and on its military exploits. Nevertheless their hopes of regaining their independence persisted and they did not spare efforts to realize them. The 1897 defeat had the effect of encouraging the pagan populations, mainly Gwari, with whom Bida and notably Kontagora had warred since their establishment, to take the offensive. Insecurity was consequently aggravated in the two emirates. By 1899 the R.N.C. had become aware of the necessity to differentiate between slave-raiding for its own sake and emirs attacking subject peoples who revolted and refused to pay their taxes in the hope of getting R.N.C. aid.[30]

As stated earlier, the R.N.C. had reconciled itself to the return of Abubakar as Emir. When Wallace visited Bida in 1899 R.N.C. acceptance of Abubakar was sealed by a promise that when the British government took over the administration Nupe's old boundaries would be restored to it.[31] Both the Makun and the Emir therefore welcomed the Lugard administration. It held out hope to them rather than fear of expropriation. Bida accepted the proclamation.[32] Although friendly with the British, the Makun was loyal to his Emir and acted as go-between for the two parties.[33]

The subsequent rupture between the British and Nupe forced the Makun, always anxious to avoid extremes, to adopt an attitude of sitting on the fence. He justified Bida's raids of neighbouring pagan territories on the grounds that they were necessary reprisals but, at the same time, he made his non-involvement in them and his friendship to the British clear.[34]

Nupe and Kontagora's hostility to the British from 1900 had been touched off by the W.A.F.F. survey parties sent to explore the region between the Kaduna river and the Bauchi highlands early in that year. The three parties under Lt-Col. Morland,

30. N.A.K. LOKOPROF, Lok. file 22, R.N.C. to W. Watts, 4 Aug. 1899, loose sheets inside Lokoja court Record Book.
31. N.A.K., S.N.P.7/3/40, Alder Burdon to H.C., 7 April 1902.
32. N.A.K. KADCAPTORY, Box 45, item 26, Arabic Letter Book, nos. 8, 129.
33. *Ibid.*, nos. 49, 82, 107, 125, 131, 133, 135, 155. All from the Makun pleading with the British for peace and professing his friendship.
34. Only rarely did the Makun accuse Abubakar and exonerate himself, see Arabic Letter Book, *loc. cit.*, nos. 135, 155.

Cole and Lt. Monck-Mason were to go up the Kaduna, Okwa and Gurara rivers respectively. All three parties encountered considerable opposition from many villages and towns on their way. They therefore had to use force.[35]

Nupe's view, strongly advanced by the Makun, was that their rupture with the British was caused by British interference in their affairs, contrary to the understanding arrived at between them and the Emir Abubakar during Wallace's visit in 1899. The R.N.C.'s promise on that occasion amounted to a revocation of the treaty of Kosoji of 1897. British interference in 1900 was thus seen as surprising fresh evidence of their hostility and a breach of their pledge. Nupe claimed that pagan tribes, like the Gwari, had taken the opportunity of the white man's presence to raid their territories as did other pagan tribes in Kontagora. On various occasions both the Makun and the Emir wrote to Lokoja to explain that Nupe raids were reprisals against tribes who raided their farms and that the British detachment at Wushishi also raided their farms and villages and caused a great deal of unrest.[36] The British denied the charges as early as February 1900. Lugard sent stern warnings, mingled with threats, to Bida and Kontagora not to attack functionaries of his government and assured them of the dire consequences that would be attendant on what he described as their slave-raiding.[37]

Even though ready to accept settlement of the impasse between them and the British, Bida's and Kontagora's hostility increased because the British did not heed their protests. Lugard, with his troops away in Ashanti, could not repress Nupe's hostility. By July 1900 there were talks of an alliance against the British between Bida and Kontagora.[38] The tension increased as the year wore on. The Emir of Nupe stressed the breach of contract

35. Lugard, *Annual Report*, 1900, pp. 7–8. Lt-Col. Kemball travelling near Keffi in June 1900 could only obtain food for his troops by using force on the local population. He gave 6–12 lashes to various village heads in the neighbourhood of Keffi, to obtain food from them. Kemball to H.C. (from a village about 20 miles north of Keffi) 21 June 1900, enclosed in Resident's report, Middle Niger Province, June 1900; N.A.K. LOKOPROF, Letter Book no. 2.
36. Nupe's case is stated in letters from both Makun and the Emir to the British at Lokoja, see Arabic Letter Book, *loc. cit. passim.*
37. See Arabic Letter Book, *loc. cit.*, nos. 6, 7, 8, 21, 23, 24, 73, 74, 77, 81 (from the Emir of Lapai), 91, 101, 153.
38. Arabic Letter Book, *loc. cit.*, nos. 22, 65.

implicit in stationing a 'marauding' force on their territory after the clear promise that the British would be friendly towards them. Nupe was divided into three parties, each identified with past emirs who had maintained Nupe's independence against European encroachment. The Emir Maliki's and Emir Majigi's parties were for peace with the white man while the Emir Masaba's party, appropriately enough, was for war.[39] Abubakar explained to Lugard that alliance between Nupe and Kontagora, which Lugard saw as evidence of hostility, was an age-old tradition.

Convinced that the intention of the two emirates was to attack the W.A.F.F. station at Wushishi, Lugard hastened to the scene with Major O'Neill and some troops. O'Neill held the villages near Wushishi and started guerrilla warfare against Kontagora and Bida, defeating their patrols in many skirmishes. Kontagora raided close to Jebba, threatened the Niger Company's station at Raba and attacked British canoes on the river. In subsequent engagements in December O'Neill cleared the Emirs' forces on both banks of the Kaduna.[40] On 19 December he pursued the fugitive Bida forces into the city and attempted unsuccessfully to arrest the Emir.[41] The projected alliance, which was intended to include Ilọrin, was thus nipped in the bud by the British forces. As soon as the W.A.F.F. troops returned from Ashanti a full-scale attack by the British on Bida and Kontagora was undertaken early in 1901.

The operations against Kontagora and Bida were led by Lt-Col. Kemball with a total of ten officers, three N.C.O.s, 323 other ranks, three Maxim guns, and two 75 mm guns at his disposal. This total included two small contingents from Illo and Argungu detailed to prevent the Emir of Kontagora from escaping towards Sokoto and to head off any reinforcement that might attempt coming to him from Yauri and Gwandu. On 31 January 1901 an advance party of the British expedition was held up by heavy Kontagora fire at Udara (about four miles north of the city) for seven hours. The combined British force advanced in square formation against Kontagora on 1 February. It was met by the Kontagora army, estimated at 5000; armed mostly with

39. *Ibid.*, no. 65; C.O. 446/10, Lugard to C.O., 8 August 1900.
40. C.O. 4461/11, Lugard to C.O., 27 Dec. 1900; C.O. 446/14, Lugard to C.O., March 1901.
41. *Ibid.* In fact, O'Neill barely managed to escape with his life.

arrows and trade guns. The arrows fell thick among the British army at the approach to the city. The Kontagora army charged intrepidly. But when the British replied with volley firing the issue was settled in 'two minutes' with one casualty on the British side and about fifty on Kontagora's side. The remaining Kontagora horsemen were chased into the city with artillery fire. Soon after, the city was almost completely deserted. Two hundred bags of gunpowder were captured. A force was immediately sent after the fugitive Emir but, failing to catch up with him, it returned after four days.[42]

A single extant letter from the Emir, Ibrāhīm, to the Caliph indicates that the Caliph had previously given him instructions on the defence of his emirate. The letter, written shortly before the attack on Kontagora, urgently appealed to Sokoto for fresh directions.[43] Nothing seems to have come from the appeal. Perhaps it was overtaken by events. The British left a garrison of 100 rank and file and an officer in Kontagora.

In the meantime Lugard, based at Wuya, had tried unsuccessfully to persuade the Emir of Bida to submit to the British. The Makun and the Lapeni honoured Lugard's invitations but the Emir refused on three different occasions to meet Lugard. On 19 February, therefore, British forces, some 300 strong, advanced on Bida. The Emir had fled, but the remnant of Bida forces prevented the British soldiers from entering the town.[44]

Only when the Makun submitted to Lugard did the British army march into Bida. The fugitive Emir, Abubakar, was declared deposed and Lugard, even though he doubted the Makun's loyalty to the British, proclaimed him the new Emir of Bida. A flying patrol sent after Abubakar captured three of his important chiefs. A large number of his followers later returned to Bida out of frustration, but the Emir escaped, although with a reduced following, including six of his chiefs.[45] The protracted British struggle for sovereignty over Bida had at last come to an

42. For the Kontagora expedition see C.O. 446/14, Lugard to C.O., 21 March 1901; N.A.K., S.N.P.7/2, file no. 2363/1901. Lugard to C.O., dispatch relating to field operations, 31 Aug. 1901.
43. Corr. I, no. 57; reference is made in the letter to instructions previously sent by the Caliph.
44. N.A.K., S.N.P.7/2, no. 2363/1901, Lugard to C.O., 31 Aug. 1901; C.O. 446/14, Lugard to C.O., March 1901.
45. C.O. 446/14, Lugard to C.O., Feb. 1901; N.A.K., S.N.P.7/2, no. 2363/1901, Lugard to C.O., 31 Aug. 1901.

end as the emirate, left with no alternative, bowed to superior force.

It is not clear what the immediate reaction among Bida people was. The flight of the Emir, however, is indicative not only of his and his followers' fear of British military power but also of their unwillingness to live under the conquerors. A garrison was left in Bida to ensure peace. The restoration to Nupe to its pre-1897 boundaries did go a long way to assuage resentment.[46]

The full implications of a European government were as yet not grasped. The non-establishment of an effective administration after the 1897 campaign would seem to have suggested that conquest would not mean loss or change of authority. The proclamation of 1 April 1901, abolishing the legal status of slavery, was the first clear indication of the full import of European administration. Quite apart from the assertion of British sovereignty over Nupe, which it meant, it also involved a disruption of the traditional, social, economic, and political structure. Many slaves absconded, with the result that famine broke out in Nupe. Section 4 of the proclamation, which made returning runaway slaves to their owners illegal, encouraged a tendency for slaves to abscond. This was contrary to the law and custom in the Caliphate which insisted on the restitution of runaway slaves.[47]

It was with the gradual awareness of the full implications of European conquest that full-scale discontent of the Nupe was revealed. They were rudely shocked by British exercise of their power as shown by the capture of the fugitive Emir of Kontagora, Ibrāhīm, and his transportation to Lokoja in chains in March 1902. This event caused great consternation in Bida and, according to the Resident, 'a distinct air of insecurity and distrust almost amounting to sulkiness prevailed'. The British-appointed Emir (the Makun) shared the fear and the resentment, as evidenced by his *'Id al-kabīr* speech in 1902, in which he despondently pointed out to his subjects that they had to obey or face the alternative of imprisonment.[48] If Ibrāhīm could be so treated, observed the Emir, no one in Bida, himself included, could hope for better treatment from the British. The usurpation of the authority of the Caliph by the British was harped on. It was held in Bida that,

46. N.A.K., S.N.P.7/3/40, Alder Burdon to H.C. (Conf.), 7 April 1902.
47. N.A.K., S.N.P.7/3/40, Alder Burdon to H.C. (Conf.), 7 April 1902.
48. *Ibid.*

granted Ibrāhīm had committed serious offences, the proper authority to try and to punish him was the Caliph and not the British. Whatever enormities might be charged against Ibrāhīm, the feeling prevailed in Bida that he had been driven to excesses by the British, who had caused his subjects to repudiate his authority. British policy of ousting the legitimate Emir and putting another in his place at the point of bayonets if necessary, which was now becoming clear, meant, as Burdon again points out, that the new Emir was never fully recognized, was looked upon with contempt, and was liable to taunts of treachery.[49] Whatever the scale of resentment, the force behind British rule sufficed to drive it underground. As long as Sokoto was not conquered, Lugard realized that the zealous Muslim and the 'Fulani party' would remain as powerful and hostile as he noticed they were.[50]

The situation in Nupe had changed since 1897. But the anger felt at British conquest and rule had not changed. After the return of British troops from Ashanti, the Lugard administration acted swiftly. They succeeded in preventing an alliance which was being talked of between Nupe, Ilọrin and Kontagora. Kontagora and Bida were therefore dealt with separately. In Bida a strong force had not been amassed as was done in 1897, apparently because of division into parties within the emirate. It appears that only the Masaba party was bent on military resistance at all costs while the other two parties, including the Makun, considered the British irresistible. Consequently opposition to conquest was not nearly as vigorous as in 1897.

ADAMAWA

Far from Kontagora and Nupe, Adamawa was already feeling the pangs of European conquest. In 1898–99, the Germans, determined on effective occupation of their share of Adamawa (seven-eighths of the emirate), sent forces under von Kamptz against Tibati. The reigning Lamido, Amalamu, was taken prisoner and

49. The account of Bida resentment is based on a long memorandum on the shortcomings of British policy with special reference to Bida, written by the Resident of Bida Alder Burdon. N.A.K., S.N.P.7/3/40, Burdon to H.C., 7 April 1902.
50. C.S.O. 1,27/2 (Conf.), Lugard to C.O., 15 March 1902.

one of his relations was installed in his place.[51] The already strong garrison in Tibati was further reinforced early in 1900 and plans were mooted for German penetration as far as Garua.[52] Zubeir, the Emir of Yola, was informed of the European (Christian) attack on Tibati and of the confusion in which this had put the people.[53] Zubeir, apprehensive of European threat as ever, saw this threat as coming from the Germans. However, the Germans did not advance beyond Tibati until after the British conquest of Yola in September 1901.

This latter event was merely the culmination of two decades of Yola's hostility to the British. It will be recalled that since 1896 Zubeir had been driven into friendship with the British by his fear of Rābiḥ. Until 1900 the British had not done anything to forfeit this friendship. They must therefore, in the Emir's view, have appeared as friends who had promised to protect him and his territory. The British, whose attempts to exceed the bounds of normal friendly commercial relations the Emir had been able to foil for two decades, would not have appeared to be a serious threat to Adamawa since they had no military post there. Even after they had sent their Proclamation in 1900, the British did not feel strong enough to attack Yola until after the return of the troops from Ashanti and the Kontagora and Bida campaigns. Meanwhile they had engaged in hostilities against the Tiv, who had threatened the R.N.C.'s station at Abinsi. In October 1899, among other outrages, the Tiv had killed all the crew of a British canoe. In December 1899 they attacked a telegraph construction company with a W.A.F.F. escort, near Ibi. In July 1900 a W.A.F.F. expedition took reprisals against them.[54] But the Tiv were a pagan people and traditional enemies of Adamawa. Hence British attack on them, even if Yola knew about it, would not be considered as a direct threat to Adamawa emirate.

But contrary to Zubeir's belief, the British considered him their main obstacle to control on the Benue. Early in 1900 the Lugard government sent its Proclamation and remonstrances to

51. C.O. 446/12, Lascalles, British Ambassador in Berlin to F.O., 13 Jan. 1900, precis of an article in *Kolon. Zeitung* of 13 Jan.
52. N.A.K., S.N.P.1/2, C.O. to H.C., 14 June 1900, encl., Lascalles to F.O. of 30 April 1900; *ibid.* Lascalles to F.O., 3 Feb. 1900 puts garrison at Tibati at 500 strong.
53. N.A.K. KADCAPTORY, Box 38, file no. 5, letter no. 3. From a man called Maikari to Zubeir, Emir of Yola.
54. C.O. 446/10, Lugard to C.O., 3 Aug. 1900, 'Munchi Expedition'.

Zubeir to stop slave-raiding and obstructing trade, but the Emir reaffirmed his refusal to have anything to do with white men.[55] In July 1901 charges of slave-raiding against Yola gave place to specific charges of Yola hostility towards the British. These were no conciliatory offers.[56] Zubeir forced the Niger Company (the new name of the R.N.C.) at Yola to pull down their flag and instructed them to quit their station or be prepared to trade from a hulk.[57] From July to August 1901 Yola's hostility to Europeans mounted and a British expedition against the Emir was being seriously considered, with a view to deposing him.[58] A suggestion was made that Faḍlallāh b. Rābih might even be put in his place![59] Zubeir's stand was that the British had no right to intervene in his affairs, as such intervention would amount to a breach of the agreement between him and them.[60]

In August the British Colonial Office approved the sending of an expedition against Yola. Zubeir would be reinstated if he accepted the terms of a letter of appointment identical with another one previously given to the Emir of Bida, failing which one of his relations would be put in his place.[61] The end of September was the latest time an attack could be made on Yola since the river would be too shallow for navigation thereafter.

A force of thirteen officers, seven N.C.O.s, 365 rank and file, two 75 mm guns and four Maxims left Lokoja for Yola on 26 August and reached the Niger Company Station near Yola on 2 September. A messenger sent to the Emir with Lugard's terms was turned out of Yola without the letter he carried having been touched, let alone read. The Emir threatened that he would drive the British army into the river. At 1 p.m. Yola forces attacked the

55. N.A.K. Yola Provincial Archives. J.1. 'Collected Histories', 1905–31.
56. Cf. Perham, *Years of Authority*, p. 48. Perham justifies the attack on Yola on the grounds that it was only undertaken after Lugard had given 'conciliatory offers' and also because Yola was a great centre for the slave trade.
57. C.O. 446/15, Wallace to C.O., 3 July 1901.
58. C.O. 446/16, Tels. Wallace to C.O., 4, 5 and 6 Aug. 1901.
59. C.O. 446/20, Lugard to C.O., 26 July 1901.
60. C.O. 446/16, A. W. Ricket to Wallace enclosed in Wallace to C.O., 22 July 1901. Ricket reported that the Emir of Yola threatened to stop European trade at once if the Niger Company did not return to him twenty-five slaves he was sending to Sokoto which the company captured at Muri.
61. N.A.K., Yola Province Archives; Acc. no. 1, A.1., vol. i, H.C. to Commander W.A.F.F.

British but were beaten back into the city within ten minutes. The Emir's palace was shelled from a long range. The shell-fire replies from Yola fell wide. The British advance on the place which followed was checked by heavy arrow and rifle fire. Yola soldiers resumed firing shells. At this point a British party made an intrepid dash and within five minutes it captured two Yola guns, which had done havoc among the British troops. The way to the palace wall which was most stubbornly defended was thus opened. The wall was cleared by bringing a 75 mm gun into operation at close range. The palace gate was rushed and the palace itself was taken in a few minutes. The mosque close to the palace, which was obstinately defended, was destroyed. On the morning of the 3rd the audience chamber of the palace was blown up and several houses in the town were sacked.[62]

The considerable expenditure of ammunition by the British and the number of casualties indicate the heat of the battle of 2 September.[63] British casualties were put at two men killed, six dangerously, eight severely and twenty-five slightly wounded, while Yola's losses were estimated at fifty killed and about 150 wounded. Yola's determined resistance failed largely because it was unmatched by skilful operation of firearms, of which they had an ample supply.[64] It is important always to bear in mind the fact that, in their engagements with the emirates, the British had not only skill on their side but also superior weapons. Apart from the obvious advantage of having Maxims, the use of quick-firing guns and high-explosive shells, which were not available to the emirates, enabled the British to score rapid and decisive successes. However, though the British casualties at Yola were light, seldom did European troops suffer casualties as heavy at the hands of an African army in those days.

62. Account of the Yola campaign is based on C.O. 446/16, Wallace to C.O., no. 433 of 26 Sept. 1901, encl. T. N. L. Morland's Report; also in N.A.K. SNP7/2 Acc. no. 2363/1901, Resident Upper Benue Report, 28 Oct. 1901, in N.A.K. Adamawa Provincial Archives Acc. no. 1, A.1, vol. i.
63. C.O. 446/16, encl. Morland to Wallace in despatch no. 433 of 26 Sept. 1901. The British artillery expended ten shrapnel shells, nineteen cases of ammunition, two star shells and four rockets. The infantry expended 4264 rounds of ammunition.
64. The British army captured 105 loaded and fused shells, 60 French rifles, an unspecified but large number of other firearms, 1000 rounds of small ammunition, some bullets and over a ton of gunpowder,

The Emir, Zubeir, fled to Gurin with a large following after the battle of 2 September with the British troops hot on his heels. He escaped capture. On about 5 September 1901 he wrote to the Caliph to report the capture of his town by the Christians and his flight.[65] The letter raises a significant point, in that Zubeir referred to the Christians' (British) conquest of Nupe (in February) of which he had heard before but did not believe. It would be interesting to know how many other emirates did not take news of the Christians' conquests seriously and the effect this might have had on their preparations, not to talk of their consideration of the necessity to co-operate with their neighbours. For the next two years Zubeir was constantly on the move and remained a baffling problem to the British and to the Germans. He had enough followers to fight the latter at Garua in 1901 (18 November), and again in 1902 in alliance with the ruler of Marua, on which occasion he suffered heavy losses.[66] His avowed intention was to leave the country, taken over by infidels, for Mecca. He was killed by Lala pagans in February 1903.[67] The fall of Yola hastened German occupation of their share of Adamawa, which may be considered established when a Residency was set up at Garua, with von Puttkamer as Resident, in October 1903.

In the meantime, after their success at Yola on 2 and 3 September 1901, the British were confronted with the problem of filling the vacancy left by Zubeir. Negotiations persuaded Bobo Ahmadu (Aḥmad), Zubeir's brother, to desert Zubeir and take up the emirship of Yola. He was made British Emir of Adamawa (or rather of Yola), on 8 September, at a ceremony in which he accepted Lugard's letter of appointment. Morland's expedition left Yola on 9 September. A garrison of one company of the W.A.F.F., under Captain Barker, was stationed there as a guarantee of order.

A lull followed the fall of Yola. The new Emir seemed to the

65. Corr. IX, no. 112.
66. C.O. 446/22, Lugard to C.O., 19 Feb. 1902. Further details on Zubeir's flight in N.A.K. Yola Prov. Archives Acc. no. 1, A.1., vol. i, Reports no. 1, Oct. 1901, no. 4, Jan. 1902, no. 10, Aug. 1902, no. 11, Sept. 1902; no. 12, Oct. 1902, no. 17, March 1903. C.O. 446/27, Lascalles to F.O., 2 May 1902, encl. in F.O. to C.O., 14 May 1902. C.O. 446/22, Lugard to C.O., 19 Feb. 1902; C.O. 446/25, Lugard to C.O., 7 Oct. 1902.
67. N.A.K. Yola Prov. Archives, vol. ii, Report no. 24, Oct. 1903.

British to be accepted by Yola people but resentment simmered beneath, as subsequent years showed. Zubeir continued to send letters to Yola. In his first letter he urged Ahmadu to follow him to a new country, seeing that the Qur'ān forbade mixing with unbelievers. He was thus urging on Ahmadu and his subjects the canonical obligation of *hijra* from a land dominated by infidels. Zubeir wanted to know what the *'Ulamā'* thought of the destruction of the mosque—an incident which caused great discontent as the Resident confirmed.[68] By December 1901 tension was high in Yola. Fulanis between Yola and Marua were restive, but, according to report, they cautiously sat on the fence to see if the Germans at Garua would support Zubeir or Ahmadu.[69] The Emir, Ahmadu, felt dissatisfied with the division of Adamawa between the Germans and the British completely to his disadvantage. His loyalty to the British was therefore highly doubtful. By means of large presents he endeavoured to ingratiate himself with the Germans at Garua with a view to being accepted as Emir of German Adamawa as well as of the British section.[70] His disaffection to the British was driven underground when in April 1902 Col. Morland arrived in Yola and issued a stern warning to him to be loyal. Ahmadu thereafter accepted the inevitable. Yola Fulani were sullen in an insolent manner, according to the Resident, but expressed their sullenness in a way to which exception could not be taken.[71]

In Adamawa the traditional pagan enemies of the emirate—tribes such as the Bachama, Batta, Verre, Chamba, Mumuye, among many others—were so hostile to the British that numerous expeditions had to be sent out to suppress them during 1902. So insecure did the pagan hostility render the emirate for British officers that the Resident felt that only a military Resident could cope with the situation.[72] In May 1902 the Yola populace broke

68. Yola monthly Reports *loc. cit.*, Report, Upper Benue Province of 28 Oct. 1901. Zubeir also wrote to other towns in Adamawa and continued to write in 'inflammatory language' to Yola. It is said that in December 1902, his messenger succeeded in dropping two letters concealed in the hollow of a guinea-corn stalk in Yola mosque. He announced his intention to go to Mecca in one of the letters.
69. Yola monthly Reports, vol. i, no. 2, November 1901.
70. C.O. 446/23, Lugard to C.O., 21 July 1902. Yola monthly Reports, nos. 5 and 6, February and April respectively.
71. Yola monthly Report, no. 6, April 1902.
72. For the resistance of pagan tribes (e.g. Bachamas, Battas, Yundams,

loose from British control. Without any incitement by influential persons in Yola they seized the opportunity of the Resident's absence on tour to attack the British fort in the town. Moreover, the Resident, Mr Barclay, was convinced that the ordinary people were disloyal both to the British and to the Emir. They saw the British as infidels and the Emir as a traitor. The Resident aptly summed up the popular revolt as an indication of 'the direction in which the cat would like to jump'.[73] Yola followed what was clearly the pattern of reaction to the British occupation elsewhere: the awareness of British power did not kill mass resentment but only drove it underground.

THE INVASION OF BAUCHI AND THE SUBMISSION OF GOMBE

Farther afield on the eastern marches of the Sokoto Caliphate, the exploits of the French, which resulted in the defeat and death of Rābiḥ on 22 April 1900, had affected the policy of both the emirates in that direction and of the British towards the remnant of Rābiḥ's forces now under the command of his son, Faḍlallāh.

French pursuit of Faḍlallāh westwards into the sphere of the British represented an urgent challenge to the latter which had to be met if they were not to lose Bornu to the French. From the beginning of 1901 to October, the British received insistent pleas from Faḍlallāh for aid and recognition as ruler of Bornu.[74] A W.A.F.F. escort from Ibi visited him at a place two miles from Birguma, north of the Gongola, from June to July 1901.[75] The arrangements to send an expedition to make Faḍlallāh ruler of Bornu having been completed, British plans were foiled by the French defeat of Faḍlallāh and his death at Gujba in the British sphere in October 1901. This event, however, merely underlined the urgency for British action in Bornu to forestall occupation by the French. Since a British expedition to Bornu must pass

Longudas), see Yola monthly Reports, nos. 6, 7, 8, 9, April to July 1902.

73. Yola monthly Report, no. 7, May 1902.

74. Records of Faḍlallāh's negotiations with the British are scattered in various volumes in the C.O. 446 series, notably vols. 11, 15, 16, 17, 18, 19, 20, e.g. see C.O. 446/15, Lugard to C.O., 12 April 1901, contains three letters from Faḍlallāh to Hewby in 1900 pleading for help.

75. C.O. 446/16, McClintock to H.C., Report 2 Sept. 1901.

through Bauchi and Gombe, the expedition sent included in its programme the submission of those emirates.

In the meantime as Faḍlallāh moved west during early 1901, he had established contacts with the emirates of the eastern marches, notably with Gombe.[76] His central plea was for trading relations. The Emir of Gombe agreed, while the Emir of Bauchi refused to have anything to do with him.[77] However, Kano merchants and merchants from Azare, Chinada, Missau and Hadejia did trade with Faḍlallāh.[78] It seems clear that the erstwhile hostile attitude of these emirates to Faḍlallāh had changed. Two explanations are possible: (1) that Faḍlallāh, fighting against Christians, was regarded as fighting the enemies of the Caliphate; (2) that his killing (in battle) of Ḥayat, an enemy of the Caliphate whose lieutenant, Jibrīl, was a thorn in the flesh of the eastern emirates, won for him the friendship of these emirates. It seems, nevertheless, that despite the goodwill that Faḍlallāh enjoyed in the eastern emirates, Sokoto disapproved of the emirates trafficking with him.[79] The immediate dangers to the Caliphate in this direction was Jibrīl Gaini and, possibly, the more remote French army in Bornu.

The British organized the 'Lower Bornu Expedition' in January 1902, to go to Gujba and assert their authority over Bornu. The expedition was ordered to go through Bauchi and to establish garrisons in important places along its route. It was further charged to break the power of Jibrīl Gaini or, if he was found pliable, to recognize him as sub-chief or even principal chief of 'Lower Bornu'.[80] A Resident in 'Lower Bornu' was to be

76. Corr. X, nos. 93, 94, 100, 193 (1900–01). Faḍlallāh b. Rābiḥ to 'Umar Emir of Gombe. The writer asks for peaceful co-existence and co-operation against the enemies of God and the prophet and to be given trading facilities. And nos. 91, 92, 'Umar Emir of Gombe to Faḍlallāh, sending Kano, Azare and Chinada merchants to trade with Faḍlallāh.
77. Corr. X, no. 178, 'Umar of Bauchi to 'Umar of Gombe; Corr. X, nos. 146, 149, 151.
78. Corr. X, no. 100, Faḍlallāh to the Emir of Gombe, 'Umar. Faḍlallāh agreed with 'Umar that Jibrīl Gaini was the master of artifice and added that if God wills, his affair would crumble.
79. Corr. X, no. 53, Wazir Bukhārī to 'Umar, Emir of Gombe: 'This is to inform you that we have seen your letter and the information in it concerning the descent of the son of Rābiḥ Faḍlallāh to the bank of your river. Do not trust him. . . .'
80. By Lower Bornu was meant south-western Bornu and the adjoining emirates of the Caliphate.

appointed.[81] The expedition, consisting of seventeen Europeans, 500 rank and file, 900 carriers, three Maxims and two 75 mm guns under Col. Morland, left Ibi on the Benue on 23 January 1902.

The Proclamation and another letter sent by Wallace to Bauchi late in 1901, asking the Emir to send his representative to pay homage to the High Commissioner, had been unanswered.[82] It seems from the evidence of Wallace, who accompanied the expedition, that the people of Bauchi knew of the coming of white men but did not know what was their intention. A reconnoitring force of the expedition which turned back at Kanna (less than fifty miles south of Bauchi) had led Bauchi people, it seems, to believe that the white men were not coming for them. Bauchi apprehensions were aroused by a letter written by Wallace from Dul (also about fifty miles south of Bauchi) promising war if Bauchi wanted it and intimating that the white man would take charge of the emirate. Bauchi responded by sending a messenger to meet the expedition, now very close to the town, with assurances of their acceptance of the white man's terms. Bauchi wanted peace at all cost. Wallace at this point was uncompromising. The reply, he said, had come too late. In the meantime—about twenty miles from Bauchi—Wallace, finding no other excuse for British invasion, had despatched yet another letter, in which he stated quite clearly that the Emir would be deposed for oppressing his people, as exemplified by the massacre of the people of Gwaram—a matter which, it will be remembered, had already been settled by Sokoto.

Wallace stood firm on the threats contained in his last letter. The expedition was now less than ten miles from Bauchi. Bauchi's messenger turned back. Time was too short for Bauchi to discuss Wallace's reply and take steps to defend itself. The enemy was already at its gates. In the evening of 15 February Bauchi reassured the expedition they would do all the white man asked. The possibility of Wallace refusing Bauchi's welcome of the second letter does not seem to have been considered. There

81. N.A.K., S.N.P.15/29, instructions to T. N. L. Morland, 26 Dec. 1901 enclosed in Lugard to Wallace (Conf.), 12 Jan. 1901.

82. The messenger of the British who delivered the second letter had been sent out of town after a night's stay, see N.A.K., S.N.P.15/7, Upper Benue Resident's Report 10 Dec. 1901. The receipt in Bauchi of the Proclamation of 1 Jan. 1900 as late as in 1901, suggests that many emirates, particularly in the east (which was little known to the British) did not know of it until perhaps even later.

was no reason why Bauchi should have supposed that the white man would not be satisfied with their unequivocal acceptance of his own terms. Bauchi's defence was consequently unorganized.

On the morning of the 16th, the British forces moved to the city wall in square formation.[83] A parley took place between the leading officials of the town and the expedition. In the evening the officials told the British that their people were quite prosperous and happy under the Emir, 'Umar, and did not wish to see him deposed, but that since the expedition insisted on a new Emir, they selected Chiroma (heir-apparent) Muḥammad out of fear.[84] During the night of the 16th the Emir, 'Umar, escaped, followed by thousands.

Bauchi embraced the lesser of two evils. There was talk of fighting the white man.[85] But in the face of the strong W.A.F.F. contingent Bauchi could take no positive action. On the morning of 17 February, as the British force marched through the town, no women or children were to be seen. The town was put on a fighting basis. All the adults were armed. W.A.F.F. soldiers guarded all the thoroughfares that led to the palace, their Maxims and other guns ominously trained on the masses of armed Bauchi adults as the expedition marched to the palace and seized it.

From the Emir's palace, Wallace formally proclaimed the deposition of 'Umar and the installation of Chiroma Muḥammad to the leading officials and the masses. Realizing the deep resentment of the Bauchi people, Wallace had no choice but to grant their demands, which were aimed at preserving their independence and their social structure as well as their ties with, and obligations to, the Caliph. He yielded to protests against the stationing of an army inside the city. The garrison would be outside the city walls. The new Emir protested against the abolition of slavery which would destroy the basis of Bauchi economy, but was told emphatically that while continuation of domestic slavery would be considered, raiding and trading in slaves must stop. Bauchi's anxiety regarding its future relations with Sokoto was

83. My interprepation of the negotiations with Bauchi and the occupation is based on a lengthy report by W. Wallace in N.A.K., S.N.P.15/29, Wallace to Lugard, 20 March 1902.

84. The real attitude of Bauchi to British occupation contradicts Perham's assertion in *Years of Authority*, p. 51, that 'bonfires were lit by the people to show their joy at his (the Emir's) deposition'.

85. N.A.K., S.N.P.15/29, Wallace to Lugard, 20 March 1902.

1 The treaty between the Caliph 'Alī (Aliyu Baba) of Sokoto and Dr Barth (on behalf of the Queen of England), 1853

2 Maxim gun in action

resolved by Wallace's promise, that its allegiance to the Caliph and the Muslim religion would not be tampered with. As regards tribute to Sokoto, about which the people were also anxious, they were allowed to continue to pay, as long as slaves did not form part of it. The Emir consented to sign his letter of appointment only after these assurances had been given.

The impression must have been that in spite of the British presence things would go on exactly as they had under the Caliphate. Bauchi, apart from being unprepared, was fully appreciative of the futility of opposing the British by armed force. The obviously reluctant acceptance of the British made a policy of caution essential for the administration. There was calm on the surface, but the Resident, Charles Temple, acknowledged that 'the extreme timidity of all classes of natives, is, however, a great obstacle to our administration'.[86]

Bauchi understood the British terms to mean that since their laws and customs were not to be interfered with the traditional powers of the Emir and his officials were to remain completely intact. The Emir and his officials were 'extremely nervous and impatient over the white men's inspection of their activities'.[87] A request by the Resident, that the Qāḍī (Hausa: *Alkali*) of Bauchi should come to see him, was viewed as a breach of the promise that their laws and customs would not be interfered with, while the Emir met the Resident's request for labour to build a fort for the W.A.F.F. with an assurance that such a move would result in the flight of the population of Bauchi town, who would then follow the deposed Emir *en masse*. The British soldiers were openly cursed in the streets of Bauchi.[88]

As late as September 1902 the new Emir of Bauchi had not visited the Europeans since the fall of the town. Even though installed by the British he persisted in acting as if the British had no control over him. Under the nose of the Resident he collected fifteen loads of cloth to send to Sokoto as tribute.[89] In the meantime the fugitive Emir was a source of considerable anxiety both to the British and to the new Emir. Considered a centre of

86. N.A.K., S.N.P.15/39, C. L. Temple, Bauchi Report no. 2, March 1902.
87. N.A.K., S.N.P.15/38, C. L. Temple, Bauchi Report, 8 March 1902.
88. N.A.K., S.N.P.15/39, C. L. Temple, Bauchi Report, March 1902.
89. N.A.K., S.N.P.15/42, C. L. Temple, Bauchi Report, Sept. 1902.

subversive intrigue, 'Umar was captured in October, tried and deported to Ilọrin, where he arrived in January 1903.[90]

The neighbouring pagan tribes who, being traditional enemies of the emirate, might have been expected to welcome the conquerors of Bauchi, detested the advent of the white man as much as did Bauchi. A friendly message sent by the Resident to the chiefs of the Dass shortly after the occupation of Bauchi was not replied to by many of them, while the chief of Dot went to the extent of not only sending a message considered impertinent by the Resident but also had the bearer of the Resident's message beaten up.[91] The Shiri killed a policeman of the Resident in May and only after 130 of them had been killed in a village called Fesmu did they agree to pay tribute to the British administration.[92] Complaints against the predatory acts of Dan Yaya, ruler of Ningi (an inveterate enemy of Bauchi) and his implacable hostility to the white man compelled Temple to send an expedition against the tribe in July 1902. The force, under Captain Monck-Mason, finally broke the power of the Ningi, who had been a threat to neighbouring emirates since the middle of the nineteenth century but were now ranged, not in direct alliance but as co-belligerents, on the same side as Bauchi against European invasion. Dan Yaya was killed along with fifty of his supporters and half of Ningi town was burnt down as a warning to others.[93]

From Bauchi the 'Lower Bornu expedition' moved on to Gombe. The Emir received the expedition hospitably, because he saw it more as an ally against his mortal enemy, Jibrīl Gaini, than as an enemy.[94] Gombe's attitude illustrates the localism of the emirates, which is constantly emphasized in this study, as well as the effect of preoccupation with internal enemies on

90. See above, pp. 224–5. That Bauchi had been occupied under *force majeure* cannot be disputed. See N.A.K., S.N.P.15/43, C. L. Temple, Bauchi Report, Oct. 1902.
91. N.A.K., S.N.P.15/38, Bauchi Report, 8 March 1902.
92. N.A.K., S.N.P.15/40, Report, Bauchi Province, 16 April 1902, encl. report on tour of 23 April to 3 June 1902.
93. N.A.K., S.N.P.15/41, report on tour of 23 July to 3 Aug. 1902.
94. N.A.K., S.N.P.15/41, Emir of Gombe to Mr Temple, received 18 Aug. 1902, shows the submission of the Emir. This submission does not seem to indicate utter weakness on the part of Gombe. In Sept. 1902 the Emir was reported camped at Bajoga with a force comprising 3–4000 horsemen, see *ibid.*, report on tour of 9 Aug.–3 Sept. 1902 by C. L. Temple.

their ability to resist the European invaders. The Emir, 'Umar, having been duly 'recognized', the expedition left Gombe on 25 February in search of Mallam Jibrīl, and reached Tongo, where the latter was, on 1 March. Near Tongo Jibrīl's men, estimated at 600 cavalry, armed mostly with arrows, spears and swords with, it seems, very few firearms, attacked the British expedition suddenly. They fought most courageously against the steady fire from the British square formation, many of them advancing as close as 100 yards from the square in an attempt to rush it. In the end they gave way under the heat of British fire, leaving sixty of their men dead on the battlefield. Tongo was shelled and set on fire. Jibrīl's power was at last broken.[95] The next fortnight witnessed a game of hide and seek, grim for both sides, during which the fugitive Jibrīl was chased through Gombe emirate by the British until the Mallam, at last deserted by most of his followers, threw himself on the mercy of the King of Burmi —newly appointed by Morland—who gave him up to the British. Jibrīl, estimated to have been seventy years old, was taken prisoner to Lokoja, where he died in 1907.

The Jibrīl assignment completed, the 'Lower Bornu Expedition' moved to Gujba, left a garrison of one company there and then set out on 17 March for Maiduguri. The garrison at Gujba was to prove important in the next phase of the events which led to the fall of the Caliphate by reason of the panic it created in the eastern frontier emirates late in 1902.

THE OCCUPATION OF ZARIA

To return to the emirates of the west, the conquest of Kontagora and Bida had provided the British with an opportunity for establishing a garrison at Zaria as a jumping off place for their ultimate advance on Kano and Sokoto. In 1899 the Bishop Tugwell C.M.S. Mission, out to carry Christianity into the heart of the Caliphate, had received some welcome at Zaria on its way north. Following their ignominous expulsion from Kano the members of the expedition had again returned via Zaria. The Emir of Zaria now became distinctly hostile, having taken the cue from

95. N.A.K., S.N.P.15/29, Morland to Lugard, 16 March 1902. N.A.K., S.N.P.15/30, Gujba, 16 March 1902, report on field operations by T. N. L. Morland.

the Kano example. He was, however, induced to allow them to settle at Girku south of Zaria. The Emir of Zaria was reported to have been influenced by the example of French conquests in Damagaram. This, he judged, counselled extreme caution in dealing with Europeans, the implication of whose military power was not in doubt.[96]

Early in 1900 Col. Kemball of the W.A.F.F. had visited Zaria and made pledges of peace and friendship with the Emir. The Emir gave him a very friendly welcome. However, Kemball's collision with the Zaria towns of Remo and Kaje, which he burnt, and his boast that the territories of Zaria would pass under British rule and that slavery must stop, changed Zaria's friendship to fear and anxiety. The Emir wrote a letter to Lugard, a copy of which he sent to Sokoto, stressing the correct constitutional position, that he (the Emir) had no power to divest himself of the powers and control Kemball wanted him to be stripped of, because he was merely an agent of the Caliph, who set him over his territory to enjoin goodness and prohibit evil. The Emir pointed out that Kemball's claims were a breach of his earlier promise of peace and friendship.[97] About May 1900 the messenger of the British, Adamu Jekada, taking the Christians' (British) tribute to Sokoto, was detained in Zaria to await the Caliph's decision as to whether or not he should proceed.[98]

With this background it was not possible for the British to continue friendly relations with Zaria for the rest of 1900. But their victory over Kontagora and Bida in 1901 strengthened their hands. The fugitive emirs, in particular Ibrāhīm of Kontagora, set to raiding villages claimed by Zaria. This caused Zaria considerable anxiety, especially as neither repeated letters nor appeals by the Emir to Ibrāhīm effected anything to stop his raiding. At the end of his tether, Ibrāhīm is said to have set at naught the Caliph's instructions to desist from raiding Zaria

96. For the Tugwell mission see N.A.K. LOKPROF. Letter Book, Agency Mark no. 2; Resident's Report no. 11, 28 June 1900; C.O. 446/7, Lugard to C.O., 17 Aug. 1899; C.O. 446/14, Lugard to C.O., 27 Feb. 1901; see also E. A. Ayandele, *The Missionary Impact on Modern Nigeria* (London, 1966), pp. 129–32.

97. N.A.K. KADCAPTORY, Box 45, item 26, Arabic Letter Book, no. 47, Muḥammad Lawal (Emir of Zaria) to Wallace.

98. Corr. IX, no. 30, Wazir Bukhārī to Amīr al-Mu'minīn 'Abd al-Raḥmān—the tribute is described as *al-hadiya 'uhidat wa 'urifat*; in Corr. VI, no. 76, it is described as *Mal al-amāna.*

territory.[99] There is no evidence that I have come across to explain the purpose of Ibrāhīm's raids and his disobedience of the Caliph. The suggestion one can make is that he needed new territory in which to settle his large following, as well as adequate provision beyond the limits of the hospitality he could reasonably expect from Zaria. His action would thus be a desperate struggle for survival.

In these circumstances the Emir of Zaria had no alternative but to accept the offer of help against Ibrāhīm, which the British had been pressing on him persistently. Lugard, who had all along directed his efforts to making Zaria invite the British, jumped at this opportunity of entering in the guise of a friend, without fighting.[100] In March 1902 the British fulfilled their pledge. Ibrāhīm, with a following, according to Lugard, of about 20,000,[101] camped at Maska, not far from Zaria town, fled at the approach of a W.A.F.F. force of 50 mounted infantry and 100 infantry under Lt. Porter. He was captured with a large part of his following but Abubakar (who had been camped close to him with a following estimated at about 12,000), escaped northwards. Ibrāhīm was sent down in chains to Lokoja for trial.[102] Early in April a garrison was stationed near Zaria and in mid-April Captain Abadie arrived there as Resident of 'Zaria Province'.[103]

No sooner had the British garrison and the Residency been established than the Emir and the people of Zaria became restive and impatient of the presence of Europeans in the emirate. They had expected help but not European settlement in Zaria. Immediately after the capture of Ibrāhīm an observer in Zaria wrote, 'Zaria is immensely relieved but still between the devil and the deep sea; ourselves and Sokoto his suzerain'.[104] The Emir informed Abadie that if the Caliph instructed him to fight

99. C.O. 446/22, Lugard to C.O., 15 March 1902; also in N.A.I., CSO 1/27,2.
100. *Ibid.*; see also C.O. 446/16, Wallace to C.O., 2 Aug. 1901. Contrary to Lugard's claim (echoed since by virtually all writers on the subject) that the Emir of Zaria appealed to him for help (e.g. *Years of Authority*, p. 93) it was Lugard who offered help to Zaria.
101. *Annual Report*, 1902, p. 103; also R.H.B.E., S.64, Report on Kontagora, 1904.
102. R.H.B.E., S.87, vol. i, Popham-Lobb to Goldie, 8 May 1902. N.A.I., C.S.O.1/27, 2, Lugard to C.O., 15 March 1902.
103. R.H.B.E., S.64, Popham-Lobb to his mother, 6 May 1902.
104. R.H.B.E., S.64, R. Popham-Lobb to his mother, 11 March 1902.

the white man, he would.[105] The presence of the British in Zaria excited the hostility of Kano so much that as early as March 1902 the British were already seriously considering an attack on Kano. British troops were moved in from Bauchi to Zaria and also from Yelwa.[106] Zaria was from then on incapable of taking military action against the British. The Emir reported his dilemma to Sokoto as well as Kano[107] and expressed his anxiety over the fact that the British troops intended to advance on Kano 'when they have completed what they want to do with us'.[108] Kano therefore knew of the imminence of a British attack at least one year before the event. In vain the Emir of Zaria, now fully regretting his acceptance of the white man's help, requested the British, on three different occasions, not to bring their force from Yelwa to Zaria.

Zaria could do no more than threaten the British and refuse to cooperate with them. Yet had the Emir but known, the British in Zaria were well aware of their own inability to do anything in the town because, from their observations, they feared that if they applied the slightest pressure, at least half the town's population would run away.[109] Even though they had cleared the slave market they dared not interfere thereafter with the slave trade. The trade went on surreptitiously under their nose. Relationship between the British and Zaria deteriorated as the months went by in 1902.[110]

It was important for the British to prevent the Emir from fleeing, as they were convinced that if he did most of the town would follow him and he would then almost certainly join forces with Kano, with which place he was in regular communication. As a measure of defence Kano had posted mounted men in various places on the Zaria–Kano road. In August the British

105. *Ibid.*
106. *Ibid.*, R. Popham-Lobb to mother, 26 and 27 March 1902, and 25 April 1902.
107. Corr. IX, no. 120, from Magaji Dalhatu b. 'Uthmān to Aliyu Emir of Kano: 'I have also heard news that the Christians are coming . . . from the Bauchi road. I tell you we are in terrible trouble. We can neither sit nor stand nor sit [live] with them.'
108. *Ibid.*, nos. 119, 121; Corr. VI, no. 68, from Emir of Zaria, Muḥammad Lawal to Amīr al-Mu'minīn 'Abd al-Raḥman.
109. Popham-Lobb to mother, *loc. cit.*, 25 April 1902 and 6 May 1902.
110. *Ibid.*, Popham-Lobb to mother, 6 and 26 May, 6, 8–9 and 24 Aug. and 1 Sept. 1902.

posted three patrols of the W.A.F.F. on the Zaria–Katsina, Zaria–Bauchi, and Zaria–Kano roads respectively, to arrest the Emir of Zaria if he attempted to flee, as well as to prevent reinforcement from the emirates to the north reaching him. Skirmishes ensued between Zaria gunmen and the patrols. Daily the Emir grew more recalcitrant. By cautious hedging he refused British demands, e.g. for labour or to return runaway criminals. It became clear that the Emir had to go if the British were to remain securely in Zaria.

On 25 August a company of the W.A.F.F. sent by Lugard arrived in Zaria. From then the city walls were patrolled every night to prevent an attack on the garrison. During mid-September Abadie ordered the Emir to prepare to go to meet Lugard. Delegations of the people pleaded on his behalf. Twelve of the finest palace horses were sent to the British as a peace-offering. Nothing availed. The Emir refused to be moved out of town, avowing that he recognized neither the British nor the Lugard government. The city gates were put under guard. The streets were packed full with bowmen. A group of W.A.F.F. men pushed through to the palace and there met the raging Emir coming out. He was arrested and taken away. Fear seized the city all of a sudden. The Galadima Suleiman was appointed to act in the Emir's place. The fall of Zaria had become a reality.[111]

The first three years of the Lugard administration had witnessed the fall of the southern emirates and of Bauchi and Gombe to the British. The inadequacy of the emirates' defence arrangements as well as of their military equipment to meet the European challenge had been clearly demonstrated. The garrisons stationed in the conquered emirates ensured that no appreciable help could come from them to the rest of the Caliphate. Rather than fight at all, or continue fighting when it was realized that the odds were heavily against them, the rulers of most of the conquered emirates had found escape in flight, a lesser evil than falling into the hands of Unbelievers. The flight of the Emirs of Kontagora, Bida, Adamawa and Bauchi was not merely avoidance of a victorious enemy but also *hijra* from lands which had fallen under the rule of Unbelievers. This is clear from the flight of the Emir of Adamawa from Yola.

Perhaps more significant in this respect than the mere flight of

111. *Ibid.*, Popham-Lobb to mother, 14 Sept. 1902.

emirs was the large number of people who abandoned everything to follow them. The opposition to British conquest was best expressed by the mass emigration of people which took place immediately after the British conquest. It is clear from this emigration as well as from the sullen attitude of those who remained behind, that there was enough popular resentment at British conquest on which to base popular general anti-British risings. However, resentment was driven underground by the presence of British troops.

Another significant observation which can be made on the British conquest is that the British-made or British-supported emirs did not and could not give the type of leadership required to continue the anti-British resistance. In Bida, Bauchi and, to some extent, in Adamawa, the real import of the British conquest, which, if realized early enough, might have stiffened popular resistance, only became clear after the emirates had had experience of the imposition of British rule and realized that it ran counter to local political susceptibilities and traditional exercise of political authority. The emirs, as British appointees, could not lead resistance without running grave risks to themselves.

In Iḷọrin and Gombe the British occupation had been facilitated by existing political situations, which played into British hands. With regard to the will of the people to resist it is instructive to note that the pagan tribes in Adamawa and Bauchi resented the British conquest as vehemently as the Muslim emirates. For the first time since the establishment of those emirates, the traditional enmity between *Dār al-Islām* and *dār al-ḥarb* receded to the background and yielded place, at least temporarily, to a common detestation of foreign conquest.

Finally, British tactical moves which ensured the isolation of the emirates from one another foiled any chances there might have been of the emirates allying to resist British conquest. The British successfully isolated Ilọrin from Bida and Kontagora, Kontagora from Bida, and the latter from Yauri, Gwandu and Sokoto. It must be borne in mind that, apart from the fear of British military power, Ilọrin's incentive to ally with Bida was probably dulled by the fact that the British did not actually attack Ilọrin. With regard to Bauchi and Gombe, the latter's readiness to accept British military aid against Jibrīl Gaini meant that the particularist interest of Gombe ruled out the possibility of an anti-British common front between the two emirates. As in

Gombe, so in Zaria, the British were able to dig themselves in by adroitly exploiting the particularist anxiety of Zaria which induced the Emir to embrace British offer of help against the fugitive Emir of Kontagora.

Given the local setting within the Caliphate in which pre-occupation by each emirate with its local defence and other security problems overrode the awareness of the general European threat, the success of the British method of piece-meal occupation can be readily understood. The quick despatch with which the British military occupation was accomplished from one place to another put the emirates in a state of quandary which rendered them incapable of co-operative efforts. With the southern emirates and Bornu fallen, the British were brought into direct confrontation with the northern emirates of the Caliphate.

Chapter 8
The fall of Sokoto

DIPLOMATIC RELATIONS BETWEEN SOKOTO AND LUGARD, 1900–02

The conquest of the southern emirates had further reduced the Caliphate's potential for resistance. As real overthrow could, however, be considered complete only after the fall of Sokoto, the occupation of that city had been the ultimate aim of the British from about 1898. It will be recalled that in that year the R.N.C. had attempted, but failed, to instal a British Resident in Sokoto with the Caliph's consent. All the same, on assuming office as British High Commissioner of 'Northern Nigeria', Lugard had no alternative but to continue with the policy, discredited by experience, of peaceful negotiations aimed at persuading the Caliph to surrender his sovereign powers to the British. It was less risky than showing hostility. It is not possible to say categorically that Lugard had no hopes whatsoever that his negotiations with the Caliph might succeed but for all practical purposes this was a stop-gap policy to be pursued only so long as the British had no alternative.

As already mentioned, the departure of a large number of his troops to Ashanti meant that Lugard was not in a position to take strong military action in the Caliphate throughout 1900. Even with the troops' return from Ashanti the British forces appeared to be not strong enough to undertake a conquest of Sokoto immediately. Without the precondition of a firm British hold on the southern emirates any British force sent against Sokoto or the northern emirates would run the risk of being cut off and crushed by the emirates at its rear. Any precipitate British move to occupy Sokoto by force before the end of 1902, when the southern emirates as well as Bornu had been occupied, was therefore out of the question.

From 1900 to 1902, while the occupation of the southern emirates was in progress, Lugard was compelled to direct his diplomatic efforts to allaying the fears of the Caliph, as far as circumstances permitted, representing the British to him in a friendly light. In this connection Lugard ensured that his troops engaged in no serious military operations close to Sokoto until the British were fully prepared to face the consequences of such a move.

Besides other problems of military combination between the emirates, the preoccupation of the northern emirates with their fear of the French, as has been shown, seems to have been sufficient to keep them out of the contest between the British and the southern emirates. This factor left scope for Lugard's diplomacy. During late February 1901, by which time Kontagora and Bida had fallen to the British, the Rev. W. R. Miller, then at Girku, concluded from complaints that reached him from the northern emirates that the latter feared the French far more than the British. The Emir of Katsina, for instance, wrote: 'Your fellow countrymen are giving me trouble coming to and fro [*sic*] my country.'[1] Since their establishment in the 'Third Military Territory' (comprising Dosso, Arewa, Maradi and Zinder) in 1900, the French had, owing to the barrenness of their new territory, had to send their columns through the northern emirates on their journeys between Say and Zinder. The journeys of the French columns through their territories brought the French threat nearer home to the northern emirates, the more so as these columns commandeered beasts of burden and foodstuffs from them.[2]

It appears also that the northern emirates remained apparently unconcerned with the fate of their southern neighbours because they did not have precise knowledge of British intended moves. That the British struck intermittently also meant that their expedition must have caught many emirates by surprise. Thus, while Kontagora and Bida were conquered early in 1901 (January to early February), Yola was not attacked until September of that year and Bauchi not until February 1902.

1. C.O. 446/14 (Conf.), Lugard to C.O., 27 Feb. 1901, encl. no. 3, extracts from Miller to Lugard, containing complaints from northern emirates against the French including a letter from the Emir of Katsina to Miller which reads in part, 'your fellow countrymen [Europeans, i.e. the French] are giving me trouble coming to and fro my country'. Miller observed that fear of the French was more dominant in the emirates than fear of the British.
2. C.O. 446/11, no. 219, Lugard to C.O., 21 Sept. 1900.

Yet the essential loyalty of the emirates to the Caliph, though weakened by the military occupation of the southern emirates, was not broken. In about March 1901 the Wazir of Gwandu was on a tribute-collecting round which brought him to Bida.[3] In April 1902 the Wazir Bukhārī was in Zaria on a similar mission.[4] The office-holders of Bauchi had insisted, at their conquest, on the maintenance of their connections with the Caliph. Lugard himself testified that the conquered emirates continued to send their tribute surreptitiously to Sokoto.[5] As long as Sokoto had not fallen the emirates, including those which had been conquered, continued to look up to the Caliph as their overlord. Lugard observed that the allegiance of the conquered emirates was divided between the Caliph and the British and that until Sokoto and the powerful northern emirates were conquered, 'Yola, Bauchi and Zaria [which, he observed, were in a state of unrest] will never settle down'.[6]

In spite of the temporary necessity imposed on Lugard by circumstances to pursue a peaceful policy towards the Caliph, he could not successfully pursue such a policy. The British conquest of the southern emirates was clearly incompatible with Lugard's offer of friendship to the Caliph. At best his peace policy, realistically appraised, amounted to no more than an attempt to demonstrate to the Caliph the futility of resisting the British, hoping thereby to make him realize the wisdom of capitulating without fighting. Albeit the manner in which Lugard executed his policy of conciliation towards the Caliph also rendered it highly improbable that he would convince the latter.

It will be remembered that Lugard's sending of his Proclamation to Sokoto and Gwandu in 1900, announcing the establishment of a British administration of the Caliphate, had evoked the hostility of both the Caliph and the Emir of Gwandu.[7] In so far as the proclamation claimed sovereign power over the Caliphate for the British it was not only a breach of the Caliphate–British treaty relations, as understood by the Caliph, but also a hostile act of usurpation. Moreover, in his anxiety to win the Caliph's

3. N.A.K., S.N.P.7/3/40, Burdon to Lugard, 7 Apr. 1902, for visit of Wazir of Gwandu to Bida.
4. R.H.B.E., S.64, Popham-Lobb to mother, 6 May 1902.
5. C.O. 446/25, no. 597, Lugard to C.O., 21 Nov. 1902.
6. *Ibid.*
7. See above, pp. 221–2.

friendship, Lugard had overreached himself when, in a covering letter which he sent to Sokoto with a copy of the Proclamation, he went out of his way to emphasize that the Queen, whom he represented, ruled over many Muslim countries with subjects more numerous than those of the Padisha (Sultan ʿAbdul Ḥamid II of Turkey, 1876–1909). The promise given in this letter, that the British would not interfere with the Muslim religion would be rendered odious by the unmistakable threat of conquest conveyed by the assurance which Lugard gave to the Caliph that '... as it is in those countries [viz. Muslim countries under British rule] so it will be in this'.[8] This first diplomatic move towards the Caliph by Lugard was an act of defiance which created an unfavourable atmosphere for future negotiations.

Throughout 1900 Lugard received no reply to his Proclamation either from Sokoto or Gwandu. Identical letters from Wallace to the Caliph and the Emir of Gwandu, instructing them to address their letters to Lugard direct were similarly not answered.[9] Besides these letters the Lugard administration made no further attempts during 1900 to contact Sokoto and Gwandu. The Emir of Gwandu is said to have forwarded his own copy of Lugard's Proclamation to Sokoto while Sokoto sent a copy to Kano.[10] The reality of the threat of conquest, implicit in the Proclamation, was forcibly brought home to the Caliph in 1901 and 1902 by the fall in succession of Kontagora, Bida, Yola, Bauchi and Zaria to British arms. In all the conquered emirates, with the exception of Ilọrin where the Emir co-operated with the British, the reigning emirs were declared deposed ostensibly on grounds of oppression and slave-raiding but in reality for opposing the British. New emirs were appointed on the authority of the British and, as has been shown, often against the will of the people.[11]

The British-appointed emirs had to accept letters of appointment, the conditions of which leave no doubt that real power was to lie thenceforth with the British. The emirs were required to obey all the laws of the protectorate, especially laws against

8. Arabic Letter Book (Lokoja), *loc. cit.*, letter no. 17, Lugard to Caliph, 1 Aug. 1900.
9. *Ibid.*, Letters nos. 2 and 3.
10. N.A.K. KADCAPTORY, G.O.K.1/1/4, Box 45, Sharpe to Wallace, Tel. 12 Mar. 1901.
11. Cf. occupation of Bauchi, Yola, Zaria and Ilọrin.

slave-raiding and importation of liquor, to give the Resident every assistance in the performance of his duties and to be guided by his advice in the establishment and procedure of native courts, tribute assessment and other matters as well as to obey the High Commissioner 'to the utmost in all matters whatsoever'. Further, the emirs undertook not to put any restrictions on traders or impose any levies on them, except with the consent of the High Commissioner. The British administration promised to support and protect the emir, as long as he kept the terms of his appointment and assisted in the construction of roads, telegraphs and other works of 'pacification', good government and progress. Minerals and waste and uncultivated lands were declared Crown property and thenceforward all titles by whomsoever could be acquired only from the Crown. The letter of appointment closed with a charge by the High Commissioner to the new emir to be obedient in all the above, to refrain from lip-service and deceit, in return for which the government promised not to interfere with his religion as long as it did not involve acts contrary to the laws of humanity and oppression of his subjects.[12]

The letter of appointment was in effect a condensed statement of the philosophy and programme of indirect rule as later established by the Lugard administration in Northern Nigeria. Besides the deference paid to the Muslim prohibition of alcoholic drinks and the qualified promise not to interfere with the practice of Islam, the letter of appointment was a declaration of British sovereignty which was bound to affect profoundly the pre-colonial administrative structure and functions. The emir in theory became a mere executive functionary of the British, weaned from his allegiance to the Caliph. It is against this background of British usurpation of the Caliph's and emirs' sovereign powers that the British diplomatic moves with Sokoto from 1901 to 1903 should be appraised.

After the fall of Kontagora and Bida in January and February 1901 respectively, British attempts to impose an Emir on Kontagora failed. Following the conquest Lugard appointed the Emir of Yauri to rule over Kontagora. As he proved unsatisfactory the Mayaki of Bida was appointed in his place shortly after.[13] The Mayaki, being an imposed 'foreigner' in Kontagora, similarly

12. C.O. 446/16, H.C. to C.O., 26 Sept. 1901, encl., no. 2, Morland to Wallace.

13. Lugard, *Annual Report*, p. 135.

proved unsuitable. After the failure of the two arbitrary and rash appointments to the Kontagora emirship, Ibrāhīm, the former Emir, was reinstated in April 1903 after he had sworn lifelong loyalty to the British.[14]

Meanwhile, following the flight of the Emirs of Bida and Kontagora, Lugard had written a letter to Sokoto to explain that he had been forced to depose both emirs because of their slave-raiding and oppression of their subjects and for attacking officials of the British administration, all of which, he argued, proved their unfitness to rule.[15] Lugard sought justification for appointing the Makun as Emir of Bida in the fact that he (the Makun) was next in the line of succession to the emirship. This was to convince the Caliph that the British did not wish to infringe the constitutional arrangement in the Caliphate. In his letter Lugard expressed his hope to resolve the dilemma he faced in Kontagora by appealing to the Caliph to appoint:

> a just man who will rule with justice. If he acts justly, I will enrich him and support his power. If you select a man such as I have mentioned and you give him a letter from yourself, let him come to me with it and I will appoint him Emir and gladly instal him on the throne of the Emir of Kontagora with pomp. But before you send such a man you are permitted to warn him thoroughly that if he acts dishonestly, heedlessly or if he is a hypocrite, he will be faced with the same consequence as befell the last Emir of Kontagora, Al-Gamashin.

In other words real power lay with Lugard, while the Caliph was to play the role of a useful adviser. Granted that the emirs were guilty of all Lugard accused them, it was an open usurpation of the Caliph's prerogative for him to have proceeded not only to depose them but also to arrogate to himself the power to appoint new emirs in their places. Far from being friendly overtures to Sokoto, as Lugard thought, his letters to date amounted to insulting acts of hostility to, and defiance of, the Caliph. As if to enrage the Caliph further, in the same year (1901), Wallace wrote to him to inform him of the British intention to put a Resident in Sokoto and to urge upon him the wisdom of accepting this act as inevitable.[16] Needless to say, these letters were not

14. R.H.B.E., S.61, E. J. Lugard, 'Journal', 1903–05.
15. N.A.K. KADCAPTORY, Box 45, G.O.K.1/1/11, Lugard to the Amīr al-Mu'minīn 'Abdullāh ('Abd al-Raḥmān was the Caliph's name). See Appendix V, English version translated from Arabic by Major Burdon.
16. C.O. 446/16, Wallace to C.O., 2 Aug. 1901.

acknowledged. Assurances to the Caliph that the British were anxious to maintain Fulani rule over the Caliphate fell flat. It was not the business of any foreigner.

For the rest of 1901 it became virtually impossible for Lugard to communicate with Sokoto. Wallace reported to Lugard in October that all his efforts to get his letters to Sokoto by sending them through the W.A.F.F. officer commanding at Illo for onward transmission had failed.[17] By July 1901 it was obvious that the Caliph was not prepared to accept overtures of friendship. Lugard therefore formulated a policy of taking Sokoto by surprise by advancing on it rapidly, adequate care having been taken to keep his preparations secret. By so doing, he argued, Sokoto would be forced to capitulate even to a small British-led force.[18]

Lugard, anxious to re-open diplomatic relations with Sokoto, approached Lord Cromer in Egypt, who made arrangements with Reginald Wingate in the Eastern Sudan to send two Sudanese African officers, who were born in Sokoto and Kano respectively, to Northern Nigeria as a means of continuing negotiations with the Caliph. Lugard hoped that their being Muslims and natives of the land would place them in an advantageous position to act as a link between himself and the northern emirates; they would impress British power on the people by disseminating news of the defeat of the Mahdists of the Eastern Sudan and the loyalty of the Muslim powers of the Nile provinces to the British.[19] However, it was being conquered like the Sudan that the Sokoto emirates dreaded. There was also talk of employing Gottlob Adolf Krause, a German traveller versed in the Hausa language, as a diplomatic agent to the northern emirates.[20] This fishing about for suitable contacts that would presumably be acceptable to the northern emirates indicates the complete breakdown of communications between Lugard and those emirates by the end of 1901. Lugard complained about the fruitlessness of his efforts to contact the northern emirates and his inability and that of his men to obtain news of events beyond the immediate ken of their garrisons.[21] The unwillingness of the northern emirates to

17. N.A.K. KADCAPTORY, Box 45, G.O.K.1/1/13, 29 Oct. 1901.
18. C.O. 446/21, Lugard to C.O., 4 July 1901.
19. C.O. 446/17, Lugard to C.O., 22 Dec. 1901.
20. Lugard to C.O., N.A.I., C.S.O.1/27, 2, 19 May 1902.
21. *Ibid.*

3 75 mm. gun in action

4 Waiting to attack: the British expedition before the walls of Kano, 1903

capitulate without fighting was obvious. It is not known what the Sudanese officers achieved for Lugard, if anything; but they arrived at Lokoja late in 1902. One was sent to join Captain Merrick's garrison at Argungu to contact Sokoto, and the other to Zaria, to contact Kano.[22]

It seems that Lugard's insistence on the prestige attached to his office and the power he represented rendered negotiations with Sokoto less likely to be fruitful. A policy advocated by Burdon (Resident of Bida), which would ensure the Caliph's real control over the emirates as near complete as possible stood a greater chance of success than Lugard's diplomacy, which involved taking the law into his own hands. Early in 1901 Burdon urged on Lugard the wisdom of handing over Ibrāhīm, Emir of Kontagora, to Sokoto and nerving the Caliph by judicious diplomacy to deal with him as his lawful suzerain. Acting on this policy, when (about March 1901) the Wazir of Gwandu came to Bida to collect tribute, Burdon had secured his friendship and confidence by declaring that he would not interfere with him and his joy at seeing him comforming with the laws of his land. He was thereby able to communicate a message to the Emir of Gwandu, a message which was duly reciprocated in March when the Wazir returned with a friendly letter from the Emir, accompanied by Magajin Garin Sokoto. The communication by Gwandu to Sokoto of Burdon's assistance to the Wazir in the collection of tribute seems to have won for him the friendship of Sokoto.[23] But whatever basis of good relations might have been thus established by Burdon with Sokoto and Gwandu would, it can be surmised, have been destroyed by Lugard's presumptuous letter to the Caliph over Bida and Kontagora. Perhaps Lugard need not be blamed too much for his own more barefisted diplomacy, seeing that it is difficult to envisage any amount of friendship which could have persuaded the Caliph to abdicate sovereign powers voluntarily to the British. Commenting on Burdon's policy, Lugard wrote: 'No doubt, the policy of trying to make omelettes without breaking eggs has the cordial support of the section generally known as "Exeter Hall" in England. It is not the way our Raj has been established in India or elsewhere.'[24] There was truth and realistic appraisal of the problem which

22. C.O. 446/24, Lugard to C.O., 20 Sept. 1902.
23. N.A.K., S.N.P.7/3/40, 7 Apr. 1902.
24. N.A.K., S.N.P.7/3/40, Lugard to Burdon, 17 Apr. 1902.

confronted the British in the Caliphate in this statement. However, early in 1902 Lugard succeeded once again in contacting the Caliph.

A letter from Lugard to the Caliph about Bauchi and the fugitive Emirs of Bida and Kontagora, despatched on 18 March 1902, brought matters to a head. In the letter Lugard informed the Caliph that he had heard of the latter's unsuccessful efforts to check 'Umar of Bauchi's oppression of his subjects and that if the Emir resisted British soldiers, whom he had sent to Bauchi, he would depose him and put the next man in the line of succession in his place. He also reported the capture of Ibrāhīm of Kontagora by W.A.F.F. soldiers and stressed the desire of the British not to deprive the Fulani of their rule but to ensure that they ruled justly with 'reason and forbearance'. He, Lugard, had ordered that Ibrāhīm of Kontagora should be brought to him for judgment.[25] Suleiman, Lugard's messenger to Sokoto, reported that he was coldly received there and was told to tell whoever had sent him that there was none who could put the country right but God. He reported further that in all the Sokoto towns he passed through people were anxious to know if it was true that the white men were coming. There was prevailing fear of the prospect of the white man's approach. Consequently people were apparently resolved to flee, fully realizing that resistance would be futile.[26]

In May 1902 Lugard reported the receipt of a very hostile letter from Sokoto, in which the Caliph said that he did not wish that anyone from among the white men should live with him, and that between him and them (the white men) there could be nothing but war as commanded by God Almighty.[27] By May 1902 Lugard was already more than ever convinced of an eventual military clash with Sokoto, but this had to wait as he, with whom the initiative rested, though anxious to settle with Sokoto, was not prepared as yet to make an immediate advance. He, however, regarded the Caliph's letter as a declaration of war. The Caliph's

25. N.A.K. KADCAPTORY, G.O.K.1/1/3, Box 45, from Governor Lugard to Amīr al-Mu'minīn 'Abdullah (i.e. 'Abd al-Raḥmān) (see Appendix VI).
26. N.A.K. KADCAPTORY, G.O.K.1/1/22, Box 45, Alder Burdon to H.C., 28 May 1902.
27. F. D. Lugard, *Annual Reports*, 1902, p. 159 (see Appendix 6). The original of this famous letter has not been found but this is not to suggest that it never existed.

reply to Lugard's letter of March 1902 about Bauchi was written in the same tone of defiance as the one just mentioned.[28] This letter sums up Sokoto's attitude, that the intervention of the British in the Caliphate's affairs was uninvited, unwanted and offensive, and that it must stop. With this letter Lugard's diplomacy had exhausted itself and, as he had earlier put it, 'diplomacy ceases when either party refuses to receive the agent of the other, to read his letters or to reply'.[29] The impasse would be resolved only through war. The rest of 1902 was spent by Lugard and by Sokoto and Kano in preparation for war.

Lugard's diplomacy towards the Caliph between 1900 and 1902 which involved avoiding any serious military clash with the northern emirates was rendered even more futile by his contradictory military strategy which was designed to put the British in an advantageous position to complete the conquest of the Caliphate. This policy was spelt out by the establishment of military posts at convenient striking distances from the unconquered emirates. It aroused the most lively apprehensions of those emirates and invoked reactions of hostility and fear in varying degrees among them.

In 1900 a W.A.F.F. military post was established at Illo ostensibly to ward off the French. In the same year a section of this force was detached to Kengakoi. After a lull of three years, from 1898, a column from Kengakoi under Captain Keyes attacked Raha and Kalgo in Gwandu emirate in March 1901 'as a punishment for slave raiding'. Raha was sacked and Kalgo, which had been deserted at the approach of the expedition, was burnt down.[30] By the end of June the situation in the country north-east of Illo in Beibei, Jega and Gwandu was greatly disturbed by the march of a British-led force to Argungu. A letter sent to the Emir of Gwandu by the commanding officer, Lt. Johnson, evoked a hostile reply.[31] The British force was compelled to retire to Illo, which it reached on 14 July. The expelled ruler of Raha took the opportunity to retake his town. There were rumours of a combination of Jega, Gwandu and Tambawel to

28. N.A.K. KADCAPTORY, G.O.K.1/1/23: Amīr al-Mu'minīn 'Abd al-Raḥmān to Governor Lugard (see Appendix VIII). It was received by Burdon at a place called Dagidda on 28 May 1902.
29. N.A.K., S.N.P.7/3/40, Lugard to Burdon, 17 Apr. 1902.
30. C.O. 446/15, Wallace to C.O., 14 May 1901.
31. N.A.K. KADCAPTORY, Box 45, G.O.K.1/1/18, C. V. Keyes to H.C., July 1901.

resist the British.[32] It seems that the return of the British troops to confinement at their Illo base prevented a war. In the circumstances Lugard rejected a suggestion by Wallace, that Jega be occupied by force and an ultimatum sent from there to Sokoto. Such a move, Lugard surmised, would precipitate a war with Sokoto, a contingency for which he felt as yet unprepared. In June 1902 Argungu, close to Sokoto and Gwandu, was occupied by a British force under Captain Merrick.

Far away from Sokoto on the eastern frontiers of the Caliphate a small incident—the sending of a column of the W.A.F.F. from Gujba (in Bornu) to Katagum in mid-December 1902—caused panic in the emirates there.[33] The column drove away the Sarki of Yaiyu and installed his brother in his place.[34] It visited several places in Katagum and the leader of the expedition, Captain Dunn, wrote to the Emir that Yaiyu belonged to Bornu.[35] The anxiety generated by this visitation is illustrated by the flight of the Emir of Missau, Aḥmad, on hearing news of the column's approach. He fled westwards with a considerable following and camped at Chediya in Kano emirate. His intention was to go to Sokoto if the column moved westward. He returned to Katagum after an absence of twenty-nine days, on hearing of the return of the British column to Bornu. Missau, Katagum, Azare and Jama'ari—all feared that the expedition was to go westwards. They all wrote to the Emir of Kano, Aliyu, not soliciting help but merely keeping him informed.[36] Just as Aḥmad of Missau fled so also did Sarkin Azare with his people. They remained in a place called Dogon Jeji until the British column had returned to Bornu.

The solution that commended itself to the emirates of the eastern marches was not to organize resistance against the British but to flee before the arrival of their army, as they had done during the approach of Rābiḥ's army in 1896–97. Recognizing that they had no force to resist the European successfully it became a general pattern for many to flee from him rather than

32. *Ibid.*
33. Corr. IX, no. 123, from Tafida of Missau to Amīr al-Mu'minīn Attahiru, states that Aḥmad of Missau fled at the approach of the British on the 8th of Ramaḍān. This fixes the date of Aḥmad's flight to 9 Dec. 1902. Aḥmad returned after twenty-nine days, on 7 Jan. 1903.
34. Corr. IX, nos. 116, 118.
35. Corr. IX, nos. 118, 123.
36. Corr. IX, nos. 114, 115, 116, 117, 118, 123, 124.

wait to live under his authority. In any case the return of the expedition to Bornu territory alleviated the fear of the eastern emirates which were thenceforth apparently lulled into a false sense of security. By the end of 1902 there was no part of the unconquered emirates which had not been alerted to the dangers of European conquest.

The choice before the emirates not yet conquered by 1902 was either to submit unconditionally to expropriation or to meet force with force. Although there was awareness in the Caliphate that its military strength could not match that of the British, there was also pious hope, expressed in prayer, that God would not permit infidels to triumph over the Caliphate. It was believed that whatever the results of military engagements with the Europeans might turn out to be, there was always the chance, be it ever so slim, that the Caliphate might be victorious in the end and thus preserve its Muslim faith and Muslim character. Indeed the greatest fear in the Caliphate was not merely the loss of political sovereignty but particularly the loss of their faith which, it was believed, would follow conquest or tame submission.

PRELUDE TO THE KANO–SOKOTO EXPEDITION

Throughout the first half of 1902 reports reaching Lugard from the interior, particularly about Zaria, Kano and Sokoto, all served to persuade him to make up his mind that a British advance on the northern emirates was not only imperative but would have to be undertaken with the least possible delay. The British establishment of a garrison at Zaria had increased the apprehensions of the northerm emirates. Rev. Miller reported in February 1902 that the Amīr al-Mu'minīn and the Emirs of Kano and Katsina had accused the Emir of Zaria of the crime of following the white man and allowing people from farther south to buy horses and other things from Zaria for the white man's use.[37] The Emir of Zaria denied the charges vehemently.[38]

Reports of Kano's preparations for war were pouring in to Lugard. During 1902 the rebuilding of Kano walls and the erection of strong gates were completed, while towns in the emirate, acting on instructions from Kano, similarly rebuilt their walls

37. N.A.K. KADCAPTORY, G.O.K.1/1/13, Miller to Lugard, 6 Feb. 1902.
38. *Ibid.*

and re-dug the trenches surrounding them. Kano procured large quantities of arms from Tripolitanian merchants and runaway W.A.F.F. soldiers, while, according to Rev. Miller, the Arabs in Kano were prepared to assist the Emir in the event of a fight.[39] Muḥammad, the Emir of Bida, remonstrated in vain with Aliyu, Emir of Kano to surrender peacefully to the British, urging that the latter were prepared to maintain the religion of Islam and traditional authority.[40]

Consequent on reports of stockpiling of arms in Kano and the implacable hostility of the Emir to white men, Lugard wired the Zaria garrison on 25 March 1902 to warn them that it might be necessary to advance on Kano 'at once'.[41] In fact Lugard was not prepared to march on Kano 'at once'. By April the Lugard government had decided to attack Kano after the rainy season of 1902.[42] The British were encouraged to go for Kano by information received to the effect that only the King was bent on fighting but that the traders and peasants were for submitting to the British even though they all detested the white man.[43] Also, Kano was known to have been weakened by a recent war with Hadejia.[44] Late in April a caravan from Katsina passing through Wushishi had reported to Lugard that the Emir of Kano had made it known that if any white man came to the city he would be killed.[45] A few weeks earlier an English trader, Grey, had been

39. *Ibid.*, see also N.A.K. KADCAPTORY, G.O.K.1/1/13, Miller to Lugard, 4 Mar. 1902. Miller had reports from three different sources to the effect that three loads of arms were brought by Arabs to Kano on or about 6 Feb.
40. N.A.K. KADCAPTORY, G.O.K.1/1/16, Burdon to Lugard, 5 Apr. 1902.
41. R.H.B.E. S.64, Popham-Lobb to mother, 26 Mar. 1902.
42. Popham-Lobb to mother, 6 Apr. 1902. In another letter written by Popham-Lobb to his mother on the 27th, he stated clearly that the British expedition to Kano was planned for Feb. 1903 or sooner. See also Perham, *The Years of Authority*, p. 87 ff. for Lugard's preparations for the Kano expedition, and D. T. M. Muffet, *Concerning Brave Captains* (London, 1964), pp. 62–8, 69 ff.
43. Popham-Lobb to mother, 6 Aug. 1902.
44. Popham-Lobb to mother, 26 Apr. 1902. Also *Labarum Hausawa*, vol. ii, pp. 69–70. The war which took place in the dry season of 1901–02 was caused by the Emir of Hadejia's seizure of Miga in Kano emirate which Yūsuf had promised him in return for his help during the Tukur revolt (1893–95). This help the Emir of Hadejia did not give.
45. N.A.K. KADCAPTORY, G.O.K.1/1/21, Lugard to Resident of Zaria, 29 April 1902.

turned back from Kano by a show of force.[46] The complete breakdown of diplomatic relations between Lugard and Sokoto by May 1902 finally demonstrated the futility of peaceful negotiations to effect British acquisition of sovereignty over the Caliphate.[47] This should have been obvious at least to Lugard from his assumption of office.

The breach between Sokoto and Kano on the one hand and the Lugard government on the other was complete. The situation deteriorated further as the year wore on. Lugard claimed that he received 'a well-authenticated report' that in October 1902 the Emir of Kano had set out to attack the British garrison at Zaria, but had had to turn back on receipt of news of the death of the Amīr al-Mu'minīn 'Abd al-Raḥmān.[48] In November Captain Merrick reported from Argungu that Fulani chiefs were gathered in Sokoto with intention to oppose Europeans by force.[49]

The feeling of insecurity among the British in 'Northern Nigeria' created by these reports was enough to convince Lugard of the necessity of settling with the northern emirates and Sokoto. He, however, had to make a convincing case to justify his war policy to the British Colonial Office and the British public, who were pressing for avoidance of war with the northern emirates of the Caliphate. The rise and fall of the barometer of public opinion in Britain, to which the Colonial Office was most sensitive, really belongs to the history of British imperial policy and need not concern us here.[50] All the same it must be noted that the Colonial Office's insistence on a peaceful policy made it essential for Lugard to prove that war was being forced on him by circumstances under which adherence to a peaceful policy would jeopardize essential British interests in the Caliphate and perhaps serve merely as prelude to a greater disaster than could result from the risk he was then braced to take. Aware of the blame he would incur if the expedition failed, Lugard took more than usual care to see that his preparations in troops, arms and provisioning were likely to ensure success.

The attitude of the Colonial Office apart, Lugard also had to

46. N.A.K. KADCAPTORY, G.O.K.1/1/16, Lugard to Burdon, 19 April. 1902.
47. See Appendices VII and VIII for the Caliph's letters.
48. Lugard, *Annual Reports*, p. 76.
49. N.A.K., S.N.P.15/9, Merrick to Lugard, 21 Nov. 1902.
50. For an account of Lugard–Colonial Office relations at this time, see Perham, *The Years of Authority*, p. 93 ff. and Muffett, *Concerning Brave Captains*, pp. 69–78.

reckon with the attitude of the subjugated emirates of the south, who, as already mentioned, continued to maintain their allegiance to the Caliph.[51] There was widespread belief in the conquered emirates that the European invaders would soon quit. Had they not evacuated Bida and Iḷorin in 1897 after conquering them? Even assuming that the white man had no wish to quit hopes were widely entertained that if he dared the might of Kano and Sokoto his defeat, which was deemed almost certain, would force him out.[52]

It was Lugard's view that the northern emirates of the Caliphate had thrown a challenge to British power which could only be disregarded at the grave risk of losing face and creating a situation in which disrespect for, and disobedience to, the British would spread in the subjugated emirates.[53] Pent-up resentment at British conquest, known to be widespread, was believed certain to break out once there was reason to hope that rebellion would be successful. On the other hand similar consequences were bound to follow the defeat of the British in battle by any emirate.

With the fear which gripped the emirates of the eastern marches when the British column at Gujba marched to Katagum in December 1902, the restiveness of Kano and Sokoto and the resentment of the conquered emirates, it seems more likely than not that if the myth of the invincibility of British forces was once exploded by defeat in the impending battles with Kano and Sokoto, the whole Caliphate would be united in hunting them down. Lugard was convinced that the time had come for taking a decisive step through application of strong measures.

MAGAJIN KEFFI AND THE MURDER OF CAPTAIN MOLONEY

Lugard found a *casus belli* in the murder of Captain Moloney at Keffi in October 1902. However, the so-called provocation to

51. See ch. 7, and also C.O. 446/25, Lugard to C.O., no. 597 of 21 Nov. 1902. 'The settlement of the three provinces (i.e. Kano, Katsina, Sokoto) will settle unrest in Yola, Bauchi, Zaria, who will never settle down until these states have given their allegiance to the British.'
52. 'Paramount chiefs in this country await result and if action deferred they would attribute to fear of them' (i.e. Kano and Sokoto). *Ibid.*, also C.O. 446/30, Lugard to C.O., Tel. 13 Dec. 1902.
53. F. D. Lugard, *Annual Report*, 1902, pp. 74–6.

war which Lugard saw in Moloney's murder was a mere excuse meant really for the consumption of the Colonial Office and the British public. It was not the first time a British officer or British-protected person had been killed in the Caliphate. In October 1900 the Hon. David Carnegie had been killed in the village of Tawari in Kotonkarfi district.[54] Lugard on that occasion considered a punitive expedition to the particular village sufficient for the restoration of such British prestige as might have been lost through the incident. Again, in August 1902 a C.M.S. missionary, the Rev. Bako, and one Samuel Obeya had been attacked near Abuja; the former died in the encounter. Even though there were reasons to implicate Nasarawa in the crime, Lugard was satisfied with sending an expedition to Abuja only. Once the expedition had wreaked vengeance on Abuja, Lugard did not immediately bother with the open resentment of the town.[55]

A great deal of obscurity, occasioned by the contradictory evidence of eye-witness accounts, surrounds the murder of Captain Moloney.[56] The broad outlines of the incident are, however, clear. The Magaji of Keffi, Dan Yamusa, the Emir of Zaria's representative at Keffi responsible for overseeing the affairs of this faraway sub-emirate, was feeling the pinch of British interference in Keffi affairs. The British forbade annual Keffi raids against pagans like the Dari, Amba, Riri and Mada[57] which, though traditional and legal, were branded as mere slave raids by the British.

On 3 October 1902 Captain Moloney, the Resident at Keffi, decided to bring the Magaji under British control and curb what he called his excesses by calling him to a conference in front of the Emir's palace, presumably to cajole him to submission. The Magaji ignored several summonses to appear before this tribunal. A final message carried by the Assistant Resident, Webster, to the Magaji was not only ignored but the bearer was manhandled

54. C.O. 446/11, Lugard to C.O., 21 Jan. 1901.
55. See N.A.K., S.N.P.15/31 on the Abuja expedition.
56. The story of the murder of Captain Moloney is reconstructed from Mr Webster's report in C.O. 446/26, Lugard to C.O., 15 Dec. 1902; Col. Beddoes's report—*ibid.* The evidence of Hassan Keffi recorded by Muffett, *op. cit.*, pp. 63–8; Mr Silva's evidence recorded by Mrs C. Larymore in her book, *A Resident's Wife in Nigeria* (London, 1911), pp. 50–2.
57. Evidence of Hassan Keffi as recorded by Muffett, *op. cit.*, p. 64.

by the Magaji's men and thrown into the *Zaure* (entrance hall) of the compound.[58] Shortly after Webster's escape the Magaji came out mounted and armed with two pistols.[59] He was followed by armed retainers. Meanwhile Moloney had despatched Webster to call in W.A.F.F. men.

All the reports are agreed that Moloney's African agent, Audu Timtim, was responsible, through his lies, for fostering hostile relations between Moloney and the Magaji. It seems certain that the Magaji first attacked Audu Timtim by shooting him. Moloney, on the other hand, was the victim of one of the numerous arrows fired by the Magaji's retainers. Finally Audu was cut down with the sword by Barga, one of the Magaji's followers, while another of his men, Mallam Dabo, cut off Moloney's head.

Some of the sources maintain that Moloney died of Magaji's gunshot, but Silva, an African hospital dresser who prepared Moloney's body for burial, maintained that he died of an arrow-wound which pierced his carotid artery.[60] Col. Beddoes, on the authority of Ibrāhīm, another African agent of the British, reported that Moloney was hit in the neck by an arrow. While Beddoes maintained that the Magaji shot the arrow, Silva held that the latter did not carry arrows. It seems unlikely that having armed himself with pistols the Magaji would have carried a bow and arrows—an encumbrance which would seriously hamper his use of his pistols should the need arise.[61] The only guilt that can attach to the Magaji is indirect, in that one of his followers killed Moloney. Whether or not he had the intention of killing Moloney remains a matter of conjecture. It must be noted that he had ample opportunity to do so before shooting Audu. That he did not in fact do so would suggest that he had no intention of killing Moloney.

On the day of the incident the W.A.F.F. soldiers, in an engagement which lasted till 4 p.m., sacked Keffi, killing many. The

58. Hassan Keffi denied that Webster was manhandled in the Magaji's compound but Webster in his report claimed that he was.
59. See Hassan Keffi's evidence, *loc. cit.*, p. 66.
60. Silva's evidence, *loc. cit.*, p. 51, he declared that there was only an arrow wound on Moloney's neck and that the Magaji was not armed with a bow.
61. It is also unlikely that the Magaji, within a short space of time, killed two people (Audu and Moloney), one with a pistol and the other with an arrow.

Magaji, followed by a large crowd and cattle, fled northwards, his intention being to go to Kano and thereby avoid the white men at Zaria.[62] In addition to a column under Col. Beddoes from Keffi several columns were sent out from Zaria to catch the Magaji. Furthermore, Lugard set a price of £40 on his head.[63] At Girku the Magaji narrowly escaped capture by cutting down the suspension bridge over a river after he and some of his followers had crossed it. He thereby made it impossible for the British column on the other side to continue the chase immediately. He reached Kano late in October.

In Kano the Magaji, Dan Yamusa, was given a hero's welcome by the Emir, Aliyu. For Lugard, this was the last straw. Kano had not only shown consistent enmity to the British and turned itself into a 'cave of Adullam' for all the enemies of the white men, but the Emir had given his approval to the murder of a high official of the British administration.

Lugard argued that failure to pursue the Magji to the utmost parts of the Caliphate and bring him to book would lead to a widespread contempt for the British, which could easily result in constant uprisings and bloodshed. He wrote: 'The lives of the men who are, to the best of their ability, doing the Empire's work here and honestly working for the good of these people would not be safe.'[64] Lugard was right, but so was the Emir of Kano; they were enemies, each anxious to protect his interests. In the circumstances of the relations between the Caliphate and the British at that time it is difficult to see how failure to arrest a culprit who had sought refuge in unconquered territory could have produced contempt for the British. With regard to Sokoto Lugard did not feel that any further argument for attacking the town was necessary beyond the Caliph's letter received in May 1902, in which he declared that a state of war existed between him and the British. The welcome given to Magajin Keffi at Kano was an excuse for war too good to be missed.

In February 1902 Lugard had indicated the probability of sending a force against Sokoto by December of that year.[65] In September he had included in his draft estimates for 1903–04

62. Popham-Lobb to mother, *loc. cit.*, 15 Oct. 1902.
63. *Ibid.*
64. C.O. 446/30, Lugard to C.O., 15 Jan. 1903.
65. C.O. 446/26, Lugard to C.O., 7 Oct. 1902, extract from a dispatch dated 15 Feb. 1902.

provisions for increasing the strength of the W.A.F.F. in Northern Nigeria, for the ostensible reason that considerations for the safety of the Anglo–French boundary commission would require a force at full strength to accompany it.[66]

Approval was given by the British Colonial Office for the increase of the forces by a third battalion of 1000 men and 400 mounted infantry.[67] Further, in the Northern Nigeria draft estimates for 1903–04, provision was made for thirteen administrative provinces including Sokoto, Kano and Katsina.[68] Not only therefore had a British attack on Kano and Sokoto been decided on before the murder of Captain Moloney, but Lugard was already making preparations for the expedition. His mind thus made up, he made no efforts at this stage to open negotiations with the newly installed Caliph at Sokoto, Muḥammad al-Ṭāhir (Attahiru).[69] He shifted the responsibility of making peace moves to the new Caliph by arguing that since he failed to withdraw the threat of war made by his predecessor, ʿAbd al-Raḥmān, the Caliph, Attahiru, had given tacit approval to the latter's policy.[70]

As the British war-fever increased, the Emir of Kano became more implacable in his hostility. Late in December 1902 he was said to have made a proclamation forbidding caravans of traders from leaving Kano for the southern emirates as they had been doing almost daily.[71] It was essential, from Lugard's point of view, to take swift action, as the only means of preventing the northern emirates from forming a military confederacy which

66. N.A.I., C.S.O.1/28, 3, C.O. to Lugard, enclosed in despatch no. 597, 23 Jan. 1903. Lugard's case for having more troops to enable him provide a strong escort for the boundary commission is fully stated in another dispatch of 28 Aug. 1902, quoted *in extenso* by Muffett, *op. cit.*, p. 58.

67. *Ibid.*

68. C.O. 446/25, Lugard to C.O., 21 Nov. 1902; also in N.A.I., C.S.O.1/28, 3, Lugard to C.O., 21 Nov. 1902, for quotation from this despatch, see Muffet, p. 73.

69. See Muffett, *op. cit.*, p. 69. Muffett's implied argument that if Lugard was not irrevocably bent on war he should have made fresh contact with the new Caliph is largely irrelevant. The situation had gone beyond peaceful negotiations. In any case, Sokoto had never considered its sovereignty as negotiable.

70. C.O. 446/30, Lugard to C.O., 15 Jan. 1903.

71. C.O. 446/30, Lugard to C.O., 10 Jan. 1903. Information collected from a large caravan which arrived at Wushishi on 10 January.

might turn out to be too formidable for his forces.[72] The British success in the ensuing expeditions to Kano and Sokoto must be ascribed in part to the dispatch with which they were organized and executed. Hence, apart from strengthening the protectorate's forces and the garrison at Zaria, supplies of food were moved up to Zaria from the end of November. There was, for instance, a food depot thirty miles from Zaria, on the Zaria–Kano road.[73] Other preparations also received Lugard's prompt attention. In late November 1902 he gave instructions for the mobilization of fifty officers and N.C.O.s and over 1000 rank and file, with five 75 mm guns and seven Maxims.

Lugard decided to advance against Kano at the beginning of January 1903.[74] In the meantime Captain Merrick, who was in Argungu with 250 men and a 75 mm gun, was instructed to take up a strong defensive position there as a threat to Sokoto's flank which would effectively deter Sokoto forces from joining up with Kano.[75] Kano would therefore be dealt with without aid from Sokoto or Gwandu. The preoccupation of the more easterly emirates with fear of the British garrison at Gujba completed Kano's isolation.

THE TAKING OF KANO

Col. T. N. Morland was appointed by Lugard to command the British Kano expeditionary force with Lt-Col. A. N. Festing as second in command. Morland advanced from Zaria towards Kano on 29 January with a force of twenty-four officers, twelve N.C.O.s, two Medical Officers and 722 rank and file, made up of 550 foot, 71 artillery men and 101 mounted infantry. The expedition had four 75 mm guns and four Maxims.[76]

72. R.H.B.E., S.65, draft memo. by Lugard (unused), p. 222.
73. C.O. 446/30, Lugard to C.O., 15 Jan. 1903. It was rumoured in January that this depot had been burnt by Kano men and the Chief of the village beheaded for being friendly with the British.
74. C.O. 446/26, Lugard to C.O., 12 Dec. 1902, and C.O. 446/26, Lugard to C.O., Tel. no. 127, 23 Dec. 1903, and C.O. 446/30, Lugard to C.O., 15 Jan. 1903.
75. *Ibid.*
76. C.O. 446/31, General Kemball to Lugard, 9 Apr. 1903, enclosed in Lugard to C.O., no. 156b of May 1903. For dispute over whether Morland or Kemball should command the expedition see Muffett, *op. cit.*, p. 80 ff. and Perham, *The Years of Authority*, p. 95 f.

As part of Kano's war plan the chief of Gaya, a town on the Zaria–Kano road, and all the headmen of the towns on the border of Kano with Zaria, had been instructed to resist European advance at Bebeji.[77] Therefore, when Morland's expedition arrived there on the first of February the inhabitants refused its offer of a peaceful parley. The town gate was blown open with shell-fire which killed the headman who had taken his position behind it. The town fell an easy prey to the superior weapons of the British and the expedition resumed its march to Kano.

The towns and villages between Bebeji and Kano, which had been fortified with a view to holding up the British advance, were deserted at the approach of the British expedition.[78] An important aspect of Kano's plan was thus rendered of no effect. On 2 February Morland's force camped at the Challawa river—about six miles from Kano, from where it advanced on Kano city at 6 a.m. the following morning.[79]

In the meantime a proclamation in Hausa from Lugard to the people of Kano had been sent ahead when the expedition left Zaria. In it Lugard assured the people that the British had no quarrel with anyone, except Magajin Keffi and those who had welcomed him to Kano with marks of honour. They would attack no one except those who elected to fight.[80] Apparently, this proclamation, which was to have been posted in public, had not been received, or if received it was, understandably, not heeded by Kano people.[81] The division of Kano, in the mind of Lugard, into those who would oppose the British and others evokes no more than theoretical interest.

The situation in Kano at the time of the expedition's approach was complex. The Emir had left for Sokoto since 2 January with

77. N.A.I., C.S.O.1/27, 3, Lugard to C.O., 8 Feb. 1903, F. D. Lugard, *Annual Reports*, 1903, p. 86.

78. *Ibid.* See also *Labarun Hausawa*, vol. ii, p. 70. Aliyu had built many fortified villages south of Kano. Perham, *The Years of Authority*, pp. 108–23 and Muffett, *op. cit.*, pp. 91–104 contain accounts of the conquest of Kano. Factually my account overlaps with these earlier works. References are made to them as considered appropriate but in general I have relied more on the original sources.

79. C.O. 446/31, Lugard to C.O., no. 156b, encl. Kemball to Lugard: Report on Kano-Sokoto expedition, 9 Apr. 1903.

80. C.O. 446/30, Lugard to C.O., 23 Jan. 1903, encl. no. 1.

81. The Morland expedition advanced on Kano without any parley with the Kano people. Lugard's instruction was that the expedition should wait for a reply to the proclamation before advancing to fight.

all his principal officials and the headmen of the western districts of the emirate and their forces. It seems that Aliyu's visit to Sokoto was to pay homage to the new Caliph, Attahiru, as was customary for emirs at the accession of a new Caliph.[82] About mid-December he had written to the Caliph to inform him of the advent of the British to Katagum and their subsequent return eastwards to Bornu. At that time Aliyu had said that since he received this news and information about the movement of the white men's troops from Bauchi to Zaria he had heard nothing more.[83] It therefore appears that even though a British attack on Kano was expected, it was not definitely known by 2 January, when Aliyu left Kano, that the attack was imminent.[84] The attack on Kano if and when it did come was apparently expected to come from the east.[85]

According to Hassan Keffi's evidence the purpose of Aliyu's visit was to pray at the graves of his forebears at Wurno, for which purpose he spent nineteen days away from Sokoto.[86] D. J. M. Muffett's view that Aliyu went to settle a rift between himself and the new Caliph arising from the Tukur revolt, is not tenable, in view of the fact that Aliyu had been reconciled with Sokoto since about 1895.[87]

Even though the Emir of Kano might have been ignorant of the imminence of a British attack, he had nevertheless put Kano in a state of defence before his departure. In view of his subsequent behaviour and in the light of the fact that he is said to have left

82. Waziri Junaidu, *Ḍabṭ al-Mulṭaqatāt*, f. 74a.
83. Corr. IX, no. 124.
84. Muffett, *op. cit.*, p. 95. Eye-witness account by Hassan Keffi who with Magajin Keffi had accompanied Aliyu to Sokoto. The 1st of Ramaḍān 1902, was 2 December of that year. The 'Id al-Fiṭr would therefore have fallen on 2 January, the day Aliyu is said to have left Kano. Would the Emir have left the city on the day of the Ramaḍān feast? It may be that even 2 January was not the day of Aliyu's departure from Kano.
85. A letter written to Aliyu by Sarkin Shanu Muḥammad when the former was away to Sokoto and referring to the British who had come to the Eastern Emirates assures Aliyu that the Christians had departed from the land of the Muslims 'to their own country'. See Corr. IX, no. 122, see also *Labarun Hausawa*, vol. ii, p. 70. Aliyu and Madakin Kano had disagreed over Aliyu's departure. The Madaki feared that the Europeans would arrive during Aliyu's absence but Aliyu did not think so.
86. Hassan Keffi's account, *loc. cit.*, p. 95.
87. See above, p. 102; cf. Muffett, *op. cit.*, p. 98.

instructions for the defence of the city, the likelihood that he left Kano for fear of the British cannot be ruled out. This conjecture is, however, contradicted by his continuance of his journey towards Kano from Sokoto, even when he had heard of the fall of Bebeji and his initial refusal to accept news of the fall of Kano as true.[88] His desertion of his troops (discussed below) on receiving confirmatory news of the defeat of Kano was apparently dictated by despair caused by the *fait accompli*, rather than fear of facing the British in battle. Other emirs had similarly fled from the British after the conquest of their capital cities. However, Aliyu's absence with the notables of Kano and a large number of cavalrymen did mean a serious depletion of Kano's total force of resistance.

It was a strongly fortified city that Col. Morland's force had to face. At 8 a.m. on 3 February 1903, their mounted infantry exchanged shots with a Kano scouting patrol at a distance of 800 yards from the formidable walls.[89] The walls were 'in a marvellous state of repair'. They were 30 to 50 feet high, 40 feet thick at the base, with a ditch running round them. At the top the walls were four feet thick with loop-holes four feet from the top through which defenders could shoot at the enemy. The ditch 'was divided into two by a dwarf wall, triangular in section, which ran along its centre'. The gates, in themselves weak, were set in massive entrance towers about 50 feet long and so tortuous that they could not be easily reached by shell-fire.[90]

The walls were reported to be strongly held by Kano soldiers as the British approached. At a distance of 400 yards, the British force directed fire from the Maxims and the 75 mm guns at the Zaria gate. Neither the gateway nor the walls could be properly breached by gunfire. After one hour of heavy shelling at the Zaria gateway, the British force was unable to effect an entrance and the walls proved impervious to the 75 mm gunfire.

Morland, in a moment that must have been one of near frustration, moved on to another gate to the west of the Zaria gate (Kowbuga gate) leaving a force to hold the Kano defenders of the

88. See below, p. 275.

89. CD.1433, Col. Morland's report to Lugard on the Kano expedition. N.A.I. CSO1/27, 3, Lugard to C.O., 8 Feb. 1903; my account of the conquest of Kano is based on the above as well as C.O. 446/31, no. 156b, Lugard to C.O., encl. Kemball's report, 9 Apr. 1903, and also on Lugard's *Annual Reports*, 1902, p. 86 ff.

90. Lugard, *Annual Report*, pp. 86–7; R.H.B.E., S.65; notes on Kano, 1903 by Lugard.

5 View from inside the walls of Kano, 1903

6 General Lugard and his staff, 1903

first gate at bay. While about 450 men attacked the second gate, patrols of mounted infantry kept watch on their flanks until a small breach was made in the gateway.[91] A party under Lt. Dyer, stormed the gate, aided with ladders previously designed for scaling the walls. The advance of Dyer's party might have been checked by the Kano soldiers holding the walls but for the fact that their firing, though heavy, was ill-directed. Dyer's party was therefore able to make an opening through which they entered the city. The Kano soldiers withdrew from the walls, while those holding the gate took fright from the heavy firing of the British force and fled.

Kano resistance was broken. An attempt by the defenders of the Zaria gate to relieve those of the other gate (Kowbuga gate) was completely foiled by a few shrapnel shells burst among them. A party of British mounted infantry scouted the circumference of the walls to prevent Kano men from fleeing from the city. It is said that 200 Kano men, discovered in the attempt to escape, were killed by this patrol of mounted infantry. Once inside the city, the British expeditionary force met with no resistance until it reached the Emir's palace which, though stoutly defended by Sarkin Shanu, Muḥammad, was taken by assault. Sarkin Shanu died defending the palace.

Morland estimated the Kano fighting force at 800 cavalry and 5000 foot. Of these 300 were said to have been killed. Aliyu's arsenal in the palace was found to contain 'every conceivable kind of ammunition' and 350 firearms were destroyed.[92] The fact that in spite of the heavy firing of the Kano soldiers the British casualties were: none killed, except three horses, and only fourteen wounded, shows that the defenders must have been surprisingly unskilled in the use of firearms. It must be added, however, that their firearms were relatively few and inferior to those of the British expedition.

With the conquest of Kano events had worked out as Lugard hoped. Morland, in accordance with Lugard's instructions, assumed the Residency of Kano in the meantime. Soon after the occupation he had posted Lugard's proclamation, written in Hausa, in the market-place. In this proclamation (an apologia for British action) the attack on Kano was blamed on the Emir who it was said, in spite of peace offers made to him, had elected war

91. Morland's and Kemball's reports on the expedition, *loc. cit.*
92. Kemball's report, *loc. cit.*

by welcoming Magajin Keffi to Kano with honour as well as maintaining an implacable hostility to the British. Kano, the proclamation emphasized, was thenceforth British territory. Aliyu was declared deposed: subsequent emirs would be appointed on the authority of the High Commissioner in consultation with the local electors. The proclamation further enjoined everybody to carry on his normal business with full assurance of protection by the British, who would ensure the rights and security of all. Slaves who felt ill-treated could complain to the Resident, who had been empowered to set them free if he thought fit. All friends of Magajin Keffi were declared enemies of the British government and any one who captured him would receive a reward of thirty pounds in cash or kind. No one could bear arms without a permit from the new government and anyone in possession of arms was to hand them over to the Resident within three days.[93]

The Galadiman Kano was named to act as Emir until a new one was appointed. As the Galadima had gone with the Emir, Aliyu, to Sokoto, it meant in fact that there was an interregnum in Kano, without anybody to hold the 'regency'. The import of the proclamation was the complete abrogation of the Caliph's authority in Kano in favour of a British regime. The British determination to uphold the rights of Kano people against molestation and injustice was demonstrated a few days later by the public execution of a W.A.F.F. soldier charged with killing a native of Kano in the market.

The British terms did not win the active support of the Kano people, but as long as the troops were in Kano, resentment to the British could not be shown openly. The atmosphere in the city was, nonetheless, not one of joy, even though normal life went on unobtrusively. According to Captain Abadie resentment was merely driven underground.[94] Lugard was, indeed, apparently overawed by the fall of Kano and feared that it might open new problems of insecurity for his men. From Zaria he wrote to Brigadier-General Kemball, who arrived in Kano from Zungeru on 13 February to take over command from Morland, in terms which suggest that he thought the expedition to Sokoto should be held up.[95] In spite of the assurances he gave to the British

93. C.O. 446/30, Lugard to C.O., 23 Jan. 1903, encl. no. 2.
94. Muffett, *op. cit.*, pp. 112–13, quoting Abadie to Lugard.
95. C.O. 446/31, Lugard to C.O., 17 May 1903.

Colonial Office that his forces were adequate for the purpose of conquering Kano and Sokoto, Lugard had had fears that the expedition might come to grief. In December 1902 he had expressed his fears to his brother: 'If I don't come to grief over the Kano–Sokoto business with my inadequate forces, there will be a big step forward in the next twelve months.'[96]

Meanwhile, Kano people who could find a way had escaped from the city after the battle of 3 February. On 14 February Kemball was able to confirm that a large body of fighting men, consisting of fugitives from Kano, the headmen of the various districts and towns of the emirate with their soldiers, was gathering at a place about sixty miles to the north-west of Kano.[97]

Near Kaura Namoda Aliyu of Kano, returning from Sokoto, had heard news in the meantime of the fall of Bebeji and had sent back to Sokoto for advice. When he reached a town called Birnin Goga he heard news of the fall of Kano but would not believe it.[98] The Kanawa were desperate after the fall of Kano. In spite of the failure of their first resistance it was evident that they meant to fight another day by rallying the forces of the whole emirate.

The British also realized that they could not be complacent. They made arrangement to transfer one company each of the Southern Nigeria and Lagos reserves to Zaria and Argungu respectively for the security of those places and the southern and western flanks of the expedition. Kemball gave orders for the force at Kano to move out to meet and scatter the hostile gathering of Kano fighters before it could become too formidable.[99] A garrison was left to guard Kano.

As Morland advanced towards them, the gathering of Kano soldiers retreated, intending to join up with their returning Emir. The only hope of a successful resistance by Kano depended on the forces of Aliyu being able to circumvent the British troops coming from Kano and retake their city. Morland, aware from the first that Kano might try its fortunes in another battle, had written to Sokoto and Katsina identical letters couched in terms of friendship and conciliation, albeit mixed with threats of a

96. R.H.B.E., S.62. F. D. Lugard to E. J. Lugard, 13 Dec. 1902.

97. C.O. 446/31, Lugard to C.O., no. 156b, encl. Kemball's report on Kano-Sokoto expedition, 9 Apr. 1903.

98. Muffett, *op. cit.*, p. 103. Eye-witness account by Hassan Keffi. See also *Labarun Hausawa*, vol. ii, pp. 70–2, for an account of Aliyu's return from Sokoto. This account is rather similar to Hassan Keffi's.

99. Kemball's report, 9 Apr. 1903, Kano-Sokoto expedition, *loc. cit.*

permanent British occupation and establishment of British authority. The two cities were urged not to contest the inevitable by fighting, seeing that although the British wanted peace they were prepared, if necessary, to fight. In all events they would not interfere with the Muslim religion.[100] In spite of the threatening tone of the letter, or perhaps because of it, Katsina, a town which had trembled for years under the fear of French occupation, promised neither to assist Kano nor harbour Magajin Keffi, Yamusa. The Caliph delayed sending a reply. The British now had a free hand to deal with Aliyu's forces without fear of attack from Katsina.

The last week of February 1903 was filled with uncertainties and great anxieties both for the Kano men and for the British expedition. At Birnin Goga Aliyu had finally confirmed the fall of Kano from one Salama, who with Sarkin Shanu had defended Kano palace against Morland.

The Emir seems to have been completely upset by the news. At dawn on 24 February he fled his camp with a few followers, including the Galadima.[101] During that day the party of Magajin Keffi, Dan Yamusa, also deserted the main body of the Kano army and returned to Sokoto. The Kano force had thus suffered an irreparable loss in numbers and more important still, in morale. That it did not disintegrate immediately was owing largely to the leadership provided by Salama and Wazirin Kano who assumed control at once and rallied the remnant of the army, about 3500 strong, to return to Kano. The journey from Kaura Namoda to Kano at that time of the year was under normal circumstances difficult because of the scarcity of water. Both the Kanawa and the British were put at great inconvenience by this factor.

Everything now depended on whether or not the British would succeed to head off the Kanawa from their advance towards their city. On their part, the British had no precise idea as to which of the several possible routes Aliyu's force would take.[102] The expedition had reached Ummadau on 22 February. Here they drew up a master plan for heading off Aliyu and his warriors.

100. For text of Morland's letter to Sokoto and Katsina, see *Annual Reports*, Appendix 6, 1902.

101. For an account of Aliyu's flight, see oral evidence recorded by Muffett, *op. cit.*, pp. 101–4; also *Labarun Hausawa, loc. cit.*

102. See Map No. 5, p. 278.

Having got information that Aliyu intended to march from Birnin Goga via Kammane, to the north-west of Ummadau, a mounted infantry patrol under Lt. Porter was despatched to head him off from that direction.[103] This route, which was not the most direct to Kano, had the advantage for Kano people of passing close to Katsina. The Kano forces might hope for Katsina aid in case of an encounter with the British. However, with Aliyu's flight on the 24th the plan of the Kanawa to march through Kammane, if in fact there had been such a plan, was shelved. The main force under Morland was to march through Duru (to the south of Ummadau) and Modawa (west of Duru) to Kaura Namoda. Should the Kanawa decide to return to Kano by the southern and more direct route they would be stopped by Morland's force. To ensure that the Kanawa were effectively cut off from all approaches to Kano, another patrol of forty-five mounted infantry under Lts. Wright and C. L. Wells was sent out to deflect south-west from Duru to Kotorkwoshi, and from there to follow the caravan route from Zaria and Kano to Kaura Namoda. This force left Duru on the 24th.

After the flight of Aliyu the people of Kano left Birmin Goga on the 24th and travelled via Kaura Namoda and Modawa to Kotorkwoshi which they reached on 25 February. Here their advance party of about 200 encountered Lt. Wright's patrol. A skirmish ensued in which the Kanawa lost about fifty killed and many wounded. The main Kano force retreated but were engaged again with Lt. Wright's patrol in fierce battle on the morning of the 26th near Rawiya, a few miles north of Kotorkwoshi.[104] Wright put up a most stubborn and disciplined resistance to the Kanawa fighters who, he said charged his square formation relentlessly for well over an hour. In addition to frequent charges, the Kanawa kept up a steady fire from about 100 yards distance but they could not take Wright's square by assault. Their intrepidity cost them dear. After they had lost sixty-five killed, including the Wazir and more than ten chiefs, many within about fifteen yards of the British guns, Kano

103. The accounts of the British advance from Kano, their despatch of forces to Ummadau and engagements with Kano forces are based on Kemball's Report, 9 Apr. 1903, *loc. cit.* See also Map no. 5. See Muffett, pp. 117–26 for a detailed account of the advance of Sokoto.

104. Muffett, *op. cit.*, pp. 119–26 for a more detailed description of the battles of Kotorkwoshi and Rawiya, including oral traditions about the battles; also Perham, *The Years of Authority*, pp. 115–17.

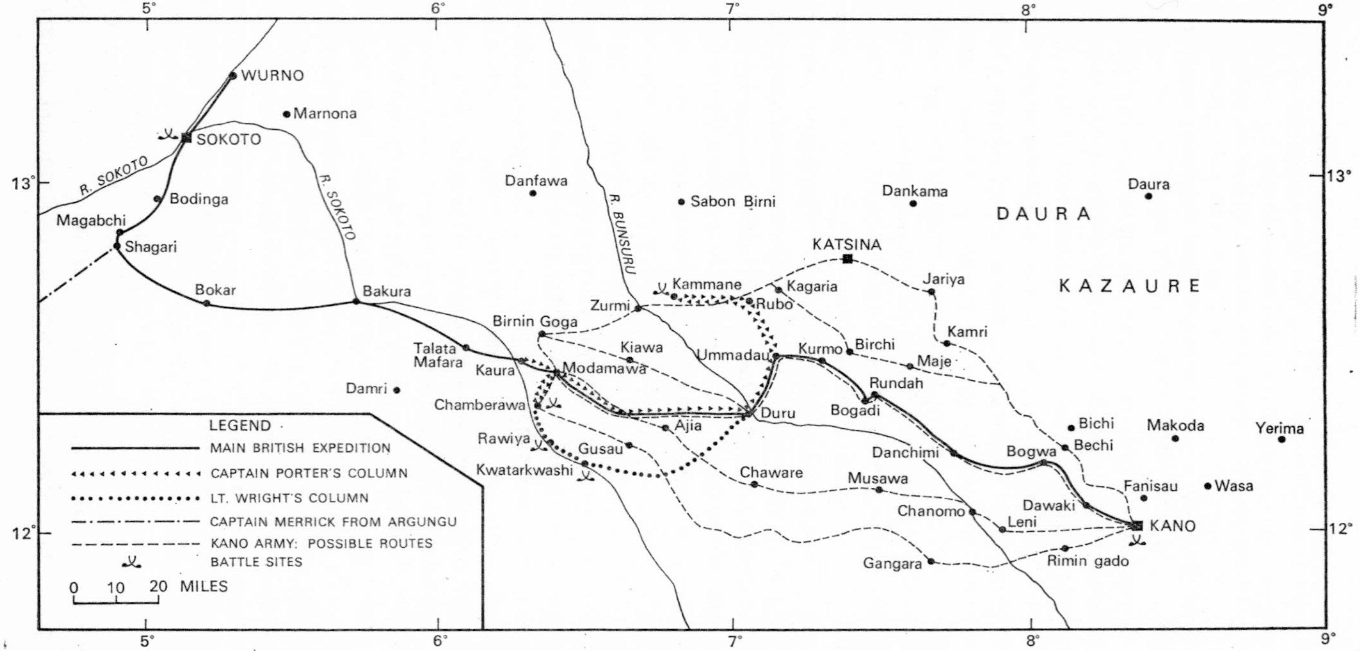

The routes of the Kano-Sokoto expedition

men retreated much demoralized by the loss of their leaders. Lt. Wright's casualties were only three horses killed and one man wounded. From thenceforth serious resistance by Kano men was at an end.

Later in the day a group of the fugitive Kano fighters was scattered by Lt. Porter's patrol at a watering place in a village called Kamberawa. Lt. Porter had had various skirmishes on the Ummadau–Kammane route but having learned of Aliyu's desertion of his army he had joined up with the main force under Morland at Modawa on the 25th.

After the battle of Kotorkwoshi Abbās, Womban Kano returned to the city. He had returned with a large following, emboldened and presumably encouraged by a letter he received from Lugard promising him appointment as Emir if he submitted peacefully.[105] On 6 March 1903 the Wombai, Abbās, with a following of about 2500 cavalry and 5000 foot (this figure excluded numerous Kano combatants from Aliyu's following who had left for their different villages) surrendered to Lugard.[106] The latter permitted them to enter Kano only after he had made them surrender their firearms. A further indication that Kano fighters were poorly equipped in firearms is that only 120 rifles were collected from the large crowd. Lugard appointed the Wombai as Emir-elect and with that Kano military resistance was, more clearly than ever, at an end. The rest of the Kano army returned to Sokoto.

THE BRITISH OCCUPATION OF SOKOTO

All the detachments of the British expedition converged on Kaura Namoda on 27 February. Nothing now stood between them and a march on Sokoto. Kano was broken, Katsina had acquiesced, strong garrisons held the conquered cities of the Caliphate and there was a strong British force at Argungu, under Captain Merrick, ready to dash on Gwandu or Sokoto at the shortest notice if it became necessary.

But this complete isolation was only one aspect of Sokoto's

105. Eye-witness account recorded by Muffett, *op. cit.*, p. 125 claims that the letter was brought to Abbās at Malikawa by messengers one of whom was Adamu Jekada.

106. F. D. Lugard, *Annual Report*, 1902.

difficulties. The election of the Caliph, Muḥammad Al-Ṭāhir b. Aḥmad (Attahiru I), in November 1902, had not been smooth. The succession had been disputed by the sons of ʿAlī (Aliyu Baba) b. Muḥammad Bello, whose choice, Muḥammad Al-Ṭāhir b. ʿAlī, is said to have been the more popular candidate. The backing of the powerful Marafa, Muḥammad Maiturare, and the fact that Al-Ṭāhir b. ʿAlī stepped down to avoid conflict, had made the peaceful appointment of the new Caliph possible.[107] The suppressed resentment of the sons of ʿAlī b. Muḥammad Bello meant that Sokoto was internally divided at a most critical time.

Besdies, opinion was divided in Sokoto over what the attitude to the British should be. Some counselled peace, some fighting, and some, apparently the majority, were for a *hijra* from Sokoto before the arrival of the British.[108] The Caliph, Attahiru, decided on emigrating before the British arrived. It appears he was a pious man. He is reported to have desired to go to Mecca a month after his succession.[109] It seems that on receiving Morland's letter, sent from Kano, he had sent to the district heads of Sokoto's hinterland for their opinion regarding the attitude that should be adopted to the British. The districts, like Sokoto, did not seem to have a ready or easy answer.

The Wazir, Bukhārī, seems to have discussed the matter earlier with Aliyu, Emir of Kano (most probably during the latter's visit to Sokoto in January 1903). Aliyu suggested that the Muslims should emigrate. In a letter he had written, most probably after he had heard of the fall of Kano to the British and his flight from Birnin Goga, he reiterated the necessity of emigrating—an opinion which the Wazir already held.[110] Aliyu pointed out in this letter that emigration seemed to him the only way of preserving the religion of Islam 'as these dogs have surrounded us and threaten to overcome us'. Whatever might have been the Caliph's precise views on *hijra* from Sokoto, he

107. For the succession dispute on Sokoto, see Last, *The Sokoto Caliphate*, pp. 140 and 175. Also C.O. 446/31, Lugard to C.O., 22 Mar. 1903.
108. Wazir Junaidu, *Ḍabt al-Multaqaṭāt*, f. 75a.
109. *Ibid.*
110. Corr. IX, no. 125, Aliyu, Emir of Kano to al-Wazīr Muḥammad Bukhārī. I suggest that this letter would most probably have been written after Aliyu had learnt of the fall of Kano because up to that point, he had made preparations to fight. He gave no indication of emigrating before the decision was forced on him by news of the occupation of Kano.

aided Aliyu's emigration. The latter, who left Birnin Goga and went northwards, intending to go to Mecca, was provided with many copies of a letter of introduction bearing the Caliph's seal and addressed to the Emir of Gobir (Chibiri), asking the latter to permit Aliyu to travel safely through his territory.[111]

Opinion on emigration was not unanimous in Sokoto. The Marafa, Muḥammad Maiturare, counselled strongly against any suggestion of emigration because he was convinced that such a move would destroy the morale and the obedience of their subjects. It was best, he advised, to await events and to emigrate if and when circumstances dictated.[112] With his powerful position in Sokoto the Maiturare's opinion may have contributed to the hesitation with which Sokoto awaited the British. Nevertheless, opinion in favour of emigation seems to have been strong in the town. In this respect it is interesting to note that, having finally decided on emigrating before the British arrived, Sokoto people had in fact begun preparations. Sandals, mules, donkeys, camels and other necessaries for the journey had been procured and a date (unknown) had actually been fixed for the commencement of the *hijra*. In the midst of the preparation news of the approach of the British was received.[113]

In the meantime the British expeditionary force had left Kaura Namoda on 3 March. Between Kaura Namoda and Bakura Morland received a reply to the letter he had written from Kano to the Caliph. The Caliph's excuse for not sending an earlier reply was that he had sent to his various districts to call in his councillors but that they were taking a long time to arrive. Even then the Caliph could not give a definite reply but asked Morland to wait until his council had met after which he would communicate their (the council's) decision to him.[114]

On receipt of news of the British approach all ideas about emigrating had to be given up. The Caliph's letter to Morland may therefore be seen as a design by the Caliph to enable him

111. Corr. VII, nos. 124, 125, 126, 127, 128, 129.

112. Corr. IX, no. 128.

113. *Ḍabt al-multaqaṭāt*, f. 75a. See also R. A. Adeleye, 'The dilemma of the Wazir: The place of the *Risālat al-Wazīr ila ahl al-ʿilm wa'l-tadabbūr* in the history of the conquest of the Sokoto Caliphate', *J.H.S.N.* iv, no. 2 (1968), pp. 292–3 for discussion of preparations in Sokoto before the attack.

114. C.O. 446/31, tr. of Caliph's letter to Morland, encl. no. 1, in Lugard to C.O., 22 Mar. 1903.

to play for much needed time while Sokoto was being put in a state of defence. According to Last the preparations included praying and procuring of charms against bullets.[115] At this point when a British attack was already imminent, the armies of the hinterland districts were called in to Sokoto and preparations to resist the British were hurriedly embarked on.[116] The Caliph pitched camp with his army outside the walls of Sokoto after the afternoon prayers on Friday 13 March. Sokoto scouts reported that they found no trace of the approaching enemy on that day and again in the early morning of Saturday. Many therefore concluded that the British would not come.[117] The hurriedly organized army of Sokoto awaited events.

While Sokoto was preparing its resistance the British army had left Bakura on 7 March. On the 10th it arrived at Shagari on the Sokoto–Gwandu road.[118] From there Morland sent to Captain Merrick to join up with him. Merrick arrived on the morning of the 11th with his company to bring the British force up to a strength of twenty-five officers, five N.C.O.s, two medical officers and one medical N.C.O., sixty-eight gunners, 656 rank and file, 400 carriers, four Maxims and four 75 mm guns.[119]

With the movement of Captain Merrick's force from Argungu to Shagari, the Emir of Gwandu, apparently terrified, sent a letter to the British expedition, saying that he would not fight. A small force was left at Shagari while the bulk of the expedition proceeded to Sokoto. By the afternoon of 14 March the British expedition was only four miles from Sokoto. Towards the evening of that day the first skirmishes took place between the scouting patrol of the British and that of Sokoto. The Sokoto scouts were driven back to their camp, on the south-west suburb of the city, with a loss of twelve killed.

Early in the morning of the 15th the British expedition reached a ridge 1½ miles from the city walls from where they saw the

115. Last, *op. cit.*, p. 140.
116. C.O. 446/31, Lugard to C.O., 22 Mar. 1903, encl. no. 2, Kemball to Lugard, 19 Mar. 1903, information collected by political officers. *Ḍabt al-multaqaṭāt*, f. 75b.
117. *Ḍabt al-multaqaṭāt*, f. 75b.
118. C.O. 446/31, Lugard to C.O., 22 Mar. 1903, encl. no. 2; Kemball to Lugard, 19 Mar. 1903, on which the account of the military engagement between Sokoto and the British is largely based.
119. *Ibid.*, Perham, *op. cit.*, pp. 126–7, Muffett, pp. 129–34, for other accounts of the conquest of Sokoto.

southern wall lined with troops estimated at 2000 horse and 4000 foot. The Sokoto warriors were armed with spears, arrows, and old guns. The Caliph commanded the centre, Ibrāhīm, Sarkin Rabah, the left flank, and Muḥammad Maiturare the right.[120]

At the bottom of the valley separating the ridge (from which the British had first seen the Sokoto army) from the plain on which Sokoto stood, the British army, now in square formation, was attacked by an advance guard of the Sokoto army, while their horsemen tried to go round the flanks of the British, apparently with the aim of encircling the invaders. As the British column advanced up the slope of the valley, the Sokoto defenders harassed it by rifle shots which did little damage, instead of rushing the square at this stage.

The British force brought their guns and Maxims into action on reaching the west of the valley slope. The main body of the Sokoto army was discomfited in less than twenty minutes, except for a group which surrounded and defended the Sokoto flag tenaciously until they were killed. The flag was thereupon captured. Shortly afterwards, it was stolen, but was ultimately found with the Caliph from whom it was recaptured at Burmi.[121]

The British square wheeled to the right to attack a large number of Sokoto soldiers assembled south-east of the city walls. These bolted without awaiting British fire, hotly pursued by the mounted infantry. By 9.30 a.m. Sokoto resistance had been broken in an operation which lasted less than 1½ hours. Sokoto had lost about a hundred killed, while British casualties were a mere two carriers wounded and two soldiers severely wounded.

THE SUBMISSION OF SOKOTO

With the fall of Sokoto the idea of emigrating, which had been prevalent before the sudden arrival of the British, found spontaneous expression. The Caliph, Attahiru, fled eastwards while the British column, which entered Sokoto at about 11 a.m., barely an hour after the rout of Sokoto's army, found it practically deserted. The whereabouts of the Caliph were as yet unknown either to the British or to Sokoto people. The Wazir, Muḥammad al-Bukhārī, and a large number of people emigrated northwards

120. Information supplied by Nagwamatse: Muffett, *op. cit.*, pp. 132–3.
121. Muffett, *op. cit.*, pp. 193, 211.

to Marnona.[122] Others fled in different directions. The British expedition, victorious but finding nobody to arrange peace terms with, withdrew from the city at about noon and pitched camp on the banks of the Bakura river. When Col. Morland visited Wurno the following day the town had also been deserted.

The majority of the Sokoto officials, like the Wazir, could not contact the Caliph that Sunday. The result was that many could not follow him on his *hijra*. At Marnona that night (Sunday 15 March) the people, including the learned men, gathered round the Wazir, all in a great dilemma. Emigration, they realized, would not be easy at that time of the year with the scarcity of water and of food to reckon with, and because 'the Christians' (Europeans) had established themselves on all the roads. The Wazir therefore ordered that everyone should leave him and find his own way of escape, but the people refused.[123]

It was a moment of great uncertainties for the Sokoto community, and in particular for the Wazir on whom leadership had devolved. The dilemma was resolved by the *'Ulamā'* who on the basis of 'Uthmān b. Fodiye's stand *in Masā'il Muhimma* on the fourth question dealing with relations between Muslims and Unbelievers, recommended that in order to preserve Muslims from harm, it was permissible by *ijmā'* for the Imām or his agent to give friendship to unbelievers when the Muslims live in fear of them and are not strong enough to oppose their power.[124] Even then, such friendship must be with the tongue only and not with the heart. In short, it must be a feigned friendship to be maintained only until such a time as the Muslims were strong enough to reassert their independence and authority.[125]

On the strength of this recommendation the Wazir wrote to the British in Sokoto and went northwards to Dinawa to await their reply. On Thursday 19 March he returned to Sokoto, still fearing

122. Muḥammad Bukhārī, *Risālat al-Wazīr ila ahl al-'ilm wa'l-tadabbūr*, f. 1, see R. A. Adeleye 'The dilemma of the Wazīr', *loc. cit.* Introduction, text and translation of the *Risālat*, pp. 285–311. Arabic pp. 299–305, tr. pp. 306–11.

123. *Ibid.*, p. 306.

124. *Ibid.*, pp. 306–7, 309.

125. For discussion of the law in support of the temporary suspension of *jihād* and signing peace treaties with unbelievers, see Majid Khadduri, *War and Peace in the Law of Islam*, pp. 65–6, and Majid Khadduri and H. J. Liebesny, ed., *Law in the Middle East*, vol. i, pp. 359, 360, 364–7.

that the British might not allow the free practice of Islam but force their own religion on the people.[126] It was only when he discovered that the British were prepared to guarantee the free practice of Islam with no prejudice to the five pillars of the faith that the Wazir reconciled himself to the situation. He entered Sokoto the same evening with a large crowd that had emigrated with him. As was done in Kano the returning *emigrés* of Sokoto had to surrender their firearms to the British before they were allowed into their city.

In the meantime Lugard, who had been following hot on the heels of the expedition, arrived in Sokoto on 19 March. The following day Sokoto officials met at Lugard's request and nominated Muḥammad Al-Ṭāhir b. 'Alī b. Muḥammad Bello (Attahiru II) as sultan.[127] On the 21st Lugard formally installed Attahiru. The ceremony took place in the afternoon in the centre of the town. The British troops 'with guns and Maxims mounted, formed three sides of a large square'. The Sultan elect and the Sokoto notables took their positions on a rug in the centre of the square. Lugard then delivered a homily on the necessity for the Sultan, as he called him, and his officials and indeed all their subjects, to learn British ways and of the British to learn the ways and laws of Sokoto people. The religion of Islam was fully guaranteed. Lugard shook hands with the new Sultan. The 'royal' trumpets of Sokoto were, with Lugard's permission, played. A public prayer 'recited aloud by the criers', brought the ceremony to an end.[128]

On the 23rd the bulk of the British army returned to Kano under Col. Morland. Major Alder Burdon was left behind as Resident with a garrison of 200 troops barracked about a mile outside the city walls. With these events the overthrow of the Caliphate by the British had become assured. But as will be seen in the sequel, the people of the Caliphate were far from accepting the British conquest as a final settlement of the struggle which the Caliphate had put up against European encroachment for more than two decades.

126. *Ibid.* For date of return, see 'Abd al-Qādir b. Muḥammad al-Bukhārī (Machido) *Tanīs al-Ikhwān*, 1906; also C.O. 446/31, Lugard to C.O., 22 March 1903.

127. With the seizure by the British of the Caliphate's sovereignty the Caliphate had fallen and there could be no Caliph. Hence I refer to Attahiru II as Sultan.

128. C.O. 446/3, Lugard to C.O., 22 March 1903.

CONCLUSION

The comparative ease with which Sokoto fell to the British force may be accounted for by the necessary inadequacy of the hurried preparations of the city to meet the enemy. The Sokoto battle was, however, illustrative of British battles with the already conquered emirates of the Caliphate, and indeed of many a European battle with Africans in the nineteenth and twentieth centuries generally. It is tempting to conclude that African armies which fell easily to such European-led forces did so because of lack of determination to resist the European onslaught. But for the Sokoto Caliphate such a conclusion would be wrong, for in all the battles in which the British confronted the emirates, the intrepidity with which the African armies charged the enemy forces was repeatedly remarked upon. The explanation of the results of these battles therefore must be sought for in factors other than personal valour.

It is well known that African states fell to Europeans in battle because of the latters' military superiority in strategy as well as in weapons. Strategy can be of supreme significance where the methods of warfare of the enemy are known. In this respect the Africans and the Europeans shared a common disadvantage by the fact that they were largely mutually ignorant of one another's methods of warfare. Yet in the final analysis superior weapons gave the Europeans the upper hand. Besides, having met many emirates in battle, the British officers had experience of methods of warfare in the Caliphate which the more northerly emirates, facing Europeans for the first time, did not have.

During the nineteenth century firearms were coming into the Caliphate in increasing numbers. The number and type of firearms cannot be ascertained but such knowledge is hardly essential to an understanding of the courses of the battles fought between the Caliphate and Europeans. It is clear from the light casualties which the armies of the emirates were able to inflict on the British expeditions, even when the former were reputed to have engaged in heavy firing that they were hopelessly unskilled in the use of firearms which consequently did not appreciably increase the effectiveness of their resistance. Besides the inability of the emirates' armies to use effectively such firearms as they had, the longer range of the vastly superior Europeans' weapons was decisive. To use their arrows and spears effectively the Sokoto army had to come close to the British square formation. The range of arrows and spears was of course very short range for the rifles of the Europeans, not to talk of their Maxim and big guns. At the close range from which the African weapons could be used with deadly effect, their superiority in numbers ceased to be of any advantage to them because they could then be easily routed.

With this consideration it is obvious that the decision of the armies of the emirates to fight the British in open battle, instead of fighting from behind the city walls and from the trenches that surrounded them, was a fatal tactical blunder. In this respect it is pertinent to draw attention to the vehemence of the resistance of Yola and Kano people who rendered the task of the British forces more arduous by forcing them to fight siege battles. The capture of Yola and Kano cost the British more dearly both in expenditure of ammunition and time and in the number of casualties than the capture of Kontagora, Bida and Sokoto, whose armies met the British in open fields.

Chapter 9
The final destruction of the Caliphate

With the installation of Attahiru II as Sultan of Sokoto by Lugard the protracted duel—diplomatic as well as military—between the Caliph and his emirs on the one hand, and the British on the other, was resolved in favour of the latter. The conclusion of the battle outside the walls of Sokoto signalled the demise of the Caliphate as a polity by reason of its loss of sovereignty to infidels. The conquest and the futility of *en masse* emigration from infidel authority enabled Lugard to establish the basis of a British administration in spite of the patent resentment in Sokoto. He paid due deference to the susceptibilities of the Sokoto people by allowing and encouraging their high officials to elect a new 'Caliph' in the traditional manner.[1] The council of electors comprised the Wazir, the Galadima, the Marafa, Sarkin Burmi, Sarkin Zamfara and Sarkin Kebbi.[2] Lugard's overture was rendered successful in the circumstances by the existence of a ready candidate in the person of Attahiru II, who had lost the election in November 1902 when a succession crisis had been only narrowly averted.[3]

The reality of British sovereignty was demonstrated by the fact that the new Sultan was installed by Lugard and given insignia of office—a turban and a gown—in the same way as the Caliph had appointed his emirs in the days of the Caliphate. The destruction of the Caliphate was further emphasized in a speech by Lugard in which he outlined the duties of the Sultan.[4] The latter was deprived of political control over the emirates. The all-important right over appointment and deposition of emirs was formally transferred to the British.[5] Thus the Caliphate's central govern-

1. See Last, *The Sokoto Caliphate*, pp. 179–80.
2. *Ibid.*, the traditional officials that took part in the election were the Wazir, Magajin gari, Magajin Rafi, Galadima, the *amīr-al-jaish*, Sarkin Kebbi, and the Ardo'en of the Sullebawa Fulani.
3. Last, *op. cit.*, p. 140.
4. Lugard referred to Attahiru II as Sultan.
5. Lugard, Appendix III of *Annual Reports*, 1902.

7 The submission of chiefs, place unknown, 1903

8 Mai Wurno (r.) and his Wazir at Mai Wurno in the Sudan, October 1928

ment was dissolved and with it the political obligations and subservience of the emirs to Sokoto. The Sultan was in fact no more than an Emir of Sokoto. His position, which Lugard recognized, as religious head of the former territories of the Caliphate was, outside the Sokoto heartland, more honorific than functional. It meant at best that he was politically the first among equals. The passing away of the Caliphate was unequivocally signalled by Lugard when he said:

> The Fulani in old times under Dan Fodio conquered this country. They took the right to rule over it, to levy taxes, to depose Kings and to create Kings. They in turn have by defeat lost their rule which has come into the hands of the British. All these things which I have said the Fulani by conquest took the right to do now pass to the British.[6]

From the ruins of the Caliphate one of the most important factors that survived was contained in Lugard's promise that the British would allow the free practice of the religion of Islam. Lugard devoted the rest of March and April to putting what he believed were finishing touches to the establishment of British rule on a formal and firm basis. He left Sokoto on 22 March 1903, and on the 28th he arrived at Katsina whose Emir, it will be recalled, had earlier indicated his peaceful submission to the British.[7] Nonetheless Lugard observed that the people of Katsina were in such an obvious state of panic on his approach that he had to induce the Emir to meet him outside the walls and lead him into the city.[8] He discovered that there was a war party[9] in the city who were deterred from showing open hostility only by their realization of the foolhardiness of such a course of action. On 29 March the Emir and the *Masu Sarauta* (office holders) accepted the conditions of British rule as outlined by Lugard.

Lugard left Katsina after he had installed the Emir and completed arrangements for the building of a Residency and barracks for a small garrison (to be quartered outside the city) which he left behind.[10] He attested to the restiveness of the people of Katsina at the time of the occupation but claimed to have

6. Lugard, *Annual Reports*, pp. 163–4, Lugard's second address at Sokoto, 21 March 1903.
7. See above, p. 276.
8. C.O. 446/31, Lugard to C.O., no. 159, 22 April 1903; also Lugard, *Annual Report*, 1902, p. 100.
9. Perham, *Years of Authority*, p. 132.
10. *Annual Report*, 1902, pp. 100–1.

arrived at an amicable settlement with the town before his departure. He wrote: 'I believe that I succeeded in transforming the feelings of great fear and apprehension which existed at the time I arrived (in spite of the friendly letters I had sent) into one of cordiality and friendship.'[11] The small W.A.F.F. garrison and Katsina's awareness of their inability to successfully challenge the British militarily were in fact the surest guarantee of that feeling of 'cordiality and friendship' which Lugard claimed to have evoked by negotiation.

On 2 April 1903 Lugard arrived in Kano where he formally installed the Emir-elect (the Wombai, Muḥammad Abbās, 1903–19) on the 4th.[12] On 7 April he brought to an end the interregnum in Zaria by appointing and installing the Wombai, Aliyu Dan Sidi, grandson of Mallam Musa (the first Emir of Zaria) as Emir.[13] There was a flicker of the erstwhile Caliph's authority over Zaria in that, in appointing Aliyu, Lugard had sounded the opinion of both the Sultan and the Wazir of Sokoto. In reality their opinion was merely advisory and not decisive.

On 14 April Lugard arrived at Zungeru and departed from there on leave to Great Britain on the 22nd. He must have felt satisfied at this point that all cause for anxiety about the British tenure in the Caliphate had been removed. However this was far from being so, as the *hijra* of the Caliph Attahiru I was to show only too clearly.

The hostility of the ordinary people of the Caliphate to European conquest was unmistakable. One significant aspect of the resentment of the masses was that it was Islamic in character. At a time of crisis the *Umma* fell back for sustenance on the Islamic values on which the Caliphate was founded and which largely sustained it to its fall. In the few months following the fall of Sokoto, the British were confronted with the problem of suppressing an opposition which entailed a reassertion of the basic unity of the Caliphate, symbolized by the Caliph. This unity had been forced into abeyance under the pressure of British conquest. Yet it is clear that a deep feeling of hostility simmered underneath the British bayonets. After the fall of Sokoto, resistance was resumed with a vehemence and a tenacity of purpose which

11. C.O. 446/31, Lugard to C.O., 22 April 1903.
12. Lugard, *Annual Report*, 1902.
13. *Annual Report*, 1902, p. 102, and C.O. 446/31, Lugard to C.O., no. 159, 22 April 1903.

threatened the establishment of British power. It found an opportunity for immediate expression in the *hijra* of the Caliph Attahiru I, and in the rise of several Mahdists between 1903 and 1906.

The flight of most of the ruling emirs with large followings after the conquest of the southern emirates was, as already suggested, in the nature of *hijra* from lands occupied by infidels.[14] There was, doubtless, a strong element of dissembling in the submission of those who remained behind. This was clearly the case in Ilọrin, Nupe, Yola, Bauchi and even in Gombe where submission to the British was ostensibly voluntary. The manner of Katsina's submission and subsequent events there indicate that its acceptance of British rule was not wholehearted. When the Emir of Kano, Aliyu, deserted his troops at Birnin Goga, he embarked on *hijra* following his own counsel earlier conveyed to Sokoto, that all Muslims should evacuate their territories in view of their inability to repel European invasion. The Caliph provided him with letters of introduction to Sarkin Gobir (Tsibiri) to facilitate his journey through the latter's territory.[15] Sarkin Gobir detained and later handed over Aliyu to the British probably more out of fear of them than out of Gobir's traditional hostility to the Caliphate. The Sarki offered his submission peacefully to Lugard while the latter was on his way to Katsina from Sokoto. Aliyu of Kano was brought from Tsibiri to Sokoto by Captain (later General) Foulkes[16] and was subsequently exiled, at first to Yola and then to Lokoja, where he died in 1907.

The submission of the Sokoto authorities to the British, following the Wazir's consultations with the '*Ulamā*', was clearly an act of *taqiyya* (dissembling). Those who returned to Sokoto did so grudgingly as the only choice open to them. The discontent in Sokoto was observed by the British Resident, Burdon, even after the installation of Attahiru II.[17] This resentment was shared by the Wazir himself. After submitting to the British the Wazir was again grieved at heart and confused about the legality of accepting British rule. In his confusion he wrote to one Aḥmad b. Sa'd, whom he described as 'the learned and wise', to

14. See above, p. 247
15. Corr. VII, nos. 124–7. Aliyu was said to have intended to go to Mecca.
16. C.O. 446/31, Lugard to C.O., 22 March 1903.
17. C.O. 446/31, Wallace to C.O., 27 May 1903, encl. report of Resident of Sokoto, Burdon.

help him resolve his doubts. In a lengthy reply[18] Aḥmad b. Sa'd urged the Wazir to see that victory of infidels over *Dār al-Islām* was not new in history. He referred the Wazir to the example of the fall of Baghdād to Hulagu the Mongol in A.D. 1258 and the eclipse which overtook the Abbāsid Caliphate therefrom. The Caliphate, he observed, did re-emerge after that gloomy phase.[19] In the same way, continued Aḥmad b. Sa'd, and even earlier, Mecca had fallen to the Qarmaṭians who took away the Black Stone. This event had been only a temporary eclipse as God caused the Black Stone to be returned later.[20] Aḥmad argued that, just as God had healed these misfortunes for the earlier Caliphate so, it must be hoped, He would do for the Sokoto Caliphate. Besides, argued Aḥmad, it would be wrong for the Muslims to emigrate from their land as this would change it from the *Dār al-Islām*, which it was, to a land of unbelievers. Since the Christians were not interested in interfering with Islam but only in worldly things, negotiation for a truce with them was legal for the Imām or his agents in a situation wherein the Muslims could not fight. It was only after reading Aḥmad's exposition, which confirmed the '*Ulamā*'s earlier counsel, that the Wazir reconciled himself to the perplexing event (as he saw it)[21] of the fall of the Caliphate to infidels. However, the *hijra* of the Caliph Attahiru provided leadership to the elements in the Caliphate who could not reconcile themselves to living under infidel rule. The Caliph's movement canalized the resentment in the various emirates into one mass movement which gave expression to opposition to British rule.

THE HIJRA OF THE CALIPH ATTAHIRU

While Lugard busied himself with hurriedly installing emirs in various places and writing a self-congratulatory letter to the Colonial Office in which he subtly blamed that office for ever

18. Muḥammad Bukhārī, *Risāla*; Adeleye, 'The dilemma of the Wazir', *loc. cit.*, pp. 308–11.
19. *Ibid.*, pp. 308–9.
20. *Ibid.* The Qarmaṭians were a sect with communistic and revolutionary traits founded by Hamdan b. Qarmaṭ. The conquest of Mecca and the carrying away of the Black Stone occurred in A.D. 930. The Stone was returned to the Ka'bah in A.D. 951, see *Encyclopædia of Islam*.
21. Muḥammad Bukhārī, *Risāla*.

failing to trust his judgment completely,[22] as the conquest of Kano and Sokoto proved they ought to have done, the Caliph Attahiru had already placed himself at the head of a mass emigration that threatened to reverse all that Lugard so confidently gloried in.

When the Caliph Attahiru escaped from the Sokoto battlefield on 15 March 1903, he took with him the initiative in the struggle between the Caliphate and Europeans which had, up till then, been firmly held by the British. Hitherto the British had dictated the pace, course, timing and places of battle. From March to the end of July 1903 Attahiru forced the British, so far the aggressors, onto the defensive. The story of the Caliph's *hijra* is an epic. The chase, the gruelling hide and seek game he played with British pursuit patrols and his hairbreadth escapes are indeed fascinating. More important to the history of the fall of the Caliphate, however, was the mass movement to which his *hijra* gave rise. The spontaneity with which his subjects in the emirates —a cross-section of all classes of society—flocked to join his banner, confirmed where their real allegiance lay. Militarily subdued by the British, their cities sacked and their traditional authorities toppled or cowed to submission to an alien infidel power, the spirit of the Muslim community of the emirates had not been conquered.

The bond of Islam which had held the Caliphate together and which the Caliph symbolized was in this moment of crisis emphasized in a fashion perhaps more dramatic than at any other period in the history of the Caliphate. The traditional loyalties of the subjects of the Caliph in the emirates having been sorely tried by the British conquest, the *hijra* provided them with a means of expressing pent-up resentment and decided many who had been sitting on the fence from fear of British military power to demonstrate their loyalty openly to the Caliph and the faith which he championed.

After the battle at Sokoto on 15 March the Caliph Attahiru had escaped eastwards, followed by a large number of people. He eventually established himself for a while at Gusau. For several weeks after the fall of Sokoto there was a lull, during which the whereabouts of the fugitive Caliph were unknown either to the British or to Sokoto officials who did not flee with him. He was

22. C.O. 446/31, Lugard to C.O., 17 May 1903. For another account of Attahiru's hijra, see Muffett, *Concerning Brave Captains*, p. 143 ff.

first reported by Alder Burdon, the Resident of Sokoto Province, to Cargill, Resident of Kano, to be at Gusau on 13 April 1903. In a letter to Cargill, Burdon wrote that the Caliph was gathering people around himself and sending messages in all directions, condemning those who accepted the rule of the infidel, and declaring his intention to collect an army and march eastwards to meet the Mahdī.[23]

In Sokoto itself there was a good deal of indecision. Burdon reported in April that 'there are indications that some of the officials (the "princes") are not too loyal to either one or the other (i.e. to either the fugitive Caliph or the British)'.[24] There was, he claimed, a good deal of unrest 'amongst the middle classes, especially the farmers'. The peasant folk were trying to find a way to the Caliph, in the hope that he would lead them to the Mahdī.[25] Thus the strong tradition of the expectation of the Mahdī in the Caliphate found practical expression in the Caliph's *hijra*. During the 1880s, when the Caliphate was not threatened by similar forces which threatened the Eastern Sudan Muslims, the call to Mahdism had been rejected by the Sokoto Caliph and his emirs.

Among the Sokoto officials who accompanied Attahiru on his *hijra* were: the Alkali (*Al-Qāḍī*), Ubandoma, Dan Maji, Dan Magaji, and Sarkin Kwani, the Madaki. One of the Wazir's sons went to join him shortly after.[26] The Marafa, Muḥammad Maiturare, some of the 'royal' electors, and the *Amir al-jaish* returned to Sokoto a few days after, while Magajin Gari returned in April.[27] Many of the lower people who initially fled with the Caliph also returned because of the hardships of the road caused by lack of water and food, and also because they learned that the British were sending military patrols after them.[28]

The proposed destination of the Caliph, Muḥammad Attahiru,

23. N.A.K., S.N.P.7/6/289, Wallace to C.O., no. 388, 6 Nov. 1903. All reports indicate either that the Caliph intended to go to Mecca, to Bima or to Balda in Adamawa.
24. C.O. 446/31, Wallace to C.O., 27 May 1903, encl. report of Resident at Sokoto, Burdon. For traditions of expectation of the Mahdī in the Caliphate, see above, p. 103 f.
25. C.O. 446/31, Wallace to C.O., 27 May 1903, encl. Burdon's report.
26. *Ibid.*, and N.A.K., S.N.P.15/57, C. L. Temple's report on the circumstances which led to the death of the Caliph Attahiru, 8 Aug. 1903.
27. Last, *op. cit.*, p. 176.
28. C.O. 446/31, encl. Burdon's report on Sokoto in Wallace to C.O., 27 May 1903.

was said to be Mecca; and the purpose of going eastwards was to meet the Mahdī. Apart from the strong traditions of the expectation of the Mahdī in the Caliphate, already discussed above, a prophecy credited to ʿUthmān b. Fodiye, had specifically foretold the emigration of the faithful from the Caliphate to the Nile and the Hijāz to meet the Mahdī and pay homage to him.[29] With the ascendancy of unbelievers over Muslims not only in the Sokoto Caliphate but elsewhere, the time was most auspicious for the appearance of the Mahdī. Alternatively, the destination of the Caliph was given out to be Adamawa or Bima hill. Both the areas of Balda in Adamawa, where Ḥayat had earlier settled, and Bima hill east of the Gongola (in Gombe emirate), had legends of holiness attached to them in folklore as well as stories of the expected appearance of the Mahdī. It seems therefore that the popular appeal enjoyed by the Caliph's *hijra* arose from the religious zeal of the masses and their consequent dissatisfaction with British infidel rule. All these cannot be separated from the office and the personality of the Caliph himself who, as the Imām of the Caliphate, was the religious head whose political function it was to maintain the *Dār al-Islām* against destruction and in conformity with the *sharīʿa*.

On their way from Sokoto to Gusau the Caliph's party received news that Lugard and his escort were going to Katsina. Even though the latter were not aware of the whereabouts of the Caliph, the Emir of Katsina, Abubakar, sent messages twice, to warn the Caliph of the nearness of Europeans. On the first occasion, at Shinkafe, the Emir of Katsina sent a gift of eighteen bales of cloth and shortly after, at a place called Ruma, Katsina horsemen came to warn the Caliph of the departure of Lugard from Katsina the previous day, 30 March.[30] That the secret of

29. Amīr al-Mu'minīn Abu Bakr b. Atīq b. ʿUthmān b. Fodiye, *Risālat ilā Jamāʿat Gwandu*, Ibadan, University Library: uncatalogued. Abu Bakr Atiku (Atīq) (1837–42) claims to have heard the prophecy from the Shaikh. According to the prophecy, the people of the *ribāṭ* or their successors and the faithful among the Shaikh's followers would go on this journey guided by the light and *baraka* of the Shaikh. Apostates would not go and the majority of those who are deceivers would go west and settle among unbelievers until *al-Dajjal* (the anti-Christ) came out against them.

30. Muffett, *op. cit.*, p. 150, record of an eye-witness account. Lugard's party was the only European-led party in this area during the Caliph's flight from Sokoto.

the Caliph's movements did not leak out to Lugard speaks much for the approval his cause (the Caliph's) enjoyed, while the surreptitious help he received from the Emir of Katsina indicates the nature of the latter's loyalty to the British. However, knowledge of the nearness of Lugard's party compelled the Caliph to veer south to Gusau.

THE PURSUIT OF THE CALIPH BY BRITISH PATROLS

On 15 April Burdon sent a column of fifty men and a Maxim, under Captain Goodwin, to pursue and, if possible, capture the fugitive Caliph.[31] The column failed in its mission. From Gusau the Caliph went on to Rogo south-east of Kano where Dr Cargill, Resident of Kano, got wind of his presence on 21 April. Dr Cargill sent out two messages immediately, one to the officer commanding the British garrison at Kano, Captain Sword, and the other to the Resident of Zaria, to send out columns to head off the Caliph.

Prior to Attahiru's flight, the situation in both the districts of Kano and Zaria had been equivocal. On 20 April, a day before Cargill sent instructions to Captain Sword to head off Attahiru's progress to the east, he had ordered Captain Sword to arrest certain persons in the district of Kano who had rebelled against the Emir of Kano's authority.[32] Cargill claimed that the country around Kano was 'in a most unsettled state'.[33]

In Zaria, the districts of Gadas-Kaje to the east of the emirate had thrown off their allegiance to Zaria since late in 1902, when the Emir was exiled by the British.[34] In November 1902 Magajin Keffi had found a safe route through these districts during his flight to Kano. In all fourteen towns were in open rebellion. Letters sent to them by the Resident in Zaria were returned unopened and the bearers were discourteously treated. An expedition, under Major Crawley, sent to subdue these towns

31. N.A.K., S.N.P.7/289, Morland to Wallace, 27 Oct. 1903, encl. in Wallace to C.O. (Conf. no. 388), 6 Nov. 1903.
32. C.O. 445/18, Featherstone Cargill to Captain Sword, 20 April 1903, Enclosed in Sword to Inspector-General W.A.F.F., 22 July 1904. See also Muffett, *op. cit.*, for the flight of Attahiru and the battles of Burmi.
33. *Ibid.*
34. R.H.B.E., S.62, Residency Zaria to High Commissioner, 7 May 1903.

was unable to do so because the towns marked down for punishment had either been completely evacuated before the arrival of the expedition, or those not deserted had declared their refusal to co-operate with the white man. At a village called Karigi, for instance, the inhabitants did not just refuse to sell food to Crawley's column but proceeded to shoot arrows at them when they attempted to search their houses. At another village called Tudun Wada the gates were shut and the walls were lined with bowmen ready to give battle. All the towns repeatedly reiterated their resolve to have nothing to do with the white man, while their chiefs, leading the revolts, conveniently blamed the risings on the peasants before the white man in Zaria.[35] With the arrival of the Caliph Attahiru on the northern frontiers of Zaria, the Resident of Zaria confessed that 'the proximity of Attahiru and the accession of a new Emir [recently appointed by Lugard] has rendered the situation in Zaria itself somewhat unsettled'.[36] The underground resentment in Kano and Zaria emirates, already breaking out in revolt, was given a chance of full expression by Attahiru's *hijra*.

On 22 April Captain Sword with one N.C.O. and forty-two rank and file left Kano in a south-easterly direction to head off Attahiru's party. On the same day Lt. Crozier was despatched from Zaria with twenty-five mounted infantry.[37] Crozier's column observed signs of a hostile people east of Bebeji. He noted:

> Arriving at Bebeji we turned right and followed a mixed crowd—thousands—mostly hostile, sullen or indifferent—bow and arrow men, slaves, caravan men, camel men, horsemen, men at arms, a few headmen, hundreds of women, priests, children—tons of household gods [goods]. All the country we passed through has been burnt, looted or vacated.[38]

The little patrol had to commandeer food for the men as well as for their horses. Shortly after some bowmen from the crowd opened fire on Crozier's party, killing two men and wounding six horses. Crozier despatched a messenger to Zaria for reinforcement. The messenger was never seen thereafter.[39] Although

35. *Ibid.*
36. *Ibid.*
37. S.N.P.7/6/289, Morland to Wallace, 27 Oct. 1903, encl. in Wallace to C.O., 6 Nov. 1903.
38. F. P. Crozier, *Five Years Hard* (London, 1932), p. 157.
39. *Ibid.*, pp. 158–9.

Crozier's column killed many from among the crowd, it was forced to turn back when under renewed attack Crozier was wounded and knocked down unconscious.

Attahiru's route lay through the southern borders of Kano emirate with Zaria and Ningi, on to southern Katagum (Jamaari district), Zadawa, Missau and south-east from there to the Bima hill area on the eastern banks of the Gongola, south of Burmi, where his final confrontation with the British was to take place.

The column under Captain Sword concentrated on harassing Attahiru, whose following increased at a rate which the Residents of the neighbouring emirates found alarming.[40] Captain Sword's column was unable to capture the Caliph, who escaped falling into their hands on many occasions. Between 25 April and 6 May Captain Sword was involved in six engagements at various points on the Caliph's route, either with the rearguard of the Caliph's party, or with crowds from towns fleeing to join the Caliph. One such party was that of Magajin Keffi and Alkalin Kano who had fled after the battle of Sokoto to join the Caliph. This group was attacked by Captain Sword on 30 April near a place called Igi, east of Takai in Kano emirate. Among them were several hundreds, including women and children, from Kano and Zaria emirates, whom Sword sent back to their homes. Although Captain Sword inflicted heavy casualties on the Caliph's followers with no loss to his own column, his expedition cannot be considered successful in so far as he failed to stop the mass movement which the Caliph's *hijra* had evoked. Naturally, the presence of Sword's column prevented the mass movement from assuming even greater proportions.

Captain Sword's inability to stop the movement had necessitated the sending out to him from Kano of a reinforcement of twenty-seven rank and file and a large quantity of ammunition, under Lt. Johnson, which caught up with him on 4 May near Shira in southern Katagum. While Sword's operation was going on, a small force under Lt. Dudley Carleton with Colour-Sergeant Graham, and fourteen mounted infantry, left Kano on 6 May in pursuit of a large party said to have been led by the son

40. C.O. 445/18, Lugard to C.O., 11 April 1904, encl. 1, Captain Sword's Report, 13 May 1903: a detailed day-to-day account of his pursuit of Attahiru with enclosures of progress report letters from Sword to Cargill.

of the Caliph (probably Mai Wurno)[41] going to join his father.[42] Carleton's patrol marched farther south than that of Sword in a bid to head off the Caliph's son and prevent him from making a junction with his father. Dan Sokoto, as he is called in the official despatches, was finally overtaken at a place called Zande, south-east of Shira, on 12 May. Seventy of his men, a large number of cattle, sheep and donkeys were captured, while the rest of the party were scattered. Dan Sokoto himself escaped.

On seeing the alarming proportions the Caliph's following assumed as he moved eastwards, Captain Sword observed that the movement was such a dangerous one that he might not be able to cope with it even with the Bauchi garrison, which he had requested earlier on, unless they came to his aid very soon.[43] From Zadawa (on the borders of presentday Jama'ari district and Missau) Sword marched to Missau on 7 April. From Missau he wrote: 'We have marched for three days through country crowded with villages and towns which have been recently occupied, but have now not a soul in them, all having joined the Sarkin Musulmi.'[44]

At Missau, where Attahiru was on 6 May, the Emir, Aḥmad b. Muḥammad b. Ṣāliḥ, in alliance with the Tijanī leader Bashīr (son of the Amīr al-mu'minīn Aḥmad b. Shaikh ʿUmar of Segu who had died near Sokoto in December 1898), had camped outside the city walls since he returned in January 1903 from his flight to Kano territory on hearing news of the approach of a British column from Gujba. On his return his brother, Muḥammad al-Ḥājj (Tafida), had seized the throne and prevented Aḥmad's re-entry.[45] A civil war had raged in Missau between Aḥmad and Tafida since then until 6 May, when the former, allied with the Tijanī Bashīr, fled with the Caliph Attahiru, on hearing news of the approach of Sword's patrol. Attahiru's strength, augmented by Aḥmad's force (reported to consist of 700 cavalry) brought the total fighting force of the fugitives to an

41. See below, p. 311.
42. C.O. 446/32, encl. no. 1, Resident Kano to High Commissioner, 22 May 1903, in Gollan to C.O., 17 June 1903.
43. C.O. 445/18, Sword's Report, encl. 1, in Lugard to C.O., 11 April 1904; also report in N.A.I., C.O.S.1/27, 3, Gollan to C.O., 17 June 1903.
44. *Ibid.*, encl. Sword to Cargill, 7 May 1903.
45. Corr. IX, no. 123, from Muḥammad Al-ḥājj to Amīr al-Mu'minīn, Muḥammad Attahiru.

estimated strength of 1000 cavalry, 2000 bowmen and 100 guns and rifles.[46] From the military point of view the threat to the British posed by Attahiru's survival loomed even larger than before. The understandably friendly welcome given to Sword at Missau notwithstanding, the route behind and ahead of his column was bristling with hostility.

Far away from the centres of rebellion, Wallace, the Acting High Commissioner at Zungeru, did not hear of the risings until 4 May.[47] Thenceforth reports reaching him from the Residents of Kano, Zaria and Bauchi tended to confirm his worst fears. In Kano, Cargill found the same disaffection as Burdon had observed in Sokoto both among the 'princes' and the peasants. Many of the chiefs of Kano territory, he discovered, had gone off to join the fugitive Caliph while the Emir, Abbās, assured him that many of the *masu sarauta* left behind, were disaffected.[48] Cargill warned the princes against following Attahiru, on pain of losing their positions and property. Those princes who had already left Kano territory were declared deposed and liable to trial for treason should they ever return. Chief among the officials of Kano were the Alkali and the Madaki, the latter renowned for his religious zeal. To the chiefs and the generality of his subjects, the Emir of Kano, presumably at the instigation of Resident Cargill, sent circulars and threatening messages to dissuade them from following Attahiru.

The rising in Kano was not limited to the official class. In his first report to Wallace (the Acting High Commissioner) on the matter on 24 April 1903, Cargill had emphasized that half the population of towns had tied up their bundles and followed the Caliph. This he noted was particularly the case among the 'farmers of smaller towns'.[49] Reports reaching Cargill from Captain Sword and passed on to Wallace, stated that the Caliph's route between Gola and Fejowa (west of Igi on the river Katagum in Kano territory) was strewn with 'loads of cloth and food in indescribable confusion', and that to allow Attahiru to sit down

46. Sword's report, *loc. cit.*, pursuit of Attahiru.
47. N.A.K., S.N.P.7/6/289, Wallace to C.O., no. 388, 6 Nov. 1903, encl. Morland to Wallace, 27 October 1903.
48. C.O. 446/31, Wallace to C.O., no. 183 of 20 May 1903, encl. 1, and encl. 2, Resident Kano to High Commissioner in Wallace to C.O., no. 194 of 27 May 1903.
49. C.O. 446/31, encl. 1, in Wallace to C.O., no. 183 of 20 May 1903.

in one place for even a week, would mean virtually the whole population joining him *en masse.*[50] Finally, in May, Cargill reported that the movement started by Attahiru was rapidly assuming proportions of a *jihād* which might pitch the entire Muslim population against the British if not checked immediately.[51] So great was the throng following Attahiru that Sword wrote: 'Attahiru's following is immense; his people are said to take from sunrise to mid-day passing.'[52]

Reports from the Residents reaching Zungeru from the occupied emirates all told identical stories of disaffection especially in the northern emirates. Regarding Zaria (never settled since the British established a garrison there), the Resident reported that there were cases of men who had disposed of all their property to follow the Caliph. The Chief and officials of Makarfi (about twenty miles east of Zaria) had all joined the Caliph, while four senior urban officials under the nose of the Resident in Zaria itself, had bolted to follow him, taking with them hundreds of their people and their property.[53] Summarizing the situation in Zaria, the Resident noted that 'Attahiru's presence is having a distinctly bad effect'.[54]

C. L. Temple, reporting from Bauchi, expressed alarm at the turn the rising was taking and asked headquarters at Zungeru for reinforcements.[55] Further reports from Captain Sword asserted that 'the Sarkin Muslumi has now many thousands of people with him. The whole population from Kano to the Gongola have joined him.'[56] The report, though probably exaggerated for effect, emphasized the urgent necessity of organizing a strong British force to hunt the Caliph down.

One thing the rising had made clear to the British was that their presence in the Caliphate would be guaranteed not by love from any class of the society but by superior military force. They quickly bestirred themselves. On 9 May Captain Sword's column

50. C.O. 446/31, encl. 2, in Wallace to C.O., no. 194 of 27 May 1903.
51. C.O. 446/31, Wallace to C.O., 3 June 1903, encl. 1, 15 May 1903.
52. *Ibid.*, encl. 2, Sword to Cargill, 28 April 1903
53. R.H.B.E., S.62, Resident Zaria to Wallace, 7 May 1903.
54. C.O. 446/31, Wallace to C.O., no. 194, 27 May 1903, encl. Resident Zaria to Wallace.
55. C.O. 446/31 (Gollan to C.O., 9 June 1903); encl. 1, Temple to High Commissioner, 20 May 1903.
56. *Ibid.*, encl. 2, Sword to Temple, 16 May 1903; also in N.A.I., C.S.O. 1/27, 3.

was strengthened by a force, under Major Plummer, which had been despatched from Bauchi on the 5th. This brought the total force pursuing Attahiru to four officers, one N.C.O. and 130 rank and file, equipped with fourteen boxes of ammunition and two Maxims.[57] The combined force pursued the Caliph along the right bank of the Gongola river from Malala, as he made direct for Bima hill. While he (the Caliph) continued his flight to Gwoni, in the Bima hill area on the left bank of the Gongola, Captain Sword halted at Burmi on the morning of the 13th, in the erroneous belief that Attahiru was there.

THE FIRST BATTLE OF BURMI

Burmi, the erstwhile headquarters of Mallam Jibrīl Gaini, whose power had been broken in 1902 at the battle of Tongo, was still the stronghold of his followers imbued with religious zeal and hatred for the white man. As the one-time headquarters of Jibrīl, Burmi was a centre of Mahdism. It was strongly fortified by a high well-built wall surrounded by a deep trench connected with the interior by underground passages.

The gate of Burmi was open as the Sword expedition approached, but the hostility of the people was evident. The Chief of the town, Mallam Musa, a reputed Mahdist and lieutenant of the captured Jibrīl, refused to parley with the expedition and made it quite plain that white men would not be allowed into the town.[58] On attempting to enter with a section of his company, Major Plummer was welcomed with a shower of arrows which started fierce fighting, as hundreds of the inhabitants rushed enthusiastically to the walls chanting war songs. After about an hour the Burmi defenders retired into the city, but Plummer's force had similarly been compelled to retreat in the face of the defenders' fire. The offensive was soon after resumed

57. N.A.K., S.N.P.7/6/289, Morland to Wallace, 27 Oct. 1903; encl. in Wallace to C.O., no. 388 of 6 Nov. 1903.
58. The battle of Burmi of 13 May 1903 is reconstructed from Captain Sword's report of his pursuit of Attahiru, *loc. cit.* Morland's report of 27 Oct. 1903, in N.A.K., S.N.P.7/6/289 enclosed in Wallace to C.O., 6 Nov. 1903, and C. L. Temple's 'Report on the circumstances attendant on the flight, pursuit and death of Attahiru', N.A.K., S.N.P.15/57, 8 Aug. 1903.

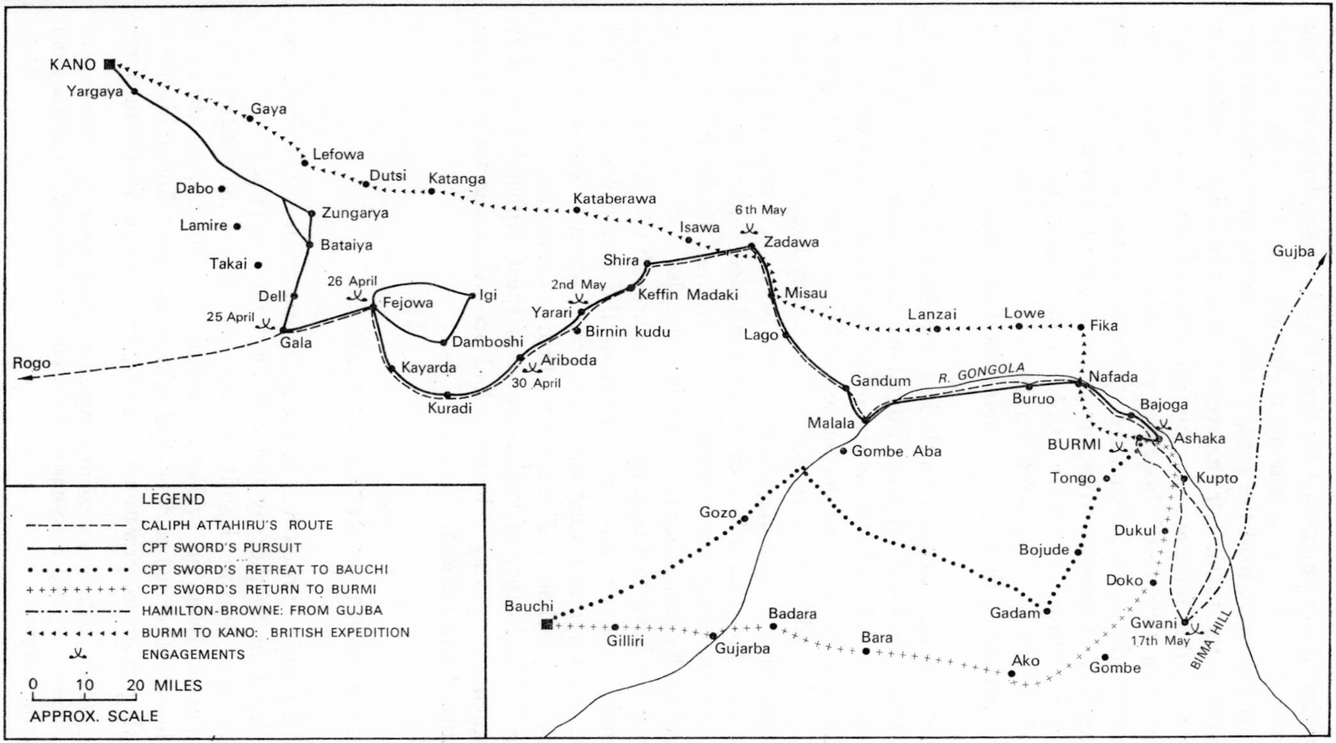

The flight and pursuit of Attahiru I

by the Burmi people led by their Chief, Musa. In spite of the great execution done among their ranks by the Maxims, the Burmi fighters held the gate, waiting for the enemy to attempt entering the town. For the second time, the British expedition attempted to force an entry but was compelled to withdraw, this time to a distance of about 600 yards from the wall from where they tried in vain to bombard it. As the battle progressed large numbers of people, from the neighbouring towns were entering the town by other gates. The morale of the Burmi defenders on and behind the walls remained unbroken. Even the women played their part, bringing food and water to the fighting men.

By 6 p.m. when the battle had raged for about seven hours, Sword, whose column had suffered over sixty casualties including two soldiers killed and several officers and many men wounded, admitted defeat. The desperate condition of the British troops is evidenced by the fact that although they had fired more than 10,000 shots, excluding the guns and Maxims, and had inflicted on the Burmawa a loss of about 250 killed (including Mallam Musa) the latter were nevertheless undaunted. Reckoning that an attempt by him either to meet a British column then approaching from Gujba or to retreat by the route through which he had come would be dangerous on account of the hostility of the local people, Captain Sword withdrew from Burmi to Bauchi under cover of darkness. The defeated British expedition (the first so far in the history of the conquest of the Caliphate) arrived at Bauchi on 23 May. The crisis had become embarrassing to the Lugard government.

THE PURSUIT OF ATTAHIRU RESUMED

The Caliph himself had in the meantime been driven from one hideout to another by the column from Gujba led by Major Hamilton-Browne. Hamilton-Browne's column had scattered his camp at Gwoni on 17 May.[59] Attahiru's followers, hundreds of whom had turned back or died at various points during his flight owing to severe privations resulting from lack of food and water

59. Hamilton-Browne's column captured much baggage: tents, about 400 lb of powder, 63 guns, 18 camels, 25 donkeys and 2 mules, from the Caliph.

as well as the sheer fatigue of the journey, had been further depleted.[60] If Captain Sword had not been forced to commit the error of judgment of turning back instead of going forward to meet Hamilton-Browne's column, the Caliph would almost certainly have been caught in a pincer movement which would have compelled him to either surrender or give battle to the British in the open field, where their superior weapons and drill would have put an end to his hitherto uncontrollable rising.

At this point Attahiru wrote to C. L. Temple, the Resident at Bauchi, pleading for friendship and permission to leave his territories, which had passed under the white man's power, and go unmolested on his travels.[61] At the same time, he had written to the Wazir of Sokoto to withhold the emigration to meet him as there was no food where he was.[62] The projected emigration from Sokoto, said to have been backed by all the high officials there, has been identified with a plan by the Marafa, Muḥammad Maiturare, to join Attahiru.[63] Temple insisted that he would accept Attahiru's plea for friendship only if he surrendered himself unconditionally to the British. This was unacceptable to the Caliph, since his desire was to have nothing to do with the white man and to escape from his jurisdiction. There was, however, no other course open to Temple and, considering that the letter was said by one of Attahiru's followers[64] to have been a ruse designed to give the Caliph time to prepare his defences, Temple's action seems justified.

60. C.O. 446/32, Wallace to C.O., no. 244, 8 July 1903, interview with brother of Emir of Kontagora, a deserter from Attahiru's following at Burmi.
61. C.O. 446/32, Gollan to C.O., 17 June 1903, encl. 3, Temple to Wallace, 27 May 1903. Temple received another letter from the Caliph in the same vein in June, see encl. 1 in C.O. 446/32, Wallace to C.O., 15 July 1903.
62. C.O. 446/32, Wallace to C.O., no. 244 of 8 July 1903. Captain Hamilton-Browne reported that he also received a letter from Attahiru in which the latter asked for permission to proceed to Mecca.
63. Muffett, *op. cit.*, p. 192, information collected from the son of the Marafa of Sokoto, Muḥammad Maiturare.
64. The son of the Emir of Kontagora, see C.O. 446/32, Wallace to C.O., no. 244 of 8 July 1903.

THE SECOND BATTLE OF BURMI

From the first battle of Burmi, the cause of the Caliph began to weaken in face of the British forces gathering against him. When the first definite news of the *hijra* was received at Zungeru on 4 May, Col. Morland had wired Zaria to send reinforcements. On 23 May a column consisting of sixty mounted infantry and eighty rank and file under Brevet-Major Barlow, which had left Zaria on the 8th in response to Morland's wire, reached Gombe Abba. In the meantime the Caliph's party, encouraged by the defeat of the British at Burmi, had retired to that stronghold. The force under Barlow was not strong enough to attack Burmi, but he moved on and established himself at Ashaka, a fortified town about two miles east of Burmi.[65] On reaching Ashaka on 31 May, he was reinforced by Lt. Lawrence on 1 June with forty rank and file—part of Hamilton-Browne's patrol which had driven Attahiru out of Gwoni.

On the same day Barlow's attempt to reconnoitre Burmi with fifty mounted infantry drew the Burmawa out of the city, ready to give battle. A stiff fight followed, in which the Burmi fighters, defiant of the heavy volley-firing by Barlow's men and undeterred by heavy casualties—in dead and wounded—inflicted on them, followed the retreating British soldiers intrepidly back almost to Ashaka.[66] Barlow, however, kept the Burmi people on their toes by patrolling the neighbourhood of their town in order to cut off their food supplies and their communication with other neighbouring towns hostile to the British. On the 18th Burmi took the offensive against Barlow when in a night attack they burnt the outer town of Ashaka and were only repulsed from the inner town in the small hours of the morning of the 19th.[67] The Burmawa attacked Ashaka again on the 22nd but were repulsed by the British garrison which had now been brought up to a strength of seven officers, 180 rank and file and two Maxims by

65. N.A.K., S.N.P.7/6/289, encl. Morland to Wallace, 27 Oct. 1903, in Wallace to C.O., no. 388 of 6 Nov. 1903.
66. C.O. 446/32, Wallace to C.O., Tel. no. 59, 5 August 1903. C.O. 446/32, Wallace to C.O., 14 Sept. 1903, and 15 July 1903, encl. 2, Barlow to Temple, 4 June 1903; also N.A.K., S.N.P.7/6/289, Morland's report encl. in Wallace to C.O., no. 388 of 6 Nov. 1903.
67. *Ibid.*, Morland's report.

the arrival of reinforcements under Captain Hamilton-Browne and Captain Sword.

Throughout the first week of July Barlow was out with a strong column to reduce to submission the hostile towns around Burmi, while Captain Sword continued to harass Burmi itself and to engage in several skirmishes with its inhabitants.[68] Their two previous attempts against Ashaka having failed, the Burmawa had concentrated on self-defence. With the subjugation of the neighbouring towns by Barlow, Burmi was effectively isolated.

The lot of the Burmawa became more and more desperate without their knowing it immediately, as British forces were being mustered from all directions. Half a company of infantry and a large stock of ammunition had been ordered from Zaria to Bauchi in June. On 13 June Major Marsh had left Lokoja with 165 rank and file and a 75 mm gun. On 23 July he reached Nafada, where Barlow had retired after subjugating the towns in the neighbourhood of Burmi.[69] With the arrival of Major Marsh the force massed to attack Burmi was 500 with twenty-five officers, four Maxims and two 75 mm guns. In London news of Captain Sword's defeat had prompted the Colonial Office to alert Sierra-Leone, the Gold Coast, Lagos and Southern Nigeria to be ready with reinforcements in case of need.[70]

On 26 July Major Marsh approached Burmi from the south-west, having marched south from Nafada the previous day. Captain Sword's column at Ashaka was to guard the south-east route from Burmi and Hamilton-Browne was in charge of the north-west approach to the town. Thus hemmed in, the beleaguered town waited desperately for the arrival of the enemy. The attack on it was opened from the south-west at about 11 a.m. on the 27th Captain Sword's column from Ashaka having made a junction with Major Marsh. The walls were bare.[71] The Burmi

68. *Ibid.*

69. *Ibid.*; C.O. 446/32, Wallace to C.O., Tel. 1 Aug. 1903.

70. Muffett, *op. cit.*, p. 189.

71. My account of the final battle at Burmi is based mainly on Major Plummer to O.C. Bauchi, 31 July 1903, encl. 1 in C.O. 446/32. Wallace to C.O., no. 328 of 18 Sept. 1903; and encl. 2 Brevet-Major Barlow's report; also N.A.K., S.N.P.7/6/289, Wallace to C.O., 6 Nov. 1903, encl. Morland to Wallace, 27 Oct. 1903; and N.A.K., S.N.P. 15/57; 'Temple's report on the circumstances attending the flight, pursuit, and death of Attahiru'—8 Aug. 1903. See also Muffett, *op. cit.*, p. 197 ff.

defenders lay hidden in trenches. The British artillery blew open the two gates on the south-west but the Burmawa did not as yet return the fire.

After about one hour a storming party under Major Plummer advanced to enter the city. As soon as they were within arrow range the defenders in the trenches unleashed a hot arrow fire supported by flanking fire from a few guns and rifles, which halted Plummer's advance. To save the situation a reinforcing party under Major Marsh dashed from behind, but no sooner had it come within the arrow range of the defenders than Major Marsh was hit by a poisoned arrow which killed him within half an hour. The desperate defence of the town was temporarily broken by about 1 p.m., when the attackers entered it. Inside the British fought from house to house and set fire to the houses. But about an hour later the heat of the conflagration compelled them to withdraw. As soon as it subsided, the Burmawa retook the offensive, fighting doggedly from the walls, in spite of the guns and the Maxims, which were kept very busy. The town was again entered by one company of the British force while the rest went round the walls. The British suffered heavy casualties during this attack but they inflicted more on their enemies.

A lull followed, the Burmi resistance seemed at an end, but the defenders soon rallied and resumed the offensive. Captain Sword at the head of the company within the town was compelled to send for reinforcements. With fresh reinforcements sent into the town by Barlow, the British faced the last desperate struggle of the Burmawa at about 5.30 p.m. near the mosque and the Emir's house. Barlow records that this last phase of the battle was severe and that the Burmawa resistance was most determined. By 6 p.m. Burmi opposition was completely quelled. Both the mosque and the Emir's house lay in ruins.

In terms of the doggedness of the defenders of the Caliphate the last battle of Burmi was the most severe opposition ever faced by the British in the course of their conquest of Northern Nigeria. It was also the best organized. The defenders of Burmi fought with determination and a ferocity which can only be ascribed to the zeal of Muslims fighting in *jihād*. In the face of heavy losses on their side and heavy firing from the British the defenders held out in their trenches where many of them were shot or bayoneted.[72]

72. C.O. 446/32, Wallace to C.O., no. 328 of 18 Sept. 1903, encl. 2, B, Major Barlow's Report on the battle of Burmi.

Some advanced to meet the storming party of the British at the risk of certain death.[73]

The heavy casualties inflicted on the Burmi defenders, estimated at over 600 killed, testify to the unyielding and desperate nature of their resistance. Time after time they refused to accept defeat until hopelessly broken. The Caliph Attahiru, who had been in the mosque when the attack on the town began, placed himself at the head of a party which held up Captain Plummer's first attempt to enter the town for over an hour. He fell, with about ninety of his men in a heap round him,[74] near the gate of the town through which the British entered.

Among those killed at Burmi were virtually all the leading Sokoto officials who fled with the Caliph, most of those from Kano, Magajin Keffi—Dan Yamusa—while there were many from other emirates such as Katagum, Missau, Bauchi (including the Wazir who was killed), Gombe, Kontagora and Nupe.[75] A list of those killed,[76] by no means exhaustive, gives an indication of how representative of the Caliphate was the community that stood against the British at Burmi.

Although the British casualties were few—Major Marsh, four rank and file and six carriers killed, and about ninety, including a few officers, wounded[77]—the total was by far the highest number of casualties ever inflicted on the British throughout their conquest of the Caliphate. In his report Major Plummer held that his second entry into Burmi would have been of great difficulty but for 'the bold handling of the guns and the great support of the mounted infantry'. In the final analysis British success, as aptly put by Wallace, was due largely to 'the great stopping power of our bullets, mark IV, which was one of the principal factors leading to our success. Without this ammunition our success would have been doubtful.'[78] Superior arms and

73. C. L. Temple's Report on the circumstances attending the flight, pursuit and death of Attahiru, *op. cit.*
74. *Ibid.*
75. C. L. Temple, 'Report on circumstances . . . et seq.', *op. cit.* A list of the Chiefs in Burmi on the day of battle. There is a claim that Magajin Keffi survived Burmi and migrated to Mecca.
76. *Ibid.*
77. C.O. 446/22, Wallace to C.O., Tel. no. 63, 16 Aug. 1903; and Morland's report, 27 Oct. 1903, encl. in desp. no. 388, Wallace to C.O., 6 Nov. 1903 in N.A.K., S.N.P.7/6/289.
78. C.O. 446/32, Wallace to C.O., 18 Sept. 1903.

ammunition, rather than superior morale or even military strategy, explain the British victory.

To the defenders of Burmi, the vast majority of whom were ordinary peasant folk who risked all to defend their land and their religion and hundreds of whom paid the last price in this endeavour, Wallace, an enemy, paid an appreciative and well-deserved compliment. He wrote: 'Our recent experiences show that the poorer people and the numerous chiefs collected at Burmi, knew how to die when facing the enemy.'[79] It was the best and the most glorious they could do in the circumstances.

By the morning of 28 July Burmi had been completely deserted, but as if to put its defeat beyond any doubt, the British expedition completed its thorough destruction. Bajoga, whose inhabitants had aided Burmi, was found completely deserted on the 29th and again the British expedition, scouring the surroundings of Burmi in a mopping up campaign, burnt down the town.

Burmi marked the end of military resistance to the British on a sufficiently large and effective scale to have a chance of reversing the overthrow of the Caliphate. There were subsequent revolts, but these did not constitute a serious threat to British tenure. For the first time the ground was prepared for the establishment of an effective British administration. This does not mean that victory in battle automatically resulted in sincere acceptance of British rule by the emirates. Years of a clever mixture of tact, patience and use of force, when unavoidable, were needed to consolidate the British victories over a people of whom the vast majority were known to have been dissembling. But the last reasonable hopes of a reversal of the British conquest died at Burmi. It marked the definite end of an epoch.

Throughout the greater part of the Caliphate, disaffection to British conquest had reared its head openly all through the duration of Attahiru's *hijra*. Temple discovered that, in spite of all appearances of loyalty, large quantities of foodstuffs had been sent to Burmi, a few days before its fall, from Bauchi (actually Maimadi) with the connivance of influential Bauchi officials.[80] Shortly after the fall of Burmi the successor of Mallam Musa in Burmi had found honourable welcome and hospitality in Jalingo, capital of Muri. Throughout the month of July the Resident of

79. *Ibid.*
80. *Ibid.*

Kano observed that 'there continues to be a certain amount of unrest and uncertainty of attitude among the natives which renders administrative work a farce'.[81]

Among important men who escaped from Burmi were Abubakar, deposed Emir of Bida, Aḥmad b. Ṣālih, Emir of Missau, Bashīr b. Amīr al-Mu'minīn Aḥmad b. Shaikh 'Umar, Galadiman Ako, Mai Wurno (Muḥammad Bello). Of these both Abubakar and Bashīr fell into British hands to join the band of exiled rulers. Aḥmad, Emir of Missau, escaped in an adventurous journey, through Bauchi and Adamawa to the Eastern Sudan.[82] So did Mai Wurno, son of the Caliph, Attahiru. They settled first at Shaikh Ṭalhat on the banks of the Nile where they were later joined by a large number of people, including those survivors of Burmi and other people from various emirates whose thirst for the *hijra* to the east was not killed by the defeat at Burmi. About thirty years later, this band of fugitives from the fallen Sokoto Caliphate made a new home in Mai Wurno across the Nile, opposite Shaikh Ṭalhat.[83]

To what extent the emigration of the leaders to the Eastern Sudan was a *hijra* from the rule of unbelievers is a matter for speculation and research. The Sudan was, from their point of view, already under infidel rule—the British. Although they finally settled in the Eastern Sudan their intended destination had been Mecca.[84] Belief in previous prophecies of the emigration of the Faithful from the Caliphate to the Nile and the Hijaz probably strengthened their hopes of preserving their religion in the Holy Land. Howbeit, emigration must be seen as, at least in part, a registration of protest against the British conquest. How much of such resentment unexpressed in flight was left over in the Caliphate remains to be seen.

81. C.O. 446/32, Wallace to C.O., no. 328, 18 Sept. 1903.
82. For a description of Aḥmad's escape, see *West Africa*, 6 Feb. 1920.
83. *Ḍabṭ al-Mulṭaqaṭāt*, f. 75 (b). For account of the Emigration to the Sudan, see G. J. F. Tomlinson and G. J. Lethem, *History of Islamic Propaganda in Nigeria* (London, 1927).
84. On the authority of Ibrahim Mukoshy (Ibrāhīm b. Maimūna bt. Muḥammad Bello, i.e. Mai Wurno, b. al-Ṭahīr b. Aḥmad b. 'Atīq b. 'Uthmān b. Fodiye) born at Mai Wurno, the original intention of the *émigrés* from the Sokoto Caliphate was to go to Mecca. They were discouraged from going there by the community of Shaikh Ṭalhat, who welcomed them to the village. Shaikh Ṭalhat of Macina, after whom the village is named, had settled in the Eastern Sudan with a large community earlier on in the nineteenth century.

It is all too easy when dealing with a Muslim society to lapse into a determinist interpretation of their history. By paying attention to known norms and values expected of, and accepted by, such a society, there is a temptation to interpret their actions within a straitjacketed framework of the 'Islamic Way'. The realization of the difficulty of making the distinction, often a very fine one, between actions motivated by Islamic obligations or otherwise does not provide the historian with an adequate excuse to proceed as if such distinctions do not exist or that, even if they do, they do not matter. Vehement opposition to foreign conquest is not peculiar to Muslim peoples, neither is flight from an overwhelmingly powerful enemy. These reactions arise from basic human instincts. During the wars of European imperialism such reactions can be illustrated from the history of many an African people. It must be clear from the brief allusions to non-Muslim peoples within the perimeter of the Caliphate that they too were as anxious to preserve their independence against European encroachment as they had consistently been against the Muslim emirates throughout the nineteenth century. In fact their final submission to British rule was the result of numerous expeditions which continued to be sent against them years after the overthrow of the Caliphate.

It is a commonplace of Islam to note that there has not been a pure Muslim state in history. Islam owes its success partly to its adaptability to differing cultures. As aptly put by Hampate Ba: 'En Afrique l'Islam n'a pas plus de couleur que l'eau; c'est ce qui explique son succès, elle se colore aux teints de terroirs et des pierres.'[85]

The Sokoto Caliphate was no exception to this appraisal. It shared with other non-Muslims the same universal human instinct of self-preservation in its resistance to European conquest. But over and above this, its resistance was clearly within the context of the Islamic overtone which had characterized its organization and its relations with Europeans throughout the nineteenth century. The manner in which it sought preservation from European infidel rule as revealed in this work, was manifestly through the application of Islamic ideas. To mention one crucial example: the scale of emigration from the conquerors and the long distances involved were perhaps not paralleled in any

85. V. Monteil, *L'Islam noir* (Paris, 1964), p. 41, quoting Amadou Hampate Ba's remarks to a stranger.

other African country, certainly not among non-Muslims, during the wars of European conquests. Even after the final destruction of the Caliphate by the breaking of its most vehement resistance, resentment continued to find expression within the framework of Islamic beliefs.

Chapter 10
Aftermath, 1903-1906

With the breaking of the resistance to the British at Burmi and the death, flight or capture of the most prominent leaders of the Caliphate's opposition to European rule, the establishment of British rule was guaranteed against overthrow. As the new Sultan Attahiru II, who should have been the leading figure around whom the forces of discontent could rally, proved particularly loyal to the British the Caliphate was deprived of central leadership. Such leadership had died at Burmi with the Caliph Attahiru I, who had fought to sustain it to the bitter end.

In August 1903 two messengers were said to have arrived in Yola with two flags around which the supporters of the fugitive Caliph were expected to rally.[1] This may well have been part of a plan by the Caliph, posthumously unfolded, to mobilize resistance throughout the Caliphate. Even if it is assumed that Caliph Attahiru knew nothing about the mission of the two messengers to Yola, it would seem that those who were responsible for sending them believed in his leadership and relied on him as a symbol of the Caliphate's struggle against infidel adversaries.

By way of contrast the loss of central leadership in the Caliphate, occasioned by the death of Attahiru I at Burmi, was highlighted by a circular which the Sultan Attahiru II sent to the emirates at the instigation of the British Resident of Sokoto,[2] announcing the fall of Sokoto and his appointment by the British. By this circular the Sultan formally announced his resignation of the traditional role of the Caliph to exercise final control over the emirates.

The loyalty of Sultan Attahiru and of several emirs, like those of Bida and of Kano, to the British may have been no more than pragmatic resignation to the inevitable by these rulers. But this resignation signalled the doom of the forces of resistance to British rule.

1. N.A.K. Yola Prov. Archives, vol. ii, Gowers, Report no. 22, August 1903.
2. *Ibid.*

The demise of the Caliphate left a vacuum of power with regard to central control over the emirates which the British found relatively easy to fill in the absence of any other leader of the stature and sway of the Caliph in the former Caliphate. Nevertheless the forces of discontent did not die completely with the Caliph Attahiru. There were, among the emirs appointed or recognized by Lugard, those who either did not personally accept the British rule wholeheartedly as a final settlement of the Caliphate–European struggle or who, realizing the resentment of their subjects to European rule, were too frightened to show their loyalty to the British too openly.

During a tour of the conquered emirates in 1904 Lugard deposed the Emir of Katsina because he had persistently given trouble since the occupation and had been opposing the British administration secretly 'in every way'.[3] In Bauchi the Emir, Muḥammad, who, it will be remembered, had been appointed at British insistence and in spite of the patent desire of Bauchi people to let the then Emir, 'Umar, continue in office, had been impatient from the time of his appointment with the Resident's interference in the administration of the emirate. He was reluctant to take a public oath of allegiance to the British when Lugard visited him in 1904.[4] During the same tour Lugard found that, like the Emir of Bauchi, that of Gombe was reluctant to take an oath of allegiance to the British publicly.[5] Lugard, commenting on the Emir of Gombe's reluctance, observed: 'Though its Emir was friendly, it appears that the population of its large walled towns had acquiesced but sullenly in the British rule.'[6] The Emir, however, like that of Bauchi, took the public oath at Lugard's insistence in spite of the disaffection of his subjects.

In Yola, which had been a hotbed of disaffection to the British since its occupation in 1901, the Emir, who was reported as being 'sensitive to public opinion', was also reluctant to take the oath of allegiance to the British publicly.[7] The Resident of Yola, W. F. Gowers, commenting in 1903 on the Emir of Yola's attitude to the British, had written: 'The Emir of Yola I believe to be friendly in the sense that he sees on which side his interest

3. Lugard, *Annual Reports*, 1904, p. 241.
4. *Ibid.*, p. 262.
5. *Ibid.*, pp. 258–9.
6. *Ibid.*, p. 255.
7. *Ibid.*, p. 262.

lies, but his friendliness to us is largely due to the fact that he is personally unpopular with his Fulani subjects.'[8] According to the Resident, the Emir of Yola was looked upon by his co-religionists as a usurper.[9]

The unpopularity of the Emir, Bobo Aḥmad, of Yola was well illustrated by the sympathy which Aliyu, ex-Emir of Kano, evoked in the town. He was brought to Yola with the ex-Emir of Zaria, Muḥammad Lawal, in May 1904. Soon after Aliyu's arrival in Yola about 300 of his followers from Kano arrived to join him. Crowds of people in Yola flocked to see him.[10] So popular was he that the Resident felt that he dared not put him under guard at the British fort because the populace, certain to conclude that the Emir of Yola had colluded with the British to persecute him, might become disturbingly restive. Therefore, although Aliyu was supposed to be in captivity, he had many followers with him and he lived like a second Emir. The most the Emir of Yola could do was to instal one of his chiefs in Aliyu's compound ostensibly to watch over him.

Aliyu in Yola, a symbol of resistance against the British, was, among the Yola populace, a hero. The Resident observed that he had both the inclination and the power to make mischief.[11] He remained truculent. He was said to be in correspondence with a certain son of the Caliph Attahiru called Mamudu (Maḥmūd) who was a refugee in Lafia.[12] The latter confessed to the British that he was in correspondence with Aliyu but only by way of sending salutations. In one of two letters to Aliyu seized from Mamudu, the latter wrote: 'Have patience. I am praying as you are, continue to pray and soon you may hope to get good news and you will see me again.'[13]

In September 1904 Aliyu, apparently trying to organize an anti-British resistance, was said to have sent envoys to the Emir of Keffi.[14] The Emir of Keffi, when questioned by the British Resident, denied any knowledge of the embassy but the British

8. N.A.K. Yola Prov. Archives, vol. ii, Report no. 19, May 1903.
9. C.O. 446/31, Wallace to C.O., 3 June 1903, transmitting news of the Emir Zubeir's death and comments by the Resident of Yola.
10. N.A.K. Yola Prov. Archives, vol. iv, G. N. Barclay, Report, May 1904.
11. *Ibid.*
12. N.A.K., S.N.P.7/5/285, G. W. Webster, Report no. 21, Sept. 1904.
13. *Ibid.*
14. *Ibid.*

discovered that he had received messages, the purport of which was that he should 'look out for the promised Mahdī and have a little patience, it was not for long'. It was probable, as Webster, Acting Resident of Keffi surmised, that emissaries were going not only to the Muslim emirates but also to the pagans to educate them to the idea that the stay of the British would be short. Indeed it is said that there was a widespread belief that the British were like a stream after the storm which would soon dry up with the passing of the rains.[15]

The feeling of resentment at the British occupation was widespread. It was, for instance, impossible for the British to assert their control over Kontagora until the ousted Emir, Ibrāhīm, was restored to power. Even after his restoration Ibrāhīm continued to behave as if British power was of no consequence. In June 1903 J. R. Lumley, in charge of Kontagora province, convicted the Emir on a charge of slave-raiding, deposed him and sentenced him to three months' imprisonment.[16] But Lugard, aware that British hold on the Caliphate rested on such slippery grounds that they had no choice but to uphold the dignity and power of the emirs, reversed Lumley's judgment and reinstated Ibrāhīm.[17] As late as 1906 Major Sharpe, Resident of Kontagora province, noted in one of his reports that the people persistently refused to obey British orders transmitted through the district chiefs:

> All along the Niger [he wrote] the islanders and riverain villages refuse to obey orders and defy police going there in couples. I cannot enforce the law thoroughly throughout the outlying parts of the province, nor collect tribute and licences unless I have more force at my disposal to back up my orders and those of my assistants.[18]

Judging by the reactions of the masses to the *hijra* of the Caliph Attahiru, and the persistence of opposition in the emirates in the years after 1903, it would seem that many of the emirs were playing a forced role in showing loyalty to the British against the wishes of many of their subjects. There were, however, a few who were consistently adamant in their opposition to British rule.

15. Last, *The Sokoto Caliphate*, p. 140, quoting a poem in Hausa from F. Edgar's collection. N.A.K. KADCAPTORY (3, 6).
16. N.A.I., C.S.O.1/27, 3, Gollan (Chief Justice), Ag. High Commissioner to C.O., 16 June 1903.
17. N.A.I., C.S.O.1/28, 3, C.O. to H.C. (Northern Nigeria) 2 Sept. 1903.
18. N.A.K., S.N.P.7/7, file 4637, Report by W. S. Sharpe, no. 35.

In this connection the Emirs of Gwandu and Hadejia were perhaps the most vehement in their opposition, the former acting surreptitiously while the latter showed open hostility. The Emir of Gwandu had, before the occupation of Sokoto, professed himself friendly with the British. It will be recalled that when the British expedition was on its way to Sokoto in 1903 he had submitted to it peacefully. Yet between 1903 and 1906, when he was deposed for his role during the Satiru revolt (discussed below), he was repeatedly warned by the British for his disaffection.

THE HADEJIA REVOLT, 1906

Hadejia had neither been conquered nor had it submitted to the British by the end of 1903. In December 1903, when a sub-province of Kano was established with headquarters at Katagum, Hadejia was grouped with Katagum. Albeit when an assistant Resident, Captain Phillips, visited the town during the same month (Dec. 1903) he received an unfriendly welcome.[19] Thereafter Captain Phillips had had to sit tight at Katagum. Hadejia's attitude became openly truculent during 1904. E. J. Lugard (F. D. Lugard's brother) observed that while the Emir was prepared to be courteous to white men, he wanted them to have nothing to do with his rule and regarded himself as completely independent.[20]

During his tour of 1904 Lugard had prevailed on the Emir of Kano to plead with the Emir of Hadejia to accept British rule. The Emir of Hadejia, in reply to Emir of Kano's letter, accepted the latter's counsel.[21] When Lugard visited Katagum in mid-December 1904, although the Emir of Hadejia was the last of the surrounding emirs to visit him, he did come ultimately. He made his submission formally to Lugard. A peaceful relationship was then established between the British and the Emir, so much so that a British garrison was established outside Hadejia walls on 9 January 1905.

19. N.A.K., S.N.P.15/83, Larymore to High Commissioner, 4 March 1904; and R.H.B.E., S.61, E. J. Lugard, Jottings, 1903–05, p. 174 f.
20. E. J. Lugard, Jottings, 1903–05, *loc. cit.*
21. Lugard, *Annual Report*, p. 245; see Emir of Hadejia's reply p. 249; and Abdulmalik Mani, *Zuwan Turawa Nigeriya ta Arewa* (Zaria, 1956), pp. 154–5.

However, the establishment of the British garrison at Hadejia seems to have been the one factor which exacerbated Hadejia hostility to the British. Aware of British activities in the conquered emirates, the people of Hadejia were living in constant fear of a British attack. The Emir therefore prepared to meet such an eventuality. By April 1905 there were rumours in the city of a British plan to attack the town. The King consulted his headmen and ordered all adult males to remain in the town and not to sleep on their farms.[22] Hadejia's hostility was rendered even more intransigent by a rumour which gained much ground that the British intended to depose and deport the Emir.[23] A letter from Cargill, Resident of Kano, denying the authenticity of this rumour did nothing to dispel Hadejia's apprehensions.[24] It was well known that the British had so acted in many emirates during the course of their occupation. For all practical purposes British control over Hadejia was non-existent. The discontent in Hadejia became progressively more pronounced as the year 1905 wore on. Lugard reported that the attitude of the people 'was consistently marked by chronic obstruction'. A soldier of the Hadejia British garrison had been killed, apparently with the sanction and in the presence of the Emir, and an attack on the garrison itself seemed to have been seriously considered.[25] News of a revolt at Satiru and the annihilation of a W.A.F.F. company there in February 1906 was received with general rejoicing in Hadejia. Lugard reported that 'all work on government buildings was stopped and the Emir's messenger no longer came to the Resident'.[26]

The Lugard administration felt compelled to take decisive action against Hadejia. An expedition was despatched from Kano on 10 April 1906 to resolve the impasse. Lugard's ultimatum, asking for the prompt surrender of the 'ring-leaders' involved in the killing of the W.A.F.F. soldier and for the levelling of a portion of the town wall (to facilitate entry to the British forces in case of need), was flatly rejected by the Emir, and its bearer was struck on the face as a mark of humiliation. In the battle which followed the British forces, having entered the city, were engaged

22. N.A.K., S.N.P.15/83, Larymore to H.C., 4 March 1904.
23. *Ibid.*, encl. (Cargill Resident Kano), 5 June 1905.
24. *Ibid.*, Cargill to Lugard, 18 July 1905.
25. N.A.K., S.N.P.15/93, Cargill to Lugard, 9 May 1905; Lugard, *Annual Report*, p. 378.
26. *Ibid.*

for five hours in a fierce battle with Hadejia soldiers led by the Emir in person. The Emir and three of his sons fell in the encounter. The Chiroma (heir-apparent) was thereafter appointed by the British as the new Emir.[27]

The revolt of Hadejia was the last serious revolt which confronted the British in any of the emirates. It differed from Burmi in that it was a localized affair in which only the Hadejia army participated. Further, whereas Hadejia had formally submitted to the British before the rising, the Burmi war was a continuation of the Caliph's struggle against the British. The Hadejia incident was therefore a revolt, whereas Burmi was not. However, the resentment at British rule in Hadejia was probably no more than similar resentment in some of the emirates—Adamawa for instance. The difference between Hadejia and other occupied emirates was that in Hadejia, unlike in other emirates, traditional leaders of the people solidly and openly associated themselves with the discontent of the people. In a sense it can be said that the overthrow of the Sokoto Caliphate by the British was carried out above the head of the masses. Even though the masses had participated actively in the battles of resistance to British conquest, they were not similarly involved in acquiescing in British rule. Against the opposition of apparently substantial portions of the emirates' populations, the British depended for the consolidation of their conquest on emirs who, backed and coerced by British military power which they could only defy at their own peril, ceased to be the symbols of the aspirations of their subjects with regard to the important question of opposition to foreign and infidel rule. Yet the emirs who showed their loyalty to the British and thereby rendered the establishment of colonial rule easier, whatever their other motives for so acting, cannot be correctly

27. *Ibid.* Contrary to the claim in Lugard's Report that no atrocities were perpetrated in Hadejia after the conquest, it is clear from Miller–Lugard correspondence on the matter in 1907 that a great deal of killing followed the conquest. Miller wrote: 'With regard to (Sokoto) and Hadejia the whole ugly story is common property and none are more pronounced and vehement in their condemnation of the atrocities than officers and political men here themselves' (see R.H.B.E. S.62, Miller to Lugard, 11 Sept. 1907; see also *ibid.*, Miller to Lugard, 24 Dec. 1907, in which he wrote: 'It would be worth Leopold of Belgium's while to pay ten thousand pounds to get hold of what we know about this'; also *ibid.*, Wallace to E. J. Lugard: 400 killed at Hadejia said to be a conservative estimate.

described as despicable time-servers. Force is the last hope of resistance. The best forces which the emirates could field had been overwhelmingly defeated by the British in various battles. Thereafter, having been pushed to the end of their tether, the obvious choice for the rulers was to reconcile themselves to accepting British suzerainty, at least as a pragmatic policy.

MAHDIST RESURGENCE

The anti-British forces stood for independence and the survival of Muslim rule. From the motivation viewpoint, they can be likened to the reformist forces grouped under ʿUthmān b. Fodiye against infidel rule at the beginning of the nineteenth century. With the overthrow of the traditional leadership in the Caliphate provided by the Caliph and his emirs, leadership of the resistance movement was taken up by many pious mallams scattered throughout the Caliphate. Such mallams expressed their opposition through the Mahdist idea. They presented themselves either as the Mahdī or his precursors. Their religious propaganda throve on the widespread belief that the British power in the Muslim emirates was destined to be of short duration. Indeed the time in the Caliphate was most opportune for nursing hopes of the appearance of the Mahdī. In Muslim belief the Mahdī is expected to appear in the last days, before the end of the world. He is to fill the world with justice, then rid it of oppression and make Islam supreme. There could therefore be no time more appropriate for this appearance than one during which the Caliphate and other Muslim countries were convulsed by imperial conquest by infidels and the cause of Islam seemed to be at its nadir.

As early as 1902 a mallam, Maizanna, had proclaimed himself Mahdī in Nupe and had invited people to drive out Europeans and the Emir of Bida, Muḥammad, who owed his appointment to the British. He obtained a numerous following from among the masses but as these were militarily unorganized the incipient revolt was easily curbed by his arrest and imprisonment for a term of six months. A heavy fine was imposed on some of the ring-leaders.[28]

Indeed expectation of the Mahdī was widespread in the Muslim emirates during the British occupation. The subject calls for a

28. Dupigny, *Gazetteer of Nupe Province*, p. 25.

deeper study than can be accomplished in the necessarily brief outline attempted in this work. It will be recalled that the *hijra* of Caliph Attahiru was closely associated with the expectation that he would lead his followers to the Mahdī. He is said to have accepted Mahdism on taking up refuge in Burmi.[29] Commenting on the rise of Mahdism in various parts of the Muslim emirates Lugard wrote: 'I do not think a year has passed since 1900 without one or more . . . Mahdist movements.'[30] The activities of several Mahdist or forerunners of the Expected Mahdī, all preaching expulsion of the British, made 1906 a crisis year for the British administration in Northern Nigeria.

Early in 1906 a Muslim preacher in Kontagora drew attention to the impending end of British rule and exhorted people to stop paying taxes to the British administration. He also predicted the advent of 'a terrible thing with 70,000 guns' which would come from the four corners of the earth. It seems that with the widespread belief in the imminent appearance of the Mahdī went also the expectation of some mysterious force which would wipe out British rule. At the same time as the Kontagora preacher was carrying out his mission two similar preachers appeared in Jebba and Yelwa respectively.[31] At this time also several preachers with large followings appeared in Bauchi and Gombe emirates, preaching the extermination of all unbelievers, particularly the Europeans. They proclaimed the imminent advent of the Mahdī on Bima hill and created considerable excitement among the masses. These movements were promptly curbed by the British administration before they could become serious threats. One of the mallams was tried and sentenced to death, another was deported and two others fled, one to Kuka and the other to Wadai. In Mandara also, in German territory, there was a strong Mahdist movement which based itself on a strong belief in the imminent appearance of the Mahdī in Balda (in Adamawa) or on Bima hill. The movement was promptly suppressed by the Germans, while Bima hill in eastern Gombe was occupied by British troops and a fort was built there.[32]

All the Mahdist movements of the early years of the twentieth century in Northern Nigeria were sporadic incipient revolts.

29. Last, *op. cit.*, p. 141, n. 109.
30. *Annual Report*, p. 367.
31. *Ibid.*, p. 408.
32. N.A.I., C.S.O.1/27, 6, Lugard to C.O., 9 May 1906.

Their significance lies in the fact that they indicated underground discontent with the establishment of British rule which expressed itself in revolts which were Islamic in character. The various movements were not coordinated, nor did they develop sufficient militancy in their scattered localities before they were stemmed by the British administration.

THE SATIRU REBELLION

The Mahdist propaganda which resulted in the famous Satiru revolt of February 1906 best illustrates the aims of the scattered Mahdist movements and the potential danger they posed to European rule if they were not checked.

The main events of the Satiru revolts are well known.[33] Briefly stated, the Sokoto heartland itself had, to all appearances, been remarkably calm and loyal to the British. This claim was, however, largely a reflection of the submission of the traditional authorities to the British. Islamic propaganda against British rule went on beneath the calm surface. In 1904 the chief of Satiru, fourteen miles north of Sokoto, had proclaimed himself Mahdī, but was promptly arrested by the Sultan of Sokoto.[34] He died in jail while awaiting trial. His son, Isa, who succeeded him, remained loyal to the cause of the Mahdī. Early in 1906 Satiru was again organized for rebellion under the leadership of Isa, egged on by a mallam called Dan Makafo[35] (his real name was Shuaibu), who had escaped from the neighbouring French territory. When on 14 February a party of British mounted infantry marched to the village to nip the rebellion in the bud, if possible by negotiation, they were ferociously attacked by the rebels who, fighting with simple weapons, bows and arrows, spears and even hoes and axes, annihilated it. Hillary, the acting Resident of Sokoto, two white officers and twenty-five men of the mounted infantry lost their lives in the encounter.[36] The rifles of the dead British soldiers and the Maxim gun which the expedi-

33. See Margery Perham, *Years of Authority*, p. 247 ff. and Lugard, *Annual Report*, 365 ff.
34. N.A.I., C.S.O.1/27, 6, Lugard to C.O., 7 Mar. 1906, encl. Burdon to Lugard, 21 Feb. 1906.
35. *Ibid.*
36. N.A.I., C.S.O.1/27, 6, Lugard to C.O., 21 Feb. 1906, encl. Telegram from Ambursa.

tion brought with it but which, because it was some distance behind at the time of the attack, it had not been able to use, were captured by the Satiru rebels.

So far as the records have revealed the rout of the mounted infantry at Satiru was the most dramatic reverse which British troops ever suffered in Northern Nigeria. It therefore caused British officials great anxiety. For some days after the foregoing Satiru incident the British feared that their conquest of the Caliphate might be reversed if other emirates took their cue from Satiru. An expedition comprising 573 rifles, Maxims and big guns was hurriedly assembled and reinforcements were requested from Southern Nigeria. All that was needed to topple British rule was the co-operation of all emirates. But, on the occasion of the Satiru rising, they failed to take up the struggle where the Burmi defenders had left it.

The traditional leaders of the emirates, the emirs, had become apparently reconciled to British rule either out of sheer fear of the consequences of revolting against the British power or out of a realization that British rule was not as bad as they had feared before they were conquered. They lacked the will, and certainly the leadership, to turn the Satiru success into a starting point for a general revolt which Lugard, with the forces at his disposal, would have been unable to suppress.

The Sultan and the emirs, like those of Kano, Bida, Bauchi and Zaria, promptly dissociated themselves from the rebellion and offered military help to the British.[37] The leader of the Satiru revolt had appealed about 16 February to the Sultan to join him. His appeal was unheeded. On the 17th the Marafa of Sokoto advanced to Satiru with a force of 3000 men but had to turn back because his men refused to fight.[38] Clearly the failure of the Satiru rebellion must be explained, at least partly, by the identification of the traditional establishment of the erstwhile Caliphate with the British cause. The Emir of Gwandu, who had all along remained disaffected to the British, had initially promised co-operation with the Satiru rebels if the Sultan supported them,

37. See *Annual Reports*, 1905–6; also R.H.B.E., S.62, Lugard to C.O., 28 Feb. 1906; and N.A.I., C.S.O.1/27, 6, Lugard to C.O., report on Satiru, 7 March 1906; also *ibid.*, Lugard to C.O., 14 March 1906, encl. Burdon's Report, n.d.

38. R.H.B.E., S.62, Lugard to C.O., 22 Feb. 1906, and N.A.I., C.S.O.1/27, 6, Lugard to C.O., 14 Mar. 1906, encl. Capt. Ruxton's Report.

and later again promised it if they achieved further successes against the British.[39] The refusal of the Sultan and most of his emirs to support the rebellion was a clear indication of the completeness of the destruction of the Caliphate.

Mallam Isa had died on 16 February and his place was taken by Mallam Shuaibu (Dan Makafo). The strong British expedition marched on Satiru on 10 March and routed the rebel forces who fought with fierce determination to the bitter end. The village was thereafter destroyed and on the 11th the Sultan pronounced a curse on anyone who tried to cultivate the land or build on the site of the village.[40]

At Satiru died the last vehement Mahdist military opposition to British rule in the Muslim emirates. In the subsequent weeks the native court at Sokoto was busy with the trials, which were followed by numerous executions of the rebels including Mallam Shuaibu.[41] Early in April 1906 the Emir of Gwandu was deposed for persistent opposition to the British, culminating in his attitude during the Satiru revolt.[42]

The Satiru rebellion was symptomatic of the malaise of opposition to European rule which had perforce to organize secretly, not only in the emirates of the Caliphate but also in the adjoining French territory of 'Niger'. In fact the rebellion at Satiru was an extension of similar disturbances which the French had had to deal with in Zaberma late in 1905. Mallam Shuaibu had played a prominent role in these disturbances. Besides Mallam Shuaibu a certain mallam from Sokoto was reported to have been actively engaged in anti-European religious propaganda which had led to the Zaberma rebellion, in which several Frenchmen and soldiers lost their lives.[43]

The anti-European religious propaganda had also spread to

39. N.A.I., C.S.O.1/27, 6, Lugard to C.O., 9 May 1906.
40. N.A.I., C.S.O.1/27, 6, Lugard to C.O., 21 Mar. 1906 and Lugard to C.O., 14 Mar. 1906, encl. Burdon's Report.
41. See Miller–Lugard correspondence in 1907 on the Satiru and Hadejia rebellions, *loc. cit.*
42. See N.A.I., C.S.O.1/27, 4, Lugard to C.O., 26 April 1904, memo. on Emir of Gwandu; also N.A.I., C.S.O.1/27, 6, Lugard to C.O., on deposition of Emir of Gwandu, 5 Apr. 1906; also Lugard to C.O., 9 May 1906 on the same matter.
43. N.A.I., C.S.O.1/28, 6, Lugard to C.O., 19 Oct. 1906, encl. extracts from French Consul-General at Dakar to Ministre des Colonies, Paris, 10 Sept. 1906.

Zinder and, according to French officials, even beyond to the east. In 1907 the Emir of Zinder, Aḥmad, was deposed for his involvement in a plot to wipe out the French military post and French officials in Zinder early in 1906. In an enquiry which followed the abortive Zinder plot it was discovered that the plotters were in close contact with the organizers of the Satiru rebellion as well as with other neighbouring Muslim territories. It was even reported that the Sultan of Zinder sent a letter to the Emir of Kano at the same time as he sent one to Mallam Isa of Satiru before the revolt in the latter place. The Emir of Kano is said to have written in his reply: 'Tell the Sultan to prepare because we are going to raise troops [*faire colonne*] against the whites.'[44]

The alleged reply of the Emir of Kano to Zinder's appeal, completely incompatible with his reported loyalty to the British during the Satiru revolt, raises the very important question of what, their actions apart, was the real feeling of the leaders of the Muslim emirates of the Caliphate towards the British.[45] The reason given by the Emir of Zaria for supporting the British during the Satiru revolt—that he could not violate the oath of allegiance to them which he had sworn on the Qur'ān[46]—may well provide a clue to the loyalty which the British got from the emirs generally.

The reactions to the Satiru revolt and the successful establishment of the British administration in Northern Nigeria by 1906 indicated clearly that the Caliphate had given up the struggle against the Europeans because, after the initial British conquest, they were unwilling to champion revolts which they reckoned would only bring terrible retribution at the hands of the British. This pragmatic attitude on the part of the Sultan of Sokoto and the emirs accounted largely, and in a sense perhaps more significantly than the initial wave of the overwhelming British military victories, for the successful establishment of British rule over the Sokoto Caliphate.

44. *Ibid.*; and Gouverneur-Général de l'Afrique Occidentale Française au Ministre des Colonies, 6 July 1907, encl. report on attempted revolt of Zinder, 10 June 1907, in A.N.S.O.M., A.O.F. XVI, 16.
45. The Emir of Kano's possible complicity with the rebels of Zinder is however compatible with an attempt which he made to attack the Resident of Kano, Cargill, in 1908, following the deposition of three of his sons from office by the British q.v. R.H.B.E., S.63, Oliver Howard to Lugard, 21 May 1908.
46. R.H.B.E., S.62, Lugard to C.O., 28 Feb. 1906.

Although revolts after 1903 against the establishment of British rule may be likened to the death-twitch, resentment at the foreign occupation survived the total collapse of armed rebellion by 1906. The vehemence and the nature of the resistance through the years of British occupation showed clearly that the spirit of the Islamic pivot of the Caliphate and the desire to remain independent had not necessarily collapsed with the loss of sovereignty. Recognition by British colonial administrators of the vitality of the Islamic heritage in the late Caliphate, as revealed during the occupation and the possibly over-exaggerated respect they paid to it, provided a basis of co-operation between the conquerors and the conquered. As yet neither the emirs nor their subjects wholeheartedly reconciled themselves with British conquest. Although the British now exercised sovereign powers over the Caliphate and the pre-conquest structure was modified in many important respects, the authority of the emirs was enhanced in subsequent years through the operation of the British policy of indirect rule. But during the period up to 1906, with which this book deals, the emirs were in no position to foresee this other advantageous side of British rule. Hence it became clear that, as office-holders under infidel rule, the emirs and the old ruling classes were not 'time-servers carrying on an empty meaningless pageant'.[47]

47. R. A. Adeleẹyẹ, 'The dilemma of the Wazir', *op. cit.*

Appendices

The translations of the documents given in the Appendices are as near literal as possible.

Appendix I
Treaty conceded by the Shaikh of Bornu ʿUmar b. Muḥammad al-Amīn al-Kānemī, to the British Government, 5 August 1851[1]

What God wishes suffices. [Seal]
The help of the slave is
with God: ʿUmar b. Muḥammad
al-Amīn al-Kānemī.

In the name of God the merciful the beneficent. Praise be to God Lord of all peoples, the peace of God be upon our Lord, Prophet and master, Muḥammad, the best of all Prophets and messengers, and upon his family and his companions all. To continue, the document of the state of the English [i.e. England] containing stipulations which shall be mentioned in this legal document, has reached the revered exemplary of leaders, the flower of leaders, the celebrated, the most glorious, the eminent, the most happy, the shining light of the Kingdom of Bornu and the happiness of these Islamic regions, the most mighty, the most famous, the most fortunate, the dazzling Imām, the illuminating lamp of his time and a perfect jewel. He is in his place; my master, the Shaikh ʿUmar, son of the one who knows God well; my master, the Shaikh Muḥammad al-Amīn al-Kānemī. May God surround him with his gracious help. This sublime Imām has considered the stipulations of the documents and his disposition to its contents. He has ordered one of his scribes to write down his stand on each of the six stipulations which came from that state. [England]. The answer is, in reality, according to the stipulation of the *Hanīfī* (Islamic) religion. We shall set down the stipulations and answer them according to the principle of the accepted *sharīʿa*.

1. F.O. 93/17/1.

The first Stipulation

That the English shall not be prevented from entering the land of Bornu and all its territories and from journeying in them. That their settlers shall be as friends of its [Bornu territory] people as long as they remain in it and that their persons and their property shall not be endangered. They shall also not be prevented from travelling at the time they wish and the same condition shall apply to [the movement of] their possessions. The answer to this is: They shall not be oppressed and their persons and property shall not be endangered by any one. They, with their possessions, shall not be hindered from journeying and leaving at the time they desire.

The second Stipulation

That the subjects of the English Queen [*Sulṭāna*] shall be equal with the people of Bornu with regard to all the goods they may wish to buy or sell throughout Bornu territories and that the ruler of Bornu shall ensure to them that no preference shall be given to any trader of other races. The answer to this is: they shall not be hindered from buying and selling whatever is legal for them according to the *sharīʿa* of Muḥammad (the peace of God be upon him). But with regard to illegal things such as slaves, copies of the Qur'ān and the like, no. However, with regard to there being no preference between them and other races, if those others are Christians, they shall not be given preference over them since the religion of all Christians is one and the same religion to us and as such [they are entitled to] the same protection [*dhimmī* status]. This is the answer.

The third Stipulation

That the roads shall be safe throughout the land of Bornu, and the English traders shall not be prevented from carrying their goods from one town to another nor from roaming about in the country and moving from one town to another and that other traders shall not be prevented from passing through and trafficking with them. The answer to this is: They shall not be hindered from all this if there is no disobedience of the pure *sharīʿa* involved.

The fourth Stipulation

That the English Queen (*Sulṭāna*) shall have the right to appoint an agent to live in the land of Bornu to see to the welfare of the

English on the basis of the stipulations. That the agent shall be honoured and protected and his words shall be heeded and that the safety of his person and whatever belongs to him shall be guaranteed. The answer to this is: She shall have the right to instal this agent and his safety and whatever belongs to him shall be guaranteed. But other than this, he shall be treated according to what is enjoined on us by the *sharī'a* since it will not be proper for us to exceed its limits.

The fifth Stipulation

That the ruler of Bornu, my master, the Shaikh 'Umar al-Kānemī, shall expend his energy in the matter of the correspondence of the subjects of the English Queen which may be sent to them and which they may send to their country. The answer to this is: This is an easy thing which does not call for his expending his energy. There shall be no occurrence of losses with regard to this or anything you will find distasteful.

The sixth Stipulation

That the ruler of the land of Bornu shall make a law and give an indication about the conclusion of these conditions and that he shall publish them [i.e. make them known] from the time of their conclusion and throughout their duration. The answer to this is: We shall give an indication according to the condition of the country and the locality and in line with the manner in which we have conceded these stipulations to you.

This is the sum-total of what we wrote down with regard to the stipulations. Indited in the morning of Tuesday the 7th of Shawāl 1267 A.H.[2] May the kindness of God be with its writer, Amen.

2. Tuesday 5 August 1851. According to Dr Barth (vol. iii, p. 473), the Shaikh signed the Treaty on 31 August 1851. This would imply that the Treaty was handed over to him on the 31st. The final conclusion of the treaty, i.e. after the approval of the British government, took place on 3 Sept. 1852 (see A. A. Boahen, *Britain, the Sahara and the Western Sudan*, p. 205).

Appendix II
Treaty granted to the British Government by the Amīr al-Mu'minīn, Aliyu, of Sokoto, 2 May 1853[1]

To continue, the Sultan [sic] of the state of the English [i.e. England] whose name [lit. his name] is Victoria, wishing to conclude a treaty (*amāna*) of buying and selling [i.e. commerce] with the sultan of the Muslims, sent 'Abd al-Karīm, Henry Barth. The Emir of Sokoto, 'Alī—the Amīr al-Mu'minīn—having heard and understood the discourse of 'Abd al-Karīm, the messenger of the Queen of England, gave his consent and granted to the English a treaty of commerce on the following conditions:

Traders from England shall travel under safe-conduct throughout the territories of the Amīr al-Mu'minīn, 'Alī, with their children, their property and their mounts and they shall lose nothing—not even a tether—as they come and go at their good pleasure. Neither in speech shall they hear that which may be loathsome to them nor shall any oppressor harm them.

No Governor in the territories of 'Alī shall lay hold of them nor shall any danger befall them. They shall return safely with their property and their honour inviolate.

If any one indebted to them delays payment, Amīr al-Mu'minīn 'Alī shall recover the debt for them from the debtor.

If any of them 'i.e. the English traders' dies, the Amīr al-Mu'minīn shall extract the tenth (*'ushr*) from his property and the remainder shall be in the custody of the Amīr al-Mu'minīn until the nearest to his territory among the agents of England 'i.e. consuls' sends for it.

They shall traffic in everything except slaves for the Amīr al-Mu'minīn will not allow them to purchase slaves. This is all. Peace.

Date of Inditement
23 Rajab 1269 (2 May 1853).

1. F.O. 93/97/1.

Appendix III
Letter from Amīr al-Mu'minīn 'Abd al-Raḥman to the Royal Niger Company,[1] c. 1899-1900

In the name of God the Merciful the beneficent, the peace of God be upon the noble Prophet.

[seal]
Amīr al-Mu'minīn 'Abd al-Raḥmān

To the Royal Niger Company Limited. The fullest regards and the purest of greetings. To continue, that you may know that we have received your letter and we understand your words.

But, as for us, our Lord is Allah (may He be exalted), our creator and our possessor. We take [i.e. go by] what our Prophet, Muḥammad (upon him be peace) brought to us. As He [God] said: Whatever comes to you from the Messenger take it—the verse—[i.e. of the Qur'ān]. Thus, we shall not change it for anything until our end. Do not send to us after this. Peace.

1. N.A.K. KADCAPTORY, G.O.K.1/1/2.

Appendix IV

Lugard's Proclamation of 1 January 1900: Arabic version sent to the Caliph and the emirs[1]

SHOUTING[2] OR THE CLARIFICATION OF MATTERS

In the name of God, and that is sufficient. The peace of God be upon the noble prophet.

That all people may hear and accept these words. Previous to this time and until now, the Royal Niger Company (*'ajam*) were the great and noble white people who held these territories of the Niger (*'ajam*). They were white men, that is *Ture*[3] (*'ajam*), great and noble, in these Niger territories (*'ajam*). They were the people who settled disputes between white men like themselves and they made war on black people and subdued all their kings, sultans, chiefs and emirs, by force. They were friendly with those who heeded their words and obeyed them. They compulsorily arrested those who committed crimes. They made laws, tried and imprisoned people who perpetrated satanic [i.e. evil] deeds. By their laws, they prevented the perpetration of venomous crimes as well as great sins such as homicide, slavery, raiding of the poor people and similar things. They did good in settling quarrels about the matter of land and all other matters besides.

No doubt it was Her Majesty the Queen of England (that is *Sarauniyā Ture*)[4] who sent the Niger Company to carry out all that they did during their time. They were upright in their deeds.

However, at this time, with effect from these days, the Queen, that is *Sarauniyā Ture* (*'ajam*), has indeed forbidden the Royal Niger Company from making war on people and from possessing

1. N.A.K. KADCAPTORY Box 45, item 26 (Arabic Letter Book), no. 1.
2. تصريح Declaration is intended, not تصريخ . The document, as can be seen from the Arabic copy, is full of grammatical errors which are not pointed out here since the intention is merely to translate.
3. *Turawa*, Hausa for white people, is intended.
4. Hausa for Queen of England.

soldiers. They shall not exercise judgment in anything between the people in any matter whatsoever. They shall make no law neither shall they exercise rule from this day and for ever. However, the Niger Company were engaged in commerce in the land, selling and purchasing goods. This then is their sole function in the Niger territories (*'ajam*), from this time and for ever.

Also, now, the great Queen of England, that is *Sarauniyā Ture* (*'ajam*) has chosen new people of hers and has sent them here to administer the Niger territories, to command good and prohibit evil in the land as well as to possess an army, discourage trade in alcoholic drinks and in slaves, and in order that they may chastise all who perpetrate evil deeds, make peace among disputing parties and those who quarrel over matters of land and to order properly all matters that shall come before them.

Further, the Queen has sent here a man from among her people to hoist the flag, meaning *tuta*,[5] of the Queen. As for the Niger Company, they shall fly a new flag from henceforth and it shall be a trading flag only.

The Queen, that is *Sarauniyā Ture* (*'ajam*), is satisfied with the treaties and stipulated conditions which existed between the Niger Company and the Kings, Emirs, the Sultan and chiefs of the Niger territories. The Queen shall fulfil all of these to them. But it is up to you to fulfil all your treaties and their stipulations with the Niger Company to the Queen—*Sarauniyā* (*'ajam*). If any one goes against such treaties and stipulations, the Queen —*Sarauniyā* (*'ajam*)—will take it up with him as well also the messenger of the Queen, who is the agent, that is, governor. The Queen—*Sarauniyā*—has accepted all lands of the Niger Company from their hands. This means that all the lands which the Niger Company bought previously now become the property of the Queen with the exception of their stores—i.e. their commercial stores—which alone, will remain theirs.

I inform you that the name of the messenger of the Queen is Lugard. He is the representative, i.e. governor. He is the one who has authority over all white men. He is the commander of the army and he has authority over the Queen's people. The Queen sent Lugard here to be her mouthpiece and to lay down the law. All the affairs of black and white peoples are in his hand.

Therefore, I, called governor Lugard, the representative agent of the Queen—*Sarauniyā*—commanded that this letter be written

5. *Tuta*, Hausa for flag.

and sent to all the great emirs as well as to their people that they may hear and understand all it contains. If any one wishes to talk to me, let him send to me.

Furthermore, all the territories have been taken from the hands of the Niger Company (*ʿajam*) and have been divided into three parts. The first of the divisions is Nupe (*ʿajam*), Yarubawa (*ʿajam*) and the extent of the river Niger. The territory beginning from Idah (*ʿajam*), and going as far as Jebba (*ʿajam*), is under the power of Mr Wallace who has stopped working for the Niger Company and has taken up service under the Queen—*Sarauniyā*. He is under the direction of governor Lugard (*ʿajam*), the representative.

This is what I have to say for the moment. Completed.

God save the Queen

O God, grant peace to Muḥammad and the family of Muḥammad. Peace.

Appendix V
Letter written by Lugard to the Caliph ʿAbd al-Raḥmān about the fall of Kontagora and Bida,[1] March 1901

In the name of God the merciful the beneficient, the peace of God be upon our noble prophet. From governor Lugard, the Governor, Emir of the whites, with greetings and salutations and increase of honour. To the Amīr al-Mu'minīn in the city of Sokoto, ʿAbdullāh[2] b. Atiku, the late Amīr al-Muslimīn. You are the Emir and the head of all Muslims, you are the refuge of all Fulani emirs in these territories. It is from you that they seek counsel and direction.

I, whose name is Jan [sic] Lugard [ʿ*ajam*], the governor in these territories, wish to inform you about the following news. During many years, the Emir of Bida as well as the Emir of Kontagora (ʿ*ajam*), have been oppressing their people. They have been well known for being unsuitable for the position of emir. Only since a short while ago, they have been destroying the towns and villages in the neighbourhood of their towns in search of slaves. They have been killing many of the people of the villages surrounding their towns. They destroyed all the towns surrounding their towns until all the people of the towns fled. All the fields and the cultivators lie idle without being productive. They [i.e. the fields] have not been sown. In any case, both these Emirs, the Emir of Bida and the Emir of Kontagora, according to their whim, without any real reason, attacked (in the sense of launching war on) my people when my people were on a peaceful journey with mails, travelling on land and on the river by boat. They (the two Emirs) seized and stole the mails from my people who were holding them. Then they stole all the goods in the boat. Because of these evils of theirs, I have taken their crowns from them and banished them. Then I put my troops, i.e. soldiers, in the neighbourhood of their towns to guard the people

1. N.A.K. KADCAPTORY G.O.K.1/1/11.
2. The correct name of the Amīr al-Mu'minīn was ʿAbd al-Raḥmān.

and restore security there. Then I made Makun (*'ajam*) the new Emir of Bida in the place of Abubakar. This is to assure you that I wish to be friends with all Fulani and that I want to be the lover of your religion—the religion of Islam—so long as the Emirs are just to their people, rule with justice, give just orders and do not oppress their people.

With regard to the affair of the town of Kontagora (*'ajam*), in the night, evil people wanted to burn the town. These evil people may have been slaves whom their masters had oppressed or our carriers, i.e. labourers, who came there with our troops, who sought to do this. But throughout that night, my officers, i.e. my chiefs, ordered every soldier to put out the fire. They put it out and saved the town from destruction. It is my wish that all the people of Kontagora (*'ajam*), should return to their town and live there in security and be under a just Emir. This letter is to ask you to select, by yourself, a just man who will rule with justice. If he acts justly, I will enrich him and support his power. If you select a man such as I have mentioned and you give him a letter from yourself, let him come to me with it and I will appoint him Emir and gladly instal him on the throne of the Emir of Kontagora (*'ajam*), with pomp. But before you send such a man, you are permitted to exhort him thoroughly that if he acts dishonestly, heedlessly or if he is a hypocrite, he will be faced with the same consequence as befell the last Emir of Kontagora, Al-Gamashin[3] (*'ajam*). Greetings from your true friend, Lugard.

3. Nagwamatse.

Appendix VI
Letter from Lugard to the Caliph ʿAbd al-Raḥmān about the British expedition to Bauchi and the deposed Emirs of Kontagora and Bida, dispatched 17 March 1902[1]

In the name of God, our refuge and our sufficiency. Praise be to God in his oneness. Peace and blessings be upon the pure Prophet, his noble family and his party of the pure ones.

From Governor Lugard who is the chief of all the white men because authority over all the troops (called soldiers) is in his hand and in his hand also is authority over all the territories and towns. To the Emir of the Muslims by the name of *Muʿalim* ʿAbd Allāh in the town of Sokoto. A thousand greetings and two thousand times, peace—that shall endure day and night. These greetings are sent to you together with other members of your entire community. We inquire after your health and the health of all your community. May God prolong your life with sound health and wellbeing. If you ask about me, I am in a like condition.

To continue, the reason for sending this letter of mine to you, is to inform you that news has reached me that you sent a letter to the Emir of Bauchi and that you told him in that letter to abandon oppressing his poor subjects and that he should not touch them with any evil. The Emir of Bauchi had refused and was not pleased with the word you sent to him and what you informed him about concerning the path of reason. Because of this, I, Governor Lugard, have resolved to send to him my warriors (called soldiers) to prevent him from practising oppression. However, I do not know at present whether the Emir of Bauchi will fight with my people. If he fights with them, the most likely thing is that it will not be possible for him to remain Emir after that. Know that much as I do not like to expel the Fulani as well

1. N.A.K. KADCAPTORY, G.O.K.1/1/3.

as all Muslims from their territory, I desire that they should rule with reason, if the Emir of Bauchi is expelled for disputing with my soldiers, of his own accord, I shall endeavour to seek who is next to him in the line of succession to the emirship to succeed him and take his place, provided that person knows the law of the land very well.

Similarly, besides this, news has also reached me that the Emir of Kontagora (*ʿajam*), and the Emir, Abubakar, refused what your Wazir told them; that they should forgo disturbing the peace in Zaria territory. For this reason, the Emir of Zaria requested assistance from me and I have sent my troops (soldiers) to both of them [Emirs of Kontagora and Bida] to help the Emir of Zaria to drive away those who cut off the roads. After this, know that peace and concord rest with him who seeks them and hardship with him who seeks it. This, and peace be upon him who follows the right path.

[P.S.] After writing the above, I received news that my troops (soldiers) captured the Emir of Kontagora and the Emir of Wushishi. I, Governor Lugard, desire that all their people be in their (two) towns, i.e. that they should be settled in their towns. But, as for the Emir of Kontagora (*ʿajam*) and all his chiefs, I have ordered that they be brought to me for trial. This and peace.

Appendix VII

Letter from the Caliph ʿAbd al-Raḥmān to Lugard, received about early May 1902[1]

[Seal]

From us to you. I do not consent that any one from you should ever dwell with us. I will never agree with you. I will have nothing ever to do with you. Between you and us there are no dealings except as between Musulmams and Unbelievers ('Kafiri'), War, as God almighty has enjoined on us. There is no power or strength save in God on high. This with salutations.

1. Copy of translation in *Annual Reports*, p. 159. The original has not been discovered.

Appendix VIII
Letter from the Caliph 'Abd al-Raḥmān to Lugard, received 28 May 1902[1]

[SEAL]

In the name of God.

To Governor Lugard. To continue, know that we did not invite you to put right [affairs in] Bauchi or anywhere else, not to speak of your interference in putting [the affairs of] the country and districts in order. We do not request help from any one but from God. You have your religion and we have our religion. God is our sufficiency and our excellent agent. There is neither might nor strength except in God, the exalted, the almighty. This and peace.

1. N.A.K. KADCAPTORY, G.O.K.1/1/23.

Notes on Sources

The sources used for the reconstruction of the history of the Sokoto Caliphate in the nineteenth century can be divided broadly into published and unpublished. The published materials consisting of books, journals and newspapers fall under the following classifications:

1. Accounts of European travellers in Northern Nigeria in the nineteenth century.
2. Books on oral traditions of the emirates in Hausa, compiled or inspired by early British administrators.
3. Histories of the various emirates compiled by early British administrative officers from oral traditions collected by them.
4. Histories of Northern Nigeria written by British administrators and other amateur historians.
5. A few books, recently published, written by scholars working in the field of Northern Nigerian history and society.
6. Journals. These are subdivided into two heads:
   (*a*) Contemporary journals of learned societies (nineteenth century).
   (*b*) Journals of learned societies of the twentieth century.
7. Newspapers. These consist mainly of newspapers published in Lagos during the late nineteenth century as well as others published in France on colonial affairs. Where newspapers published in Britain are cited, the relevant articles were found enclosed in official despatches and other correspondence in British archives. German papers cited are taken from translations enclosed in official despatches in British and French archives.
8. Official publications. These consist of Northern Nigeria Gazettes, Northern Nigeria Blue Books, Military Reports, Command papers of the British Government and Annual Reports on Northern Nigeria.

A general remark which can be made about the published sources on Northern Nigerian history in the nineteenth century is the paucity of the information which (relative to their volume) can be gleaned from them. Another general observation is that with the possible exception of H. A. S. Johnston's work, there is no single publication which attempts to give a history of the area in any systematic form. These sources are, nonetheless, of great value to research into the history of the Sokoto Caliphate and Northern Nigeria in general. They serve as an indispensable starting point.

1. The chief value of the travellers' accounts lies in the fact that they provide contemporary information about several areas through which the travellers journeyed. In this respect the Travels of Major H. Clapperton, Denham, John and Richard Lander, R. K. Oldfield, Dr H. Barth, Dr W. B. Baikie, G. Rohlfs and Robinson are outstanding. Information which can be derived from them, particularly their judgments on the historical situations which they observed, as distinguished from the bare facts which they recorded, cannot always be taken as gospel truth. Being *passagers* their first impressions were not always correct representations of what actually obtained. Even such a close and penetrating observer as Dr Barth arrived at the conclusion that the Sokoto Caliphate had become effete and was already disintegrating by the mid-nineteenth century, his evidence being the revolt of Bukhārī of Hadejia and the chronic state of warfare which he observed in other places, notably in the Gwandu and Sokoto areas. As Dr Last correctly points out in his book, the account of P. L. Monteil on Sokoto is not a reliable guide to the institutions and offices of that place. More need not be said on the European travellers seeing that Dr Last has already made a competent assessment of them. It is, however, pertinent to point out that the travellers' accounts do not cover all the emirates of the Caliphate.

The riverain emirates of the Niger–Benue waterways, particularly those bordering on the Niger, are more adequately covered than any other part of the Caliphate. Sokoto itself was visited by Clapperton, Barth, Flegel, Thomson, Monteil and Wallace. Sokoto, Gwandu, Zaria and Yola were relatively more frequented than other emirates.

2. An important source for the history of the Sokoto Caliphate is provided by oral traditions as recorded by some British administrators. Here we are concerned with such sources in Hausa. There are a few publications of this class but most outstanding among

them and most useful are, the collections of R. M. East in *Labarun Hausawa da Makwabtansu* (2 vols, Zaria, 1931/1932), and *Litafi na Tatsuniyoyi na Hausa* by Francis Edgar. On these again, it is convenient to refer to Dr Last's comments. More recently publications have appeared in the Hausa language by Gaskiya Corporation in Zaria, which record oral histories and legends. Useful examples of such works are *Tarihin Fulani*, by the Waziri Junaidu of Sokoto which is a translation of the author's *Ḍabt al-Multaqaṭāt*; and another book is Abdulmaliki Mani's, *Zuwan Turawa Nigeriya ta Arewa* (Zaria, 1957). In one major respect, the latter, which attempts a description of the coming of Europeans to Northern Nigeria, is disappointing. It takes, and in fact reproduces, the official early British administration's viewpoint on the history of Northern Nigeria, which is not always correct. In many instances, the book, which is in no way critical, gives accounts which can be identified as coming straight from the *Annual Reports*. However, it contains useful translations of letters (from their Arabic originals) concerning the coming of the British. English versions of many of these letters are contained in Backwell, *The Occupation of Ḥausaland 1900–1904* (Lagos, 1927). Another book in this class is *Kano ta Dabo Cigari* (Zaria, 1958) by Abubakar Dokaji, which traces the history of Kano from Barbushe to the reign of ʿAbdullāh Bayero b. Abbās (d. 1953); it concentrates particularly on the nineteenth and twentieth centuries for which period it complements and supplements the *Kano Chronicle*.

Still on published sources in Hausa, attention must be drawn to publications of Hausa translations from Arabic documents. R. M. East's collection (cited above) includes Muḥammad Bello's *sard al-Kalām*, *Tarīkh Kano*, translated and expanded to include chronicles on the reigns of rulers after Muḥammad Bello (d. 1893). In the extension of the chronicle to cover twentieth-century Emirs of Kano, are oral histories about the British conquest of Kano. The oral traditions in D. J. M. Muffett's *Concerning Brave Captains* (London, 1964) relating to this event, read very much like the accounts in *Labarun Hausawa*. Also available in *Labarun Hausawa* is the most comprehensive indigenous written account of the history of Nupe called 'Litaffi Chude' (i.e. Tsoede) by Imām ʿUmar b. Muḥammad b. Al-Hasan b. Adam of Bida (date unknown to me). I have used the Arabic version of this book (*Tarīkh mīn bilād Bida wa Tarīkh al-bilād mīn bilād Gbara*), which I discuss below. Apart from these translations in *Labarun Hausawa* there is also a translation of ʿAbdullāh b. Fodiye's *Ḍiyā' al-ḥukkām* published by Gaskiya Corporation.

3. On oral histories, perhaps the richest source so far available in English, while fresh collections from the field by trained historians are awaited, lies in the collections of early British officers (administrative and military) published in the Gazetteers of the various provinces of Northern Nigeria. There is a temptation to look down on these accounts as the results of amateur investigations. But each attempts a comprehensive history of an emirate and they provide a starting point for further enquiries. However, the Gazetteers were not published for every province.

Besides straightforward accounts of the political history of the emirates, the Gazetteers contain useful information on ethnology and traditional customs. For the period beginning from 1900, they supply data on British administration and personnel which are not otherwise easily accessible while they are valuable for the administrative history of Northern Nigeria in the first two decades of this century. Indeed most of the compilations or history books written by British administrative officers, on which until recently we depended heavily for our knowledge and interpretation of Northern Nigerian history, were based largely on the accounts in the *Gazetteers*.

4. With regard to the nineteenth-century history of the Caliphate, oral traditions collected and interpreted by British officers belong to the same class as the Gazetteers. These are works such as Arnett's *History of Sokoto*, Major Burdon's *Northern Nigeria: Historical Notes on certain emirates and Tribes* (London, 1909), Hogben's *Muhammedan Emirates of Nigeria* (revised and enlarged by Hogben and Kirk-Greene as *The Emirates of Northern Nigeria* (Oxford University Press, 1966). Worthy of particular attention among this group is *History of Adamawa* by Karl Strumpell (Hamburg, 1912, mimeographed), a collection in English translation of oral traditions covering the various districts of Adamawa. This book, a copy of which can be found in the Library of Yola Provincial Secondary School, and on microfilm in Ibadan University, gives detailed historical and ethnographical information. In this class also falls Tilho's *Documents Scientifiques*, volume ii, which contains useful material on the nineteenth-century histories of the emirates of the northern frontiers

of the Sokoto Caliphate and their neighbours in Ahir, Damagaram and Damerghou and their interrelations.

For the history of European activities in the Caliphate during the last quarter of the nineteenth century there are a few memoirs written by participants in the events. Such are Seymour Vandeleur's *Campaigning in the Nile and Upper Niger* which contains an invaluable account of the Nupe–Ilọrin conquest by the R.N.C. in 1897, and *British Nigeria* by F. Mockler-Ferryman, who accompanied Macdonald on his mission in 1889. The books of European travellers during this period also fall into this class.

With regard to French penetration, I have found the works of Jean Darcy, H. Blet, Gabriel Hanotaux and A. Martineau, *France et l'Angleterre*; *Cent années de rivalités coloniales en Afrique*, *France d'outre-mer* and *Histoire des colonies françaises* respectively, most valuable. With particular reference to Rābiḥ's conquest of Bornu and the French penetration of that area, *Rabah et les Arabes du Chari* and *La chute de l'Empire de Rabah* by M. Gaudefroy–Demonbynes and Captain E. Gentil respectively, contain very useful, and in the case of Gentil detailed, information.

There are several books written by early British administrative officers and other amateur historians. These, such as Charles Orr, *The Making of Northern Nigeria*, Flora Lugard, *A Tropical Dependency*, Larymore, *A Resident's Wife in Nigeria* (more of a traveller's account than anything else), Allan Burns, *History of Nigera*, are of limited value for serious research. They do attempt a sketch of Northern Nigerian history in the nineteenth century and after, but their viewpoint is purely that of Lugard's administration (which is in itself useful) and information given in them, with few exceptions, can be obtained elsewhere. They echo identical interpretations to such an extent that it seems a fair comment to say that, to have read one is to have read all. The authors of these books have been the apostles of the view that the Sokoto Caliphate was decadent and was on the verge of collapse when it was conquered by the British, who are therefore seen as the timely Messiah. The books of the Rev. W. Miller must however be regarded as standing in a class by themselves. Though biased, they are the result of long contact, as well as patient and often penetrating observation and they contain valuable factual information.

5. Recent books written by scholars such as Nadel, Perham,

Flint, and M. G. Smith are well known. One may, however, remark that with regard to the present study, Perham and Flint adequately cover the events of the European (particularly the Anglo–French) rivalry. While Flint is particularly useful for the history of the R.N.C. Perham's treatment of the British Colonial Office policy is detailed. With regard to this particular study, D. J. M. Muffett's *Concerning Brave Captains* (London, 1964) deals with the British conquest of Kano, Sokoto and the Burmi battle. It also attempts to analyse Lugard's diplomatic moves towards the Caliph. The book has no great merit as a piece of critical analysis, but the documents quoted, often *in extenso*, are very useful. One serious limitation of the book is that the locations of almost all the documents used are either not mentioned or not properly indicated.

6. The journals used in this study are listed in the Bibliography in two groups, those of the nineteenth century and those of the twentieth. The main difference between the two groups is that the nineteenth-century articles are based mainly on the observation of the authors who were usually travellers, while those of the twentieth century are the results of historical investigations made by their authors from varied sources.

7. The newspapers published in Lagos in the late nineteenth century carry occasional articles and references to events in 'Northern Nigeria'. The researcher has, however, to go diligently through their pages for the occasional relevant article. The most useful of these papers is the *Lagos Observer*. The issues from 1884, and particularly from 1886 to 1890, contain many articles on R.N.C. activities on the Upper Niger and on the Benue. Of the overseas newspapers, the most rewarding is the *Bulletin du Comité de l'Afrique Française*, published in Paris from 1891. It is a fruitful source of information on French activities as well as those of the British and Germans during the era of European scramble in Africa. It contains not only accounts of European travellers but also articles on French colonial policy as well as on the European colonial rivalries. For French colonial policy and its execution in our area of study, the *Bulletin* is an invaluable source.

In addition to the above sources, a general reading in the field of Islamic history and institutions was found useful as providing a necessary background to understanding the significance of events in the Sokoto Caliphate's history. Publications used in this respect can be identified easily in the Bibliography.

A. UNPUBLISHED SOURCES

The unpublished materials for this study are located in the University of Ibadan Library and in archival institutions in Nigeria, Great Britain and France.

1. Nigerian Archives

The University of Ibadan Library

Materials here consist mainly of books in Arabic written by the Sokoto *Majāddidūn*—'Uthmān b. Fodiye, 'Abdullāh b. Fodiye and Muḥammad Bello—and some books written during the colonial period, as well as a few uncatalogued letters, mainly from collections of the correspondence of the Emirs of Bauchi. The books have been commented on by D. M. Last. Not many of these have been used for the purpose of writing this book and only such as are actually cited in the notes are included in the Bibliography. Some—*Kitāb al-Farq*, *Tazyīn al-Waraqāt*, *Ḍiyā' al-ḥukkām*, *Infāq al-Maisūr*—have been published as indicated in the Bibliography.

The second group, a collection of ninety letters from the Emirs of Bauchi's correspondence, are on microfilm in Ibadan (M.42–43) and have been recently reproduced in photocopies awaiting cataloguing. Many of the letters have been translated into English by A. N. Skinner. These letters, which are exchanges between Bauchi on the one hand and the Caliphs of Sokoto, Emirs of Kano and a few other emirates, cover mainly reigns of the Emirs of Bauchi; Ibrāhīm, 'Uthmān (Usman) and 'Umar. They deal with such topics as appointments, slavery, expeditions against pagan peoples (especially the Ningi), and the sending of military contingents to Sokoto. The letter of appointment of the first Emir of Bauchi, Ya'qūb, which may be from the original, is included in this collection. There are also scattered letters on microfilm and in photocopies at the Ibadan Library which are cited in this book.

Centre of Arabic Documentation Institute of African Studies, Ibadan

There are many useful works, correspondence, poems and books on microfilm or in photocopies at the centre. I wish to draw particular attention to the history of Ilọrin by Aḥmad b. Abubakar (nicknamed Ọmọ Kokoro) *Ta'līf Akhbār al-qurūn min 'Umarā' bilād Ilọrin*. This work, a translation of which has been published by Dr B. G. Martin, is a chronicle of the Emirs of Ilọrin and their chiefs. It retails popular traditions about the origin of the town and attempts a brief history of the reign of successive emirs, mentioning their wars and the places they conquered. The story is carried to shortly after 1900. The author is disappointingly brief, almost silent, on the disputes in Ilọrin between the emirs and their war chiefs in the 1890s and the first few years of this century.

National Archives of Nigeria

The material from the Nigerian National Archives (N.A.) are from the Kaduna and the Ibadan branches (N.A.K. and N.A.I. respectively).

The sources from N.A.K. fall into two main groups:

i) Correspondence of the Sokoto Caliphate from the last two decades of the nineteenth century.

ii) Despatches of the colonial administration and records of the administrations of the various provinces relative to the British occupation.

i) Correspondence of the Sokoto Caliphate 1886–1903

This correspondence consists mainly of:

a) Xerox and photocopies of letters in the possession of Waziri Junaidu of Sokoto contained in the files of the Wazir Muḥammad Bukhārī. They are contained in eight files referred to in this work as Corr. I–VIII (N.A.K. Sokprof 25). These letters (about 600 in number) are the same as those referred to by D. M. Last. Many letters in Corr. VIII are duplications of letters in Corr. I–VII.

b) A collection of the originals of 131 letters (N.A.K. KADCAPTORY, 44) captured from the house of the Wazir Muḥammad Bukhārī in 1903 (Corr. IX). Translations of these letters were published by H. F. Backwell in *The Occupation of Hausaland* (Lagos, 1927), while there is a set of unpublished translations in (N.A.K. KADCAPTORY, 48b) by Captain Merrick. The translations used in this work are my own.

c) 227 letters collected from Gombe (Corr. X) are in N.A.K. KADCAPTORY, 38 covering the period 1898–1902. In reality, these letters are about 223 since about 4 are duplicated in the file.

These letters, mainly correspondence between the Caliphs and their emirs as well as a few inter-emirate exchanges, deal with topics ranging through appointments, intra-emirate disputes, instructions from the Caliph, recovery of absconded slaves, tribute and gifts, wars and truces and finally the coming of Europeans and Rābiḥ Faḍlallāh. Group (*b*) in particular, is richer than the others on the coming of Europeans and the threat of Rābiḥ. In (*c*) there are a few letters dealing with the relations with Rābiḥ Faḍlallāh, including two written by Faḍlallāh b. Rābiḥ Faḍlallāh (1901). This group also contains about thirty-six letters on the Galadiman Ako revolt and letters from the Emir of Bauchi, 'Umar, between (1898–1902) to the Emir of Gombe and the Caliph. Letters about the Jibrīl Gaini revolt are contained mainly in Corr. II and IV and in the Gombe letters.

The common difficulty with using the correspondence of the Caliphate is that they are, almost without exception, undated. Approximate dates are derived from internal and external evidence such as known dates of the writers and their recipients, dates of incidents mentioned and, in a few cases, the mention of the day of month and week. The letters are however of immense importance for the reconstruction not only of the events in the Caliphate's history during the late nineteenth century but also the nature of the emirate's relations with the Caliph and with one another as well as the working of the Caliphate's machinery of government. As they are rather disconnected and do not cover all emirates, these letters are useful for reconstructing only a general picture of the Caliphate and also as providing bases for further investigations.

Also in N.A.K. (G.O.K. series) there are originals of letters in various files, cited in the book, about the relations between the British and the Caliph, 'Abd al-Raḥmān. In N.A.K. KADCAPTORY 45, item 26, there is an *Arabic Letter book* of the R.N.C. and the early British administration from 1899. Included in this collection are a few letters from Sokoto, exchanges between the riverain emirates (notably Nupe) and the British administration. There are several intelligence reports written by Adamu Jekada on the situation in the hinterland emirates between 1900 and 1902. Adamu Jekada, a native of Kano, was initially employed by the R.N.C. as a political officer. His services, in the same capacity, were inherited by the Lugard administration.

Other sources in Arabic

As mentioned above, most of the books I used have been adequately commented on by D. M. Last. I wish, however, to draw attention to two which are representative of another class of work by the *'Ulamā'* during the colonial era: chronicles of various emirates. The longest and most informative of such works is *Tarīkh Umarā' Bauchi* (Ibadan 82/377) by an Imam of Bauchi, Muḥammad b. Muḥammad Bello b. Aḥmad b. Idrīs al-Sudānī (written *c.* 1912). The author gives a comprehensive history of Bauchi Emirs and their wars from the *jihād* of the Emir Ya'qūb, up to the British occupation, as well as perhaps the most comprehensive available recorded history of Ningi. There is a shorter version of the book by the same author (82/378) called *Tarīkh Bauchi.* On Gombe, there is a history; *Tabyīn Amr Buba Yero*, probably written by a certain Alkali Garga. It does provide a framework of the history of the Emirs of Gombe and their wars. A copy, in his own hand, was kindly lent to me by Professor H. F. C. Smith. Another book in the same class is *Tarīkh min bilād Bidā wa Tarīkh al-bilād min bilād Gbara* (N.A.K. KADCAPTORY 2, item 22) by Imām of Bida, 'Umar b. Muḥammad b. Al-Ḥasan b. Adam (date unknown). It is detailed on the coming of Dendo to Nupeland and the early history of Nupe emirate up to the death of Masaba. A Hausa translation is in *Labarun Hausawa da Makwabtansu* (see above). A photocopy of an anonymous document on the biography of Amīr al-mu'minīn Aḥmad b. Shaikh 'Umar b. Sa'id of Segu written by one of his students, describing his flight with his followers and their settlement in Sokoto territory is kept in (N.A.K. KADCAPTORY 43, 7), Muḥammad al-Bukhārī: *Risāla al-Wazīr 'ila ahl al-'ilm wa'l-taddabūr*, an apologia on the action of the Wazir of Sokoto explaining his action with respect to the British after the conquest of the city in 1903 is in the possession of Wazirin Sokoto, Junaidu. An edited version by the present author is cited in the Bibliography.

ii) Archives of the British administration (N.A.K.)

These consist of documents in the S.N.P. and G.O.K. series and the Provincial archives series (e.g. Sokprof, Lokoprof, Ilọrin prof. Bauchiprof, and KADCAPTORY). These archives contain mixed material ranging through despatches to and from the British Colonial Office, military and provincial reports, written by military and administrative officers. Besides the Archives of the provinces, I found S.N.P. 1, 7 and 15 most useful for my purposes. In the series from the provinces oral histories collected and recorded by early administrative officers are to be found, as well as detailed reports on contemporary events. Special mention must also be made of Francis Edgar's collected oral traditions in Hausa (N.A.K. KADCAPTORY 3, items 3–36), some of which have been used in this work.

The sources used in the Ibadan archives (N.A.I.) need little or no comments since they are mainly despatches from 1899 between the W.A.F.F. and the British administration of Northern Nigeria on the one hand and the British Colonial Office on the other. These are contained in C.S.O. 1/27 and C.S.O. 1/28 series.

a) Military Museum Zaria. The sources here consist of valuable documents on the activities of the R.N.C. constabulary and the W.A.F.F. No. 1602, cited in this book, is a record of R.N.C.'s 'punitive expeditions' in the Niger–Benue area. The Museum is also useful for the purpose of identifying military equipment used by the British in the Caliphate. There are also albums containing interesting photographs.

b) British Archives. The P.R.O. sources on the history of the Caliphate for our period fall into the following groups:

(i) Treaties

Originals in Arabic of treaties signed by the Caliph of Sokoto and the Shehu of Bornu with Dr Barth, acting on behalf of the British government, are in F.O. 93/17. Copies, and sometimes originals, of English versions of treaties signed with the Caliphs of Sokoto, ʻUmar and ʻAbd al-Raḥmān and various Emirs are contained in F.O. 2/167. The originals of these latter treaties in Arabic are not extant.

(ii) British activities in the Caliphate 1880–99

Documents, mainly correspondence, of the N.A.C. and the R.N.C. with the British foreign office are contained in the series, F.O. 83 and F.O. 84. Material on N.A.C. and R.N.C. contained in these series are scattered and disconnected and contain little on local situations in the 'Upper Niger Territories'. F.O. 27 contains material on Anglo–French rivalry in West Africa. F.O. 101 (the archives of the British Consulate in Tripoli) is a fruitful source of information hitherto untapped for the late nineteenth century. The facts that can be gleaned from these series relate mainly to Rābiḥ Faḍlallāh's activities in Bornu and events in the Northern Nigerian emirates in general. These were collected from letters written by North African merchants resident in the area or through information supplied by such merchants returning to Benghazi or Tripoli. F.O. 2/118 is devoted to British policy towards Rābiḥ with scattered incidental information about Rābiḥ's activities. There is in this volume an account (a sort of diary in Arabic) by one Sherif Ḥasan who visited Rābiḥ. He records incidental information on emirates of the Caliphate, e.g. Kano.

C.O. 537 series (particularly vols 11–16) is a valuable source of information on Anglo–French rivalry and military build-up. In this series, there are intelligence reports compiled for the I.D.W.O. C.O. 445 and C.O. 446 are of course well-known sources. The former consists of W.A.F.F. despatches on Northern Nigeria to and from the British Colonial Office from 1897 while vols 1–32 of the latter consist of similar despatches of the early British administration up to the fall of the Sokoto Caliphate. The earlier volumes of C.O. 446 deal mainly with the W.A.F.F. during the period of transition from 'R.N.C. regime' to British government rule. Indeed, the C.O. 446 volumes, covering the early years of the occupation of Northern Nigeria, contain a high proportion of despatches on military operations.

C.M.S. House, London. The papers of the 'Upper Sudan Mission' from 1880 are a valuable source for the history of Northern Nigeria. The series G3/A3/O1 have been used in this book but it cannot be said that this in any way exhausts the C.M.S. sources on Northern Nigeria.

Rhodes House, Oxford. The papers here can be divided into the R.N.C. papers and the Lugard papers. The R.N.C. papers in the series S.58, S.85, S.87 and S.101 (the last two being Lord Scarborough's papers) which have been used in this work, contain material relating to R.N.C. activities in the Caliphate. They contain valuable memoranda, minutes of annual meetings and letters.

The Lugard papers used, S.95 (diaries published by Perham in 4 vols, London, 1964) S.60, S.61, S.62, S.63, S.64 and S.65, deal with sundry matters relating to events in Northern Nigeria during the last few years of the nineteenth century and the beginning of the twentieth. They contain memoranda and sundry correspondence with a large number of individuals as well as official despatches. Among the most outstanding individuals Lugard corresponded with were Chamberlain and Rev. Miller. S.64 must be classified separately. It contains letters of R. Popham-Lobb to his mother providing valuable information on the occupation of Zaria, particularly on the complexion of local attitude to the British.

2. French Archives

The Bibliothèque Nationale

The Bibliotheque Nationale, I found useful as a source of rare books relating to French activities in the Western Sudan during the era of the European scramble and also for French newspapers devoted to colonial affairs. Of the latter group the *Bulletin du comité de l'Afrique Française* is the most useful (q.v. supra) others in the same group are: *La Dépêche Coloniale*, *Journal officiel de la République Française* and *Le Figaro.*

Archives Nationales

Two sections of the Archives Nationales (*Section d'outre-Mer* and *archives diplomatiques et Documents*) were found most useful. The sources from *A.N.S.O.M.* (section d'outre-Mer) in the series, Afrique I–VI contain very rich and extensive materials on French explorers in the Western Sudan and equatorial Africa from 1880–99 as well as diplomatic despatches between the French government and Great Britain and Germany. Under the head *Missions* are records of explorers. The head '*Missions 7*' contains dossiers which deal exhaustively with Lieutenant Mizon's expeditions to the Benue and include his diaries. The lengthy despatches of Mizon (in Afrique III, 14–16) are very detailed and contain material not only on the explorer's activities but also on local situations. The Mizon papers can be easily cross-checked from the rich internal evidence as well as from R.N.C. sources. The R.N.C. sources dealing with the Anglo–French rivalry on the Benue (1890–93) can also be cross-checked with the Mizon's papers. Using the Mizon papers and other French sources with R.N.C. sources has enabled me to reconstruct a more comprehensive account of Anglo–French rivalry on the Benue.

In A.N.S.O.M., also, the series Soudan I–IV contains vast material on the foundation of the 'Troisième Territoire Millitaire' which later became the 'République du Niger'. Under this head are also records of the A.O.F. which contain relevant material on the 'Troisième Territoire Militaire'.

The file *Traités 12* contains treaties made with African rulers in Western Sudan. These are usually in the French versions.

Archives diplomatiques et Documents (*Archives of the Minister for foreign affairs*) *A.N.S.E.*
In the series Afrique 57 and 86 are to be found diplomatic exchanges between France and Great Britain relevant to the Anglo–French rivalry in the Niger–Benue basins and the Sokoto Caliphate. There are, in this connection, incidental material on French explorers, missions and merchants from about 1880. Much of the material in these archives is duplicated in the *Section d'Outre-Mer*.

On the whole the sources from the French national archives are useful for reconstructing the French role in the events which culminated in the overthrow of the Sokoto Caliphate. This role is of such significance that no serious scholar working in this field can neglect it. It must not be presumed that the French archives have been exhaustively used in this work. In this respect the subject imposes obvious limitations. However, the indications in this book of the value of the French Archives will, it is hoped, draw the attention of scholars to this important source for Nigerian history.

3. Oral Traditions

The present writer is convinced of the value of oral traditions in a work of this nature. However, such traditions as have been used have been taken second hand from publications and documents. With the vastness of the territory of the old Caliphate which it would have been necessary to tour, it was not possible to carry out any fieldwork. Besides travellers' accounts and books of the Sokoto *mujāddidūn*, the records used in the introductory chapter have the status of recorded oral traditions. It is hoped that extensive fieldwork which would necessarily be called for in writing the history of the emirates will produce a clearer and more detailed picture than is presented herein. With regard to the collapse of the Sokoto Caliphate, there is the important consideration that oral traditions of the actual conquest of Sokoto and the flight of the Caliph, Attahiru, is surprisingly still too intimate a thing for those who preserve them for us to extract from them yet.

4. Maps

Map No. 1 is based on the Tribes of Nigeria, scale 1:100,000 of 19. Maps Nos. 2–4 are based on Northern Nigeria administrative map scale 1:1,500,000, ref. 100/215/5–66. Boundaries of the Caliphate shown in Map No. 3 are approximate. The production of a reasonably accurate map of the boundaries of the Caliphate must depend on exhaustive field work and collection of oral traditions. Maps 5 and 6, as indicated on them, are based on contemporary maps of the I.D.W.O. while they provide adequate diagramatic illustrations, they must not be taken as accurate. Provincial maps of Northern Nigeria, scale 1:1,000,000 have also been used for location and checking of place names for all the maps.

Bibliography

The nature of the material is such that a classification into primary and secondary sources would not only be arbitrary in a number of cases but would also be confusing. The bibliography is therefore divided into two parts: Contemporary Sources and Later Works. The bulk of part I is primary, while part II is largely secondary.

Abbreviations are listed on p. xi.

A. CONTEMPORARY SOURCES

1. Manuscript Books in Arabic

Some of these have been published and a few translated as indicated.

ʻAbd al-Qādir b. Muḥammad al-Bukhārī, *Tanīs al-Ikhwān bi dhikr al-Khulafā' al-uẓma fi 'l-sūdān* (N.A.K. KADCAPTORY 1, 3).

ʻAbdullāh b. Fodiye, *Tazyīn al-Waraqāt bi jamʻ baʻḍ mā lī min al-abyāt* (Ibadan, 1964; Mss Ib. 82/465).

—*Ḍiyā' al-ḥukkām fī mā lahum wa ʻalaihim min al-ahkām* (ed. Mecca; Mss Ib. 82/4).

—*Idāʻ al-Nuṣūkh* (ed. and trans. M. Hiskett, *B.S.O.A.S.* xix, 1957, pp. 551–9).

Abu Bakr. b. Atīq b. ʻUthmān b. Fodiye, *Risāla ila Jamāʻa Gwandu* (Ibadan, uncatalogued).

Ahmad b. Abu Bakr, *Ta'līf Akhabār al-qurūn min ʻUmarā' bilād Ilọrin* (C.A.D., uncatalogued).

Bello, Muḥammad b. ʻUtḥmān b. Fodiye, *Infāq al-Maisūr fī Tarīkh bilād al-Takrūr* (ed. C. E. J. Whitting, London, 1957).

Bello, Muḥammad b. ʻUthmān b. Fodiye, *Tanbīh al-Ikhwān ʻalā Aḥkām al-amān* (Ib. 82/254).

Bello, Muḥammad b. ʻUthmān b. Fodiye, *Sard al-Kalām fī ma jarā bainī wa bain ʻAbd al-Salām* (Ib. 82/212).

—*Rauḍāt al-Afkār* (tr. H. R. Palmer, *J.A.S.* vol. xv, 1916).

Garga, Alkali (?), *Tabyīn Amr Buba Yero.*
Hayat, b. Sa'īd, *Miftāḥ al-khairat wa mazīd al-barakat li'l-dhakirīn Allāh Kathīran wa'l-dha kirat* (Ib. 82/384).
Ḥayāt b. Sa'īd and Al-Mahdī, *Al-Khitābāt al-Mutabādilat bain al-Imām al-Mahdī wa al-Shaikh Hayatu* (4th ed., Khartoum, 1962).
Junaidu, Al-ḥajj (Wazirin Sokoto), *Ḍabt al-Multaqaṭāt* (Ib. 82/31).
Muḥammad, Bukhārī, *Kitāb fī mā jarā bainī wa bain Amīr Hadejia wa Yūsuf* (N.A.K. KADCAPTORY 2, 30).
—*Risāla al-Wazīr ila ahl al-'ilm wa tadabbur* (Waziri Junaidu Sokoto).
Muḥammad b. Muḥammad Bello b. Aḥmad b. Idrīs al-Sudānī, *Tarīkh Umarā' Bauchi* (Ib. 82/377).
Sa'īd, al-ḥajj, *Tarīkh Sokoto in Tadhkirat al-Nisian* (trans. C. E. J. Whitting (Kano, 1949).
—*Sīrāt Amīr al-Mu'minīn Ahmad b. Shaikh 'Umar b. Sa'īd* (photocopy in N.A.K. KADCAPTORY 40, 7).
—*Tarīkh Kano* (Ib. 82/212).
'Umar, b. Muḥammad b. al-Ḥasan b. Adam, *Tarīkh min bilād Bida wa Tarīkh al-bilād min bilād Gbara* (N.A.K. KADCAPTORY 2, 22).
'Uthmān b. Fodiye, *Bayān Wujūb al-hijra 'ala 'l-'ibād* (tr. F. H. El-Masri).
—*Kitāb al-Farq* (tr. M. Hiskett, *B.S.O.A.S.* xxiii, 1960; Mss Ib. 82/397).
—*Ta'lim al-Ikhwān bi'l-Umūr 'allatī Kafarnā bihā Mulūk al-Sūdān* (Mss Ib. 82/254).
—*Tanbiḥ al-Ikhwān ala aḥwāl arḍ. al-Sudān* (Mss Ib. 82/212).
—*Wathiqāt ila Jamī'ahl al-Sudān* (trans. A. D. H. Bivar, *J.A.H.* ii, no. 2, 1961; Mss Ib. 82/399).
—*Naṣa'ih al-Ummat al-Muḥammadiyya* (collected by F. H. El-Masri).
'Uthmān b. Fodiye, *Masā'il Muhimma* (Ib. 82/86).

2. Archival Materials

Nigerian National Archives Kaduna (N.A.K.)

i) G.O.K. 1/1/1–46, 1899–1902.
Records from the Governor's Office, Kaduna.
ii) S.N.P. 1. 1900–01 despatches and reports.
iii) S.N.P. 7/1–6. 1900–06 despatches and reports.

iv) S.N.P. 15. 1900–06 despatches and reports.
v) Provincial records classified under individual provincial heads.
vi) SOKPROF 25. Correspondence I–VIII: Letters from the files of Wazirin Sokoto Bukhari (1886–1910).
vii) Correspondence IX: KADCAPTORY, 44. 131 letters captured from the house of Wazir Bukhari in 1903.
viii) KADCAPTORY 38. Correspondence X: Gombe letters.

National Archives Ibadan (N.A.I.)
i) C.S.O. 1/27, 1899–1906.
ii) C.S.O. 1/28, 1899–1906.

Military Museum, Zaria
W.A.F.F., records No. 1602.

University of Ibadan Library (Ib)
i) Sundry correspondence in Arabic, head 82.
ii) Microfilms nos 42–43: Correspondence of the Emirs of Bauchi.

Public Records Office, London
i) F.O. 2/118 and FO 2/167.
ii) F.O. 27 C. 1880–99. Scattered documents relating to Anglo–French rivalry in the Niger–Benue basins.
iii) F.O. 83 } C. 1880–99. Documents relating to R.N.C.'s activities.
iv) F.O. 84 }
v) F.O. 93/17/1. Treaty between the Caliph Aliyu and Great Britain in 1853 and Treaty between the Shaikh of Bornu and Great Britain.
vi) F.O. 101. 1890–1900. Correspondence of the British Consulate at Tripoli.
vii) C.O. 147. 1897–98. Despatches relating to the R.N.C.
viii) C.O. 445. W.A.F.F. despatches, 1897–1903.
ix) C.O. 446. Despatches of the British Administration of Northern Nigeria, 1899–1903.
x) C.O. 537. 1897–1900. Despatches and intelligence reports of the I.D.W.O.

C.M.S. House, Salisbury Square, London (C.M.S.)
G3/A3/01. 1880–82: Papers of the upper Sudan Mission.

Rhodes House, Oxford (R.H.B.E.)
i) *R.N.C. Papers*: S.58, S.85, S.87, S.101.
ii) *Lugard Papers*: Sundry correspondence. S.60, S.61, S.62, S.65. Letters of R. Popham-Lobb to his mother, S.64. Diaries, S.95.

Archives Nationales: Section do'utre-Mer, Paris (A.N.S.O.M.)
i) Afrique I–VI, 1880–99.
ii) Missions 7.
iii) Soudan I–IV.
iv) A.O.F. I–XV.
v) Traités 12.

Archives Diplomatiques et Documents, Paris (A.N.S.E.)
Afrique 57 and 86.

3. Printed Books

Allen, W. and Thomson, T. R. H. *Narrative of the Expedition to the Niger River in 1841*, 2 vols, London 1848
Baikie, W. B. *Narrative of an Exploring Voyage up the Rivers Kworra and Benue in 1854*, London 1856
Barth, H. *Travels and Discoveries in North and Central Africa*, 5 vols, London 1857
Blanc, E. *Routes de l'Afrique Septentrionale au Soudan*, Paris 1890
Burdo. *Niger et Benoué*, Paris 1880
Clapperton, H. *Journal of a Second Expedition into the Interior of Africa*, London 1829
Crowther, S. A. *Journal of an Expedition up the Niger and Tshadda Rivers*, London 1855
Crozier, F. P. *Five Years Hard*, London 1932
Darcy, J. *France et l'Angleterre: Cent années de rivalité coloniale en Afrique*, Paris 1904
Denham, D. and Clapperton, H. *Narrative of Travels and Discoveries in Northern and Central Africa in the years 1822, 1823 and 1824*, London 1826
Flegel, E. *Vom Niger–Benue Briefes aus Afrika, Von Edward Karl Flegel*, Leipzig 1890
Gaudefroy-Demonbynes, M. *Rabah et les Arabes du Chari*, Paris 1905
Gentil, E. *La chute de l'Empire de Rabah*, Paris 1902

Hastings, A. C. G. *The Voyage of the Dayspring*, London 1926
Houdas, U. V., ed. *Tedzkiret en-nizian*, Paris 1901
Hourst, E. A. L. *Sur le Niger et au pays des Touaregs*, Paris 1898
Joalland, Lt. *Le Drame du Dankori*, Paris 1931
Joalland, Lt. *Du Niger au Chad*, Rouen 1902
Laird, M. and Oldfield, R. A. K. *Narrative of an Expedition into the Interior of Africa*, London 1837
Lander, R. *Record of Captain Clapperton's Last Expedition to Africa*, 2 vols, London 1830
Lander, R. and Lander, J. *The Travels of Richard Lander and John Lander into the interior of Africa*, 2 vols, London 1836
Lander, R. and Lander, J. *Voyage Down the Dark River*, London 1832
L'Enfant, E. A. *La Grande Route du Chad*, Paris 1904
Mizon, L. *Une Question Africaine*, Paris 1895
Mockler-Ferryman, A. F. *Up the Niger*, London 1892
Mockler-Ferryman, A. F. *British Nigeria: A geographical and historical description of the British possession adjacent to the Niger, West Africa*, London 1902
Monteil, P. L. *De St Louis à Tripoli par le lac Chad*, Paris 1894
Richardson, J. *Narrative of a Mission to Central Africa 1850–51*, London 1853
Rohlfs, G. *Quer Durch Afrika*, 2 vols, Leipzig 1874
Robinson, C. H. *Hausaland or Fifteen hundred miles through Central Sudan*, London 1896
Robinson, C. H. *Nigeria, our latest Protectorate*, London 1900
Shaw, F. L. *A Tropical Dependency*, London 1905
Vandeleur, S. *Campaigning in the Nile and Upper Niger*, London 1898
Whitting, C. E. J., tr. *History of Sokoto*, Kano 1949

4. Contemporary Articles

Baikie, W. B. 'Notes on a journey from Bida in Nupe to Kano in Hausa', *J.R.G.S.*, vol. xxxvii, 1867
Crowther, S. A. 'Notes on the Niger', *R.G.S. Proc.*, vol. xxi, no. 6, 1877
Hutchinson, E. 'Ascent up the river Benue in August 1879 with remarks on the systems of the Shari and the Benue', *Proc. R.G.S.*, new series, vol. ii, no. 5, 1880

Lefroy, Lt. R. N. Visit to Masaba in September 1862. *Proc. R.G.S.*, vol. viii, no. 2, 1863

Macdonald, C. M. 'Exploration of the Benue and its Northern tributary the Kebbi', *Proc. R.G.S.*, new series, vol. xiii, no. 8, 1891

Thomson, J. 'Sketch of a journey from the Niger to Sokoto', *Journal of the Manchester Geographical Society*, vol. ii, 1886

Thomson, J. 'Niger and Central Sudan Sketches', *Scottish Geographical Magazine*, vol. ii, no. 10, 1886

Thomson, J. 'Up the Niger to the Central Sudan', *Good Words*, vol. xxvii, 1886.

Wilmot, Commodore. 'Resources of the Niger as regards legitimate trade', *Proc. R.G.S.*, vol. viii, no. 2, 1864

5. Newspapers

The Lagos Observer, 1882–90

Lagos Weekly Record, 1892–93, 1897–98

The Lagos Times, 1880–83, 1890–91

Le Figaro, with particular reference to 1899–1901

La Dépêche Coloniale, reference 1900–01

Journal Officiel de la République Française, reference 1898–1901

Bulletin du Comité de l'Afrique Française (B.C.A.F.), 1891–1902

6. Official Publications

Northern Nigeria Gazette, 1900–06

Northern Nigeria Blue Book, 1900–06

Annual Reports on Northern Nigeria, 1900–11, London 1911

Cd 1433, vol. xlv, 1904, 'Correspondence relating to Kano'

Cd 3620, vol. lvii, 1907, 'Correspondence relating to Sokoto, Hadejia and the Munshi country'

Military Report on Nigeria, vol. i, 1939

B. LATER WORKS

1. Books

Abadie, M. *La Colonie du Niger*, Paris 1927

Arnett, E. J. *Gazetteer of Sokoto Province*, London 1920

Arnett, E. J. *The Rise of the Sokoto Fulani*, Kano 1922
Arnett, E. J. *Gazetteer of Zaria Province*, London 1920
Ayandelẹ, E. A. *The Missionary Impact on Nigeria, 1842–1914*, London 1966
Ba, Hampate, A. and Daget, J. *L'Empire Peul du Macina*, Etudes Soudanaises, I.F.A.N., Memoire no. 3, 1955
Babagoro. *History of Gombe*, typescript, Gombe Divisional Office, Nigeria, n.d.
Backwell, H. F. *The Occupation of Hausaland 1900–1904*, Lagos 1927
Benton, P. A., tr. Shultze, A. *The Sultanate of Bornu*, London 1913
Blet, H. *France d'outre-mer*, Paris 1950
Boahen, A. A. *Britain, the Sahara, and the Western Sudan, 1778–1861*, Oxford 1964
Burdon, J. A. *Northern Nigeria: Historical notes on certain emirates and tribes*, London 1909
Burns, A. *History of Nigeria*, 6th ed., London 1963
Cattenoz, H. G. *Tables de concordance des ères Chrétiennes et Hegiriennes*, Rabat 1961
Cook, N. *British Enterprise in Nigeria*, New York 1943
Crowe, S. E. *The Berlin West African Conference 1880–1885*, London 1942
Daniel, F. *History of Katsina*, mimeographed, Lokoja Provincial Office 1937
Delafosse, M. *Haut–Sénégal Niger*, Série d'études, 3 vols, Paris 1912
Dokaji, Al-haji Abubakar. *Kano ta Dabo Cigari*, Zaria 1958
Duff, F. C. and Hilton-Browne, W. *Gazetteer of Kontagora Province*, London 1920
Dupigny, E. G. M. *Gazetteer of Nupe Province*, London 1920
East, R. M. *Labarun Hausawa da Makwabtansu*, 2 vols, Zaria 1932
Edgar, F. *Litafi na Tatsuniyoyi na Hausa*, 3 vols, Belfast 1911
Elphinstone, K. V. *Gazetteer of Ilọrin Province*, London 1921
Encyclopædia of Islam, Leyden 1913
Fagnan, E., tr., and Mawardi, A. H. *Les Statuts Governementaux*, Alger 1915
Flint, J. E. *Sir George Goldie and the Making of Nigeria*, Oxford 1960
Fremantle, J. M. *Gazetteer of Muri Province*, London 1922

Geary, W. N. M. *Nigeria under British Rule*, London 1927

Growers, W. F. *Gazetteer of Kano Province*, London 1921

Hanotaux, G. and Martineau, A. *Histoire de colonies françaises dans le monde et de l'expansion de la France*, tome 4, Paris 1931

Harris, P. G. *Gazetteer of Sokoto*, 1939, mimeographed copy in Ahmadu Bello University Library

Hassan, Al-haji and Shuaibu, Naībi. *A Chronicle of Abuja*, Lagos 1963

Herman-Hodge, H. B. *Gazetteer of Iḷorin*, London 1929

Hertslet, E. *Map of Africa by Treaties*, 3 vols, London 1909

Hodgkin, T. *Nigerian Perspectives*, London 1960

Hogben, S. J. *Muhammedan Emirates of Northern Nigeria*, Oxford 1930

Hogben, S. J. and Kirk-Greene, A. H. M. *Emirates of Northern Nigeria*, Oxford 1966

Hopen, C. E. *The Pastoral Fulbe Fulani in Gwandu*, Oxford 1958

Ibn Khaldūn (Rosenthal, F., tr.). *Muqaddimah*, London 1958

Johnson, Rev. S. *History of the Yorubas*, 5th ed, London 1960

Johnston, H. A. S. *The Fulani Empire of Sokoto*, Oxford 1967

Junaidu, Wazirin Sokoto. *Tarihin Fulani*, Zaria 1957

Khadduri, M. *War and Peace in the Law of Islam*, Baltimore 1965

Khadduri, M. and Liebesny, H. J., ed. *Law in the Middle East*, vol. i, Washington 1965

Kirk-Greene, A. H. M. *Adamawa Past and Present*, Oxford 1960

Last, D. M. *The Sokoto Caliphate*, London 1967

Levy, R. *The Social Structure of Islam*, Oxford 1957

Lewis, I. M., ed. *Islam in Tropical Africa*, Oxford 1966

Mahmassani, S. R. *Falsafat al-Tashrī fī'l-Islām: The Philosophy of jurisprudence in Islam*, tr. F. J. Ziadeh, Leyden 1961

Mani, A. *Zuwan Turawa Nijeriya ta Arewa*, Zaria 1957

Meek, C. K. *Tribal studies in Northern Nigeria*, 2 vols, London 1931

Menaud, J. *Les Pionniers du Soudan*, 2 vols, Paris 1931

Miller, Rev. W. R. S. *Have we failed in Nigeria?*, London 1947

Miller, Rev. W. R. S. *Reflections of a Pioneer*, London 1936

Miller, Rev. W. R. S. *An Auto-biography: 1872–1952*, Zaria 1952

Muffett, D. J. M. *Concerning Brave Captains*, London 1964

Nadel, S. F. *A Black Byzantium*, Oxford 1942

Orr, Capt. C. W. J. *The making of Northern Nigeria*, London 1911
Palmer, H. R. *Bornu, Sahara and the Sudan*, London 1936
Palmer, H. R. *Gazetteer of Bornu Province*, Lagos 1929
Palmer, H. R. *Sudanese Memoirs*, 3 vols, Lagos 1928
Perham, M. *Lugard: The Years of Adventure*, London 1956
Perham, M. *Lugard: The Years of Authority*, London 1960
Ruxton, F. H. *Maliki Law*, London 1916
Sciortino, J. C. *Notes on Nassarawa Province*, London 1920
Shemesh, A. B. *Taxation in Islam*, Leyden 1958
Smith, M. *Baba of Karo*, London 1954
Smith, M. G. *Government in Zazzau*, Oxford 1960
Strumpell, H. K. *A History of Adamawa compiled from Verbal information*, mimeographed, Hamburg 1912
Temple, O. and Temple, C. L. *Notes on the Tribes Provinces, Emirates and States of the Northern Provinces of Nigeria*, Cape Town 1919
Tilho. *Documents Scientifiques de la Mission Tilho*, vol. ii, Paris 1911
Tomlinson, G. J. F. and Lethem, G. J. *History of Islamic Political Propaganda in Nigeria*, London 1927
Tremearne, A. J. N. *Hausa Superstitions and Customs: an introduction to folklore and the folk*, London 1913
Trimingham, J. S. *Islam in West Africa*, Oxford 1959
Trimingham, J. S. *A History of Islam in West Africa*, Oxford 1962
Urvoy, Y. *Histoire de l'Empire du Bornou*, mémoire de l'IFAN no. 7, Paris 1949
Urvoy, Y. *Histoire des Populations du Soudan Central*, Paris 1936

2. Articles

Adeleye, R. A. 'The dilemma of the Wazir: the place of *the Risālat al-Wazir ila ahl al-'ilm wa l- taddabūr* in the history of the Sokoto Caliphate', *J.H.S.N.*, vol. iv, no. 2, 1968
Adeleye, R. A. *et al.* 'Sifofin Shehu: an autobiography and character study of 'Uthmān b. Fūdi in verse', *B.C.A.D.* ii, no. 1, 1966
Bivar, A. D. H. 'Arabic documents of Northern Nigeria', *B.S.O.A.S.* xxii, 1959

Bivar, A. D. H. 'The Wathiqāt ahl al-Sudan', *J.A.H.* iii, no. 2, 1961

Chailley, Commandant. 'La mission du Haut–Soudan et le drame du Zinder', *B.I.F.A.N.*, Série B. i, no. 16, 1953

Fremantle, J. M. 'History of the region comprising the Katagum division of Kano province', *J.A.S.* x (1910–11) nos. 29 and 40, ii (1911–12) nos. 41 and 42

Hiskett, M. 'Kitab al-Farq: a work on the Habe Kingdoms attributed to 'Uthmān dan Fodio', *B.S.O.A.S.* xxiii, 1960

Hiskett, M. 'An Islamic tradition of reform in the western Sudan from the 16th to the 18th century', *B.S.O.A.S.* xxv, 1962

Hiskett, M. and Bivar, A. D. H. 'The Arabic literature of Northern Nigeria to 1804, a provisional account'. *B.S.O.A.S.* xxv, 1962

Kirk-Greene, A. H. M. 'Von Uechtritz's expedition to Adamawa, 1893', *J.H.S.N.* i, no. 2, 1957

Kirk-Greene, A. H. M. 'Expansion on the Benue, 1830–1900', *J.H.S.N.* i, no. 3, 1958

Kirk-Greene, A. H. M. 'Three forgotten explorers of the latter 19th century with special reference to their journeys', *J.H.S.N.* i, no. 4, 1959.

Last, D. M. 'A solution to the problems of dynastic chronology in nineteenth century Zaria and Kano', *J.H.S.N.* iii, no. 3, 1966

El-Masri, F. H. 'The life of Usuman dan Fodio before the jihad', *J.H.S.N.* ii, no. 4, 1963

Palmer, H. R. 'An early Fulani conception of Islam', *J.A.S.* xiii and xiv, nos. 52–54, 1914–15

Palmer, H. R. 'Western Sudan history being the Raudatu 'l-Afkāri', *J.A.S.* xv, no. 59, 1916

Perié, J. 'Notes historiques sur la région du Maradi', *Bull. IFAN* i, 1939

Perié, J. and Sellier, M. 'Histoire du population du cercle de Dosso', *I.F.A.N.* xiii, 1950

Smith, H. F. C. 'Source material for the history of the western Sudan', *J.H.S.N.* i, no. 3, 1958

Smith, H. F. C. 'A neglected theme of west African history; the Islamic revolutions of the nineteenth century', *J.H.S.N.* ii, no. 1, 1961

Smith, H. F. C. 'The dynastic chronology of Fulanin Zaria', *J.H.S.N.* ii, no. 1, 1961

Vicars-Boyle, C. 'Historical notes on the Yola Fulani', *J.A.S.* x, no. 27, 1910

Waldman, M. R. 'The Fulani *jihād*: A re-assessment', *J.A.H.* vi, no. 3, 1965

3. Unpublished Theses

Anjọrin, A. O. 'British Occupation and Development of Northern Nigeria: 1897–1914', London 1965

Gbadamọsi, G. O. 'The Growth of Islam among the Yoruba,' Ibadan 1968

Ifemesia, C. C. 'British Enterprise on the Niger: 1832–1869', London 1959

Low, V. N. 'The Border Emirates: A Political history of three North-east Nigerian Emirates *c.* 1800–1902', U.C.L.A. 1968

Ọlọruntimẹhin, B. O. 'The Segu Tukulor Empire: 1848–1893', Ibadan 1966

Index

THE MISSIONARY IMPACT ON MODERN NIGERIA 1842–1914

A Political and Social Analysis

by E. A. AYANDELE, Department of History, University of Ibadan

The emphasis in this work is on the reactions of various sections of the African community—chiefs, educated Africans, ordinary people and slaves—to missionary activity and also to other agencies linked with it, in particular the colonial administration.

Contents: The Beginnings, 1842–1875; Missionary Enterprise and the Pacification of Yoruba-land, 1875–1900; The Missions and 'Southern' Nigerian Politics and Society, 1875–1900; The Triumph of Gin; The Missionary Impact on Society. Bibliography. Index.

Demy 8vo   xx + 393 pages   Maps, Plates   Cased **$7.50**

THE SOKOTO CALIPHATE

by MURRAY LAST, Northern History Research Scheme, Ahmadu Bello University, Zaria.

An account, based largely on nineteenth-century Arabic documents from Sokoto, of the origins and history of the caliphate until the coming of the British in 1903. *It includes, in particular, a study of the role of the vizierate in maintaining the administrative and the spiritual position of the caliphate.*

Contents: The Establishment of Dār al Islām in Sokoto 1754–1817: 1168–1232 (The Community; The Jihād; The Early Caliphate); The Maintenance of Dār al Islām in Sokoto 1817–1903: 1232–1320 (The Consolidation of the Caliphate 1817–1859: 1232–1276; The Composition of the Caliphate; The Period of Security and Settlement 1859–1903: 1276–1320); The Vizierate in Sokoto 1804–1903: 1218–1320 (The Viziers, The work of the Viziers); Concluding Remarks. Bibliography. Index. Genealogies.

Demy 8vo   lxxxii + 280 pages   Maps, Plates   Cased **$8·50**

BRITAIN AND THE CONGO QUESTION 1885–1913

by S. J. S. COOKEY, Department of History, The University, Nsukka

Beginning from the emergence of the Congo Free State under the private rule of Leopold II of Belgium, this book examines Belgian interests and the consequences for the Congolese. The origins, motives and organisation of the Congo Reform movement in Britain are revealed for the first time, and its influence on British and Belgian diplomacy.

Contents: Early Evidence on Congo Maladministration; Origins of British Intervention; The Casement Inquiry and its Aftermath; The Congo Commission of Inquiry and the Royal Manifesto; International Reactions on the Eve of Annexation; the Belgian Solution; Non-Recognition; Recognition. Appendices. Bibliography. Index.

Demy 8vo   xvi + 340 pages   Map   Cased **$6.75**

BENIN AND THE EUROPEANS 1485–1897

by A. F. C. RYDER, Professor of History, University of Ibadan

A study in depth of European relationships with a West African kingdom, to which, in the course of four hundred years, most of the commercial and colonial powers of Europe turned their attention. The author's research has embraced oral tradition, art and artifacts as well as documentary material in Portuguese, Italian, Dutch and British archives.

Contents: The Benin Kingdom—Historical Perspective; Era of Portuguese Monopoly; English and Dutch Beginnings; the Capuchin Missions; The Dutch at Ughoton; The Slave-Trade Era; British Encroachment. Appendices. Bibliography. Index.

Demy 8vo   xi + 372 pages   Maps, Plates   Cased **$8.50**

NIGER DELTA RIVALRY

Itsẹkiri-Urhobo Relations and the European Presence 1884–1936

by OBARO IKIMẸ, Department of History, University of Ibadan

A study of the coastal Itsẹkiri people and their hinterland neighbours, the Urhobo. Traditionally the two groups supplied each other's economic needs, but the author shows how Itsẹkiri commercial contact with Europeans at the coast gradually gave them an advantage over the Urhobo; and how the advent of British rule, the attempt to force the two groups into the same political and judicial institutions, deepened the tension between them—a tension which remains a political factor today.

Contents: Introduction—Indigenous Antecedents; Early European Activities and Itsẹkiri-Urhobo Relations, 1485–1883; The Régime of Chief Nana, 1884–1894; The British Penetration of Urhoboland, 1891–1914; The Native Court System and the Career of Chief Dọghọ, 1900–1925; The Reorganisation of the 1930s; Epilogue. Appendices. Bibliography. Index.

Demy 8vo xviii + 288 pages Maps, Plates Cased **$10.00**

THE INTERNATIONAL BOUNDARIES OF NIGERIA 1885–1960

The Framework of an Emergent African Nation

by J. C. ANENE, Professor of History in the University, Nsukka

A pioneer work in its field. The author has studied, from field-work, oral tradition and primary documentary sources the types of indigenous frontiers—not necessarily stable—which existed before European boundary intervention, and objectively assesses the results of that intervention and its consequences for modern Nigeria.

Contents: Introduction; The Atlantic Littoral and the Problems of the Hinterland; The Eastern Boundary—I; The Eastern Boundary—II; The Western Boundary—I; The Western Boundary—II; The Northern Boundary; Conclusion. Bibliography. Index.

Demy 8vo xi + 300 pages Maps Cased **$9.00**

In preparation

REVOLUTION AND POWER POLITICS IN YORUBALAND 1840–1893

Ibadan Expansion and the Rise of Ekitiparapo

by S. A. AKINTOYE, Department of History, University of Ife

THE SEGU TUKULOR EMPIRE 1848–1893

by B. O. ỌLỌRUNTIMẸHIN, Department of History, University of Ibadan

THE NEW ỌYỌ EMPIRE

A Study of British Indirect Rule in Ọyọ Province 1894–1934

by J. A. ATANDA, Department of History, University of Ibadan